Endorsements

Lochner's book is perhaps the most important work on the Lutheran Divine Service ever produced in North America. A treasure trove of information on the history and doctrine of worship, it is a valuable resource for anyone interested in learning about the Lutheran liturgical heritage. Matthew Carver's English translation is precise, clear, and supplemented with insightful annotations. This book helps readers appreciate the beauty and richness of the Divine Service and understand better its enduring role in the life of the Church today.

Rev. Dr. Gerhard Bode
Dean of Advanced Studies, Associate Professor of Historical Theology
Concordia Seminary, St. Louis

Thanks to the expert translation of Matthew Carver, English speakers finally have the opportunity to study the *magnum opus* of Friedrich Lochner, the grandfather of liturgical renewal and recovery in The Lutheran Church—Missouri Synod. In Lochner readers will encounter a style of writing and scholarship that has all but disappeared. Lochner writes as a liturgical historian, well-versed in Lutheran liturgical history. This alone makes the work a salutary read. But Lochner also writes as a scholar and pastor well-formed by the Scriptures, the Lutheran Confessions, Luther, and Lutheran history. Lochner's approach to liturgy, ceremony, and music is neither marred by pedantry, nor by indifference and liturgical relativism. Lochner's work should be required reading for all seminarians, circuit Winkels, Lutheran musicians, and anyone interested in learning more about the beautiful and salvific gifts of God.

Rev. Dr. James Ambrose Lee II
Associate Professor of Theology, Concordia University Chicago

Friedrich Lochner wrote his *The Chief Divine Service of the Evangelical-Lutheran Church* while serving as a pastor and seminary teacher in Springfield, Illinois, 1876–1887. But this work is important well beyond its place in the history of Lutheran liturgy. Masterfully translated from the German original by Matthew Carver, this book is now fully available for the first time to English-language readers, who will benefit from Lochner's balanced and insightful views of historical and conceptual aspects of Lutheran liturgy.

Dr. Daniel Zager
Eastman School of Music

Friedrich Lochner's *The Chief Divine Service* provides a fascinating picture of church life in the Missouri Synod in 1895, giving the history of each part of the liturgy and practical suggestions on everything from the chanting of prayers to the placement of flower vases to the reason why the altar crucifix (yes, crucifix!) should ideally be made of silver rather than gold. The book is finally available in English in Matthew Carver's superb translation.

Joseph Herl, Ph.D.
Professor of Music, Concordia University, Nebraska

This is the liturgical theology taught at CTS Springfield, the original liturgical theology of the LCMS. For each part of the liturgy, Lochner gives its history, meaning, practical instructions, and several musical settings. Some of this has been preserved in our congregations, but a lot of it has been lost due to the switch to the English language at World War I. This book is the link to centuries of lost culture, beauty, and wisdom with which the Lutheran Church lived.

Matthew Carver's footnotes make this an indispensable resource for research of early Lutheran worship. He has tracked down all the church orders and even the exact wording to which Lochner alludes. In short, he has improved on Lochner's marvelous work. This is a better book than when it was first published in German. It deserves to be studied closely and used by every Lutheran pastor and congregation.

The melodies are part of the Lutheran liturgical heritage that is still preserved among German Lutherans but has been mostly lost among English-speaking Lutherans. This is all worthy of use and restoration! By using the music provided here, we could have three or four more Divine Service settings.

The translator and editors have done a remarkable job matching Gregorian psalm tones to the English text of the propers. This is a difficult task, and there are different legitimate approaches on how it should be done. They have followed Lochner's method but have applied it more consistently than Lochner himself did.

The liturgical parts in which Lutherans made significant developments were in the sermon liturgy, confession and absolution, the general prayer, and the communion exhortation—many of which are no longer in use. Here we can learn about the practices by which the Reformation faith was handed down and can consider whether these practices might now be reclaimed.

Rev. Dr. Benjamin T. G. Mayes
Chairman, Department of Historical Theology
Concordia Theological Seminary, Fort Wayne, Indiana

In his *Three Books on the Church*, Loehe had pleaded that any who presumed to revise Lutheran liturgy ought first make a thorough and careful study of the great church orders. Apparently his student Friedrich Lochner, author of this present volume, took the exhortation very much to heart. For what Friedrich Lochner did in his original *Der Hauptgottesdienst* was to ingeniously bring together the chief sections of the great church orders with their music and rubrical instructions into a form accessible for any German speaker in the nineteenth century. It was an unrivaled liturgical *ressourcement*.

And now Matthew Carver (with assistance from Jon Vieker, Kevin Hildebrand, Sean Daenzer, and Nathaniel Jensen) has done the same for us in English, giving us Lochner's work in our native tongue and in modern musical notation, and even with an ear toward the cadence of the English Standard Version.

I do not exaggerate: this is the book that I have been looking for in vain for years. It is the definitive book on the classic historic Lutheran liturgy, where that liturgy is grounded in complete continuity with what came in the centuries before. Lochner's work shows how the liturgy was purified at the Reformation and then offered to the Church in the service of the Gospel. In Lochner, the liturgy lives and breathes; it is manifestly not some museum artifact but a richly ordered way for the people of God to feast upon the twin gifts that constitute the Chief Divine Service: the Word and the Holy Sacrament.

All lovers of Lutheran doctrine and liturgy and music will want this book on their shelves, and they will all be grateful to Matthew Carver, yet again.

Rev. William Weedon
St. Paul Lutheran Church, Hamel, Illinois

Through this skilled translation of *Der Hauptgottesdienst*, Friedrich Lochner does a masterful job of pleading for a simple return to "the true, historic form of the Divine Service." Lochner follows the cry of Luther to treasure and trumpet what is most true, honorable, just, pure, and lovely (Philippians 4:8) through an intentional return to the first sources. *The Chief Divine Service* places before us the "what," "how," and "why" of the Lutheran Reformation's work of cleansing a darkened and disfigured Mass—a restoration that gave back to the faithful the Divine Service in a form wholly centered around Christ's Word and Sacrament.

Rev. Dr. Daniel N. Harmelink
Executive Director, Concordia Historical Institute

With this translation, Matthew Carver brings more people to encounter the mind of a pastoral figure that is adept in liturgical history and practice, cognizant of the ecclesial landscape of his time and circumstance, attentive to the palpable liturgical needs of a nascent Lutheran Church on the frontier, and keen on supporting and encouraging its posterity unto the same. While much has transpired in the study and practice of Christian liturgy since Lochner's time, his insight not only informs our current realities but also inspires us to better appreciate the rich diversity of the Church's "awakened, vigorous, and joyful life."

Rev. Dr. Christopher Ahlman
Associate Pastor and Director of Parish Music
Memorial Lutheran Church and School, Houston, Texas

Lochner's great work on the Chief Divine Service of the Church of the Augsburg Confession, rooted as it is in the historic liturgy of the ages, is cause for joy on the part of all who cherish it. It shows beyond a shadow of a doubt that the love for this heritage is no recent development in the Missouri Synod but has been an ongoing part of our church's life. And how delightful to find here a setting of the Gloria in Excelsis by Dimitry Bortniansky and a lovely sixteenth-century musical setting of the Nicene Creed!

Rev. Charles L. McClean
Pastor of Our Saviour Lutheran Church, Baltimore, Maryland

Friedrich Lochner is a Missouri Synod treasure once hidden in a field of dusty German tomes but now uncovered thanks to the tireless work of Matthew Carver. Pastors will find Lochner to be a rare jewel, a pastor with skill and experience in a parish where historic Lutheran customs of worship were retained, and in another where they had yet to be fully revealed. This book will also appeal to those fascinated by the early history of the Missouri Synod, by church musicians, and by those interested in all things liturgical. Go sell all you have and buy this pearl!

Rev. David Saar
St. John's Lutheran Church, Mount Forest, Ontario, Canada

Who knew that in the 1890s German-speaking LCMS congregations could have a well-informed source for upgrading liturgical music and practice? Those who had settled for liturgical essentials and then, during World War I, had gone to English services just set this book aside. This fresh translation of Friedrich Lochner's practical and sage advice contains his admirably documented research into Reformation and nineteenth-century German resources. Carefully crafted English texts are provided for its numerous musical settings. It makes this hidden gem come alive again.

James L. Brauer, Ph.D.
Emeritus Professor, Concordia Seminary, St. Louis

What a treat to have this significant resource from early in the Synod's history available in English. While one may not find all of the musical examples pertinent to our current setting, the historical and theological background that Lochner provides is a wonderful window into the treasures of the Divine Service.

Rev. Dr. Paul J. Grime
Professor, Dean of the Chapel
Concordia Theological Seminary, Fort Wayne, Indiana

Friedrich Lochner understood that the liturgy is more than just an order of service. It includes the full range of biblical texts that adorn it and the ceremonial actions that give it symbolic richness. This classic study delivers the theological and historic meaning of it all. But most important for Lochner was to restore to its center the Supper of the Lord, the Head (*Haupt*) who makes the Divine Service "chief" (*Haupt*). More than a century later, we may be more ready than ever to realize this goal.

THOMAS M. WINGER
PRESIDENT, CONCORDIA LUTHERAN THEOLOGICAL SEMINARY
ST. CATHARINES, ONTARIO, CANADA

Finally, Friedrich Lochner's *The Chief Divine Service of the Evangelical-Lutheran Church* has been translated and published by CPH. I wish I had this volume when I was studying at the seminary. One of Loehe's original *Sendlinge* and a founding father of the Missouri Synod, who taught liturgics at the Synod's Springfield, Illinois, seminary, Lochner wrote this excellent work to preserve our rich Lutheran liturgical heritage in the face of a predominately American Reformed Protestant landscape. Had this work been translated during the Synod's language transition following World War I, perhaps much of our later struggle over Lutheran worship could have been averted.

REV. DR. JOHN C. WOHLRABE JR.
LCMS SECOND VICE-PRESIDENT
EDITOR-IN-CHIEF, *CONCORDIA HISTORICAL INSTITUTE QUARTERLY*
PRESIDENT, CONCORDIA HISTORICAL INSTITUTE BOARD OF GOVERNORS

The Chief Divine Service of the Evangelical-Lutheran Church

Explained, and Furnished with Historic Church Melodies for the Preservation of the Liturgical Heritage and for the Advancement of Liturgical Study in the American-Lutheran Church

Friedrich Lochner

Translated by
Matthew Carver

Edited by
Jon D. Vieker
Kevin J. Hildebrand
Nathaniel S. Jensen

"Let all things be done decently and in order." 1 Corinthians 14:40

"Finally, brothers, whatever is true, whatever is honorable, whatever is just,
whatever is pure, whatever is lovely, whatever is commendable,
if there is any excellence, if there is anything worthy of praise,
think about these things." Philippians 4:8

CONCORDIA PUBLISHING HOUSE · SAINT LOUIS

3558 S. Jefferson Avenue, St. Louis, MO 63118-3968
1-800-325-3040 · cph.org

Originally published as *Der Hauptgottesdienst der evangelisch-lutherischen Kirche,* St. Louis: Concordia Publishing House, 1895.

Manufactured in the United States of America

3 4 5 6 7 8 9 10 11 12 30 29 28 27 26 25 24 23 22 21

Table of Contents

PART TWO: THE INDIVIDUAL PARTS OF THE LUTHERAN CHIEF DIVINE SERVICE

Frequently Cited Sources

AC	Augsburg Confession
AE	*Luther's Works, American Edition.* Volumes 1–30: Edited by Jaroslav Pelikan. St. Louis: Concordia, 1955–76. Volumes 31–55: Edited by Helmut T. Lehmann. Philadelphia/Minneapolis: Muehlenberg/Fortress, 1957–86. Volumes 57–60, 67–79, 75–79: Edited by Christopher Boyd Brown and Benjamin T. G. Mayes. St. Louis: Concordia, 2009–.
ANF	*The Ante-Nicene Fathers: Translations of the Writings of the Fathers down to A.D. 325.* Alexander Roberts and James Donaldson. Revised by A. Cleveland Coxe. 10 vols. (Buffalo: Christian Literature Publishing Company, 1885–96).
Ap	Apology of the Augsburg Confession
EA	*Martin Luthers sämtliche Werke,* Erlangen-Frankfurter Ausgabe. 67 vols. Edited by Johann K. Irmischer, et al. Erlangen/Frankfurt: Carl Heyder, 1826–57.
Hommel	Friderich Hommel. *Liturgie lutherischer Gemeindegottesdienste: cum notis musicis.* Nördlingen: Beck, 1851.
Kade	Otto Kade. *Ein feste Burgk ist unser Got: Der neuaufgefundene Luther-Codex vom Jahre 1530 . . . .* Dresden: Schrag'sche Verlags-Anstalt; Klemm, 1873.
König	Johann Ludwig König. *Die Haupt-Liturgien der alten Kirche in wortgetreuer Übersetzung.* Neustrelitz: Barnewitz, 1865.
Layriz	Fridrich Layriz. *Kern des deutschen Kirchengesangs: zum Gebrauch evangelisch-lutherischer Gemeinden und Familien.* Part 4: CXX liturgische Weisen enthaltend. Nördlingen: Beck, 1855.
Löhe, *Agende*	Wilhelm Löhe. *Agende für christliche Gemeinden des lutherischen Bekenntnisses.* Nördlingen: Beck, 1844; 2nd ed. 1853–59; 3rd ed. 1884.
Löhe, *Sammlung*	Wilhelm Löhe. *Sammlung liturgischer Formulare der evangelisch-lutherischen Kirche.* 3 vols. Nördlingen: Beck, 1839–42.

LSB	*Lutheran Service Book.* The Commmission on Worship of The Lutheran Church—Missouri Synod. St. Louis: Concordia Publishing House, 2006.
Lyra, *Ornitho.*	Justus Wilhelm Lyra. *Andreas Ornithoparchus aus Meiningen, der Zeitgenosse Luthers: und dessen Lehre von der Kirchenaccenten.* Göttingen: Vandenhoeck & Ruprecht, 1877.
Naumann	Emil Naumann. *Illustrirte Musikgeschichte: die Entwicklung der Tonkunst aus frühesten Anfängen bis auf die Gegenwart.* 2 vols. Stuttgart: Spemann, 1880–85.
Rudelbach	Andreas Gottlob Rudelbach. *Die Sacrament-Worte oder die wesentlichen Stücke der Taufe und des Abendmahls, historisch-kritisch dargestellt . . . .* Leipzig: Tauchnitz, 1837.
Schoeberlein	Ludwig Schoeberlein and Friedrich Samuel Riegel. *Schatz des liturgischen Chor-und Gemeindegesangs . . . .* 2 vols. Göttingen: Vandenhoeck & Ruprecht, 1865–72.
Sehling	Emil Sehling, ed. *Die evangelischen Kirchenordnungen des XVI. Jahrhunderts.* Vols. 1–8, 11–15 in 15 physical vols. to date. Leipzig: Reisland, 1902–13; Tübingen: J. C. B. Mohr [Paul Siebeck], 1955–.
Schultze	Viktor Schultze. *Das evangelische Kirchengebäude: ein Ratgeber für Geistliche und Freunde kirchlicher Kunst.* Leipzig: G. Böhme, 1886.
StL	*D. Martin Luthers Werke.* Edited by Albrecht F. Hoppe. 23 vols. St. Louis: Concordia Publishing House, 1880–1910.
WA	*D. Martin Luthers Werke: Kritische Gesamtausgabe.* 73 vols. in 85. Weimar: Hermann Böhlau, 1883–2009.
WA Tr	*D. Martin Luthers Werke: Tischreden.* 6 vols. Weimar: Hermann Böhlau, 1912–21.
Wackernagel	Philipp Wackernagel. *Das deutsche Kirchenlied von der ältestesten Zeit bis zu Anfang des XVI. Jahrhundert.* 5 vols. Leipzig: B. G. Teubner, 1864–77.
Zahn	Johannes Zahn. *Handbüchlein für evangelische Cantoren und Organisten.* 1st ed. Nürnberg: G. Löhe, 1871.

Foreword

Non multa sed multum. As far as books go, one ought strive not for many, but a few great ones. This is a great one. Lochner's work on the Divine Service of the Lutheran Church is, frankly, the greatest modern source in English on the topic. Scholars, pastors, seminarians, organists, church musicians, choir directors, deaconesses, and lay people who love and want to better understand the form, meaning, and practice of worship will find a clear and straight-forward depth of doctrine, history, and practice unparalleled since its publication in German by CPH in 1895. It has not previously appeared complete in the English language because of its technical breadth and depth. Finally, a century and a quarter after it appeared, Matthew Carver has provided a beautiful, accurate, and clear English translation.

In 1841, Lochner heard F. C. D. Wyneken give a stirring address calling for missionary pastors for America. In 1844, Lochner enrolled in Löhe's program in Neuendettelsau. Löhe described Lochner as "his most gifted student." In the spring of 1845, Lochner became one of the many "Löhe men" who were trained for a year in Germany, then sent to America as missionaries with the goal of shepherding vast numbers of unchurched German immigrants into the church while associating with orthodox Lutheran synods. Lochner was present with other Löhe men, Sihler and Ernst, at the first meeting with Walther and the Saxons in the spring of 1846, which led to the founding of the Missouri Synod in 1847. Like a great many of those educated and sent to American by Löhe, Lochner came to be convinced that the Missourians were correct on the teaching of the Church and the Office of the Ministry—that is, that the teaching of the Scriptures, the Lutheran Confessions and Luther himself were consistent. Yet Lochner, like his mentor, Wilhelm Löhe, also became a scholar of the liturgy.

Lochner served as pastor at Old Trinity in Milwaukee, which had a rich liturgical life and made much use of the plethora of resources available in historic German Lutheran church orders. In 1876, Lochner was called to Trinity in Springfield, Illinois, which had a much simpler liturgical life. This was the case with many congregations, depending largely on whether the pastor or membership had emigrated from South Germany, where, due to Reformed influences, liturgical life was more limited. Lochner feared that the great flourishing of the Lutheran liturgy as a result of pure doctrine might be "turned back into the austere, puritanical rite which we found in general use. We are living in a land of rank Reformed sectarianism, a land which is therefore Reformed at heart . . ." This, coupled with "less . . . tolerance for spiritual practices" and a "severe lack of precise liturgical understanding," could result in "a diminished desire to retain the liturgical legacy that has only just been regained" (xviii–xix).

Lochner knows full well the difference "between the kernel and the shell." He confesses clearly the *satis est* of Article VII of the Augsburg Confession. "To the true unity of the Christian Church it is enough that the Gospel is preached according to the pure sense, and the Sacraments administered according to the Word of God." But he writes to teach the "beauty, riches, and merits of the Old Lutheran liturgy," and make his students aware that "everything depends upon the pure Word and Sacrament, and that all ceremonies should and must only serve the end that these [Word and Sacrament] may be rightly employed, and how on the other hand the liturgy would always do this service, and that it would therefore be lamentable if, where it is introduced, it should eventually be supplanted by English Puritan austerity." Yet Lochner also warns his students against "overestimating the liturgy and introducing it prematurely."

Lochner demonstrates that the great Lutheran liturgy is catholic, lively, diverse, and doctrinally and biblically rich. He is in sympathy and dialogue with Luther, early Lutherans, great contemporaries like Löhe and Rudelbach, with the ancient church and her theologians, with Roman Catholics, and many others. He explains the many ways that Rationalism destroyed the Lutheran liturgy, and how the many different German states moved away from Luther's own views of the liturgy. This volume is the only work in English that informs the reader of the many Lutheran church orders that display great and acceptable diversity under the freedom of the Gospel.

The reader will constantly be surprised to find that practices long believed to be "Roman Catholic" have actually been practiced by Lutherans for centuries—starting with, or mostly continued by, Luther. On the other hand, the reader with find that what many have believed to be "Lutheran" in worship (long liturgies, droning chant, drudging through the service and hymnody) is as much the influence of Rationalism as anything.

Lochner produced this book while teaching at the seminary in Springfield, Illinois from 1876 to 1887. He taught his students about the Divine Service with a crystal clear hermeneutic of Law and Gospel, a precise knowledge of the freedom of the Gospel, and with a catholic depth and Lutheran passion. Now, at long last, just when we need it most, he can teach us.

Matthew C. Harrison

Translator's Introduction

Over the past few years, with the increasing interest in historical liturgics, there has been a parallel increasing interest in Friedrich Lochner, one of The Lutheran Church—Missouri Synod's preeminent liturgical scholars from the nineteenth century, and particularly in his seminal work on that subject, of which the following is a translation.[1] His book has been a recent subject of study in journals,[2] and has received positive reference at serious liturgical conferences in Lutheran circles for several years running, often with an aside to the effect: Why isn't this translated?

In fact, Lochner's *Der Hauptgottesdienst* has already been translated in part. Aside perhaps from a few articles in early issues of *The Lutheran Witness*, for example, which with little explicit citation draw sometimes literally on Lochner's text, the *first part* of the present book was translated in a somewhat condensed form by Fred H. Lindemann.[3] While Lindemann's text is generally solid and clear, it is of course incomplete, since it is missing the second part (the liturgical music component) and the appendix on liturgical stations. In addition, the condensed nature of the text, adapted to the magazine format of *The American Lutheran*, has some unfortunate omissions which may only be uncovered after careful examination. Lindemann's goal is to relate the information contained in Lochner's book and to encapsulate the arguments, while at the same time saving space and not attempting to address, but entirely skipping over, issues which had been resolved or rendered obsolete by 1951. Our intention in the present translation is to include all the material, obsolete or not. On this note, it will be observed that Lochner spends some time referencing (and refuting) certain Roman Catholic practices which no longer apply, such as the withholding of the chalice from the laity. This has all been left in place without comment. The reader will

[1] For a biography of Lochner, see Cameron A. MacKenzie, "Appreciating Friedrich Lochner: A Founding Father of the Missouri Synod," *Concordia Historical Institute Quarterly* 84, no. 3 (2011): 36–50. For a biography and analysis of Lochner's *Der Hauptgottesdienst,* see: Kevin J. Hildebrand, "Friedrich Lochner and *Der Hauptgottesdienst,*" *Concordia Historical Institute Quarterly* 84, no. 4 (2011): 10–39.

[2] For example, John W. Fenton, "Wilhelm Löhe's *Hauptgottesdienst* (1844) as Critique of Luther's *Deutsche Messe,*" *Concordia Theological Quarterly* 64, no. 2 (2000): 127–48.

[3] Published as "The Main Lutheran Service," in *The American Lutheran* 34, nos 4–10 (1951) and 35, nos 1–4 (1952). The comparative table at the end of vol. 35, no. 4 is particularly good.

know best how to inform himself concerning the particulars of liturgical changes that have occurred in the Roman Church since Lochner's time.

In addition to Lindemann's mid-century translation, references to Lochner's *Der Hauptgottesdienst* appearing in Lutheran publications in English earlier in the twentieth century show a distinct familiarity with and respect for the work as a distillation of late nineteenth-century liturgical scholarship, and a regard for the author's sentiments as possessing some authority.[4] Eventually this familiarity with Lochner seems to have subsided, except perhaps in academic circles and through secondary literature. Likewise, familiarity with German yielded to English, so that Lindemann found it beneficial to publish his English rendering in the middle of the twentieth century, albeit without adapting the musical part.

It may be seen, then, that a translation has been desirable for some time. What was perhaps less clear was to what extent it would serve its original purpose in this post-Vatican II world (the vernacular liturgy of the Roman Church not being officially sanctioned until after Lindemann's translation), and how German musical pieces might be adapted and suited to English expression. The former must be viewed from a historical perspective. Here we are given a glimpse into a bygone day, and simultaneously are made to recognize the changeableness to which even the Roman Church is subject, despite any claim to the contrary. It will, perhaps, be helpful for the interested reader to consult a modern edition of the *Graduale Romanum* and *Rituale Romanum* for clarification on which differences between Lutheran and Roman Catholic liturgies still obtain.

The efficacy and wisdom of the second point, concerning the adaptation of musical parts to English, must be judged from what is presented here. In this case, our primary concern was to conform the translation to that familiar to our modern Lutheran reader, insofar as possible, without omitting any distinct variation in the German. The closest affiliation to the old German liturgy in our *LSB* is found in Setting Three, which in turn derives from the Common Service setting found in *The Lutheran Hymnal* (Concordia Publishing House, 1941). With a few changes here and there, this wording sufficed to convey the original German. Since, however, the modern reader is no longer accustomed to the Introits, Graduals, and psalms generally as they are found in the latter hymnal (that is, the so-called Jac-

[4] Notable, for example, is H. W. Bartels, "Uniformity of Liturgy for Our English Churches," *Theological Quarterly* 14, no. 4 (1910): 193–208, which relies heavily on Lochner's work. One should also mention in this regard P. E. Kretzmann, *Christian Art in the Place and in the Form of Lutheran Worship* (St. Louis: Concordia Publishing House, 1921), which draws on Lochner's notes on the artwork and furnishings of the liturgical space, in turn drawn largely from Schultze, *Das evangelische Kirchengebäude*.

obean or King James English), the more modern wording and idiom of *Lutheran Service Book*, and particularly of the English Standard Version is used here to render these respective Propers. Generally speaking, the monodic chanted parts have been set by the translator, while the harmonized chants and songs are adapted musically by Kantor Kevin Hildebrand—here and there with the advice (sometimes unsolicited!) of the translator, whose primary concern here was to convey in standard, slightly formal (liturgical) modern English the original German, more than to conform English syllabically to the original music. Thus, especially in the monodic chanted parts, an attempt has been made to use the underlying formula of the original rather than to maintain the exact contour found with the German. This is less the case with regard to the rhythmic, harmonized musical pieces, in which a balance must be struck between recasting the tune and maintaining good liturgical English idiom. Those pieces which are otherwise familiar from *LSB* have nevertheless been produced again from the text so as to preserve the harmonization as well as any other distinctive features which may have been lost or omitted in other published adaptations, for example, the optional verses in the otherwise familiar Sanctus (p. 235), or the longer slur on the word "Israel" in the Nunc Dimittis (p. 299).

References to and citations of works in the text have been confirmed and clarified where possible. It was usually a simple matter to locate the works intended, especially copies of the ancient church orders, by referring to Lochner's main sources: Hommel and Löhe. (See below, pp. xxii–xxiii.) Of great service to the annotations in the present translation is the welcome discovery that almost all the church orders may now be found online, digitized, and provided for scholarly use by German libraries. The full titles, necessary for searching and locating these, are included in the bibliography of Joseph Herl, *Worship Wars in Early Lutheranism* (New York: Oxford University Press, 2004), 281–338.

One note regarding translation choices: Lochner's language has been rendered into a similar style of English. No special endeavor was made to shorten his lengthy sentences (though this often occurs by necessity) nor to alter his characteristic, slightly ornate, collegial lecturing style (as in Lindemann). Latin has often been supplied with English translations, or, in a couple cases of liturgical nomenclature, simply replaced with the English equivalent (e.g., "*Offertorium*" becomes "Offertory"). Technical terms are given in the usual English rendering; or where multiple choices appear, the rendering regarded as most familiar to the modern congregation.

Matthew Carver

Editors' Introduction

The translator has labored mightily to provide an accurate and readable rendering of Friedrich Lochner's *opus magnum*. The original page numbers have been maintained in brackets throughout (e.g., <123>) to assist the interested reader in comparing the original with the translation. This may be particularly useful in places where it was necessary to adapt some of the musical excerpts to fit the English translation.

Lochner's original is available electronically via Google Books, as are many of the sixteenth- through nineteenth-century sources that he cites. The translator and editors have endeavored to trace and document these sources for the scholarly reader.

Lochner's use of footnotes is less frequent than one might encounter today. He often provides bibliographic information within the body of his commentary, which this translation has, for the most part, maintained. Most of Lochner's footnotes provide extended explanations rather than bibliographic documentation. Lochner's footnotes are not numbered in the original, but rather employ an older style of asterisks and other symbols. In this translation, Lochner's original footnotes have been marked with *), and the translator's copious documentary and explanatory footnotes are distinguished from Lochner's with the addition of "—MC."

Lochner made extensive use of *Sperrdruck*—that is, spaced italic and bold type to highlight and accent important parts of his text. The translator and editors have maintained Lochner's textual emphases, wherever possible. Lochner also included a detailed Table of Contents, which, short of a modern index, also provides today's reader with a helpful guide to the main topics and subtopics.

In quoting from Luther, Lochner used primarily the Erlangen Edition (EA) and the St. Louis Edition (StL) of Luther's writings. The translator has almost always translated directly from the German or Latin quoted in Lochner's original, but has also helpfully provided cross references to the American Edition of *Luther's Works* (AE), for comparison's sake.

Special thanks are due my editorial colleagues, Nathaniel Jensen and Kantor Kevin Hildebrand. Jensen made a first pass through the translator's manuscript, working to bring it into a designated editorial style and preparing it electronically for design and layout. Kantor Hildebrand took the rudimentary music files provided by the translator, added harmonizations where needed, and then began the editing and shaping of the musical excerpts for design and layout. The editors and translator all made a final review of the manuscript penultimate to publication.

Special acknowledgment is due Chaplain Sean Daenzer for his detailed analysis of and attention to Lochner's pointing of the Introits. The editorial note on pages 82–83 is the result of his study and outlines the approach he took in pointing the Introit texts that follow. Special thanks also to Joseph Herl, who read the entire manuscript and offered valuable comments and corrections.

Final thanks are due to Lisa Moeller, who provided the first several iterations of design and layout, and to my assistant, Rachel Asburry, who proofread the manuscript for appropriate hyphenation.

Jon D. Vieker

The musical examples in this volume are provided, in nearly every instance, exactly as they were presented in Lochner's original. Modification of some rhythms, notation, and syllabification is an inevitable result of translation considerations, particularly in paraphrases of liturgical canticles. Harmonizations and voice leadings are generally unaltered and often reflect the musical standards of nineteenth-century music editing. The reader will see and hear many familiar musical examples as Lochner demonstrates the rich heritage of liturgical music as he knew it in his day. Other music examples have fallen out of use or never became fully assimilated into American Lutheran practice. Overall, this volume serves as a historical snapshot and scholarly resource rather than a practical manual for present-day practice.

Kevin J. Hildebrand

Preface

From 1876, when I received my call to Trinity in Springfield, Illinois, until 1887, when I left, I taught both congregational singing and liturgics at the Missouri Synod's seminary of practical theology, which had been relocated from St. Louis to Springfield in 1875. Through this I was inspired to take up again my earlier studies in both hymnology and liturgy. I had been encouraged and guided in these studies during my preparation for the ministry of the American-Lutheran church over forty years ago by the blessed Pastor Löhe in Franconia and by his friend Hommel, later publisher of a musical *Liturgie lutherischer Gemeindegottesdienste* [Liturgy of Lutheran Divine Services],[5] who was then working in the neighboring district. Thus over the course of more extensive studies, and with a mind toward instruction particularly in the form and manner of the Chief Divine Service with the basis of the Augsburg Confession, Article XXIV, a number of study-notes emerged which, at the request of earlier and more recent students, are now published in as detailed and exhaustive a manner as possible.

Already during the preparation of a "Paper on the Proper Center of the Lutheran Liturgy," which I had been assigned to write in 1861 for the convention of the (then) Northern District, and which, by the resolution of said convention, was printed in the June, July, and August issues of *Lehre und Wehre*, volume 8 [nos. 6–8],[6] I was moved with a desire that, for the good of this country's immigrant church, which was being built on the basis of Luther's pure doctrine and freshly and vigorously organized under the blessings of complete freedom of conscience, a capable hand might some day produce and expound on the true "Mass" referred to in Augustana XXIV as purified by Luther—as his liturgical writings, and the not-insignificant number of older church orders, along with <IV> the treasures of liturgical music from the Reformation and post-Reformation days present it, and as that Mass still asserted itself, at least in its essential forms, here and there in the old country during the age of vulgar Rationalism, despite the havoc which Rationalism wrought with the liturgy. If, in the mean-

---

5 See below, p. xxiii, n. 23. —MC.

6 Friedrich Lochner, "Referat über die rechte Mitte der lutherischen Liturgie," *Lehre und Wehre* 8, nos. 6–8 (1862): 161–80; 193–207; 225–35.

time, seeing no competent hand has undertaken the task, I have ventured to publish my notes, I am motivated in doing so not solely by a desire to serve the students which were assigned to the practical field of theological instruction more aptly than was possible through individual, brief lectures, *but also by misgivings that the old form of the Divine Service which has now come into use again may be endangered in the future. Toward the prevention of such danger, then, I hereby desire to contribute the present liturgical work.*

When I came to this country nearly a half-century ago with other brethren in order to serve the Church, the old form of the Lutheran *Chief Divine Service* [*Hauptgottesdienst*] was known and used only in a handful of congregations of Saxon and Prussian Lutherans which had immigrated at the end of the thirties for their faith, and not long after that in the Franconian colonies which were just being formed in Michigan. Although Löhe had recently published his Agenda [1844], and Hommel afterwards his altar chants and other liturgical music [1851], for the local church, we, who were gathering together the scattered fellow Lutherans which had come largely from Rationalist or Unionist congregations, were compelled and content to lay the prerequisite foundation with the pure doctrine and therefore to make do more or less with the most rudimentary forms of the Divine Service. Even so, simply on account of our doctrine, we were decried as crypto-papists by the sects, Unionists, and General Synod (which falsely called itself Lutheran)! But once an adequate doctrinal foundation had been laid, it naturally led more and more toward liturgical formation in the congregations. The Agenda of the Synod of Missouri, etc., composed "from the old Saxon church agendas," which appeared in 1856,[7] was received in our congregations everywhere. It even had an influence beyond their districts, and in the more organized congregations the Chief Divine Service could be seen in its full form as prescribed in that Agenda. <V> Even in those places where, while the Agenda was being used, there was apprehension toward liturgical singing as something "Catholic," prejudice against this also continued to vanish.

Nevertheless, not only I but also others, on the basis of various signs, are moved by the foreboding that what has, as the fruit of the pure doctrine, now become our inheritance in the liturgy may also in time to come gradually be turned back into the austere, puritanical rite which we once found in general use. We are living in a land of rank Reformed sectari-

---

[7] *Kirchen-Agende für evangelisch-lutherischen Gemeinden ungeänderter Augsburgischer Confession* (St. Louis: Concordia Publishing House, 1856). Various editions were published in subsequent years. Portions of this Agenda were published in English in *Church Liturgy for Evangelical Lutheran Congregations of the Unaltered Augsburg Confession* (St. Louis: Concordia Publishing House, 1881). —MC.

anism, a land which is therefore Reformed at heart, and it is incumbent upon the coming generation to continue to strive more and more against the influence of English Puritanism in matters of church. Furthermore, we live in an age in which there is increasingly less patience and tolerance for spiritual practices, so that in some places a somewhat abbreviated liturgical service is already found to be too long, and the preacher is urged to shorten still more. Besides this, there is frequently a severe lack of precise liturgical understanding, as may be expected under the circumstances, and consequently a diminished desire to retain the liturgical legacy that has only just been regained. And if, alas, the precious doctrine of Christian freedom should cease to be applied rightly with respect to the world alienated from God, and the antinomian spirit threaten us at long last, then as time goes on, there will be an increasing tendency recklessly to dispose of the beautiful historic ceremonies, since as adiaphora they lie entirely in the area of Christian freedom.

To offer encouragement and guidance in the study of the liturgy, and more importantly to illustrate the beauty and importance of the Lutheran Chief Divine Service and the spirit of simplicity and confession which pervades it, and to lead to an understanding of it, and to do this all in such a way that the liturgical legacy already received may also be retained among us, and if possible, become a property held even more in common—such is the intent of my presentation on the emergence and meaning of the Lutheran Chief Divine Service and its individual parts, and the purpose of the accompanying materials from the rich treasury of the historic liturgical music of our church, which even here is so richly blessed, as well as the <VI> occasional notes on practical matters, in which I naturally focus on our local need.

Yet in order that my intention may be rightly understood, I will permit myself a few more remarks.

It is well known that in recent times, and above all in the old country, very great interest has been taken in the liturgy of the early Lutherans and the Early Church, and thus of Early Church music. Liturgical study is pursued ardently, and treasure after treasure is put on display. Everywhere there is an endeavor to cultivate Divine Services once more in their ancient and beautiful form, to turn attention again to churchly customs and usages with respect to altar hangings, ringing of the prayer bells, and the like. And so strong is this liturgical current among those who are of a mind to return to authentic Lutheranism that it asserts itself here in this country. Even the General Synod, which has obviously abandoned Lutheranism since 1845, nevertheless, always desiring to be called Lutheran, cannot evade it. It would be good for people to be excited about these efforts and to hail them as the proclamation of an awakened, vigorous, and joyful life, if only they were regarded as secondary in importance, and God's Word and Luther's doctrine primary. Unfortunately, that is not the case. People only grasp for the shell and leave the kernel. Indeed, they mistake the shell for the kernel, and think that by it they will breathe the mind and spirit of Luther back into the present-day Lutheran Church. The Augustana, Article VII [:2], by saying, "*it is enough*," so emphatically stresses unanimity in the pure doctrine and true use of the Sacraments, and identifies uniformity in the ceremonies instituted merely by men as inessential to unity. Yet they place no importance on the pure doctrine, but allow disunity in doctrine to be as great as it will be, and uniformity is forged through regulations and the old Luthern liturgy. While the Apology, in the Article on the Mass [XXIV (XII), 51], testifies: "There is nothing that keeps people in church more than good preaching," it is thought that by reestablishing the outward beauty and variety of the old Lutheran order of Divine Service, the people will be brought back to the Church and kept there, instead of attending, above all, to preaching that is "good" (in the sense of the Apology [XXIV]), and experiencing beforehand the truth of this quote from the Confessions. And when people ought to recognize their increasing departure from God's Word <VII> and Luther's doctrine, and repent in sackcloth and ashes, they instead thank God for their "sense" for liturgical regulations in the Church of the present-day as though this were some spiritual gift [*charisma*] bestowed on them. May God preserve our American-Lutheran church from *this sort* of appreciation of the liturgy!

Two people do the same thing, and yet it is not the same thing! Where "the Gospel is preached unanimously according to the pure understanding and the Sacraments administered according to God's Word" [AC VII 2–3], and where the Church therefore wishes to be built upon and governed by the Word alone, there is a far different purpose for liturgical efforts. This moreover is the order that my own efforts will tend toward, and the service which I seek to perform with this work. Since in this work I am concerned solely with retaining that portion of the old liturgy which has fallen into our lap on its own merely as a result of returning to Luther's doctrine, I have not been able to speak favorably of those efforts which aimed to embellish the old Lutheran liturgy even more by all manner of "additions" from church antiquity and even from Roman rituals, and so to go above and beyond it. Thus, in my instruction at the aforesaid theological seminary, whenever I showed my students the beauty, riches, and merits of the old Lutheran liturgy, I always made them aware of the fact that everything depends on the pure Word and Sacrament, and that all ceremonies should and must only serve the end that these [Word and Sacrament] may be rightly employed, and how on the other hand this liturgy would always do this service, and that it would therefore be lamentable if, where it is introduced, it should eventually be supplanted again by English Puritan austerity. But above all, I did not neglect to warn them earnestly of overestimating the liturgy and introducing it prematurely. They were also able to see this in practice [*in praxi*] right where they were. After twenty-six years of service at one of our old congregations, which was not only advanced in knowledge but also richly appointed liturgically, I was installed in a congregation that was not yet fully ripe for the old liturgy, so that even chanting at the altar had to be dispensed with for a time. Although I was therefore unable, in the context of the Divine Service in the congregation, to demonstrate to my students all that I gave them in liturgical instruction, yet I was able to some extent to show them by my example that, and how, a Lutheran preacher <VIII> seeks to emphasize a "good sermon" and can, when it comes to proper forms with respect even to liturgical matters, be patient for a time, and, while having great love for the old liturgy and all enthusiasm for it, it is still possible by God's grace to say with Paul in this respect: "I can face both abundance and need, through Him who strengthens me, even Christ" [Philippians 4:12–13].

Finally, I will permit myself also to reference the works which I have more or less used as my sources, or which I have consulted in various ways.

Above all I have drawn on *Luther's liturgical writings*, referring constantly to his *Formula Missae* (1523) or [the German translation] *Weise christlich Meß zu halten* [Manner of Holding a Christian Mass, 1524])[8] and his *Deutsche Messe* (1526).[9] Added to these is a series of old church orders—that is to say, as many as were at my disposal. These include: The Brandenburg-Nürnberg church order (1533),[10] Veit Dietrich's *Agendbüchlein* [Little Agenda Book, 1565],[11] the Agenda of Duke August of Braunschweig-Lüne-

[8] WA 12:205–20. Cf. Luther, "An Order of Mass and Communion for the Church at Wittenberg" (1523), AE 53:15–40. The German translation, *Weise christlich Meß zu halten* (1524), by Paul Speratus, is found in StL 10:2230ff., and appears to be the text Lochner is using throughout this volume. —MC.

[9] WA 19:72–113. Cf. Luther, "The German Mass and Order of Service" (1526), AE 53:51–90. —MC.

[10] Andreas Osiander, *Kirchen Ordnung. In meiner gnedigen herrn der Marggraven zu Brandenburg . . . Wie man sich bayde mit der leer und Ceremonien halten solle* (Nürmberg, 1533). —MC.

[11] *Agend Büchlein, Darinnen angezeigt, wie die Predigt Gottes wort, und die heiligen Sacramenten, sampt ihren zugehörigen Gesengen, und anderen Ceremonien . . . sollen verrichtet werden . . .* (Frankfurt am Main, 1565). —MC.

burg (1657),[12] the Oels Agenda (1664),[13] the Schwarzburg Agenda (1675),[14] the Leipzig Agenda of Duke Henry (1681),[15] and the Magdeburg church order (1685).[16] In particular, however, I sought to make use of Dr. L. **Schoeberlein's** *Schatz des liturgischen Chor- und Gemeindegesangs: nebst den Altarweisen* [Treasury of Liturgical Choir and Congregational Song along with the Altar Chants] (Göttingen, 1865),[17] encompassing three extensive volumes, since this remarkable work is a storehouse full of historic liturgical music and a most thorough introduction to understanding the Chief Divine Service and its individual parts. In addition to this I consulted the following sources: (1) Dr. **Freytag**: *Lutherus musico-liturgicus, das ist, Luthers Deutsche Messe und Ordnung des Gottesdienstes* [Luther's Liturgical Music, that is, Luther's German Mass and Order of Service] (1871);[18] (2) J. **Lyra**: *Die liturgischen Altarweisen des lutherischen Hauptgottesdienstes* [The Liturgical Altar Chant of the Lutheran Chief Divine Service],[19] and his *Andreas Ornithoparchus von den Kirchenaccenten* [Andreas Ornithoparchus on Ecclesiastical Accentuations] (1877);[20] (3) **Löhe**: *Sammlung li-*

[12] *Agenda oder: Erster Teyl der Kirchen-Ordnung Unser von Gottes Gnaden Augusti Herzogen zu Bruns-wyk und Lunä-Burg. Wy es mit den Ceremonien, auch andern nootwendigen Sachen und Verrichtungen in den Kirchen Unserer Fürstentume Graf-Herrschaften und Landen zu halten* (Wolfenbüttel: Sterne, 1657). —MC.

[13] *Agenda, oder Ordnung derer evangelischen Kirchen im Oelßnischen Fürstenthum*... (Oels: Seyffart, 1664). —MC.

[14] *Agenda Schwartzburgica: das ist, Verzeichniß der Ceremonien* . . . (Rudolstadt: Freyschmid & Fleischer, 1675). —MC.

[15] This edition is not readily found. Instead, see *Agenda, Das ist: KirchenOrdnung, Wie sich die Pfarrherrn und Seelsorger*... (Leipzig: F. Lankischens Erben / Altenburg: G. Richter, 1672). —MC.

[16] *Chur-Fürstliche Brandenburgische Jm Hertzogthum Magdeburg publicirte Kirchenordnung. Anno 1685* (Halle: Salfeld, 1708). —MC.

[17] Ludwig Schoeberlein and Friedrich Samuel Riegel, *Schatz des liturgischen Chor- und Gemeindegesangs: nebst den Altarweisen in der deutschen evangelischen Kirche*... (Göttingen: Vandenhoeck & Ruprecht, 1865–72). Vol. 1: Die allgemeinen Gesangstücke. Vol. 2: Die besonderen Gesangstücke. Abt. 1. Die Fest- und feiertagsgottesdienste. Vol. 2: Die besonderen Gesangstücke. Abt. 2. Der Sonntagskreis des Kirchenjahres. Abt. 3. Die besonderen kirchlichen Handlungen. —MC.

[18] J. A. Freytag, *Lutherus musico-liturgicus. das ist, Luthers Deutsche Messe und Ordnung des Gottesdienstes* (Hannover: Carl Meyer, 1871). —MC.

[19] Justus Wilhelm Lyra, *Die liturgischen Altarweisen des lutherischen Hauptgottesdienstes nach ihrer Reinheit und Einheit in musikalischer Beziehung untersucht und festgestellt* . . . (Göttingen: Vandenhoeck & Ruprecht, 1873). —MC.

[20] Justus Wilhelm Lyra, *Andreas Ornithoparchus aus Meiningen, der Zeitgenosse Luthers: und dessen Lehre von den Kirchenaccenten* (Gütersloh: C. Bettelmann, 1877). —MC.

turgischer Formulare [Collection of Liturgical Formulas][21] and his Agenda of 1844, 1853, and 1884;[22] (4) F. **Hommel**: *Liturgie lutherischer Gemeindegottesdienste* [Liturgy of Lutheran Divine Services] (1851);[23] (5) Dr. F. **Layriz**: *Kern des deutschen Kirchengesangs: IV. Liturgische Weisen* [Core of German Church Music: Part 4—Liturgical Melodies] (1855);[24] (6) Dr. L. **Kraußold**: *Historisch-musicalisches Handbuch für den Kirchen- und Choralgesang* [Musicological Handbook for Church and Choral Music] (1855);[25] (7) **Vilsecker**: *Lehre vom römischen Choralgesange* [Teaching on Roman Choral Music] (1842);[26] (8) Seminary director J. **Zahn**: *Handbüchlein für evangelische Cantoren und Organisten* [Little Handbook for Evangelical Cantors und Organists];[27] (9) **Rudelbach**: *Die Sacrament-Worte* [The Words of the Sacrament];[28] <IX> (10) O. **Kade**: *Luther Codex;*[29] (11) J. L. **König**: *Die Haupt-Liturgien der alten Kirche in wortgetreuer Übersetzung* [The Chief Liturgies of the Ancient Church in Literal Translation];[30] (12)

[21] Wilhelm Löhe, *Sammlung liturgischer Formulare der evangelisch-lutherischen Kirche* (Nördlingen: Beck, 1839–42). Vol. 1. Taufe, Catechismusübung, Confirmation, 1839. Vol. 2. Beichte, 1842. Vol. 3. Ordnung der Communion oder der evangelischen Messe, 1842. —MC.

[22] Wilhelm Löhe, *Agende für christliche Gemeinden des lutherischen Bekenntnisses* (Nördlingen: Beck, 1844). A second, expanded edition, part 1, was published in 1853. A third edition, edited by Johannes Deinzert, was published in 1884. English translation found in *Liturgy for Christian Congregations of the Lutheran Faith*, trans. F. C. Longaker, ed. Johannes Deinzer (Newport, Kentucky, 1902). —MC.

[23] Friderich Hommel, *Liturgie lutherischer Gemeindegottesdienste: cum notis musicis* (Nördlingen: Beck, 1851). —MC.

[24] Fridrich Layriz, *Kern des deutschen Kirchengesangs: zum Gebrauch evangelisch-lutherischer Gemeinden und Familien.* Abt. 4: *CXX liturgische Weisen enthaltend* (Nördlingen: Beck, 1855). —MC.

[25] Lorenz Kraußold, ed., *Historisch-musicalisches Handbuch für den Kirchen- und Choralgesang: für evangelische Geistliche und die es werden wollen* (Erlangen: Deichert, 1855). —MC.

[26] Franz Joseph Vilsecker, *Lehre vom römischen Choralgesange. Zum Gebrauche für Seminarien, Geistliche, Schullehrer und Choralisten* (Passau: Pustet'sche Buchhandlung, 1841). —MC.

[27] Johannes Zahn, *Handbüchlein für evangelische Cantoren und Organisten,* 1st ed. (Nürnberg: G. Löhe, 1871). —MC.

[28] Andreas Gottlob Rudelbach, *Die Sacrament-Worte oder die wesentlichen Stücke der Taufe und des Abendmahls, historisch-kritisch dargestellt . . .* (Leipzig: Tauchnitz, 1837). —MC.

[29] Otto Kade, *Ein feste Burgk ist unser Got: Der neuaufgefundene Luther-Codex vom Jahre 1530 . . .* (Dresden: Schrag'sche Verlags-Anstalt; Klemm, 1873). —MC.

[30] Johann Ludwig König, *Die Haupt-Liturgien der alten Kirche in wortgetreuer Übersetzung* (Neustrelitz: Barnewitz, 1865). —MC.

Naumann: *Illustrirte Musikgeschichte* [Illustrated History of Music], etc.;[31] in addition to others.

I will take the liberty once more to note that, after this work was already completed, Dr. Herzog's excellent revised and expanded *Musicalischer Anhang zur Agende der evangelisch-lutherischen Kirche in Bayern* [Musical Appendix to the Agenda for the Evangelical-Lutheran Church in Bavaria] (1883)[32] came to my attention, and it gave me no little joy to know that I was in agreement with his views in all points. From his work I borrowed the setting for the melody of the Nicene Creed which had previously been made famous by Hommel.

Our preachers studying here in the land of Puritanism and immigration, where conditions are still primitive to some extent, including with respect to church architecture, have before their eyes little that is normal, and certainly a great deal that is abnormal and ungainly, so that the Church's form and practice with respect to the chancel, altar, and baptismal font are frequently misunderstood. Therefore it seemed advisable to me to discuss the sites for the liturgy in a special appendix, yet strictly with an eye to our local need. In doing so I have made partial use of an instructive writing which appeared only this year, titled, *Das evangelische Kirchengebäude. Ein Ratgeber für Geistliche und Freunde kirchlicher Kunst, herausgegeben in Verbindung mit Baurath Dr. Mothes in Leipzig und Architect Prüser in Berlin von Viktor Schultze, Prof. der Theologie* [The Evangelical Church Building: A Guide for Clergy and Friends of Churchly Art, published in connection with construction consultant Dr. Mothes in Leipzig and architect Prüser in Berlin, by Viktor Schultze, Professor of Theology] (Leipzig: Georg Böhme, 1886).[33]

May God preserve us in His pure Word and Sacrament, and grant us so to live in His Word that in the public Divine Service, any ceremonies and customs with which the hands of men may entwine the Means of Grace may be of service to the same and appear not as a contrived but as a natural and genuine adornment in the public participation in the Means of Grace in the common confession and adoration of the Most High.

F. L.

[31] Emil Naumann, *Illustrirte Musikgeschichte: die Entwicklung der Tonkunst aus frühesten Anfängen bis auf die Gegenwart,* 2 vols. (Stuttgart: Spemann, 1880–85). —MC.

[32] Johann Georg Herzog, *Musicalischer Anhang zur Agende der evangelisch-lutherischen Kirche in Bayern* (Erlangen: Deichert, 1883). —MC.

[33] Viktor Schultze, *Das evangelische Kirchengebäude. Ein Ratgeber für Geistliche und Freunde kirchlicher Kunst* . . . (Leipzig: G. Böhme, 1886). —MC.

Friedrich Lochner

Part One
The Formation and Structure of the Lutheran Chief Divine Service

Unjustly are our churches accused of having abolished the Mass. For, without boasting, *it is obvious that the Mass is celebrated among us with greater devotion and more earnestness than among our opponents.* Furthermore, the people are taught frequently and with great care why the Holy Sacrament was instituted and how it is to be used (namely, to comfort terrified consciences), by which fact the people are drawn to Communion or Mass. At the same time, instruction is also given to counter false teachings about the Sacrament. *Neither have any* ***notable changes*** *been made in the public ceremonies of the Mass, except that in certain places German hymns (to instruct and train the people) are sung in addition to the Latin responses*, since the chief purpose of all ceremonies is that the people may learn from them what is necessary for them to know about Christ.

—Augsburg Confession, Article XXIV

§1. The Divine Service of the New Testament, Its Essence and Form

<3> The external, corporate worship service of Christians is not based on any statutory (ceremonial-legal) commandment of the Lord as was the Old Testament service, nor for that matter on any commandment of His holy apostles. Rather, it is the product, expression, necessary manifestation, exercise, and operation of the internal life of the communion of saints. While this communion may be invisible in essence, it is nevertheless discernible in its existence by virtue of the Word and Sacrament through which it is created. The inward communion of the saints consists of the one, living faith of all its individual members—the outward communion, of its gathering together for the common use of Word and Sacrament, as well as for adoration and supplication and the giving of thanks and praise (Ephesians 4:3; Acts 2:42; Hebrews 10:25).

Insofar, then, as the public Divine Service is comprised of the common use of Word and Sacrament along with the exercise of prayer and praise, it is characterized as a public operation of divine love giving gifts and blessing, and of human love receiving and responding. God serves man by repeatedly offering him His salvation and by coming to him with blessing in Word and Sacrament, and man serves God by honoring His offerings of salvation in Word and Sacrament and by reciprocating His love in prayer, thanksgiving, and praise, in self-offering, and in the employment of those spiritual and bodily gifts bestowed on him, to the glory of God and the benefit of his neighbor (Exodus 20:24; Psalm 100; Matthew 18:20; Romans 12:1ff.; Hebrews 13:15–16; cf. 1 Corinthians 16:2). "To serve Christ and God," says Luther, "meant to St. Paul chiefly to do the duty which Christ had given him, namely, preaching. It is a service *from* Christ, not *for* Him, and not *from* us but *for* us" (EA 7:79). And on Christ's words, "This do in remembrance of Me," he writes, among other things: "Learn to remember Him, that is, (as said) to preach, praise, and worship, listen to and thank Him for the grace <4> revealed in Christ. When you do so, behold, you confess with heart and mouth, with ears and eyes, with body and soul, that you have not given God anything, nor can you, but that you have and receive it all from Him, yea, everything, especially eternal life and boundless righteousness in Christ. If this is done, you have made Him your true God, and by such confession upheld His divine honor. For a true God is One who gives, not receives; who helps, not is helped; who teaches and governs, not who is taught and governed. In short, He does and gives all things and has need of no man, and does all things freely by pure grace without the merit of those who are unworthy and undeserving—indeed, who are condemned and lost. Such remembrance, confession, and honor is what He desires. Behold, such divine service has hardly any glory, nor does it fill the eyes. Nevertheless it fills the heart, which heaven and earth cannot do. And when the heart is filled, then eyes and ears, nose and mouth, body and soul, and all the members are filled. For as the heart goes, all the members go likewise, and it is altogether nothing but tongues giving thanks and praise to God" (EA 23:174ff). Therefore the Apology states in the Article [XXIV] on the Mass: "A sacrament (*sacramentum*) is an outward sign (*ceremonia*) or work by which God gives us what His divine promise, tied to said ceremonies, offers. For example, Baptism is a ceremony and a work not which we give or offer to God but in which God, or the one baptizing in God's stead, baptizes us. Here God offers and gives us remission of sins according to His promise: 'He who believes and is baptized shall be saved'" [Mark 16:16]. Again: "Sacrifice (*sacrificium*) is a *ceremonia* or work that we render to God and thereby honor Him" (Ap XXIV 18). The Apology then goes on to explain that the sacrifice made by Christians is not a propitiatory sacrifice, but purely one of thanksgiving and praise for the all-availing propitiatory sacrifice of Christ.

Accordingly, if the public service of Christian worship is a natural and necessary expression of the Christian congregation's life of faith, its character must reflect this in *form* and *manner*. The latter is the concern of the *liturgy* insofar as it highlights what is spoken and done in the administration and reception of the Means of Grace on the one hand, and in the sacrificial offering of prayer, praise, and thanksgiving on the other hand.

Note: According to its literal sense and churchly meaning, *liturgy* denotes the ceremony performed in service to the Christian congregation. Thus in the <5> Article on the Mass cited above, the Apology gives the definition: "In Greek, *liturgia* properly signifies a ministry in which the congregation is served. This agrees well with our teaching that the priest is like a common waiter, serving and bringing the Holy Sacrament to those who wish to commune" [Ap XXIV 87]. In the first centuries, the Church did not commit her liturgy to writing. Basil the Great (d. 379) plainly says this: "Which of the saints has left to us the words of invocation at the consecration of the bread and of the thanksgiving and of the cup of blessing? For we are not content with what the apostle or the Gospel mention, but both before and after them we say other things, as those having great power, with respect to the mystery, receiving them from teachings not written down." (See König, *Die Hauptliturgien der alten Kirche* [The Main Liturgies of the Ancient Church].)[34] The recording of these things, which later became necessary, eventually gave rise to liturgical books, rituals, agendas, and so on.

---

[34] Cf. Basil, *De Spiritu sancto ad Amphil.* c. 27, dist. 67. Cf. Jacques P. Migne, ed., *Patrologiae cursus completus, series Graeca,* 161 vols. (Paris: J. P. Migne, 1857–66), 32:193a. Cf. Philip Schaff and Henry Wace, eds., *A Select Library of the Christian Church: Nicene and Post-Nicene Fathers: Second Series,* 14 vols. (New York, 1890–1900), 8:43. —MC.

§2. The Communion Service as the Chief Divine Service among Various Services

There is a wealth and a blessed multiplicity in the forms and manners of the public Divine Service of the orthodox Church, in which the life of faith and communion has found its free expression. She has a *service of Communion*, in which the preaching of the Word is followed by the administration of the Lord's Supper, thus adding sign and seal to the Word; a *service of preaching*, in which, primarily, Scripture is expounded and applied, or in special cases a sermon (a homily for a particular occasion) is preached; a *service of catechesis*, for establishing and furthering the knowledge of the chief articles of Christian doctrine (preaching and examination in the Catechism), and a *service of prayer and praise* in her Matins and Vespers, the brief daily morning and evening services in which, according to Luther's well-founded request, God's Word is not only read but also expounded in the briefest manner,[35] yet

[35] *) Namely, in "Concerning the Order of Public Worship" (1523), Luther writes: "Now to do away with these abuses, it should first be known that the Christian congregation is never to come together *unless the Word of God is preached and prayed, though it be in the briefest manner*. As in Psalm 101 [102:21–22]: 'When the kings and the people are gathered together to serve God, they should proclaim the name and praise of God.' And Paul (1 Corinthians 14 [:31]) says: 'that there may be prophecy, teaching, and admonishing in the congregation.' *Therefore, wherever the Word of God is not preached, it is better not to sing or read or come together.*"

"Now this is how it was done among Christians in the time of the apostles and should be done still: every morning at an early hour, perhaps four or five o'clock, let the people gather and a lesson be read, whether students or priests or whoever, just as the lessons are still read at Matins today. One or two ought to do this, or one by one, however is most pleasing. Then let the preacher, or whoever is appointed, go up and *expound a part of the same lesson*, that the others may all understand, learn, and be admonished. The first work St. Paul calls 'speaking in tongues' (1 Corinthians 14 [:26]); the second, 'expounding' or 'prophesying,' and speaking with sense and understanding. And where this is not done, the congregation is not edified by the lesson, as happened hitherto in cloisters and monasteries, where they were only blowing against the walls" (EA 22:154 [AE 53:11f.]). Consequently, that the Word of God might be expounded at Matins and Vespers, albeit "in the briefest manner," Veit Deitrich's Summaries were produced. Cf. the prologues by Dietrich and [Franz] Vierling in the Altenburg New Testament, American edition. In the latter's prologue, there is also an order for Matins and Vespers from the same time.

[See *Das Neue Testament unsers Herrn Jesu Christi* (St. Louis: Concordia Publishing House, 1892). Vierling's prologue is also found in his book of biblical prologues and epilogues, at the beginning of the New Testament, where he says, "According to the old, traditional choral singing of Matins: first, a Psalm or hymn is sung pertaining to the season . . . This song is followed by the lesson, which is done by the choralists as lectors. And they begin by reading the prologue belonging to the chapter of the Holy Bible, then the chapter, then the summary from Veit Dietrich, etc. Then the relevant *votum* or concluding blessing. After the lesson is done, a corporate prayer is read, also conforming to the various sea-

in which prayer and praise compose the bulk of the activity. <6>

On the basis of Acts 2:42 and 1 Corinthians 11, and following the pattern of the Ancient Church, the Lutheran Church considers the *Communion service* the most glorious and most important of all public services, having also fitted it out liturgically in the richest and most thoughtful manner. There is therefore a distinction between the *chief service* and the *incidental service* [*Haupt- und Nebengottesdienst*]. It is not by the Sunday or festival nor by the season nor by the liturgical richness that a service becomes a *chief service*, but (as determined by the scriptural relationship of Word and Sacrament), *when the proclamation of the Word of the Gospel is immediately followed by the administration of the Sacrament of Christ's body and blood, so that this, as the* ***seal*** *of the Word, forms the goal and keystone* of the service. All other services in which the administration of the Sacrament is not intended from the outset are rendered *incidental services*, however richly many of these may have been ordered liturgically in the past. Having regard for the interconnectedness of Word and Sacrament, as well as for Christian antiquity, when even in the days of Augustine (AD 400) the Supper was received by the whole congregation every Sunday at least, assuming there was a longing for it—the <7> *mid-morning service* which followed the early Matins service in the Reformation era and long afterward *was regularly a Communion service, and thus a Chief Divine Service,* at least in congregations of greater number. In contrast to the private masses of the papacy in which only the officiating priest receives the Sacrament, the Apology, Article VIII [33] emphasizes: "Among us, however, the people partake of the Holy Sacrament *every Sunday* willingly, without compulsion"; likewise Article XXIV [1]: "*Masses are celebrated in our churches every Sunday and on all festivals,* in which the Sacrament is offered to those who wish to use it, provided they have first been examined and absolved." Thus it was that, when for lack of communicants the Supper could not be celebrated in such a service, there was still an attempt to leave the form of the Divine Service intact in all other respects. In a number of places, however, the sermon was followed by the reading of a prescribed exhortation, such as in Pomerania (1563), Liegnitz (1594), or the delivery of a freer exhortation, as in Wittenberg (1559, 1565) and Mecklenburg (1540, 1552). In such exhortations, the lack of the communicants was lamented and a frequent use of the most worthy Supper was exhorted and encouraged (yet without constraint of the Law).

---

sons of the year. This is concluded with the prayer of the Lord Christ, which is called the Our Father after its first words, and this is spoken by the whole congregation with a loud voice. With this the daily corporate prayer concludes and is finished." See Franz Vierling, *Vorreden und Beschluß uber die Capitel der Bücher des Alten und Newen Testaments* (Breslau: Georgius Bawman, 1596). —MC.]

Note: (1) It appears that the oldest description of the Communion service is found in the post-apostolic period by Justin Martyr (d. 166). The passage, as Dr. Uhlhorn gives it in German translation in his writing, *Der Kampf des Christenthums mit dem Heidenthum* [The Battle of Christianity with Heathenism], reads:

> On Sunday, all who live in cities or in the country gather together in one place, and the memoirs of the Apostles or the books of the prophets are read, as long as time permits. Then, when the reader has finished, the president in a discourse instructs, and exhorts to the imitation of these glorious examples. Then we all rise together and send up our prayers. And when we have ceased from prayer, bread and wine and water are brought, and the president offers prayers and thanksgivings according to his ability. The congregation gives its assent, saying Amen; and there is a distribution to each one present of the consecrated things, and to those who are absent a portion is sent by the deacons. And they who are well-to-do and willing give what each thinks fit, and the collected gifts are deposited with the president, who by them succors the widows and orphans, and those who through sickness or any other cause are in want, and those who are in bonds, and the strangers sojourning among us, in short, all who are in need.[36] <8>

At the beginning of the fourth century, the Chief Divine Service was broken up into a *missa catechumenorum* (service of preaching) and a *missa fidelium* (lit., "service of the faithful" = service of the Supper). When the sermon was finished, the deacon excused the non-Christians and catechumens present with the words: "Ite, missa est!" — "Go, you are dismissed." (Hence, it seems, the German word *Messe* ["Mass"].) Thus the beginning of the *missa fidelium* especially, in contrast to the very simple acts of Communion described above, shows a greater flourish and festivity in the liturgy of the Supper. According to the eighth chapter of the so-called "Apostolic Constitutions," the *missa fidelium* began with the silent prayer of those who remained, followed by a general prayer of the church prayed by the deacon, during which the congregation interjected "Kyrie eleison" after every petition as in the Litany. After a collect prayed by the bishop, the deacons gathered the gifts of bread and wine which had been offered and prepared them for use in the Supper. Then, when the holy kiss had been passed—men to men and women to women—the bishop, being robed in a special festive garment and

[36] Uhlhorn, Gerhard. *Der Kampf des Christentums mit dem Heidentum. Bilder aus der Vergangenheit als Spiegelbilder für die Gegenwart* (Stuttgart: D. Gundert, 1899). Cited from *First Apology*, 67. See *ANF* 1:186. —MC.

surrounded by ministers of the higher orders, approached the altar, spoke the apostolic blessing (2 Corinthians 13:13) over the congregation, which replied with the words "And with thy spirit." Then antiphonally, the Bishop: "Your hearts [*Sinn*] on high!" Congregation: "We have them with the Lord." B.: "Let us give thanks to the Lord." C.: "It is meet and right." B.: "It is truly meet and right to praise Thee high above all, the truly living God. . . ." etc.

This very, very long yet thoroughly majestic prayer of thanksgiving concludes with the Sanctus sung by the whole congregation: "Holy, Holy, Holy Lord God of Sabaoth. Heaven and earth. . . ." etc. This is followed by the Consecration, another general prayer of the church with intercessions, this time being said by the bishop, then the Peace, and finally the Distribution. This last item, along with the conclusion, is described thus:

> And after all (in response to the Peace) have said "Amen," let the deacon say: "Let us take heed!" and the bishop address the people thus: "Holy things unto the holy!" and the people answer: "One is Holy, One the Lord, One Jesus Christ, to the glory of God the Father, blessed forever. Amen. Glory to God in the highest, and peace on earth, good will toward men! Hosanna to the Son of David! Blessed is He that cometh in the name of the Lord! The Lord God hath appeared also unto us. Hosanna in the highest!" And thereupon let the bishop partake, <9> followed by the elders, deacons, and subdeacons, and the lectors, singers, and ascetics; and of the women the deaconesses, virgins, and widows, and then the children followed by all the people in order, in awe and caution without noise. And let the bishop give the sacrifice, during which he says, "The Body of Christ," and let the one receiving say, "Amen." But let the deacon hold the cup and, offering it, say, "The blood of Christ, the cup of life," and let the one drinking say, "Amen." Let Psalm 33 (=34) be said (=sung) while all the rest receive, and when all men and all women have received, let the deacons bring the remnants to an adjacent room. And when the singers have finished, let the deacon say, "Having become partakers of the precious body and the precious blood of Christ, let us give thanks to Him who has made us worthy to be partakers of His holy mysteries, and let us pray," etc. The prayer of thanksgiving spoken by the bishop forms the conclusion. (See König, *Die Hauptliturgien der alten Kirche* [The Chief Liturgies of the Ancient Church].)

Note: (2) Although the *Brandenburg-Nürnberg Church Order* (1533) sought to model the Sunday service without Communion on the order for incidental services, it nevertheless became the general practice to leave the

arrangement of the chief service intact up to the sermon. This was then followed by the Litany or the Te Deum, or both in turn, as the "congregational" and "congregational thanksgiving." Or else the conclusion was limited to a congregational hymn of praise connected with a "Christian motet" by the choir, which the latter introduced, both simultaneously acting as a "Deo Gratias" upon hearing the Word of God. The Braunschweig-Lüneburg church order, however, specifies: "After the sermon shall be sung the Preface, Sanctus, the German *Paternoster*, '*O Christ Thou Lamb of God,*' a German collect for Sundays, and the closing benediction."

§3. The Mass Restored by Luther in Its Evangelical Form

As the Augsburg Confession, its Apology, and Luther's liturgical writings indicate, the *traditional name* of the Chief Divine Service was left intact and was called "the **Mass**" even in the orthodox [Lutheran] Church. This single term signifies holy service, *cultus*, and parallels the <10> Greek *liturgia,* as the Apology, Article XII [XXIV], emphasizes over against the papistic derivation thereof from the Hebrew *misbeach*, "altar of sacrifice," saying: "*Missa* and *liturgia* do not mean sacrifice; *missa* in Hebrew means a collected contribution, for it was by such means that the Christians brought food and drink to the assembly for the good of the poor. And this custom was derived from the Jews who were required to bring such contributions to their feasts, and called them *missa*." While in the Scandinavian Lutheran Church this name was always used to indicate the chief service, in the German Lutheran Church it was later abandoned, regardless of the fact that even when we were young it was customary in the Nürnberg dialect to refer to Communion as the *Amt* ["office"] and the sermon in the chief service as the *Amtspredigt* ["office sermon"].

Yet there is no doubt that the retention of the name "Mass" indicates that, in the outward Divine Service, Luther intended *to do* ***nothing new,*** *but only to return to the true, historic form of the Divine Service*. Generally speaking, the aim of Luther's whole Reformation was not negation and destruction, but restoration. It sought merely to eliminate in doctrine and life that which contradicted God's Word and had over the course of time expanded like harmful leaven. After Luther had begun the Reformation and then turned his attention to the administration of the Sacrament in the Roman Church, he exclaimed: "The words of salvation and life are shut up, even as the ark of the Lord stood in the pagan temple next to Dagon, but the ark had to clear its own way!" (Rudelbach, *Sacrament-Worte* [Words of

the Sacrament], 9.)[37] It could not elude his keen eye that the Word of the Lord had been buried, as it were, here under a host of ceremonies which deafened by their sheer weight, and distracted the attention of the faithful away from the One Thing Needful. But how did he let the ark clear its own way? Not in the manner of Zwingli and his ilk, who broke radically with the past, particularly by getting rid of those outward things which found no explicit support in the words of Scripture but only came to be adopted after the time of the apostles. Rather, Luther here proceeded with extreme caution and a sparing hand *according to principles drawn from the deepest lifespring of Scripture and of true evangelical practice.* Pursuant to this, on the one hand, he mercilessly *purged* everything that was genuine papistic leaven, and especially <11> that belonged to or even simply "smacked of" the abomination of the sacrifice of the Mass properly speaking. On the other hand, he *separated* the clutter of churchly hue from that which was in agreement with the pure doctrine and seemed to be the common property of the Church, especially that which was salutary and profitable for Word and Sacrament. "We confess," says Luther in his *Formula Missae*, "that we never intended to abolish every outward service, but rather to purge again that which has been in use hitherto, albeit corrupted with many accretions, and to show what the true Christian use is."[38] In the same way he explains in his "Concerning the Order of Public Worship" (1523): "The Divine Service which is now everywhere in use has an exquisite Christian pedigree, as does the office of preaching. But just as the office of preaching has been corrupted by spiritual tyrants, the Divine Service has been corrupted by hypocrites. Therefore, just as we do not abolish the office of preaching, but desire to restore it to its rightful place, neither is it our intention to abolish the Divine Service, but to restore it to its proper use" (EA 22:153).[39]

When Luther says that the intention was merely to purge the service "which has been in use hitherto," and to show "what the true Christian use is," yet at the same time boasts that "the Divine Service which is now everywhere in use has an exquisite Christian heritage," he is referring to the *structure of the Mass in its chief parts* as the Western Church received it from the earliest Eastern Church, possessed it until the Reformation, "albeit corrupted with many additions," and has, since 1570, retained it permanently and invariably with these accretions. We saw a picture of the original shape of the Mass in the testimony of Justin (expressed [above] in

---

[37] Rudelbach quotes in German the eighth point of Luther's *Formula Missae* (1523). Cf. Luther, "An Order of Mass and Communion" (1523), AE 53:20. —MC.

[38] Ibid. —MC.

[39] Cf. Luther, "Concerning the Order of Public Worship" (1523), AE 53:11. —MC.

§2 [page 4], note *), and its expansion in the *Apostolic Constitutions* cited in the same place. Nothing in the latter, however, smacks of a *sacrifice for propitiation.* Although in this Clementine liturgy, the bread and wine, in the lengthy prayer connected to the consecration, are referred to as sacrificial gifts, it is not a *meritorial* but a *material* offering of the elements which takes place, since it plainly says, ". . . and [we] beseech Thee that Thou wouldest look favorably upon these gifts which are laid before Thee, O God who lackest naught; and be pleased with them to the glory of Thy Christ, and send down upon this offering Thy Holy Ghost, the witness of the sufferings of the Lord Jesus, *that He may make this bread to be the body of Thy Christ, and this cup to be the blood of Thy Christ,* that they which partake thereof <12> may be confirmed in piety, obtain the forgiveness of their sins, be delivered from the devil and his deceit, be filled by the Holy Ghost, be made worthy of Thy Christ, and attain to everlasting life, inasmuch as Thou art reconciled with them." (See König, *Die Hauptliturgien* [The Chief Liturgies], 114.) But following on the gradual disappearance of the *disciplina arcani,* that is, the tenet of secrecy concerning the mysteries—Baptism, Supper, the Apostles' Creed, the Our Father—which had been practiced since the second century, the order of the *Roman* Mass developed increasingly beginning in the fourth century. While in its form, inherited from the primitive Eastern Church, it is markedly improved in clarity, effect, and beauty, nevertheless, it is at the same time sorely *corrupted* by the abominable sacrifice of the Mass at its heart, along with transubstantiation, the withholding of the cup, the invocation of saints, private masses, and masses for the dead.

This service, then—which had an "exquisite pedigree," but was later so terribly corrupted by the sacrificial abomination and other "accretions" in the papacy—Luther "*purged and cleansed,*" just as an old painting is cleansed by the removal of dust and the blots of a foreign hand and thus restored, or as a noble structure is ridded of the partly disfiguring, partly superfluous ornament of later times so that it may be seen again in the beauty of its true form. **It is in its original and beautiful form—the form which is in accordance with the Gospel—that Luther gave the Mass back to the people!**

§4. Luther's Principles and Procedure in Restoring the Evangelical Mass

What ideas Luther had in particular when reforming the Divine Service he expresses early on in his "Concerning the Order of Public Worship" (1523) as follows: "Three great abuses invaded the Divine Service. First, *God's*

Word was silenced, and was only read and sung in the churches, which was the worst abuse. Second, once God's Word was silenced, *a great many unchristian fables and lies entered in alongside it,* both in legends, songs, and sermons, such that it is destestable to see. Third, *this Divine Service was performed as a work* to earn God's grace and salvation. Then faith was destroyed <13> and everyone gave to churches and religious bodies, and wanted to become popes, monks, and nuns" (EA 22:153; StL 10:221; [AE 53:11]). The principles applied here by Luther are none other than the twofold principle of the Lutheran Church generally: the so-called formal and material fundamental principle: "*scripture* alone" and "by *faith* alone."

Accordingly, in restoring the ancient, authentic order of the Mass, Luther brought the ***preaching*** *of the divine Word, above all, to its full right.* In his view, the worst abuse was that God's Word had been "silenced," that preaching had slowly but surely been squeezed out of the Mass—just as in Roman practice today it still appears not as an organic member but more as a discretionary option, an interpolated addition, the omission of which does nothing to diminish the papistic splendor of the Mass. But in doing so, Luther gave the Mass a definite pillar of support. As the Gospel of the free grace of God in Christ, it is placed in the center, and thus comprises the fundamental idea of the whole Divine Service, so that all the liturgical parts preceding the sermon have their *preparatory* place and meaning, and those following the sermon, their specific connection to and meaning for the *appropriation and sealing* of this grace in the Sacrament of the Altar. Hence everything that was contrary to the Gospel of the free grace of God and the Sacrament *as its seal*—that in one way or another related to the doctrine of the merit of works or the meritorious performance of the Divine Service or the Mass itself—must of itself give way and disappear. The Anglican Church therefore took from the *Apostolic Constitutions* the previously quoted prayer of the material sacrifice, (which, if properly understood, is not contrary to Scripture) and incorporated it into its Book of Common Prayer almost word for word, as an "oblation" and "invocation." Nevertheless, Luther deleted it along with everything else, so that nothing anywhere would have the faintest "smell" of a sacrifice and be abused in some way or other by erring spirits. Neither will we interpret this, as many have done more recently, as an excess in Luther's reformatory zeal. On the contrary, we will thank him all the more for it.

Let us now recreate this labor of his in the examination of the order of the Roman Mass, wherein he sought to "purge" the bad and "to retain only what is best." <14>

The *Roman papistic Mass* is divided into the following parts:

I. *Initium missae solemnis.* After the priest in chasuble, led by the acolytes bearing candlesticks, has ascended to the altar and placed the covered chalice upon it, he descends, stands at the foot of the altar, makes the sign of the cross upon himself, and prays: *Introibo ad altare Dei,* etc., from Psalm 43. This is supposed to resemble the preparation of the priest at the entrance of the altar of sacrifice.

II. The *Confiteor*, or Confession: the consecration of the priest and his ministrants for the celebration of the Mass. The priest, bowing forward, speaks it while standing at the foot of the altar. At the last words of the brief prayer appended to it, he ascends the altar, kisses it, censes it, and is himself censed. Then, standing at the Epistle, or right, side of the altar, he says:

III. The *Introitus*, or the Entrance Psalmody, which varies according to season and occasion.

IV. The *Kyrie*, prayed from the middle of the altar, nine times in alternation with the altar servers.

V. The *Gloria in excelsis* with the *Et in terra,* etc., and the *Laudamus te,* etc.

VI. The *Collecta(e)*, with preceding *Dominus vobiscum*, one or several according to season, feast, and other need.

VII. *Epistola*, its reading being done in the liturgical tone.

VIII. *Graduale* ("step song") with *Alleluia* or *Tractus* (song during procession or movement to the Gospel side).

IX. *Evangelium*, read by the deacon from the left side of the altar in the liturgical tone, after he has first obtained the blessing for this from the priest and kissed his hand in return.

X. The *Credo Nicaenum*, which the priest intones from the middle of the altar. While the choir finishes singing it, the former prays:

XI. The *Offertorium*, or prayer of oblation (while pouring the wine and some water into the chalice and offering up the host along with various censings), immediately followed by:

XII. The *Secreta*, the *silent* or secret prayers. Everything that has happened after the intoning of the Credo up to this point the priest speaks and does silently with his assistants while the choir finishes the Credo. Now, however, he sings aloud the transition, *Dominus vobiscum*, etc., to: <15>

XIII. The *Praefatio,* to which the choir responds with the *Sanctus,* while the priest silently speaks:

XIV. The *Canon missae*, the silent Mass. This consists of: (a) a prayer for the Church generally; (b) an intercession for individual members of the Church (*commemoratio pro vivis*); (c) the prayer remembering the saints, beginning with Mary and her meritorious intercession (*diptycha sanctorum*); (d) the recitation of the Words of Institution or Consecration, spoken softly by the priest after and during a deep silence by all present; (e) the prayer for the gracious reception of the sacrifice now accomplished (*canon missae post consecrationem*); and (f) the prayer for the dead (*memento pro defunctis*), whom the sacrifice of the Mass is supposed to benefit. Here the singing of the choir is ended and the priest chants aloud.

XV. The *Praeparatio ad Communionem*, consisting of the singing of the Our Father and a prayer following its Seventh Petition, during which a fragment of the host is broken and inserted into the chalice, whereupon the Salutation of Peace (*Pax Domini vobiscum*) follows. Then:

XVI. The *Preces ante Communionem*, consisting of the *Agnus Dei* ("O Christ, Thou Lamb of God"), with several collects.

XVII. The *Sumptio*, the reception of the bread and wine by the priest, and the distribution of the bread to communicants, if any are present.

XVIII. The *Communio*, that is, a Bible passage varying according to season and occasion, the Antiphon of the Psalm previously sung during Communion.

XIX. *Postcommunio*, a collect with the *Ite, missa est*.

XX. *Finis missae*, silent prayer of the priest.

XXI. *Benedictio*, blessing of the people.

XXII. *Evangelium*, John 1:1–14, which the priest, still at the altar, reads or sings, whereupon the *Deo gratias* of the altar server [*Meßdiener*] forms the conclusion.

In his *Formula Missae* (1523), then, Luther designates for retention from the first part of the Mass extending to and including the Credo numbers III to X above:

I. *Introitus*, although he would prefer the actual psalms;

II. *Kyrie*, yet threefold instead of ninefold;

III. *Gloria* with the *Et in terra* and the *Laudamus te*;

IV. *Collecta*, but only one; <16>

V. *Epistola*;

VI. *Gradual* of two verses with Alleluia, or only one or the other;

VII. *Evangelium*;

VIII. *Credo* or *Symbolum Nicaenum*—followed by the sermon if it has not already preceded the *Introitus*.

According to this scheme, Luther eliminated:

(1) *Initium missae*, together with the *Confiteor*. In doing so, he regarded the *Introitus* as the proper beginning of the Mass, as indeed it was originally. The *Initium* and *Confiteor* he no doubt viewed as things for the priest himself, and the *Confiteor* contains all sorts of papistic additions.[40]

---

[40] *) The Confiteor of the Roman Mass reads: "Confiteor Deo omnipotenti, beatae Mariae semper virgini, beato Michaeli archangelo, beato Joanni Baptistae, sanctis apostolis Petro

(2) *Tractus, Proses* (rhymes), and *Sequences*; not as though these contained anything contrary to Scripture, but so as not to make the people tire of the Divine Service through superfluous length, for which reason he also limited the Gradual itself to two verses. Moreover, in the restored Mass, Word and preaching were rightly to stand out as the main focus, and everything preceding was to serve them! Necessary room had to be secured for them, even though it meant giving up one or two things that were in effect embellishments.

However, the deletions in the *second* part of the Mass, mingled as it was with the abomination of sacrifice properly speaking, were of a completely different nature. Here Luther saw "the words of salvation and life shut up, even as the ark of the Lord stood in the pagan temple next to Dagon" [AE 53:26]. From the very beginning, therefore, the *Offertorium* was dropped, since "almost everything sounds and smells like sacrifice" in it. (It was later replaced by "Schaffe in mir, Gott" ["Create in Me a Clean Heart, O God"], among other things, which still claims its position today; more on this in the proper place.) Following inexorably upon the *Offertorium* were the *Secreta* and the whole *canon missae*. Of the latter, Luther writes, "In short, what is wrong in the Mass is of sacrifice and works, which God wondrously arranges so that the priest reads almost everything secretly <17> and it is called the silent Mass.[41] But what is sung openly by the choir and among the people is almost entirely good things and hymns of praise, as if God were saying in deed that He wished to spare His Christians the silent Mass, that their ears need not hear such abomination, and so let the clergy be af-

---

et Paulo, omnibus sanctis et vobis, Fratres: quia peccavi nimis cogitatione, verbo et opere (percutit sibi pectus ter, dicens): mea culpa, mea culpa, mea maxima culpa! Ideo precor beatam Mariam semper virginem, beatum Michaelem archangelum, beatum Joannem Baptistam, sanctos apostolos Petrum et Paulum, omnes sanctos et vos, Fratres, orare pro me ad Dominum, Deum nostrum."

[I confess unto God Almighty, the blessed ever-virgin Mary, blessed Michael the Archangel, blessed John the Baptist, the holy apostles Peter and Paul, unto all saints, and unto you, brethren: that I have sinned exceedingly in thought, word, and deed (he strikes his chest thrice, saying): by my fault, by my fault, by my own most grievous fault! Wherefore I pray the blessed ever-virgin Mary, blessed Michael the Archangel, blessed John the Baptist, the holy apostles Peter and Paul, all saints, and you, brethren, to pray for me to the Lord our God. —MC.]

[41] *) This "soft and secret" reading is closely related to the papistic idea of sacrifice, since, as Bellarmine openly explains, to offer a sacrifice "is not to speak but to act, and even if it is in a certain sense also to speak, it is a speaking not in or to the congregation (*ecclesia*) but to *God*; for whoever offers a sacrifice to God is dealing with God, not with men, even though his actions have not a private but a public character, since he is not acting on behalf of himself but for the whole Church." (See [Johann Jakob] Herzog, ed., *Real-Encyclopädie für protestantische Theologie und Kirche*, s.v. "Messe," 9:395.)

flicted with their own abomination" (Jena 5:196b).[42] About the same time, of course, Luther also published his writing, "The Abomination of the Secret Mass" (1525), in which he translated and annotated it for the people, since he wanted to "uncover the devil" and, for the sake of the people, "put him in the light, so that everyone might see what a terrible, abominable thing the despicable devil is doing every day throughout the world in the silent Mass" (EA 29:118; [cf. AE 36:314]).

In his first liturgical labors, then, Luther extricated from this Canon of the Mass both the Preface and the Words of Institution—the latter as the Consecration proper, which, in conjunction with the Our Father, were not to be recited, spoken, or sung softly as in the papistic Mass,[43] but *aloud*, "so that they may be discerned by those in attendance." The Consecration was to be followed by the *Sanctus*, then the *Our Father*, and no further prayers, but the *Pax Domini* immediately following. During the *Sumptio* (distribution) the *Agnus* was to be sung. Luther accepted the *Communion sentence* (the Communion hymn soon took its place). Instead of the usual *Complet* (Post-Communion Collects), he wants another prayer, "since they have a rather sacrificial tone." In place of the *Finis missae*—the Benediction formula and the lesson from John, which in any case was the pericope for the Third Christmas Mass—Luther appointed the simple conclusion with *Dominus vobiscum — Benedicamus.* (The Lord be with you. And with thy spirit. <18> Let us bless the Lord. Thanks be to God forever!) and the Aaronic *Benediction* (Numbers 6 [:24–26]).

Thus the *Formula Missae* (1523). This liturgy of the Supper appeared in an even more simplified form in the *Deutsche Messe* (1526). In this, namely, the *Paraphrase* of the Our Father with a brief *Exhortation* is substituted for the Preface, whereupon the Consecration immediately follows, and the Distribution takes place during appropriate congregational singing. The conclusion is made by a *collect of thanksgiving.*

Yet Luther expressly states that he *does not want his Formula Missae* (1523) "*abrogated or changed*" [AE 53:62]. *And this is the order that has remained the decisive pattern for the Lutheran Church,* while of the form given in 1526, only the *Exhortation* attached to the paraphrased Our Father was included in agendas here and there, while the collect of thanksgiving found

---

42 Cf. Luther, "Admonition Concerning the Sacrament of the Body and Blood of Our Lord" (1530), AE 38:123. —MC.

43 *) "It is of particular importance that the Words of Consecration, which are alleged to effect transubstantiation as well as constitute the sacrifice, be spoken softly; they do not pertain to the congregation but only apply to the elements, in order, by magical power and effect, to produce a transformation in them, whereby the priest daily makes (*conficere* [confect] is the typical expression) the Body of Christ." (Herzog, *Real-Encycl.,* s.v. "Messe," 9:395.)

its place at the end of all of them. Specifically, it was the Saxon and Low German agendas on the one hand and the agendas of Austria and Nürnberg-Brandenburg on the other hand which adhered as closely as possible to Luther's precedent in his liturgical writings, while the South and West German agendas of Baden, Andorf,[44] Hanau,[45] Worms, Hohenlohe,[46] and later also Strassburg, took the Reformed structuring of the Divine Service into greater account. Nevertheless, although alike in their total preservation of a strict Lutheran character and every aspiration for uniformity in ceremonies, the agendas of the first sort were not bound together slavishly and pedantically, but within the confessional unity, a multiplicity was permitted even in the form of Consecration and Distribution.

Thus taking these all together, we find for the *second part* of the purified Mass the following elements retained:

I. *Praefatio* with *Sanctus*—replaced by the Exhortation in the Brandenburg-Nürnberg church order (1533)—this is the one by Volprecht included in the St. Louis *Kirchen-Agende,* p. 233ff.—while the other agendas, specifically the Saxon ones, have both the Preface *and* the Exhortation.

II. *Consecratio* with *Our Father*—now one, now the other first; along with the *Salutation of Peace* (*Pax*), though this was not adopted by all agendas. <19>

III. *Agnus Dei* ("O Christ, Thou Lamb of God") and other hymns, namely, Communion hymns, during the actual *Communio* or *Sumptio*.

IV. *Collecta* with *Dominus vobiscum* and—though not universally—the singing of the *Nunc Dimittis* ("Lord, now lettest Thou Thy servant depart in peace") preceding.

V. *Aaronic Benediction* with *Benedicamus* frequently preceding; whereupon a hymn, such as, "O Lord, we praise Thee," "Lord, keep us steadfast," etc., is appointed here and there—namely, wherever the *Nunc Dimittis* was dropped.

§5. Retention of Vestments and Their Use in Later Years

"The usual public ceremonies are retained: the order of lessons, the prayers, *vestments*, and other such things," explains the Latin Apology in the Article on the Mass.[47] Thus with respect to the vestments of the preceding time, not everything was abolished, but much was retained. In the

[44] *Andorffer Kirchen-Agende* (1567). —MC.

[45] *Hanauer Kirchen- und Schulordnung* (1659). —MC.

[46] *Hohenlohische Kirchen-Ordnung* (1578). —MC.

[47] Lochner quotes the Latin of Ap XXIV 1 (The Mass): "Servantur usitatae Ceremoniae publicae ordo lectionum, orationum, vestitus, et alia similia." —MC.

Formula Missae [1523], Luther comes at last to speaking about clerical vestments, saying:

> We have not said anything about vestments, but we think of them as we do of other similar external gestures. *We leave them to be used freely, provided pomp and other excess be avoided.* You are not more pleasing in God's sight if you wear priestly vestments while celebrating the Sacrament, nor less pleasing if you do so without such vestments. Neither does clothing commend us in the sight of God. I would prefer that they not be consecrated or blessed, as if they were then to be holier than other garments; unless a general blessing should be used, since it is by the Word and prayer, as Scripture says in 1 Timothy 4:4–5 that every good creature of God is sanctified. Otherwise, it is pure superstition and impiety brought in by the Baal-bishops of the highest and ultimate abomination of the Church, as other such things besides (StL 10:2246; [AE 53:31–32]).

How this was then regarded after this time, for example, in the church at Wittenberg, Luther writes in his treatise, "Against the Heavenly Prophets" (1525): "In the cloister we had Mass without chasuble, without elevation, in the very simplest way, like Christ's example which Carlstadt praises. Meanwhile, in the parish we continue to have chasuble, alb, altar, and elevation for as long as we wish" (EA 29:191; [AE 40:130]). <20>

The usual clerical attire consisted of a long, ankle-length black *Priesterrock* ["priest's robe"], now called the *Chorrock* ["choir or chancel robe"] or *Talar* ["ankle-length"], and a white linen garment worn over this, approximately of knee-length, called the *Alba* or *Chorhemd* ["chancel smock"]. The latter derives from the Ancient Church, in which the white garment was worn as a symbol of the peace, purity, and dignity of those persons involved in the Divine Service. Until the first quarter of our century [the nineteenth], the pastors in the Lutheran churches in Germany wore the *Chorhemd* during the administration of the Sacraments and the performance of the liturgy at the altar. It is still in use in certain churches, such as that of Thuringia, and even in a few places in liturgically impoverished Württemberg. In this country too it is, as far as I know, still being used in the handful of congregations which migrated into Texas and belong to the Missouri Synod, as well as among our local Norwegian brethren. In Saxony, in Braunschweig, in the region of Brandenburg-Nürnberg, and elsewhere, the liturgist appeared for the administration of the Supper in the proper eucharistic vestments, among which was, in addition to the *Chorrock* and *Chorhemd*, the *Casula* or chasuble, the sleeveless covering of various colors and decorated with a cross of gold brocade. For example, there is a description of the Divine Service from

Alt-Dresden from the time of the two hundredth jubilee of the Reformation, which says: "After this [the sermon], Communion begins, for which purpose the deacon, dressed in the alb and chasuble [*Meßgewand*], and accompanied by two boys specially vested for the purpose and appointed to hold the Communion cloths or veils [*Fächel*] approaches the altar [set with paten, chalice, and candles burning throughout the service and] adorned [with two linen cloths]" (*Etwas zur Kirchen-Historie in Alt-Dresden, etc.* [A Little Something about the Church History in Alt-Dresden, etc.] by M. Paul Hilscher, pastor in said city, 1721 [p. 150f.]). Similarly, in a description of the consecration of the new Friedrichstadt church in Dresden in 1730, at which Dr. Valentin Löscher gave the sermon, it says: "Then the *Te Deum laudamus* was intoned with trumpets and timpani . . . Meanwhile, the ordained pastor of the church, Rev. David Mehner [1694–1756], in a green chasuble, approached the altar and sang both the Our Father and the Words of Institution for the Holy Communion."[48] In Nürnberg, the author's native city, the chasuble was still in use during the celebration of the Supper until the year 1790. In fact, at the dedication of a Norwegian Lutheran church in Wisconsin, which the author attended about forty years ago, the synodical president at that time was vested in a chasuble. It was Rationalism which for "the improvement of religion" committed such vandalism even with regard to the office vestment, at least in the German Lutheran church. In the return to the earlier Lutheran liturgy <21> there can, for the sake of peace and for other reasons, no longer be any thought of reintroducing even the *Chorhemd*, and we can only be content with the black robe of office, the more so since even this had already become rare in this land of Reformed sectarianism when our synod was organized.

§ 6. The Use of the Vernacular and the Inclusion of the Spiritual Song in the Liturgy — The Notable Changes. The Significance of Choir Song and the Use of the Organ

Among the **more notable** *changes* to the Mass, without contest, is the *use of the* **vernacular** in the Divine Service and the *introduction* of the **spiritual song** into the liturgy. Through this change, the spiritual priesthood of all Christians, in its divinely appointed relationship to the public vocation and ministry with the Word and through the liturgy, was made effective and put into practice, and this to such an extent as had not been the case since

[48] *Kurtze, doch deutliche Nachricht, wie die Einweihung der neuen Kirche zu Friedrichstadt vollbracht worden* (Dresden: Mohrentaler, 1730), 13 (unnumbered). The consecration took place on July 11. —MC.

the time of the apostles. Thus, in addition to the pure Word and Sacrament, the Augsburg Confession is fully able to confess that "without boasting . . . the Mass is celebrated among us with greater devotion and more earnestness than among our opponents" [AC XXIV 1, German]. It is precisely in the congregation's participation in the Divine Service resulting from congregational singing that the whole fundamental idea of the Reformation, the general priesthood, finds truly striking expression—and therein lies the most fundamental difference in the concept of the Church itself.

In the papistic church, the Mass is celebrated everywhere exclusively in *Latin*, as is the whole liturgy of the Divine Service generally. It is the peculiar language of the Church, the universal language in the kingdom of the Antichrist with which papistic Rome, in a manner resembling pagan Rome, has imposed its heavy yoke upon the people, relating its use, as a language unintelligible to the people, together with the whole concept of the sacrifice of the Mass. Since the use of a foreign language entirely unintelligible to the people stands in direct contradiction with 1 Corinthians 14:1–20, it was first necessary for the Church of the Reformation to return to the original use of the vernacular in the Mass as well as in the whole Divine Service "since," <22> as Article XXIV [3] of the Augsburg Confession states, "the purpose of all ceremonies is that the people may learn from them what they need to know about Christ." True, it says "that in certain places German songs (to teach and exercise the people) are sung *in addition to* parts sung in Latin." Indeed, in his *Deutsche Messe* (1526), Luther discusses his first *Formula Missae*, published in Latin, saying: "I do not hereby intend that it should be abrogated or changed. Rather, the use of it is to be left free even as we have kept it among us until now, wherever and whenever it pleases us or reason moves us. For it is in no way my desire for Latin to disappear entirely from the Divine Service." But why? "It is all for the sake of the young," he continues. "Moreover, if I had the power, and if Greek and Hebrew were as common among us as Latin, and there were as much admirable music and song for them as there is for Latin, we would celebrate Mass and sing and read on successive Sundays in all four languages—German, Latin, Greek, and Hebrew" (EA 22:229).[49] Thus the parallel use of Latin in the Mass was only for the purpose of training young students in this language, and because Latin was more "universal" at that time, and this language had "much admirable music and song." This same reason is given in the "Instructions for the Visitors" (1528 and 1538): "Some sing German masses, some Latin masses—we leave this as it is. It seems profitable and good, wherever the majority of people are unfamiliar with Latin, to celebrate the Mass in German, so that the people may better be

[49] Cf. Luther, "The German Mass," (1526), AE 53:62–63. —MC.

able to understand the singing and other things that are read; as St. Paul says in 1 Corinthians 14 (v. 6 [16–17]): 'But when you bless in the Spirit, how shall he who stands in the position of a layman say Amen to your thanksgiving, since he does not know what you are saying? You give thanks well enough, but the other person is not edified by it.' Yet Paul also says in the same place (v. 26): 'Let all things be done for edification'" (StL 10:1665.)[50]

As early as 1520, Luther expressed the wish: "Would to God we Germans might *read Mass in German*!"[51] In 1523 there then appeared in quarto a pamphlet, *Von ordenung gottis diensts ynn der gemeyne,*[52] and not long after that, the *Formula Missae et Communionis pro Ecclesia Wittenbergensi,*[53] which, after *Paul Speratus* had promptly translated it into German, <23> the parish church in Wittenberg employed to celebrate a German Mass in 1525 on Christmas. Lastly, in 1526, as a continuation and supplement, Luther published the work, *Deutsche Messe und Ordnung des Gottesdienstes,*[54] according to which German psalms and songs were already to take the place of the Latin hymns and sequences on a set schedule.

But while Zwingli would only consider the singing of German psalms and hymns, and in sectarian fashion ridiculed *liturgical singing* and dispensed with it, *Luther here desired* the Mass to be ***sung*** as before, yet not solely in *Latin* but also in *German*, and not only because liturgical singing was previously in use and unobjectionable, but also because the sung parts of the Divine Service are generally good and in conformity with Scripture. Being as fond as he was knowledgeable about music, and assigning it a place next to theology, Luther writes in the location quoted above: "Let the sung parts in the Sunday masses and Vespers be left in place, for they are quite good and drawn from Scripture, though they may be abbreviated or expanded"; and likewise in his *Formula Missae*: "Much singing in the Mass is admirably and gloriously composed of thanksgiving and praise and has remained to this time." With the assistance of the electoral chaplain Johann Walther and Konrad Rupff, whom he invited to his house for several weeks as a "cantory," he went on to supply the *Deutsche Messe* with the notation needed for the liturgist and simultaneously with directions for liturgical singing (StL 10:235ff.).[55] True, he used the received Gregorian modes as his

[50] Cf. Luther, "Instruction for the Visitors of Parish Pastors in Electoral Saxony" (1528), AE 40:300. —MC.

[51] Cf. Luther, "Treatise on the New Testament, That Is, the Holy Mass," AE 35:90ff. —MC.

[52] Cf. Luther, "Concerning the Order of Public Worship," AE 53:7–14. —MC.

[53] Cf. Luther, "An Order of Mass and Communion" (1523), AE 53:15–40. —MC.

[54] Cf. Luther, "The German Mass and Order of Divine Service" (1526), AE 53:51–90. —MC.

[55] Ibid., AE 53:69ff. —MC.

models, yet what a veritable master this man, formerly a gifted choirboy and now a virtuoso lutenist, also proved himself to be in this pursuit! "We will be able to assert," says E. Naumann (*Illustrirte Musikgeschichte*) [An Illustrated History of Music, vol. 2] 1883),

> that Dr. Martin was fully capable of setting any church text he might choose, even if it were *not* written metrically (e.g., an Introit, Psalm, a Collect, Epistle, Preface, or a Gospel pericope), to available melodies from the liturgy of the Ancient Church, and could do so with all the changes to the melody line necessitated by the German translation, and all with the keenest perception for the accentuation and meaning of the words with respect to their particular sense and expression—considerations which presuppose in our <24> Reformer a tremendous faculty for composing and adapting rhythms and melodies. As witness to our assertion, we will here quote Johann Walther . . . who, regarding the matter touched upon, says of Luther (according to Michael Prätorius):[56] "He (Luther) himself also made and sang for me the notes over the Epistles and Gospels, and over the Words of Institution of the true body and blood of Christ, and wanted to hear what I thought about it."[57] In another passage of the same writing, Walther says: "It may be seen from the German Sanctus, among other things, how masterfully and how well he matched all the notes to the text according to the proper *accentus* and *concentus*[58] and I, too, was given cause to ask his Reverence at that time what or where he had acquired this piece of instruction; whereupon the precious man laughed at my simplicity and said, 'The poet Virgil, who is able to apply his verses and words so skillfully to the events which he describes, taught me that. In the same way, Musica should match all her notes and melodies to the text.' . . . Lastly, he was also com-

[56] Michael Prätorius, *Syntagmatis Musici Tomus Primus* (Wittenberg: J. Richterus, 1615), 452f.; cf. WA 19:50. —MC.

[57] *) "Thus the composer Johann Walther here directly designates his friend Luther as the *setter of the music*. Walther distinguishes . . . very clearly the mere *adapter* of a melody from the *inventor* of it. . . . Therefore, even if the notes over the Epistles and Gospels could all be traced back to the Latin *cantus gregorianus*, it is still certain that Luther, in this task, was frequently required to proceed with his own independent changes and transpositions to the tone to be used, following his own judgment—a process betraying a talent for which the invention of a new melody must have been far easier, relatively speaking, than the musical operations to be undertaken in the case cited" (Naumann).

[58] *) All the chants of *cantus gregorianus* are traditionally divided into *concentus* and *accentus*. *Concentus* applies to all responsorial and antiphonal singing, psalm melodies, and the choir music proper; *accentus*, on the other hand, refers to those pieces which the priest is to sing alone, such as the collects, lessons, intonations, prefaces, etc.

pletely conversant with the manner of performing Gregorian *cantus choralis*, and had made thorough study of the nature, peculiar character, and particular expressiveness of each of the individual church tones on which both the Gregorian melodies and all art music at that time were based. In this regard, Walther says of his great friend: "When forty years ago he wished to establish the German Mass in Wittenberg, he wrote to the Elector of Saxony and Duke Johannes of blessed memory, and requested his Electoral Grace to send the old songmaster at that time, *Konrad Rupff*, and myself to Wittenberg, and conversed with us on that occasion <25> regarding the notes and the character of the eighth mode. In the end, he *personally* adopted the notes of the eighth mode for the Epistle, and assigned the sixth mode to the Gospel, saying, 'Christ is a friendly Lord, and His words are pleasant. Therefore let us use the sixth mode for the Gospel; and since St. Paul is a serious apostle, let us appoint the eighth mode for the Epistle.'"[59] Thus for Luther "the characters of the individual church modes had become specific domains of musical expression fundamentally different from one another."

No less a part of the "notable" changes—indeed, rather especially so—was *the people's singing of German hymns in the Mass*. It is true that the Apology, in defense of Article XXIV [:4] of the Augustana, notes that this "is not so new," for "the people have always sung something in German in all the churches." Here the Apology has in mind the pre-Reformation hymns "Ein Kindelein so löbelich" [A Little Child so Praiseworthy], "Christ ist erstanden" ["Christ Is Arisen," *LSB* 459] "Nun bitten wir den Heiligen Geist" ["To God the Holy Spirit Let Us Pray" *LSB* 768], (stanza 1), "Gott der Vater wohn uns bei" ["Triune God, Be Thou Our Stay," *LSB* 505], and "Gott sei gelobet und gebenedeiet" ["O Lord, We Praise Thee," *LSB* 617].[60] With the latter, as Luther says in his treatise "The Private Mass and the Consecration of Priests" [1533], the Church simultaneously "cried murder at both the Antichrist and the mercenary priests of private masses," which withheld the cup from them.[61] But these popular spiritual songs in German were only

---

59 *) Mode 6 [Hypolydian Mode] is comparable to our modern C major scale, and Mode 8 [Hypomixolydian Mode] to a D minor scale without the accidentals, i. e., without B flat or C sharp [in the harmonic minor].

60 Cf. Wackernagel, vol. 2: "Ein Kindelein so löbelich" (as "Der Tag, der ist so freudenreich"), nos. 689–99, pp. 520–27; "Christ ist erstanden," nos. 39–42, pp. 32–33; nos. 935–951, pp. 726–33; "Nun bitten wir den Heiligen Geist," nos. 43–44, p. 44; "Gott der Vater wohn uns bei," no. 687, p. 519; "Gott sei gelobet," nos. 520, 989–90, pp. 748–49. —MC.

61 Cf. Luther, "The Private Mass and the Consecration of Priests" (1533), AE 38:206. Luther is pointing out that in the hymn, "Gott sei gelobet," both the body and the blood are

sung during processions and pilgrimages, or during dramatic performances in the church on high festivals, not as an integral part of the Mass itself. In the Mass, only liturgical Gregorian singing in Latin was valid. The popular spiritual song in German was only regarded as a "tolerated, extra-liturgical song."[62] Only in the Divine Services of the Bohemian Brethren did the people sing spiritual hymns in their native tongue, Bohemian.

Quite in contrast, then, to this *tolerated* status, Luther assigned to the German popular song an *integral* place in the Mass. "It was my desire," he writes, "that we might have a number of German songs for the people to sing during the Mass. Who has any doubt that those songs which only the choir sings or responds to by itself were *long ago sung by the whole church*?"[63] But by doing this, Luther was not merely returning to the practice of the Ancient Church, but was giving popular song a more *prominent* place in the Mass than it occupied in the Ancient Church, as it is to this day. After a long, long night, the <26> sun of the Gospel rose again with a brightness not seen since the time of the apostles! God had visited His people once more! And so once again one might say: "Sing to the Lord a new song; sing to the Lord, all the earth." **The true German hymn first came into being with the Reformation.**

For this purpose Luther not only took up those few German spiritual songs which already existed, though to some extent "improved and corrected in a Christian way" or expanded by further composition; nor did he only translate some of the ancient Latin hymns; but he also authored a number of hymns himself, and called for contributions from those of his friends who were capable. Thus in 1524 the first Lutheran hymnal of original hymns appeared, the *Enchiridion geistlicher Gesänge und Psalmen* [Handbook of Spiritual Songs and Psalms], containing twenty-five hymns, eighteen of them by Luther, and published by Justus Jonas—at Luther's direction, as Wackernagel conjectures.[64] Some time later that same year in Wittenberg, Walther's *Chorgesangbüchlein* [Little Choral Hymn Book] was published—a collaboration between Luther and Walther designed for teaching singing to the

mentioned, especially in stanza 1. Yet according to Roman teaching, either species of the Sacrament alone is itself both the body and blood of Christ, as taught in the *Catechismus Romanus*. See an English translation in J. Donovan, trans., *Catechism of the Council of Trent* (Dublin: James Duffy and Co., 1908), 205–6. —MC.

62 Naumann, 1:395. —MC.

63 Cf. Luther, "An Order of Mass and Communion" (1523), AE 53:36. —MC.

64 Since Lochner's day and the discovery of the *Achtliederbuch*, a somewhat different chronology pertains. See Robin A. Leaver, *The Whole Church Sings: Congregational Singing in Luther's Wittenberg* (Grand Rapids, Mich.: Willam B. Eerdmans Publishing Company, 2017). —MC.

youth, since it was through them that the congregation was to *learn to sing* in the Divine Service. Then in 1529, the Wittenberg *Gemeindegesangbuch* appeared, in the preface to which Luther expressed disappointment not only at the great flood of unsuitable songs that had appeared since the publication of the *Chorgesangbüchlein*, but also at the corruption of his own hymns, and pled for an end to the unsolicited proliferation and alteration of the hymnal. The last edition during Luther's lifetime, appearing in 1545 by V. Bapst in Leipzig and boasting a new preface by Luther, is the more complete edition of the hymnal on the interior, as well as the more beautifully decorated on the exterior. In addition to the funeral chants which had already appeared separately in 1542, it also contains a number of Collects along with their Versicles put into German. And these are not simply included as an appendix, but are dispersed throughout, so that there is a Christmas Collect with the Christmas hymns, an Easter Collect with the Easter hymns, etc., clarifying all the more readily the liturgical intent.

Luther, in conjunction with his musical friends, gave these hymns their corresponding **melodies**. In his treatise, "Against the Heavenly Prophets" (1525), he writes: "I am eager to have a German Mass today, and I am working on it; yet I really want it to have a true *German character*. The practice of *translating the Latin text* and *keeping the tone or notation* is something I can make allowance for; *yet it does not sound* <27> *natural or authentic*. Both *text and notation, accent, melody, and expression* have to flow from the *mother tongue and voice* or else it is all imitation, the way *monkeys* do!" (EA 29:203; [AE 40:141]). In order, then, that the popular spiritual song in German and the melody might flow as much as possible "from the true German mother tongue and voice," and thus "have a true German character," Luther did not seize upon *cantus gregorianus* or put new wine in old wineskins by seeking merely to underlay it with his and his friends' German hymn texts, but he took the following course.

First, he made use of *what was at hand*. In the preface to the funeral songs published in 1542, he expresses himself in the following way:

> To that end we have also used as a good model the *beautiful musical settings or songs which have been used in the papacy at vigils, soul masses, and funerals* . . . yet we have set different texts to them . . . The melodies and the notes are exceptional. It would be a pity if they perished. Yet the texts or words are unchristian and unfitting; they deserve to perish. As in all other matters also, they (the papists) far surpass us, having the most beautiful services, beautiful, majestic cathedrals and cloisters; yet the preaching and teaching which they practice in them are mainly of service to the devil and blaspheme God; for the devil is the prince and god of the world, and therefore must have whatever is

> most elegant, excellent, and beautiful . . . Thus it is that they possess so many wonderful, beautiful melodies or songs, especially in the cathedrals and parishes, and yet have adorned them with many atrocious, idolatrous texts. We have therefore divested and stripped these idolatrous, dead, and foolish texts of their beautiful music, and with it clothed the living and holy Word of God, thereby to sing, praise, and glorify the same, so that the beautiful adornment of the music in its proper use may redound to the praise and honor of its dear Maker and His Christians, and we, having His Holy Word impressed on our heart by means of sweet music, may be edified and strengthened in the faith" (EA 56:301–2).[65]

From those things already in existence he took, firstly, the *melodies of the Latin hymns.* Yet while he left the melodies for the good hymns which he translated, such as "Nun komm, der Heiden Heiland" ["Savior of the Nations, Come"],[66] among others, and "stripped the idolatrous, dead, and foolish texts of their beautiful music," this was nevertheless done by imitation or adaptation, so that the melody of the Latin text also had a "German character" for the German text. Furthermore, there were the *melodies of the popular spiritual hymns which he took from the* <28> *pre-Reformation period* to which he still applied a refining hand here and there, as for instance in "Christ ist erstanden" ["Christ Is Arisen"].[67] And finally, *there were the beautiful melodies of popular secular songs* which were stripped of many an honorable text, and many a carnal one, and furnished with a Christian one: for example, for the Christmas hymn "Vom Himmel hoch, da komm ich her" ["From Heaven Above to Earth I Come"][68] initially the tune, "Aus fremden Landen komm ich her" [From Foreign Lands to Here I Come];[69] or for the hymn, "Herr Christ der einig Gotts Sohn" ["The Only Son from Heaven," *LSB* 402] by Elisabeth Cruciger, the tune, "Ich hört ein Fräulein klagen" [I Heard a Young Woman Wailing]—an example of the use of sec-

---

[65] Cf. Luther, "Preface to the Burial Hymns" (1542), AE 53:327–8. —MC.

[66] Wackernagel 3:12f., no. 16. Cf. Luther, "From Heaven on High I Come to You" (1534/35), AE 53:289f., *LSB* 332. —MC.

[67] Wackernagel 2:726ff., nos. 935–51. *LSB* 459. This hymn is also related to Luther's "Christ lag in Todesbanden," Wackernagel 3:12, no. 15. Cf. the reworking by M. Weiße, Wackernagel 3:273, no. 309. —MC.

[68] Wackernagel 3:23, no. 39. *LSB* 358. —MC.

[69] On the melody, see Salomon Kümmerle, *Encyklopädie der evangelischen Kirchenmusik*, 4 vols. (Gütersloh: Bertelsmann, 1888–95), 3:839ff. For more on this melody and text see: William H. Otte, "From Heaven Above to Earth I Come," in *Lutheran Service Book: Companion to the Hymns*, Joseph Herl, Peter C. Reske, and Jon D. Vieker, eds., 2 vols. (St. Louis: Concordia Publishing House, 2019), 1:74–78. —MC.

ular melodies even in subsequent times, in the consideration of Luther's statement, "How is it that on profane themes (*in carnalibus*) we have so many a great poem (*poema*) and beautiful song (*carmen*), but on spiritual themes (*in spiritualibus*) such cold, sluggish stuff?"[70]

Then Luther created *original melodies*—for it remains a firm fact that the melodies to hymns such as "Ein feste Burg" ["A Mighty Fortress"][71] "Wir glauben all an einen Gott" ["We All Believe in One True God"],[72] "Vater unser im Himmelreich" ["Our Father, Who from Heaven Above"],[73] "Jesaia dem Propheten" ["Isaiah, Mighty Seer"],[74] and others, are creations of Luther. By this activity he, more so than others, became the father of our precious and popular rhythmic church hymn [i.e., "chorale"].

Accordingly, our church melodies originate from a fourfold source: (1) the imitation or adaptation of a Latin hymn, (2) the religious yet extra-ecclesial song of the pre-Reformation period, (3) the secular song, and (4) the original composition.

Yes, admittedly, it is *a* ***notable*** *change that "the people sing German songs"* in the Mass and elsewhere, and by this fact especially that *"the Mass is celebrated with greater devotion among us than among our opponents."* Our Lutheran Church is for this reason called *"the singing Church."* What a host of psalmists from all walks of life we may invoke, and among them how many a Miriam! How well the hymn has fulfilled the wish of Moses: "Would to God that all the people of the Lord might prophesy!" [Numbers 11:29] Yet chief among this great host of singers, lyrically and musically, is and remains Luther. He was such a spiritual poet and musician by God's grace that even a Paul Gerhardt does not compare with him, nor with respect to melody, a Crüger or an Ebeling.[75] For no one was so successful as he in capturing the popular tone lyrically and musically. No one was so utterly the mouth of the Church, echoing in hymn and melody that which stirred her great soul. Take for example the beautiful testimony of Cyriacus Spangenberg, who in the preface to his *Cithara Lutheri* (1569) <29> says,

> Thus Luther, in whose hymns and songs no vain or needless word is found, must be allowed to stand as the greatest and most skilled of all master singers since the time of the apostles. Everything flows

[70] WA Tr 5:274, no. 5603. Cf. *LSB: Companion to the Hymns,* 1:203.—MC.

[71] Kümmerle, 1:362ff.; *LSB* 656/657. —MC.

[72] Ibid., 4:461ff.; *LSB* 954. —MC.

[73] Ibid., 3:748ff.; *LSB* 766. —MC.

[74] Ibid., 1:648ff.; *LSB* 960. —MC.

[75] Johann Crüger (1598–1662) and Johann Georg Ebeling (1637–76) were the chief publishers and composers of original melodies for Paul Gerhardt's hymns. —MC.

> and falls from him in the most pleasing and fitting manner, full of spirit and doctrine, so that practically every word speaks its own sermon or at least a special reminder. There is nothing forced, nothing patched on, nothing broken. The rhymes are easy and good, the words apt and well-chosen, the meaning clear and intelligible, the melodies and sound sweet and sincere, and in short, everything is so fine and admirable that it has a substance and power to it; it encourages and consoles. And indeed, his equal is not to be found, much less his superior, as all good hearts who have any knowledge of Luther's *Gesangbüchlein* must confess with us, and declare that by him God has given us a high, wonderful, and exceptional gift for which we can never thank Him enough (*Cithara Lutheri,* 1569, p. 2).

Yet, having for our subject the Chief Divine Service, we cannot conclude this section without also examining the subject of *choral singing* as well as the *use of the organ*:

(a) Clearly, in both the Mass and the incidental services of the papistic Church, *the singing of the choir* plays an important role in its obligatory representation of the congregation, and is more or less polyphonic singing [*Kunstgesang*] as well. Accordingly, although the active cooperation of the congregation, specifically in the hymn, constitutes an important component of the Lutheran Chief Divine Service, it in no way suggests that choir song is to be replaced by it. Polyphonic music was also to continue to be used in service to the sacred, and employed for the multiplication and enrichment of the liturgical part of the Divine Service, for the enhancement of the festival observance, and for edification generally.

As proof that Luther still strove for something more for church singing than its confinement to congregational hymnody, we include the following passage from his writings, also cited by E. Naumann in his *Illustrirte Musikgeschichte* [Illustrated History of Music]. We hear Luther say:

> But when natural music is sharpened and polished by artistic skill, only then is the great wisdom of God seen and recognized in His wonderful work of music, in which the most amazing and bewildering thing is that one voice sings a simple tune or tenor line, while three, four, or five other parts <30> are also sung, playing and leaping around that simple, straightforward melody or tenor line as it were with shouts of joy, marvelously adorning and beautifying the melody with various characters and sounds, as if conducting a heavenly dance. They meet each other tenderly and hug and embrace sweetly, so that those who understand it a little and are moved by it are greatly astounded and think that there is nothing so amazing in the

> world as such a song adorned with many voices. But those who are not stirred by it are indeed very boorish asses" (Walch 14:411.).[76]

The ideal which he here envisioned he found realized especially in the compositions of the Netherlander Josquin [de Prez], as well as in the motets of the Bavarian chapel director [Ludwig] Senfl, whom he counted as a friend and for whom he held the highest regard. On a December evening in 1539, as he was entertaining some singers, upon quitting the table they sang him "several sublime and lovely motets" of Senfl's, and he exclaimed with warm words: "I could never dream of making such a motet even if I tore myself to pieces!"[77]

Although the compositions of *Gallus* (d. 1591), *Haßler* (d. 1612), and others show that in the Lutheran Church, *adult male choirs* were sometimes used, yet the most preferred and most frequently used was the *mixed choir*. Since it unites within it the two chief classes of voice and allows the voices a much greater range than the adult male choir, the mixed choir is also undeniably the consummate form of choir. For the Discant and Alto, however, boys' voices were formerly employed through the Latin schools. *Not until the Christmas festival of 1715 did the first instance of using* ***female voices*** *in the mixed church choir occur, when the Hamburg conductor* <31> *Mattheson had three female opera singers (!) appear in the church.* It is for this reason an unsettled question even today whether the mixed church choir should consist only of *men* and *boys* or whether *women* may also be permitted. Perhaps Palmer hit upon the correct answer here when he states (in Herzog, *Real-Encyclopädie,* s.v., "Gesang," 106f.):

> The woman must be silent in the congregation where liturgical and homiletical action is concerned; but in the domain of music, woman, too, is endowed with a spiritual gift [*charisma*] deserving of a place that is not constrained. Yet it must be admitted that, if the choir has stalls in a part of the church which gives them a preferen-

[76] Cf. Luther, "Preface to Georg Rhau's *Symphoniae Jucundae*" (1538), AE 53:324. —MC.

[77] *) Incidentally, in the *Encyclopädie der gesammten musikalischen Wissenschaften* [Encyclopedia of All Musical Sciences] by Dr. Gustav Schilling, the following can be read: "It is known that, in addition to many fine melodies, especially for his own chorales, Luther also wrote a number of motets. The library in Munich still houses a collection of his motets, titled *Symphoniae jucundae 4. vocum seu Motettae 52, cum praefatione Mart. Lutheri* (Wittenberg, 1535). Handel, who in fact studied all the extant works, is supposed to have remarked that he was indebted to this study for the best of his work. Luther's free mind first broke the fetters of the canonics which came from the Netherlands at that time and was the dominant musical style even in Italy. His friends Walther, Senfl, and Agricola assisted him honorably and faithfully in this endeavor. The first aesthetic glimmer that issued from him had a powerful effect on the Church, and eventually taking on the form of a universally warming glow, was transferred to the great wide realm of music."

> tial appearance in the sight of all, then for other, greater reasons the upper voices are better represented by boys. The aesthetic or musical consideration can more readily submit to this ethical consideration when, with careful selection and attention, the boy's voice possesses its proper beauty and is able to render exceptional service.

Since the area in our local churches usually does not afford an appropriate place for most of the choir to stand, and choir rehearsals can normally be undertaken only at night-time, it would be all the more desirable from the ethical perspective if in our churches' mixed choirs the upper voices might again be assigned to boys exclusively. Would it not be possible, especially in our city schools, to assemble a group of boys with a gifted voice, and gradually to prepare them to be proper choristers? And since people are justly pleased to hear children's voices in the congregations, would it really be so hard to motivate the congregation, or a number of its members, to have a small compensation given to the "choir students" from time to time as an encouragement to them? Then there would again be something of the Ancient Church institution of the *Kurrende* [*children's choir*], to which Luther also belonged and which he praised, and which was highly regarded, especially in the Lutheran Church, and was maintained for the blessing of church and school, and which Rationalism and its efforts to emancipate church and school increasingly pushed to the periphery. Marquardt, a pedagog in Berlin who has done much for reclaiming the student choir and *Kurrende*, argues justly: "A well organized and nurtured choir program which assists the Church in every expression of her life is not only possible and without detriment to the purposes of schooling, but gives the whole school a greater pulse from the foundation up, which exponentially increases the school's ability to educate." <32> (*Halleluja, Zeitschrift für geistliche Musik* 4, no. 17 (1884): 195).[78]

Now concerning the *purpose* of choral singing and its proper *significance* in the Lutheran Divine Service, we have no universally accepted idea which we might be able to follow. For this reason various opinions hold sway. When the introduction of German congregational singing faced great difficulties because of the initial inexperience of the congregation, the choir was required to sing the congregation's hymns to the people so that they could learn them by hearing and repetition, on which account Luther notes in the *Enchiridion* (1524), the first Lutheran hymnal: ". . . in order that

[78] *) Also in the high church segment of the Episcopal Church in this country there has already been a movement to give preference in the church choir to boys' voices again, and with admirable results. [The full title of this journal is *Halleluja; Zeitschrift für geistliche Musik in Kirche, Haus, Verein und Schule, zugleich Organ des Evangel. Kirchengesangvereins für Deutschland,* published in Hildburghausen, Gadow, Quedlinburg. —MC.]

the common Christian household may in time learn to grasp what is done by the congregation in singing and reading." Yet in the enthusiasm for the reappearance of the Gospel in those days, the people quickly caught on and only needed to be *led* and supported by the choir. However, since the choir in the Divine Service distinguishes itself from the congregation through sacred polyphony, according to Schöberlein and other recent liturgical scholars, "the choir represents the Church per se, the ideal congregation, the universal Church in contrast to the local congregation." The reasoning for this goes: "What is more natural than that the local congregation, when it gathers for worship, should feel like a member of the universal Church, to which its prayers and songs make explicit reference, and that it should therefore desire to hear the voice of the Church singing with it as it sings? Clearly, this represents an ideal element within the actual assembled congregation. For this reason the choir is to use the ideal form of polyphonic singing." But it is because of this concept of the "universal Church" and "ideal congregation" that we for our part side more with Hommel in the *practical* interpretation of what the choir signifies, and view it as a part of the congregation serving the Church with its gift [*charisma*]. Hommel says, namely:

> The *practical* interpretation of the subject is probably the best in this case as well. In no way can it (the choir) be regarded as the representative of the congregation or the mediator between clergy and congregation. But if, according to the apostolic saying [1 Peter 4:10; Romans 12:6–7], everyone is to serve the Lord with his gifts, it must be asked why those <33> who are more gifted than others in singing should not exercise this gift in the Divine Services of the church. As the Christian congregation offers up to the Lord all that it has and does, so it offers up to Him the gifts of singing which are in its midst, thereby sanctifying it. And as the idea of offering stirs up diligence in every part of the congregation to come before the Lord with the best gifts and talents, so the congregation will eagerly employ its most beautiful abilities in the offering of singing. These are the beautiful acts of service to the Lord—beautiful, lovely, and of various kinds in form as well as in relation to the spirit from which it all proceeds. Thus for the sake of a pleasing variety, a part of the congregation is allowed to step forward now and then and present its offerings in the public Divine Service, with the living participation of the others in spirit, especially to add greater glory to festivals.[79]

[79] Hommel, xi. —MC.

This interpretation of choral singing is surely also in view when venerable Dannhauer writes in his *Katechismus-Milch* [Catechism Milk]: "Singing with voices and thus praising God, whether it is done *choraliter* or *figuraliter*—with plainsong or polyphony—is for us a matter not of freedom but of obligation, since God has commanded, 'You shall not misuse My name; therefore, you are to use it rightly, and so even the voices of Discant, Alto, Tenor, and Bass can use it to honor Me.'"[80] Yet Hommel is right to conclude, "The choir should never sing unless the congregation is acquainted with the text."[81] For this very reason it is necessary for the choir director to train the singers to enunciate clearly, and it is not necessary for a new thing to be sung every time. *Good pieces that have been sung several times are performed better every time and become more and more familiar to the congregation, both of which serve all the more for edification.*

Accordingly, if the former is the *purpose* of the church's choral singing and the latter is the *significance* of it, its place in the liturgy must reflect both.

By necessity it could never be superfluous in its position *as leader and supporter of congregational singing*. Not only is the number of the melodies familiar to the congregation relatively small, and the choir's assistance necessary to increase it; and not only does rhythmic singing first need to be introduced to a great many congregations, <34> for which the support of the choir is also required; but the choir can also be useful in maintaining rhythmic singing, since in their apathy toward spiritual things people approach rhythmic singing too lightly, and too easily revert to their former laziness when singing spiritual songs, while in singing secular folk songs they always pay close attention to time and rhythm.

Yet while choral singing is to occupy an *independent* position in the Divine Service in accordance with its significance indicated above, this should not be an *isolated* position, if the choir is to serve rightly in edifying the congregation and do its part in truly beautifying the Divine Service. The music which it performs must thus be *integrated* as closely as possible with the actions of the liturgist and the congregation so that choral singing does not appear as a performance or assume the character of a religious concert—which it certainly should **not**. Experts in the field today also put great stress on this. For example, Otto Kade, music director and publisher of the *Luther-Codex*, reports concerning the grand-ducal palace choir in Schwerin (which he currently conducts with mastery and great expertise, including liturgical): "The purely external position, directed almost solely

[80] Johann Conrad Dannhauer, *Catechismus Milch, oder der Erklärung deß Christlichen Catechismi*, 10 vols. (Straßburg: Friderich Spoor, 1642–78), 1:521. —MC.

[81] Hommel, xii. —MC.

toward the delivery of religious concert pieces and having absolutely no, or a very loose, relation to the liturgy itself, has been transformed into one which is organically and closely linked with the course of the religious ceremony and integrally entwined with it, achieving the most intimate connection between liturgist, congregation, and choir." (*Halleluja* 5, no. 8 (1885): 102.) So too, Dr. G. Herzog (Professor of music in Erlangen): "Choral singing will only fulfill its true purpose when the songs to be selected occupy a close relationship with the Divine Service and are thus organically incorporated into it, have the character of true church liturgy, and are widely understood."[82] This is augmented also by the following words of Johannes Zahn, the director of the Schoolteacher's Training College in Altdorf and authority on sacred music, words worthy to be taken to heart: "Choral singing must, with respect to its delivery, be able to serve as a model for the congregation. Therefore the director has to make every effort to enable the members of the choir to execute as perfectly as possible the choir pieces to be performed, for which reason he *should, above all, select only* such compositions as do not exceed the ability of the choir to perform them. <35> He should also regard it as more commendable to perform an easy composition well than a difficult one deficiently" (*Handbüchlein . . .*).[83]

The choir, being organically integrated, may work together with the liturgist and congregation in the Chief Divine Service in the following manner:

1. It assumes those parts of the liturgy which would give the congregation more or less difficulty to perform musically. These would include the *Introits* in the psalm tone, in their original forms or in figural form; likewise the beautiful versified *Festival Kyries*.

2. If on High Festivals the original form of the Gloria is used instead of "Allein Gott in der Höh sei Ehr" ["All Glory Be to God on High"] it might be done as follows. After the liturgist intones: "Glory be to God on high!" and the congregation with the choir has sung: "And on earth peace, good will toward men," the choir then continues: "We praise Thee, we bless Thee, we worship Thee, we glorify Thee," etc., and the congregation could participate in the "Amen." The Gloria with the "Et in terra" and "Laudamus" are located below in Part Two of this work [pp. 53 ff.].

3. In antiphonal singing, the choir intones and the congregation responds, as for instance in the Double Kyrie (also included in Part Two below), for example, Choir: "Kyrie eleison." Congregation: "Lord, have mercy." Choir: "Kyrie eleison." Congregation: "Christ, have mercy." Choir:

[82] Johann Georg Herzog, *Musikalischer Anhang zur Agende für die evangelisch-lutherische Kirche in Bayern.* (Erlangen: Deichert, 1883), Preface, vii. —MC.

[83] Zahn, 140. —MC.

"Kyrie eleison." Congregation: "Lord, have mercy upon us." This especially applies to the *Te Deum*.[84] The choir, in four voices and without organ accompaniment, would intone: "Lord God, Thy praise we sing," the congregation, with organ accompaniment, would respond: "Lord God, our thanks we bring." The choir: "Father in eternity." Congregation: "All the world doth worship Thee," etc. (Yet if there is a desire to accompany the choir with the organ, somewhat softer registration should be used for it.)

4. For pleasing variety in congregational singing (Psalm 147:7),[85] the choir, at a fitting point, performs a special polyphonic selection relating to the season or festival (more details on this in Part Two below). In the same way, on occasions when Communion [Distribution] takes more time, pleasant alternation may also take place between choral and congregational singing by having an anthem or other piece relating to Communion performed between two Communion hymns or between two parts of one lengthier Communion hymn. This would be more conducive to edification than if the organist, fearing that the Communion hymn might end too soon during the Distribution, <36> should, between stanzas, play interludes longer than the hymn's stanzas themselves, the end of which the congregation would await with increasing impatience.

In this discussion of the place and use of choral singing we have had before our eyes the example of the Church as we have found it not only in orthodox agendas but also in those contemporaneous collections which contained the material for choral singing, such as Johann Spangenberg's *Kirchengesänge* (1545), the *Psalmodia sacra* of Lucas Lossius (1553), the Wittenberger *Kirchengesänge* of Johann Keuchenthal (1573), the *Missodia* etc., of Michael Prätorius (1611), and so on.

A further point on the history of choral singing. In the post-Reformation period, there was a particular fondness for setting Lutheran chorales in motet-style arrangements for use as special polyphonic pieces. The greatest achievements in this endeavor were made by the electoral chaplain Johann Eccard (d. 1611), a student of Orlando di Lasso. Later, other texts were also chosen for the choir: first, passages of Scripture, then newly written works. Yet gradually the churchly Lutheran model was abandoned in those forms. This occurred through solo arias, through different types of polyphonic singing in dramatic dialog, through the instrumental music which was supposed to accompany choral singing but increasingly came to share the

---

84 See Luther's versified adaptation of the Te Deum. WA 35:521–24; Wackernagel 3:19, no. 31; Cf. Luther, "The Te Deum" (1529?), AE 53:173ff. —MC.

85 In Luther's translation (1545) this verse reads: "Sing back and forth [*umb einander*] unto the Lord. . . ." WA Deutsche Bibel 10:581. —MC.

stage with it. Eventually, the influences of secular music, developing with imposing force in opera and chamber music, were indulged with greater and greater abandon, although [Johann] Sebastian Bach, by earnestly cultivating the chorale and the sacred character of his cantatas and passions, certainly sought to stem the tide of secularization in church music. Yet even he, still the unrivaled master in his field, no longer represents the full strength of churchly style.

Now, the choral singing in our country leaves a great deal to be desired, however much it is nurtured in many places. Its renditions are still more *concert-like* performances, and performances chiefly of modern origin at that. Therefore, if we want above all to try to regain the purpose, significance, and place of the choir—then away with the greater part of modern choir piece collections, and let us go back not merely to Bach but to the classical period of church music! Dr. Schöberlein says aptly:

> The Church has her own style in singing no less than hymnody. Though she knows the extremes of sacred sorrow and joy, yea, of jubilation in the upper choir, yet in her these extremes are contained within the bounds of chaste moderation, <37> and over all the sensations of repentance and praise so vivacious and profound, the blessed calm of God's peace reigns supreme. The harmonies, too, are free from mushy sentimentality and violent transitions; clear and pure, calm and noble their course proceeds, and thereby transports the hearers out of the sphere of subjective, worldly sensations into the realm of the sacred. The classical period for this churchly kind of singing is that of the sixteenth to the mid-seventeenth century, for in this period faith, a holy sense of community, and strict artistic form were present and pervasive. It is therefore preferable to select church music from this period. And even though the style of that period may at first seem more foreign to our musical feeling and consciousness, the relationship is no different from that which we enjoy with the hymns of the same period, which nevertheless satisfy the true needs of the congregation's faith more than the modern ones do.[86]

The same applies here to the melodies of Reformation hymns, or even the writings of Luther. At first they have little appeal, and then the longer we taste them, the better they are. If only the leaders of our church choirs would therefore try first by thorough study of older church music to develop a sense of what is genuinely churchly! Here we call attention to Dr. *Schöberlein*'s three-volume work *Schatz des liturgischen Chor- und Gemeindegesangs* [Treasury of Litur-

[86] Schoeberlein, 1:9. —MC.

gical Choir and Congregational Song], or to its abridgment, *Musica sacra,*[87] since for most people the former would be too costly.[88] Noteworthy progress in the return to the classical church music of the <38> Lutheran Church was also made in this connection by Endlich's choir and chorale book,[89] which is the musical appendix to the *Kirchenbuch* of the General Council.[90] Within the Missouri Synod, too, the recovery of musical forms has been encouraged and initiated. Here one may mention, among others, the little collection of old and new Christmas songs published in 1884 by the teacher Hermann Ilse.[91] The author of the present liturgical work cannot forbear to add to his own words the following from the preface to this collection:

> Certainly many who have been occupied exclusively with modern music will require time and effort to accustom themselves to the style present in these older settings. It will be found helpful to this end if the individual voices are first sung properly at the piano and afterwards heard together as a whole. While much of the newer material can be understood by every hearer and is almost impossible

---

87 Lochner is likely referencing this or an earlier edition of Ludwig Schoeberlein, ed., *Musica sacra: für Kirchenchöre, höhere Lehranstalten etc.*, 4th ed. (Göttingen: Vandenhoeck & Ruprecht, 1895). —MC.

88 *) The *Cantionale für die Landeskirchen des Großherzogthums Mecklenburg-Schwerin* [Cantional for the State Churches of the Grand Duchy of Mecklenburg-Schwerin], published by order of the sainted Grand Duke of Mecklenburg-Schwerin, must be a masterful work and rich treasure. The journal *Halleluja* reports the following: "It was to contain all the liturgical material for Sundays and feast-days as well as for occasional services and weekday Divine Services, such as Matins, Vespers, baptisms, weddings, funerals, etc. In 1862, his royal highness the Grand Duke therefore established a committee of six specialists: the senior church councilor Dr. Kliefoth as president; church councilor Dr. Maßmann, pastor in Wismar; church councilor Dr. Wöhler, pastor in Lichtenhagen; music director Pitschner at the seminary in Neukloster; music director Dr. von Roda at the University of Rostock . . . and music director Kade, dirctor of the Grand Ducal Palace Choir in Schwerin. Kade was also tasked with the composition of the musical apparatus and the artistic elaboration of the polyphonic settings." Since this extraordinary cantional was not available from the bookseller until just a few years ago, the publisher of *Siona,* Ph. Herold in Schwabach, succeeded in obtaining the permission for an excerpt from it. This was put out under the auspices of C. Bertelsmann in Gütersloh with the title: "Der Hauptgottesdienst des Osterfestes und der österlichen Zeit. Liturgisch-musikalischer Auszug aus dem neuen Mecklenburgischen Cantionale. Herausgegeben von M. Herold." [The Chief Divine Service of the Festival of Easter and Eastertide. Liturgical-musical Excerpt from the New Mecklenburg Cantional. Edited by M. Herold].

89 *) Johann Endlich, ed., *Choralbuch mit Liturgie und Chorgesängen zum Kirchenbuch der Allgemeinen Kirchenversammlung* (Philadelphia: J. Kohler [1879]).

90 *Kirchenbuch für evangelisch-lutherische Gemeinden* (Reading: Caxton, 1877). —MC.

91 *) Hermann Ilse, ed., *XIV alte und neue Weihnachtsgesänge für gemischte Kirchenchöre* (Brooklyn, 1884).

> for any group of singers to spoil, most of the older pieces will only be as good as the singer's ability. Regardless of the great simplicity which is characteristic of them, they are intended to be sung in a very pure manner; and, in order to be truly understood and valued, they presuppose profound immersion into the spirit of these works, which will always demand the earnestness of a Christian disposition. Little store can be set by the excuse of so many who claim that people no longer understand this kind of music. Practical experience shows that, over time, congregations can be groomed to better material; and that, on the other hand, when people have lost the taste for what is sound, no one is to blame but the musician himself.

(b) Concerning the organ and its use in the Divine Service, Luther naturally found it also present, and it would seem strange if he had excluded it from the holy place when he himself wished to see music—as art generally—put in the service of the Most High. Moreover, no instrument is so suitably and exclusively used in worship as the organ, that queen among musical instruments! While in the iconoclastic zeal of the Reformed party, organs are also known to have been destroyed; in fact, even at the Council of Trent, as a result of the <39> growing misuse of the organ for profane music which distracted from devotion, the abolishing of the organ was seriously contemplated in the papistic camp; yet in the orthodox Church it not only remained in uncontested use, but also experienced dramatic development, and found in [Johann] Sebastian Bach its still unrivaled master, even to this day, in terms of church style and performance. Thus we find that even the earlier church orders provide prescriptions for worthy organ playing.

In the Divine Service of the orthodox Church, congregational singing is accompanied and led by the organ. This has constituted its most important usage from the beginning. With respect to the harmony, however, one should keep to the older setting and not that of Master Bach, since because of its richness and independent treatment of voices, though tremendously appropriate for church polyphony, and in our view unsurpassed, it is not suited for the people's singing. Concerning organ accompaniment of liturgical singing, the necessary points will be made in their place. But on the question whether choral singing should be accompanied by the organ, Dr. J. G. Herzog remarks:

> Whether the organ should provide accompaniment or *a cappella* singing should be preferred in the evangelical *cultus* can be answered only thus: that both types are permissible according to the form of the Divine Service and the character of the composition, as well as abilities of those performing them, if we do not wish to give up a good

> percentage of the extant treasury of church music. It is not the organ accompaniment as a mediator between choir and congregation which justifies it, as many suppose, but the intimate relationship which it has with the Divine Service generally. I cannot deny that I perceive in *a cappella* singing an especially appropriate means for awakening religious devotion. In its pure, unmediated operation on the spirit, in the pristine emerging and entwining of the different vocal characters, it forms at once a richly varied contrast to accompanied congregational singing. Nothing stirs human beings so deeply as a cleanly executed piece of polyphonic singing free from accompaniment. Anyone who has ever witnessed the performance of the Bach [St. Matthew] passion will never in his life forget the amazing effect of the chorale "Wenn ich einmal soll scheiden" ["When I Shall Depart One Day"]. In liturgical worship services it [*a cappella* singing] occupies a place of special preference." (*Halleluja* 4, no. 9 (1884): 104. <40>

Yet the organ also appears *independently* in the Divine Service when it uses preludes and postludes to make musical *introductions* and *conclusions*, and interludes to *connect* liturgical ceremonies musically. And here everyone who has discernment and churchly taste must certainly join Dr. Herzog in the wish "that our church organ music, when playing independently in preludes and postludes, might increasingly reclaim the spirit of Bach and be freed from the popular style with its secular sweetness found in so many newer organ compositions, particularly in the organ sonatas which have come into fashion these days."

The *introductory prelude* must take into account the character of the Sunday or feast. Just as the bells cry, as it were, "Serve the Lord with gladness, come before His presence with singing" (Psalm 100:2), this prelude is to put the assembling congregation in the mood to say with Psalm 95: "Oh come, let us sing to the Lord; let us make a joyful noise to the rock of our salvation! Let us come into His presence with thanksgiving; let us make a joyful noise to Him with songs of praise! For the Lord is a great God, and a great King above all gods. Oh come, let us worship and bow down; let us kneel before the Lord, our Maker! For He is our God, and we are the people of His pasture, and the sheep of His hand" (vv. 1–3, 6–7). But of this prelude leading into the Divine Service, the Prelude proper, more shall be said in Part Two in the discussion of the Introit.

As for the prelude, so for the *postlude*. It is not to be treated by the organist and regarded by the congregation as merely an afterthought to be endured or as a sort of concert. Rather, its purpose is to bring the Divine Service to a fitting conclusion, as an echo of the ideas and sentiments which have been received.

The *interlude* forms a musical connection between liturgical ceremonies. This includes not only the traditional interludes played between individual hymn stanzas sung by the congregation, and the interlude that leads the transition from congregational to liturgical singing, indicating the tone for the liturgist, but also the preludes to the intermediate hymns, to the hymns within the Divine Service generally, and therefore also to the so-called Chief Hymn [Hymn of the Day]. Yet what liturgical ignorance often appears in this or that place—to say nothing of the carelessness with which many organists perform the office entrusted to them for the edification of the congregation! How long these interludes often are, including those between hymn stanzas, and even the one from the church Benediction to the closing stanza! How bored <41> the congregation becomes, waiting wearily for the singing to start. And even when the organist is not incompetent, but a master—how the liturgical chain is broken and how the whole liturgy is lost by all manner of lengthy interludes, whereas everything in the liturgy should follow one after another at a lively pace! And how needlessly prolonged the Divine Service is! If there is any notion that the liturgy must be abbreviated, let people first see whether an abbreviation of the organ music could or should be undertaken. Therefore, just as the collective interlude music should be worthy and fitting, let it also be brief. Let the so-called "hymn preludes," including that for the Chief Hymn, be *brief*; and the music between hymn stanzas even *more brief*; and the music for the intonation of the liturgist, from the Benediction to the closing stanza—and to the Creed (when there is no intonation)—*briefest of all*.

§ 7. Place of Word and Sacrament in the Genuinely Lutheran Chief Divine Service. Its Organization and Progression. Deviation of Orthodox Churches from the Normal Form in Christian Freedom

In his "Treatise on the New Testament" (1520), Luther says, "In these passages (namely Luke 22:19, 1 Corinthians 11:26, Psalm 102:22–23, Psalm 111:4–5) you see how the Mass was instituted to preach and praise Christ and to glorify His Passion and all His grace and goodness, that we might be moved to love, hope, and believe in Him, **and so upon the same Word or preaching receive a physical sign, that is, the Sacrament, as well,** that by it our faith might be equipped, confirmed, and strengthened with divine Words and signs in opposition to all sin, suffering, death, and hell, and all that is against us. And if that preaching were not to be, he never would have instituted the Mass (Supper). He was more concerned with the Word than the sign" (EA 27:167ff.).[92] The Mass is to be "the use and employment of the Gospel and distribution of the Sacrament" (*Formula Missae*) [cf. AE 53:25]; "everything done among Christians in the Divine Service" was to be "for the sake of the Word and Sacrament" (*Deutsche Messe*) [AE 53:90]. Thus the guiding idea of the Chief Divine Service, in such structure as we have now received it through Luther from Christian antiquity, is the Word of grace in preaching and Sacrament, and the same cannot be a coincidental conglomeration (a heap). It must be an ordered and organized whole both spiritually and psychologically. <42> If Word and Sacrament designate the order of salvation, should these then not have in turn designated the shape of the Divine Service to thoughtful antiquity? When, for example, we begin with the Kyrie and this is immediately followed by the Gloria, does this not suggest that in this succession of the first and second elements there is a train of thought moving upward? In accordance with the interpretation given by Löhe in the preface to the first edition of his Agenda, the present author sought in 1862, in "Referat über die rechte Mitte der lutherischen Liturgie" [Address on the Correct Center of the Lutheran Liturgy] to clarify this train of thought briefly (*Lehre und Wehre* 8 (1862): 205–6), emphasizing, however, that the Chief Divine Service finds its ultimate goal and keystone in the Supper *only insofar as the Sacrament is the **seal** of the Word*. Since no other interpretation has proposed itself to him since then, let this attempt at an interpretation stand here.

After the Introit has introduced the Divine Service, indicating the character of the Sunday or feast, the assembled congregation next humbles itself before God in the Kyrie as in a common confession of all the tragedy which Adam's fall has brought us, but ascends in remembrance of the birth of the promised Savior, the incarnation of the eternal Word, which took place on the holy feast of Christmas, up to the angelic Gloria ("Glory be to God on high," etc., and "All Glory Be to God on High")[93] and breaks forth in lofty adoration of the Three in One ("We praise Thee, we bless Thee, we worship Thee," etc., or "We praise, we worship Thee, we trust," etc.)[94] From the Hymn of Praise the congregation proceeds to prayer in the Collect, in which the desire, according to the character of the Sunday or feast, ignites in one brilliant thought. *And now the Lord comes to them in the **Word***. In the Epistle, which contains chiefly doctrine and admonition, He speaks

[92] Cf. Luther, "Treatise on the New Testament" (1520), AE 35:105ff. —MC.

[93] "Allein Gott in der Höh sei Ehr," the versified Gloria in Excelsis by Nicolaus Decius (1525), Wackernagel 3:555f., nos. 615f. See *LSB* 947. —MC.

[94] See the second line of Decius' hymn. —MC.

by the mouth of the apostles; in the Gospel of the day, which is largely proclamation of the pertinent salvation-event or one of the Lord's miracles, the *ipsissima verba* [very words themselves] are also mostly perceived at the same time. The congregation responds to the Epistle with praise of the Most High in the form of the Chief Hymn, in many places with an Alleluia preceding, while its response to the Gospel (or to both lessons collectively) is a bold and vigorous Confession of Faith, the Credo ("We All Believe in One True God," or on feasts the Nicene, Apostolic Creed). At this point they sit with Mary at the Lord's feet and rest, that they may receive in the Sermon the prophecy which accords with the faith [*or* the Creed] for the fostering of their inner life. This then leads immediately to the Church's public Confession of sins <43> and the Absolution (wherever this follows the sermon) as an exercise and application of the Law and Gospel which have just been heard. Enriched by the Word and filled with comfort and joy, they cause their communal concerns in petition, prayer, and intercession to be brought before God in the *General Prayer of the Church*, in the special *intercessions* and *thanksgivings*, and in the holy *Our Father*, which are then followed by the Thanksgiving in the Preface.

Thus prepared for the sealing of the grace received through the Word and for union with the Lord in the Sacrament of His body and blood, they approach the altar, having already brought the offering of the repentant heart in the evangelical *Offertory* through the *Psalmody*: "Create in me a clean heart, O God" from Psalm 51, and simultaneously through the *gathering of the offering*, wherever it is customary at this point, and the thank-offering of love in voluntary contributions for the charity fund, for missions, for schools, and the like. The Preface now beginning is, in name, an introduction to the Consecration, in content, the aforesaid thanksgiving in the most exalted form (Eucharist); and then, in the Sanctus, the "Thrice Holy" with Benedictus, it becomes the adoration of Him "that cometh in the name of the Lord" with His body and blood in the most worthy Sacrament. In the Our Father—here and there preceded by an Exhortation to Communion—together with the Words of the Testament, the Consecration is completed, and after the congregation in the Agnus Dei ("O Christ, Thou Lamb of God") has eminently proclaimed the Lord's death with one accord, and in the Salutation of Peace [*or* the Peace *or* Pax], wherever this is still practiced, received once more the assurance of God's grace and His good will, then the Distribution and reception of the Sacrament through the pastor follows, accompanied by the singing of the Communion hymn by all who are gathered and with the confession of the true presence of the body and blood of Christ (distribution formula). In many liturgies, when the Distribution is concluded, it is followed by the admirable practice of singing the Canticle of Simeon, the Nunc Dimittis: "Lord, now lettest Thou Thy servant depart in peace," or "In Peace and Joy I Now Depart"[95]—for what more can be desired in the valley of sorrow of powers of the world to come, than the reception of Christ's body and blood for the forgiveness of sins, for life, for salvation, and when could the longing to see the Lord face to face and to dwell with Him be greater than at that point where He draws so near to us? The conclusion of the <44> Divine Service, having now reached its climax hereby, is formed by the Collect of Thanksgiving, which is simultaneously a prayer for the blessing and fruit of the Sacrament, together with the Aaronic Benediction, as a "confirming and sealing of all the gifts of grace received in the Word and Sacrament, by one last impartation of grace"[96] from the Triune God, who in the many gives the one, and in the one gives the many.

Now as to interpreting the progression of the liturgy in the Chief Divine Service—it is certain at least that there is no form and manner so beautiful and gracious and so reflective of and conducive to the pure Word and Sacrament as the Mass purified by Luther. Since it has such a "noble pedigree," descending as it does from Christian antiquity, it is equally deserving of that which Dr. Guericke says in his *Kirchengeschichte* [Church History] concerning the explicit liturgy of the Chief Divine Service of the Ancient Church; namely: ". . . the purpose of which was to propound in a truly visual way to the consciousness of the communicants the divine and the divine-human communion of life of the faithful with Christ reciprocally, by means of communal, real participation in Christ's holy body and blood" (5th ed., 1:313–14).[97] The more this form and order is used and the more familiar it becomes, the more one must agree with Luther when he cries out enthusiastically in his "The Private Mass and the Consecration of Priests" (1533):

> *God be praised, in our churches we can show a Christian a truly Christian Mass according to Christ's ordinance and institution, and according to the true intention of Christ and of the Church!* The altar is approached by our pastor, bishop, or minister in the parochial office, who has been rightly and properly and publicly called (after having first been consecrated, anointed, and born as Christ's priest in Baptism, without regard to private chrismation). He publicly and plainly

[95] See Luther's versification, "Mit Fried und Freud ich fahr dahin," Wackernagel 3:17, no. 25; *LSB* 938. —MC.

[96] Uncited source, ultimately from Karl Friedrich Gaupp, *Praktische Theologie,* vol. 1: Die Liturgik (Berlin: G. Reimer, 1848), 1:294. —MC.

[97] Heinrich Ernst Ferdinand Guericke, *Handbuch der Kirchengeschichte*, 5th ed., 2 vols. (Halle: Gebauersche Buchhandlung, 1843). —MC.

chants the Ordinance of Christ instituted in the Supper, takes the bread and wine, gives thanks, distributes it and gives it by virtue of Christ's Words (this is My body, this is My blood. This do, etc.) to us who are present and wish to receive it. And we, in particular those of us who wish to take the Sacrament, kneel beside, behind, and around him—man, woman, young, old, master, manservant, mistress, maidservant, parents, children, even as God brings us all together there, all true holy fellow-priests sanctified by Christ's blood and anointed and consecrated by the Holy Spirit in Baptism. And in this our inborn, hereditary priestly dignity and adornment we are present, have (as depicted in Revelation 4) <45> our crowns of gold on our heads, harps in the hand, and censers of gold, and do not cause our pastor to speak the Ordinance of Christ as for his own self, but he is the mouth of us all, and we all speak them with him from our heart and with faith lifted up to the Lamb of God, who is before and with us, and feeds us according to His Ordinance with His body and blood. This is our Mass, and the true Mass, which we are not lacking.

For here, first of all, everything goes according to the ordinance and command of Christ, so that it is administered and given to the Church under both forms through the words of Christ: "Take, eat, this is My body, etc. This do in remembrance of Me." The pastor does not receive it for himself alone, as the abomination of the pope does, nor does he offer it to God for our sins and all manner of distress, as in the abomination of the pope. He does not grant it to us or sell it to us as a good work to appease God, as in the abomination of the pope, so that a blasphemous market-fair has been made of of it. Rather, he serves it to us for the comfort and strengthening of our faith. Here Christ is preached and proclaimed. Here there can be no covetousness or idolatry. Here we assuredly have the intention of Christ and of the Church. Here we need not worry whether the pastor speaks the words secretly or if he effects a change, or if he even believes; for we hear the Words of the Institution openly and speak them in our heart with him, and Christ's institution (not our doing, nor chrism) effects a change and gives us the body and blood of Christ. If the pastor disbelieves or doubts, yet we believe; if he stumbles over the words or begins to stray and forgets if he has spoken the words, yet we are present and listen and firmly believe and are sure that they have been spoken. Therefore we cannot be deceived. And because the ordinance and true faith are present, it must be certain that we receive the true body and blood of Christ. And thanks and praise be

> to God that I have lived to see the true Christian Mass and the pure, Christian use of the Holy Sacrament. I see it with delight and joy in my heart after the abominable, detestable abuse which, alas, I helped to perpetrate so many years under the abomination of the pope (EA 31:370–72).[98]

Of course the Lutheran congregations of south and southwest Germany, for the most part, adhered far less to Luther's precedent in his liturgical writings. They not only went their own peculiar way and departed substantially in liturgical matters from Luther and the rite that was becoming dominant, but, while clinging firmly to the unity in the Spirit and the doctrine of Luther, yet in formal matters yielded more or less to <46> the Reformed rite in the neighboring lands, Switzerland and France. Thus not only did [Ambrosius] Blarer, in the reformation of Württemberg, exclude from the first church order of 1536 everything in the *cultus* (with the exception of the pericopes) that was reminiscent of the Mass, but E. Schnepf and Erasmus Alber themselves gave to the Divine Service a simplicity far more Reformed than Lutheran.[99] For example, the chanting of the Words of Institution, the whole Altar service outside of Communion, all eucharistic vestments, and initially even the use of the *Chorhemd*, were abolished by these faithful Lutherans. And Brenz, who with Osiander had put the finishing touches on the Nürnberg church order with its rich liturgy, when treating the Chief Divine Service in his Württemberg church order of 1553, gave it a form which could probably not have been more sparse; namely: Latin *Introitus* or a German spiritual hymn, then a sermon and, if there is no Communion—which was offered only once a month—a hymn and benediction. Or note what a simple, sparse, and rag-tag order the Chief Divine Service of Worms (1582) was: Litany by the choir, three collects from the pulpit, a congregational hymn: "To God the Holy Spirit Let Us Pray" or a festival hymn, Sermon, Prayer of the Church, Our Father, Exhortation, public Confession and Absolution, another Exhortation, Consecration, Distribution, Prayer, Benediction. Yet even Luther did not wish to see his order of Divine Service regarded and established in any way as a law for others. And note with what vigor the whole orthodox Church explains in Article VII of its chief Confession, the Augustana: "To the true unity of the Christian Church *it is* ***enough*** [*satis est*] that the Gospel is preached according to the pure sense, and the Sacraments administered according to the Word of God. *Nor is it necessary to the true unity of the Christian Church that* ***like ceremonies****, instituted*

[98] Cf. Luther, "The Private Mass and the Consecration of Priests" (1530), AE 38:208–9. —MC.

[99] Erhard Schnepf (1495–1558) was dismissed in 1548 for opposing the Augsburg Interim. Erasmus Alber (d. 1553) wrote a number of core Lutheran hymns. —MC.

by men, should be observed everywhere. As Paul says (Ephesians 4 [:4–5]): "One body, one Spirit, even as you were called in one hope of your calling; one Lord, one faith, one Baptism."

At the same time, our present concern is the *genuinely* Lutheran Chief Divine Service, in which the good forms and rites deriving from the Ancient Church, or even those belonging to later times yet agreeing with Scripture, have been retained as much as possible, and thus "in the public ceremonies no notable change has been made." **This, moreover, is the liturgically normal and, in the Lutheran Church, formerly dominant order and rite of the Chief Divine Service.** <47>

§ 8. Table of Comparison

In order to present us with an overview of "the evangelical Mass in comparison with the Roman Mass," Löhe, in his *Sammlung liturgischer Formulare* [Collection of Liturgical Formulas] (1839),[100] provides a table in which the order of the Chief Divine Service from the most notable church orders of the Reformation and post-Reformation times is put side by side with the Roman Mass. Following this example, we conclude Part One with a table modeled on Löhe's. Naturally, we list as first Luther's two chief liturgical writings—his *Formula Misssae* (1523) [or in the German translation, *Weise, christlich Meß zu halten* (1524)] and his *Deutsche Messe* (1526).[101] These are followed by the rite of the Brandenburg-Nürnberg church order (1533), which Chytraeus calls "*fons et mater agendorum*" [the fount and mother of agendas] and which was introduced not only in Franconia but also in the Archduchy of Austria below-the-Enns [Lower Austria]; likewise also the rite of the revised Braunschweig-Lüneburg church order (1657), which was originally composed by Bugenhagen in 1528 and of which the order of Divine Service served as the basis for that of the churches in Lower Saxony and Pomerania. After these are a few normative Saxon orders, namely that of 1536, to which Justus Jonas, Spalatin, Cruciger, and Myconius lent their names, and the order of Duke Henry of Saxony, edited after the example of Elector Augustus's Agenda (1681); also, the *Agenda Schwartzburgica* (1675). The final column contains the order of the Chief Divine Service from the *Kirchen-Agende für evangelisch-lutherischen Gemeinden ungeänderter Augsburgischer Confession zusammengestellt aus den alten rechtgläubigen Sächsischen Kirchen-Agenden und herausgegeben*

[100] Löhe, *Sammlung*, 3:29ff. —MC.

[101] Lochner appears to be working primarily from the text of *Weise, christlich Meß zu halten*, the 1524 German translation of Luther's *Formula Missae* by Paul Speratus, available to him in StL 10:2230ff. —MC.

von der Allgemeinen deutschen Evangelisch-Lutherischen Synode von Missouri, Ohio und anderen Staaten [Church Agenda for Evangelical-Lutheran Congregations of the Unaltered Augsburg Confession, Collected from the Old, Orthodox, Saxon Church Agendas and Edited for the General German Evangelical-Lutheran Synod of Missouri, Ohio, and other States] (St. Louis: Deutschen Ev.-Luth. Synode v. Missouri, O. u. a. St., 1856).[102] This last column is to show that this Agenda has remained faithful to the authentically Lutheran rite of the Chief Divine Service, and in what ways it has done so.

First, a few remarks about our Table:

1. The Table should not only show which items in the "evangelical Mass" were eliminated as papistic impurities or superfluous ornament, while "in the public ceremonies of the Mass *no substantial change* has been made," but also how, despite their many variations <48> permitted in Christian freedom, a very substantial uniformity nevertheless prevails with respect to the parts of the Chief Divine Service and their sequence.

2. Also, at a quick glance over the Table, the considerable **regularity** in the Lutheran Chief Divine Service becomes apparent. Kyrie, Gloria, Collect, Epistle, congregational hymn ("Chief Hymn"), Gospel, Credo, and Sermon, and the ceremonies corollary to them, universally compose the first part of the Chief Divine Service; and while the second part shows some variation, apart from the sequence of the Our Father and the Words of the Testament, this mainly concerns the use of the Ancient Church Preface, which is replaced by the Exhortation in Luther's *Deutsche Messe* (1526) and in the Brandenburg-Nürnberg church order (1533). <49>

And yet in all its regularity, what **diversity**, and thus what *variety*, there is in the words and forms of these firmly established parts! In one, the Introits for Sundays and festivals differ; in another, the form of Kyrie, Gloria, and Creed vary textually and melodically, as Part Two will show; in another, there is a Preface not only for common Sundays but also for feasts and for the festival seasons. And what variety in congregational song! One need only consider any such congregation entrusted with these different forms and usages, and it will no doubt be difficult to perceive the complaint of *monotony* in the form of the Divine Service, or to account for the longing for changes in the liturgy expressed by preacher and congregation.

[102] See page xviii, note 7 —MC.

Table Comparing the Order of the Roman Mass

	Roman Mass	Luther		Brandenburg-Nürnberg (1533)
		Formula Missae (Latin: 1523; German: 1524)	*Deutsche Messe* (1526)	
1.	**Initium Missae**			
2.	**Confiteor**			*Confiteor*, "or whatever the priest's devotion makes him mindful to do."
3.	**Introitus**	*Introitus*. "Though we would prefer the psalms from which they were taken."	"A spiritual song or German psalm."	*Introitus*. In the villages perhaps German songs.
4.	**Kyrie** (ninefold)	*Kyrie*. "In various melodies or modes according to the distinction of the season."	*Kyrie*. Threefold, not ninefold. So also in all other church orders.	*Kyrie*
5.	**Gloria in excelsis. Et in terra. Laudamus te**	*Gloria*, etc.		*Gloria*, etc.
6.	**Collecta(e)**	A Collect	Collect	The Lord be with you. One or several Collects.
7.	**Epistola**	Epistle. Other epistle readings to be used according to desire.	Epistle	A chapter from the epistles of the apostles Paul, Peter, and John. Special introductory and concluding formulas.
8.	**Graduale** with Alleluia or *Tractus (Prosa, Sequentia)*	"Gradual, perhaps two verses with Alleluia." Yet not the long festival Graduals! Sequence and Prose only on Christmas: *Grates nunc omnes*; and Whitsunday: *Spiritus sancti*, etc. *Veni sancte*, etc.	"A German song: "To God the Holy Spirit Let Us Pray," or another, and that with the whole choir."	After the Epistle he may read an Alleluia with its verse in Latin, or a Gradual taken from Holy Scripture; which the students may also sing in Latin.
9.	**Evangelium**	Gospel. Candles and incense as desired.	Gospel	"Chapter from the Gospel or Acts." Note: the pericopes were retained.

AND THE LUTHERAN CHIEF DIVINE SERVICE

	Braunschweig-Lüneburg (1657)	Saxony		*Kirchen-Agende,* Missouri Synod (St. Louis, 1866)
		Duke Henry's Church Order (Leipzig, 1681)	Agenda Schwartzburgica (1675)	
1.				
2.				
3.		Introit "of the Sunday or feast."	"Come, Holy Spirit, fill . . ." with Collect for the Holy Spirit.	
4.	*Kyrie.* "The cantor, the fellow teachers and students, sing: "O Father, almighty God," etc.	*Kyrie eleison*	*Kyrie* of the time.	"Kyrie, God Father," etc. St. Louis Hymnal #7.
5.	*Gloria in excelsis Deo.* "By the whole congregation: 'All Glory Be to God on High,'" etc. The Lord be with you, etc.	*Gloria in excelsis Deo* and *Et in terra* in Latin.	Glory be to God, etc. Mel. according to time and feast. Congregation: "All Glory Be to God Alone" or "All Glory Be to God on High," or sim.	P.: "Glory be to God," etc. C.: "All Glory Be to God on High." Hymnal #1.
6.	Collect "of the time or feast, as relates to the Gospel."	"The Collects" in German or Latin.	"*Collecta de tempore.*" [Collect of the time]	The Lord be, etc. Versicle. Collect.
7.	Epistle "with good volume, clearly and slowly."	Epistle "in German, facing the people."	Epistle, etc.	Epistle
8.	"After reading of the Epistle, let a German Psalm or Hymn of the time be sung from the common hymnals. And the organist may play along with the singing using counterpoint, as musicians call it."	Nothing mentioned.	"A German chorale hymn, as the preacher shall choose."	Chief Hymn
9.	Gospel "recited to the congregation from our Ev. Luth. harmony, clearly and distinctly without any distortion.	Gospel "of the Sunday or feast, also read in German, facing the people."	Gospel	Gospel

	Roman Mass	Luther		Brandenburg-Nürnberg (1533)
		Formula Missae (Latin: 1523; German: 1524)	*Deutsche Messe* (1526)	
10.	**Credo**	*Credo.* Sermon here, or preferably before the Mass, since the Sermon summons people to God's Supper; the Mass is for those who have accepted the call, for believers.	*Credo.* "We All Believe" to be sung by the congregation. Sermon. General Prayer, from the pulpit or altar left free; yet "it seems that the ancients used to do it from the pulpit."	*Credo,* "which the students should sing in Latin, as is the custom, or else the people should sing the German Creed." Then on the day of rest the usual Sermon should follow. "It is known that the General Prayer came between the Sermon and the Holy Meal" (Löhe).
11.	**Offertorium**	During the singing bread and wine are brought forward.		"Song or Offertory"
12.	**Secreta**			
13.	**Praefatio** with **Sanctus**	Introduction to the Preface. *Praefatio up to "per Christum Dominum nostrum,"* whereupon a small silence follows, and then:	*Paraphrase of the Our Father with Exhortation to the Supper.*	Exhortation to the Supper (of Joh. [Wolfgang] Volprecht). Later with appended General Confession and additional (general) Absolution.
[14a.]	**Canon Missae** (a) ante consecrationem (b) commemoratio pro vivis (c) diptycha sanctorum			

	Braunschweig-Lüneburg (1657)	Saxony		*Kirchen-Agende,* Missouri Synod (St. Louis, 1866)
		Duke Henry's Church Order (Leipzig, 1681)	Agenda Schwartzburgica (1675)	
10.	"*Credo in unum Deum*" sung by the *presbyter*, and then "We All Believe in One True God" by the congregation. *Sermon* preceded by Our Father with introductory formula, and with a pulpit hymn. *Confession* and Absolution with retention. *General Prayer.* Intercessions. Excommunications, if any, etc., etc. *Our Father. Votum.*	*Credo in unum Deum* and the Latin *Patrem.* Then the Creed in German: "We All Believe." *Sermon.* Confession with Absolution, without Retention. *General Prayer*	*Credo in unum Deum* "Whereupon music is to be played and, time permitting, the [German] Creed to be sung, etc. Sermon is delivered and, to begin it, before the Our Father, a hymn of the time . . . is to be sung." *Congregational Confession. General Prayer. Intercessions*, etc.	*Creed:* "We All Believe." *Sermon* preceded by silent prayer (Our Father) and pulpit verse before the reading of the text. *Confession* with Absolution, without Retention. *Prayer of the Church. Intercessions and Thansgivings. Our Father. Votum.*
11.	"As the priest leaves the pulpit and approaches the altar, the communicants should go to the chancel, and a devout psalm of the time should be sung, that the congregation may thereby be moved to greater devotion."			Song: "Create in me a clean heart, O God."
12.				
13.	*Preface* in German with Introduction and Sanctus, of which "the most important part of the Thanksgiving consists." Brief exhortation and prayer.	*Preface* in Latin with Luther's *"Paraphrase of the Our Father"* and the *Exhortation to the Sacrament,* in front of the altar.	"German Prefaces, which are to be used on the high feasts, where they have been introduced." *Sanctus* by the choir. Luther's brief Exhortation to the Supper.	Preface with the Sanctus.
[14a.]				

	Roman Mass	Luther		Brandenburg-Nürnberg (1533)
		Formula Missae (Latin: 1523; German: 1524)	*Deutsche Messe* (1526)	
14[b].	(d) **Consecratio** (e) post consecrationem (f) memento pro defunctis	*Consecration* (loud or secretly) and Sanctus follows. During the Benedictus of the Sanctus, Elevation is permitted.	*Consecration.* And the consecrated bread is distributed immediately after the blessing and Elevation. Meanwhile the German Sanctus: "Isaiah, Mighty Seer" is sung, likewise, "O Lord, We Praise Thee," "Jesus Christ, Our Blessed Savior." Then the chalice is blessed and distributed. During this, the hymns, being already begun, are sung to the end, and as the conclusion the *Agnus Dei* is sung.	*Consecration.* After this, the Sanctus.
[15a.]	**Praeparatio ad Communionem** (a) Pater noster (b) Oratio	Our Father		Our Father. Also in Latin with the introductory words from the Mass: "*Praeceptis salutaribus moniti.*" [being admonished by salutary precepts . . .]
15[b].	(c) **Pax**	Pax		Pax. Response: Amen.
16.	Preces ante communionem: **Agnus** and prayer of preparation.	*Agnus.* Also the prayer from the Roman Mass: *Domine Jesu Christe, Fili Dei.*		*Agnus Dei.* When the number of communicants is large, "not only one *Communio* (taken from Scripture) should be sung, but some more also may and should be sung . . . such as the Responsory '*Discubuit [Jesus].*'"
17.	**Sumptio** (Taking of the Sacrament on the part of the celebrant.)	During the Agnus, the Sumptio or Communio. At the same time, from the Roman Mass: *Corpus Domini*, etc. *Sanguis Domini*, etc.		Meanwhile Communion.
18.	**Communio**	*Communio* if desired.		
19.	**Post communio**	Instead of the last Collect, which usually refers to sacrifice, the prayer from the Roman Mass: *Quod ore sumpsimus.*	Collect of Thanksgiving	Collect
20.	**Finis Missae**	Benedicamus with Alleluia.		Benedicamus, etc.
21.	**Benedictio**	Benediction from Num. 6.	Benediction, etc.	Benediction (4 forms.)
22.	John 1:1–14			Hymn: "Lord, Keep Us Steadfast in Thy Word," etc.

	Braunschweig-Lüneburg (1657)	Saxony		*Kirchen-Agende,* Missouri Synod (St. Louis, 1866)
		Duke Henry's Church Order (Leipzig, 1681)	Agenda Schwartzburgica (1675)	
14[b].	Our Father sung in German.	Our Father sung in German.	Our Father sung in German.	Our Father sung.
[15a.]	*Consecratio.*	*Consecratio.*	*Consecratio.*	Consecration.
15[b].				
16.	O Lamb of God.	*Agnus Dei* in Latin (distribution begins during the beginning of singing.)		"O Christ, Thou Lamb of God," #69.
17.	Meanwhile, Communion with further singing of Supper hymns, etc.	Meanwhile *Communion* with further singing of "Jesus Christ Our Blessed Savior." Psalm 111 may also be sung, if there are many communicants.	Communion.	Communion during singing of Supper hymns.
18.				
19.	Ps. 23 read aloud. Collect.	Collect.	Collect.	Collect.
20.				
21.	Benediction, etc.	Benediction.	Benediction.	Benediction.
22.	Hereupon let the whole congregation sing *choraliter*: "Lord, now lettest Thou Thy Servant depart in peace," etc.			Song: "O Lord, We Praise Thee," #195:1, etc., or another appropriate closing stanza.

Part Two

The Individual Parts of the Lutheran Chief Divine Service

INTRODUCTION

"The notes give life to the text."

–LUTHER[103]

§1.

The first German Mass was held on Christmas Day 1525 in the parish church of Wittenberg. It was not *spoken* but **sung**. We already know the fact that, and the method by which, Luther, working with the cantor Johann Walter, created the musical portion of the German Mass during a special three-week period of labor. Already at the beginning of 1525 he had written in his essay "Against the Heavenly Prophets": "I am eager to have a *German* Mass today, and I am working on it; yet I really want it to have **a true German character**. The practice of translating the Latin text and keeping the tone or notation is something I can make allowance for; yet it does not sound natural or authentic. Both *text and notation, accent, melody, and expression have to flow from the mother tongue and voice or else it is all imitation, the way monkeys do!*" (EA 29:203).[104]

What, then, might have induced him to undertake "notable changes" in the manner of performance also, aside from the fact that the Mass was sung not in Latin but in the *German language* and in *German manner*? Was it merely a concern over the liturgical performance coming to predominate again? The reason is a deeper one.

The ritual performed in the Christian Divine Service on the part of the pastor and congregation consists not only of speaking the Word but also of *chanting it*; for "the Word, when spoken with an elevated emotion, turns into *chanting*, according to the artistic impulse innate in man, as the mod-

[103] WA Tr 1:480 (no. 968). —MC.

[104] Cf. Luther, "Against the Heavenly Prophets" (1525), AE 40:141. —MC.

ulation of the voice fixes itself to the musical scale grounded in the physical world" (Zahn).[105] This chanting is, however, not simply metrical singing, but recitative singing. And the latter is no doubt the original. Professor Max Müller, the famous linguist (as <60> Lyra, in his *Altarweisen* [Altar Chant], quotes from his abridged edition of the sacred hymns of Indian Brahmans) states: "And it is my view that what we call 'accent,' and for us possesses no musical quality at all, was in origin purely musical *in every language* . . . I know that this idea of accent's original character needs further demonstration . . . Yet for Sanskrit it stands reasonably firm." Likewise, with respect particularly to the earliest prose, yet also to the original form of the recitation in every language generally: "The voice's *cantilene* (singing pitch) ascended noticeably at the acute accent, descended at the grave accent, and for the rest maintained a medial position."

According to witnesses of church antiquity, it is safe to assume that, following the pattern of the Jewish church, which sang the psalms antiphonally in accordance with their parallel structure (Psalm 147:7: "Sing ye *back and forth with one another* unto the Lord"), there was responsive singing in Christian services of worship from an early period. The congregation responded to the clergy's intonations and petitions by continuing, repeating, concluding, or else sealing with the singing of a simple "Amen" (*cantus responsorius, hypophonicus*) the psalm or portion of a psalm intoned by one or several of the assistants. This then gave way later in the fourth century to another kind of antiphonal singing, *congregational antiphony* proper, in which the congregation divided itself into two or more choirs—such as in choirs of men, women, boys, and girls—which sang "back," or "one to another" (*cantus antiphonicus*).[106]

---

[105] Zahn, 1. —MC.

[106] *) Eusebius, Ephraim, and especially Ambrose, the poet and singer of immortal hymns of the Early Church, also make mention of this kind of antiphonal singing. We borrow from *Siona* the following translation of the beautiful words from his *Hexameron* III, 9: "What else is the roaring of the ocean waves but a type of the congregation's joyful song? Hence the sea is often very fittingly compared to the congregation at worship. As those approaching come streaming in, it shows the first, gentle rolling of the tide; then, during the united prayer of the whole assembly, it is lifted up louder like murmuring breakers; and finally in the psalm responsories and the antiphonal singing *of men, women, girls, and boys*, it sounds mightily like the echoing of the waves in harmonious concert." [*Siona: Monatschrift für Liturgie und Kirchenmusik* 11, no. 1 (1886): 2. A footnote here states: "We excerpt this admittedly loose but tasteful translation from *Siona*, vol. III, 115. In the original, the passage reads: *Quid aliud ille concentus undarum*," etc.] — That Luther also had in view the latter form of antiphonal singing when he was arranging the German Divine Service is demonstrated not only by his translation of the *Te Deum* and the Litany, but also by the directions given for the Christmas hymn, "From Heaven Above to Earth I Come," according to which the words of the angel (sts. 1–5) were to be sung by boys only.

We know that a special kind of *congregational singing* came into the Western Church by way of Ambrose, who <61> composed metrically structured hymns and gave these a modulated melody, and it was this spiritual popular song which, through Luther, would rise to a new and imperishable life in the church of the Reformation. However, as this Ambrosian hymn singing fell into decline and at the same time a great multiplicity and confusion of melodies in churches here and there increasingly asserted itself, a new epoch of church singing dawned, that is to say, the *Roman choral singing,*[107] *or Gregorian chant* (*cantus choralis Gregorianus*). Pope Gregory I (540–604), seeking to bring about a reformation of church singing, collected the extant songs of the church which were good but had fallen out of use, improved, expanded, and organized them, assigned them places in the liturgy, established a system of music theory for rendering and setting their melodies, and in the process increased the four church modes or modal scales stemming from the Ambrosian period to eight. These same modes were retained throughout the medieval period and are still known in music today by their particular names (Ionian, Dorian, Phrygian, Lydian, etc.), even though there has been a complete shift in the whole science of music. To preserve the form of the singing which he introduced, Gregory further invented a special form of *notation*, and to cultivate it founded special *schools*, on account of which he is also graced with a special day of remembrance as patron protector of schools—which has long been kept as an annual school-festival even in the Lutheran Church. Among the prescriptions made by Gregory, one runs: "*No one can attain the office of the priesthood except he be well-versed in singing.*"

"Gregorian chant," says Zahn in his *Handbüchlein für evangelische Cantoren und Organisten* [Little Handbook for Evangelical Cantors and Organists], "is a testimony of serious Christian art and piety and has lasting value for the whole Christian Church. It is characterized especially by solemn dignity and reverence."[108] Gregory proceeded from the principle that *all singing in the church must be a bearer of the divine Word.* In order that no factors outside of God's Word might assert themselves, not only did all those elements in church singing which had been added on have to be removed, *largely* to awaken aesthetic interest, but in Gregorian chant all artistic [polyphonic] forms had to give way to the *cantus firmus.* <62> Thus a form of singing arose in which the song proceeded in unison[109] and in ex-

[107] *) This kind of singing is called *choral* because it was performed by the clergy in the *chorus*, that is, the chancel.

[108] Zahn, 13. —MC.

[109] *) "Gregorian chant, having arisen before the invention of counterpoint (composition),

tremely simple reciting tones which only became melodic at certain points in the text by the rise and fall of the voice according to certain rules. The characteristics of this style of singing are also shown by its terminology. On account of the even progress of the melodies, which for the most part change only by seconds and thirds, it was called *cantus planus* (plainchant, i.e., "regular song"). Because the melody, once it had been firmly established, could not be altered by the singers, it is referred to as the *cantus firmus* (*canto firmo,* "firmly set song"), and because this singing was not just sung by one, but sometimes by many or several at the same time, and was thus sometimes a song of the choir, it was called *cantus choralis* ("common or united song"), for which reason the precentors, who were required to know the fixed melody ("*canon*") precisely, were originally called *canonici,* and the singers in the choir led by him, *chorales*.

Yet one should not think that Gregorian chant was dragging and monotonously tedious, as the ignorant suppose based on the fact that these tones are customarily represented by notes of equal length. It has rhythm, too, in that during performance, the tones much rather maintain their emphasis by lengthening and contracting, and therefore it is only arhythmic insofar as its tones are not sung in a precisely measured tempo, as they are in the hymns of our hymnals, for example. This is also evident from the signs often inserted in ancient notation, which indicate either a quicker or slower manner of performance, and not only for individual tones, but for entire verbal and tonal phrases, for example, "t" (*tarditas* = lingering), "m" (*mediocritas* = medium movement), "c" (*celeritas* = quickness). Likewise, the following letters indicate the strength of the tone: "b" (*bene*) denotes emphasis; "bt" (*bene teneatur*), a longer hold with raised voice; "x" (*expectare*) a pause.

Because Gregorian is partly sung alone, partly sung in concert, its songs are divided into two classes: *accentus* and *concentus*. Under *accentus* belong all songs that are to be sung by one <63> person alone, and thus the sung recitations of the liturgy: the intonations, collects, lessons, prefaces, etc., which recitations more often have the lection tone or recitative tone, which in later times was called *choraliter* reading (*modus choraliter legendi*). We will revisit this point. Under *concentus* belong all the songs to be sung jointly by multiple persons, and thus all responsorial and antiphonal songs, the psalmodies, and the choir songs properly speaking. For these, specific forms were prescribed, the distinction of which related to their beginning, middle, and end.

---

was originally designed for strictly monophonic performance. Only later was it given polyphonic settings and employed in the most varying manner of the art of counterpoint; yet it resisted such use in many ways." (Zahn, [7].)

Now, it is certainly true that with Gregorian chant the people's participation in church singing formally and fully ceased, partly through the preparation which it required, partly through the exclusive use of Latin even after it had already become a dead language. As already noted in its proper place, singing was delivered entirely into the hands of the higher and lower clergy so that nothing was left for the people but merely to watch and listen. But the blessed time came when it was again exclaimed, "Everything is yours!"—therefore also Ambrose and Gregory. Luther restored to the Christian people not only an involvement and a rich participation in the church's song by introducing the popular spiritual hymn as an integral part of the Divine Service, but also the joint ownership and delightful enjoyment of *cantus Gregorianus*, which was found at last by Luther and the musical experts he had befriended. And he was the man suited to that purpose. From his school days, Luther, who was most gifted linguistically and poetically as well as musically, lived in the musical sanctuary of *cantus choralis Gregorianus*. He was as conversant with its musical grammar as he was with linguistic grammar. Concerning this Gregorian musical sanctuary so familiar to him and understood by him, we know that his judgment of music was such that, out of all the arts, he cleared for it the first place after theology, and only found it the more admirable and glorious that there was "much singing in the Mass."[110] Therefore, just as he made no notable changes in the most important parts and the general composition of the Chief Divine Service up to that point (apart from his purging it of the accretions which had spoiled it), since it had "a noble Christian pedigree"—so he likewise retained the *singing* of the Mass and the customary *manner* of the singing, since he saw in *cantus Gregorianus* the *musical form most suitable to the sacred texts*, <64> and wished to see this artistry placed into proper service to Him who is the author and bestower of all arts. Yet "every language has its own music, a different law for the ordering of its sounds." And no one knew that better than Luther, who addresses the subject in several places nor did anyone understand better how to adapt the Latin chants to a German manner than he, the author of the beautiful form of the German language which we use in church and writing, the translator of the German Bible. And to what extent his work was successful musically we have heard from the mouth of his musical collaborator, Johann Walther. Yet the latter, along with other professional musicians, did great service to the polyphony of the Lutheran Church by *combining cantus gregorianus with polyphonic settings*.

[110] Cf. Luther, "Admonition Concerning the Sacrament of the Body and Blood of our Lord" (1530), AE 38:123; WA 30^{2}:614, line 35. —MC.

Thus through Luther we came to find not only the spiritual folk hymn but also the *Gregorian music of the Church* utilized in our public Divine Service, according to need—and with German texts and "in a German manner," what is more. We have found the latter utilized in the preserved parts of the Mass, in the Ambrosian hymn of praise, in the Litany, in the canticles of Zacharias and Mary, as well as Simeon, and finally in the psalmody. And those most glorious musical testimonies in the field of spiritual folk hymns such as "A Mighty Fortress Is Our God," "Isaiah, Mighty Seer in Days of Old," and "All Glory Be to God Alone," for all their originality, did not disown their Gregorian ancestry.[111] Works such as the *Kirchengesänge* of J. Spangenberg (Nordhausen, 1545) and of J. Keuchenthal (Wittenberg, 1573), the *Psalmodia sacra* of Lucas Lossius (Lüneburg 1553 and 1579)—a highly regarded resource even in Catholic circles—the *Cantica sacra* of Franz Eler (Hamburg, 1588), the *Missale, Vesperale,* and *Matutinale* of M. Ludecus (Havelberg, 1589), the *Missodia,* etc., of M. Prätorius (1611), et al., all had their origin in the Lutheran Church. And it is in this recognition of and appreciation for *cantus Gregorianus* that we also see the characteristic distinction between the Swiss and the German, or Lutheran, Reformation. Whereas the Swiss were unfavorably disposed to it from the outset—in fact, the Second Helvetic Confession explicitly identifies it as "supremely absurd," and its exclusion from the Reformed service as "a service"—the Lutherans of central and north Germany, on the contrary, have nurtured the greatest regard for it, and show how an excellent understanding of its beauty and use can be of service <65> for furthering the Gospel. In the return to a genuinely Lutheran form of the Divine Service presently, attention has been directed back to the importance of *cantus Gregorianus* and its use in the Lutheran Church, and here the grand-ducal director of music, *Otto Kade* of Schwerin, Mecklenburg, has been of extraordinary service, not only through his *Luther-Codex*, which appeared in 1870, but also through a project strongly supported by the blessed Grand Duke Friedrich Franz II, which is: "to encourage in the congregation the preparation, employment, and appreciation of the ancient, splendid chants of the Gregorian melodic treasury—which in the Protestant Church have regrettably long since fallen into obscurity and faded away—by supplying the congregation once more with a careful selection in pleasing and suitable form for four voices."[112] Great is the praise

[111] On the Gregorian qualities of the first two, see Kümmerle, *Enzyklopädie der ev. Kirchenmusik*, 1:362ff., 648ff. On the last, see Robin Leaver, *Luther's Liturgical Music: Principles and Implications* (Grand Rapids: Eerdmans, 2007), 219, 328, 414 n. 62. —MC.

[112] *) The first part of this work [Kade], printed in 1867 at the expense of the Grand Duke, contains monophonic settings of the Gregorian tones for the Chief Divine Service, for the choir as well as for the liturgist. The second part, which appeared in 1875, contains

that this scholar of ancient hymnody ascribes to *cantus Gregorianus*. In the Preface to his *Luther-Codex*, he exclaims (among other things):

> There is no substitute in the world for the profound merit of these character types and melodic forms which the Church labored over a thousand years to perfect. No other music comes near it in terms of powerful motifs. It is the most mysterious musical language that there is in the world. It is the *most delightful possession* of a congregation which has discovered in this rich selection of melodic forms (with which *all the liturgical* texts are set not merely once, but at times twice according to their liturgical position) a *mean* where Church and artistry meet. It is the Bible set to music.[113] — Never and under no circumstance should the sense for these melodic forms have disappeared from the memory of the congregation, never should the use of these glorious character types in the Church's polyphonic composition have been given up."[114] <66>

In the article, "Der großherzogliche Schloßchor in Schwerin" [The Grand-Ducal Castle Choir in Schwerin], appearing in the religious music journal *Halleluja* in February 1884, Kade repeats this judgment almost verbatim and adds to it, "This foundation of all melodic theory . . . by itself has the power to convey the concept of church music, which is hardly comprehensible without it. The free composition, that is, a composition which does not have as its foundation this ancient, worthy *choral* chant, is excluded from the Divine Service on principle, or at very least reduced to a minimum."

In dispensing with the old, orthodox agendas, Rationalism robbed our Lutheran people of the bulk of the *liturgical chant* heritage, or at least limited its use wherever it still survived, largely to a bare minimum. But especially the people raised in this country of Enthusiasts have so absolutely lost the sense and understanding of liturgical singing that, despite all instruction and encouragement—even in many of the more informed congregations, particularly those consisting of Württembergers and other South Germans—a man must still refrain from reintroducing liturgical

---

the monophonic Gregorian melodies for the secondary divine services, Matins and Vespers, and the third part in 1880 brought the polyphonic version of the first part by O. Kade. Whether the fourth part, which was supposed to bring the harmonized settings to the second volume, has ever appeared, is unknown to me at this time. The German text was handled by Dr. Kliefoth.

[113] *) That is, "*the Vulgate set to Music!* And just as he who has learned Latin grammar has by the same token learned all the general rules for German grammar, in the same way Luther learned from this musical Vulgate the general rules which came to serve in setting Luther's Bible to melodies" (*Blätter für Hymnologie,* June 1884).

[114] Kade, 23–24. —MC.

singing at this time, if as a good Lutheran he does not wish to cause division and schism over an external order, which, although glorious and desirable, is nevertheless human. Sung responses on the part of the congregation or of the choir are accepted here and there, but in no way (they suppose) is the *liturgist* at the altar to avail himself of the Church's lection tone, for that is "*Catholic*." And even if here and there liturgical singing at the altar has asserted itself or gained acceptance, singing is largely done only *as it has been heard from others*. For it cannot be denied "that the positive precepts, the very basic fundamentals of teaching churchly accent, have been tragically lost to our own people, in an age when . . . instead of the artistry of the Church there is the arbitration of subjective taste, when for an altar churchgoers are offered the empty leftovers of a gaudy table from the salon and opera stage," and when the old liturgical accent with its ancient, robust power and simplicity was expelled from the conduct of the *cultus* "by the tyranny of the *Zeitgeist*, by which it ruthlessly subjected to the sledgehammer the capitals of gothic columns in order to paste them over with Corinthian capitals of plaster and all manner of painted stucco work" (J. Lyra).[115] And what of *choral singing*? Operatic style has so thoroughly spoiled the sense of taste in singer and <67> congregation that whoever wishes to discard those choral pieces of an operatic style and to take up the treasures of the Ancient Church's choral music is, for the present, obliged to swim against the tide.

In the meantime, a good start has been made for familiarizing oneself with the musical treasures of our Church which have fallen into oblivion and for learning about the origin of our altar liturgy, its positive precepts, and the basic elements of liturgical accent. Aside from O. Kade, these treasures have been saved by F. *Hommel* in his *Liturgie des lutherischen Gemeindegottesdienstes* [Liturgy of the Lutheran Divine Service] (1851) and in his *Psalter*, etc. (1859);[116] by Dr. F. *Layriz* in his *Kern des deutschen Kirchengesanges* [Core of German Church Music] (1855), of which vol. 4 contains 120 settings; by Ph. *Herold* and Prof. Dr. *Krüger* in their journal *Siona*, but above all, by Prof. Dr. *Schöberlein* and *Riegel* in their incomparable three-volume *Schatz des liturgischen Chor- und Gemeindegesangs nebst den Altarweisen* [Treasury of Liturgical Choir and Congregational Music with the Altar Chant] (1872); while we are introduced to the development and grammar of liturgical chant by Dr. L. *Kraußold* in his *Handbuch für den Kirchen- und Choralgesang* [Handbook for Church and Choral Music] (1855), and in particular by Pastor Justus W. *Lyra*, in *Die Liturgischen Altarweisen des lutherischen*

---

[115] Lyra, *Ornitho.*, vi-vii. —MC.

[116] Friderich Hommel. *Der Psalter nach der deutschen Übersetzung D. Martin Luthers für den Gesang eingerichtet.* (Stuttgart: Liesching, 1859). —MC.

Hauptgottesdienstes nach ihrer Reinheit und Einheit in musikalischer Beziehung untersucht und festgestellt [The Liturgical Altar Chant of the Lutheran Chief Divine Service according to its Purity and Unity Considered and Established in Regard to Music] (1873), and in connection to that, in his *Andreas Ornithoparchus aus Meiningen, der Zeitgenosse Luthers und dessen Lehre von den Kirchenaccenten* [Andreas Ornithoparchus from Meiningen, the Contemporary of Luther and His Teaching on Ecclesiastical Accentuations] (1877).[117] And as one example of the fruit of so many of the works referred to and their detailed study, one should also mention one ripened on American soil: *Choralbuch mit Liturgie und Chorgesängen zum Kirchenbuch der Allgemeinen Kirchenversammlung* [Choral Book with Liturgy and Choir Music for the Church Book of the General Church Assembly], edited by B. Endlich, which was published in this country in 1879 by J. Kohler, 911 Arch Street, in Philadelphia. This work is divided into two parts. Part 1 contains the liturgy and choral songs, and part 2, the so-called "chorales," or tunes for the songs of the hymnal, consistently presented in their rhythmic form and according to the older harmonic setting. <68> With respect to part 1, let it be noted with pleasure that the editor, besides using Schöberlein's *Schatz* as his chief sources for liturgical music, also used from earlier times Spangenberg, *Kirchengesänge* (1545), the church order of Palsgrave Wolfgang (1570), the church order of Pomerania (1563), and other older and more recent works; and also that this work contains the intonations and responsories strictly according to the pure and correct *accent*, and that it presents for the liturgist, choir, and congregation only what is reliable, only what is of the Ancient Church. May this musical work of the Church also find in our circles the attention due, especially in the interest of liturgical chant.

Addendum. Lately added to the the aforementioned works is *Der Vortrag des liturgischen Gesanges. Ein Handbuch für evangelische Geistliche, bearbeitet von H. Franke* [The Performance of Liturgical Music. A Handbook for Evangelical Divines, edited by H. Franke] (Leipzig: Carl Klinner Verlag, 1891.) (See the review in *Lehre und Wehre* 39, no. 3 (1893): 87ff.)

---

[117] *) Andreas Ornithoparchus ("Vogelsang") is one of the earliest and most influential German music teachers. In the same year in which Luther posted his 95 Theses, and quite frequently after that, Ornithoparchus published his *Musicae activae Micrologus* in Leipzig. The third book of this writing contains the theory of liturgical accent, the systematic presentation and methodical continuation of the ground rules of chanted reading. He is regarded as the original author of this field of study.

§2. For the proper execution even of Lutheran altar chant, some knowledge of the theory of church accent is needed

By church accent (*accentus ecclesiasticus*), we mean the musical line in which the syllables of any given text, according to certain rules, may be given its natural expression with regular rise and fall of the voice. Thus this accent is not grammatical but musical, and as such is distinct with respect not to rhythm but to melody. The theory of church accent is accordingly concerned with enumerating the rules for the *choraliter* reading (*modus choraliter legendi*). *In the Lutheran Church, however, accent theory deals only with the most elementary forms of Gregorian chant:* the Psalm tones according to the eight church modes, the tones for the lessons, the Words of the Testament, the prayers (Collect, Preface, Our Father), the versicles, and the benedictions.

We were already reminded in the proper place[118] that, when Luther's collaborator in the musical parts of the *Deutsche Messe* asked him who had taught him the use of the *accentus* and *concentus* so masterfully, he answered, "The <69> poet Virgil taught me that, who is able to apply his *verses* and words so skillfully to the events which he describes. *In the same way, Musica should match all her notes and melodies to the text.*" According to this principle, then, Luther employed the teaching of accent as it had been presented scarcely ten years earlier by Master Ornithoparchus in his *Micrologus*. This was done by him in his *Deutsche Messe* (1526). Lyra writes:[119] "It [the teaching of accent] at that point forms a stable chapter in the countless instructions on singing in the schools of the sixteenth century. The frequently misunderstood saying, *Accentus pater musices* ('Accent is the father of music'), was thereby changed into the flesh and blood of contemporaries whose musical education was based not, as today, on the sensual sound of musical [Lyra: "mechanical"] instruments, but on the sensible tone of the articulated human voice." How this was done is shown by the tones of the *Deutsche Messe* in the musical supplement to volume 22 of the Erlangen edition of Luther's works, as in volume X of the St. Louis edition [cf. AE 53:69ff.], which are also found elsewhere variously transposed. At the same time, we see from these in what sense Luther, in producing a Mass to be sung in *German*, shaped the modal Gregorian tones for their corresponding parts, and in so doing went above and beyond Ornithoparchus and prior tradition. The spirit of a churchly German language, awakened by the translation of the German Bible, motivated and drove Luther often—for exam-

[118] See above, p. 21 ff. —MC.

[119] Lyra, *Ornitho.*, 18. —MC.

ple, in the Gospel and Epistle tones, and in the Words of Institution—to appoint more dynamic, expressive formulas, which nevertheless bore on their brow just as solidly and clearly the imprint of specific Gregorian modes.

In the old agendas which are still available, as well as in the sophisticated compendiums of today, we certainly have enough exemplary models for the liturgical altar tones. Yet let us at the very least attempt, with the help of the above named writings of Kraußold and Lyra,[120] to furnish ourselves with a brief guide to the simplest form of liturgical singing—lest we learn liturgical singing simply according to tradition, which these days is very untrustworthy, much less according to the even more untrustworthy faculty of subjective discretion—and in this way be all the more able to study and make use of the models before us.

For this very simple form, then, Lyra classifies that tone as best which: <70>

1. Gives the greatest latitude to the *free rhythm* of well articulated, suitably moderate, unaffected speech.

2. (a) Allows for a moderate *rise* and *fall* of the *voice* corresponding to the involuntary change of pitch in solemn speaking, and (b) encourages a rich multiplicity of melodic phrases *within the most limited range of vocal intervals.*

The requirement of the first point is met by the *method of reading in a chanted manner* (*choraliter legere*) which has remained in use in the Lutheran Divine Service, and is employed not only for the recitation of the Collects but also for the responsively sung versicles as well as the psalmody whenever the voice progresses on a thematic note,[121] called the *dominant*,

---

[120] *) This includes the work of Franke, mentioned in the addendum to the previous paragraph. [See above, p. 61.]

[121] *) This reading or singing, where the voice stays on the same pitch without melodic shift of intervals, is called *in unisono* according to the terminology of the old school. Hence in Luther's *Deutsche Messe und Ordnung des Gottesdienstes* [German Mass and Order of Divine Service] (EA 22:237; StL 10:239 [AE 53:72]), when he specifies, "Then the priest reads a collect in *f* faut *in unisono,* as follows: *'Allmächtiger Gott, der du bist ein Beschützer aller. . . .'*" he avails himself of Guido von Arezzo's then-universally employed solmisation scheme (invented in 1038), to indicate the pitch for the running tone in which the collect is to be sung. In this scheme, the various pitches of song tones are represented by the syllables: ut, re, mi, fa, sol, la, si, do. This is not the place to delve into this Guidonian method. Let it suffice to note, after Lyra, that the *f* faut (or more properly, "*f* fa ut") *in unisono* means that the main or running tone, the *tonus currens*, for the collect should be the F on the fourth line of the bass clef. Luther is not saying, however, that the collect should only be sung on *f*. He only wishes to indicate the medial pitch for the collect as an example. Depending on whether the voice of the liturgist is higher or lower, the medial pitch for the collect may even be *g* or *a* or *b* or even *c*.

The second passage is also explained by Luther accordingly: "After that, the Epistle in the *octavo tono*, remaining in the *unisono* of the collect." As will be presented in more detail in its place, the Epistle and Gospel were formerly chanted from the altar in Gregorian for a length of time, keeping the same pitch but expressing rhythm by the quantitative lengthening or contracting of the vowels and the dynamic emphasis or deemphasis of the breath, <71> with pauses for breathing as appropriate to the sense, all according to the unaided guidance of linguistic instinct.

[The text is chanted with similar speed, rhythm, and emphasis to the manner in which the text would be spoken. For example, the text in bold is emphasized when speaking:

O give **thanks** unto the **Lord,** for **He** is **good** . . .
O **God,** the **strength** of **all** . . .
Blessed is the **man** who **walks** not . . .

Therefore, the singing of the text is executed as follows:]

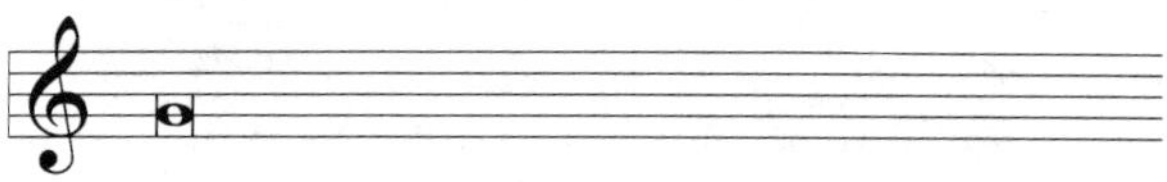

Versicle: O give **thanks** unto the **Lord,** for **He** is **good** . . .

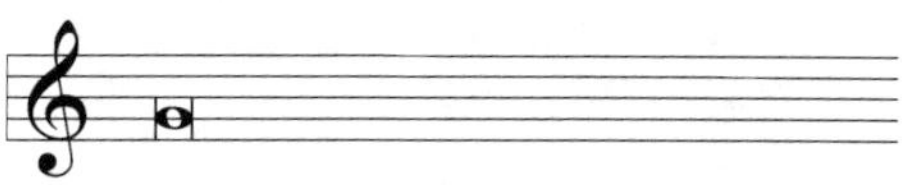

Collect: O **God,** the **strength** of **all** who . . .

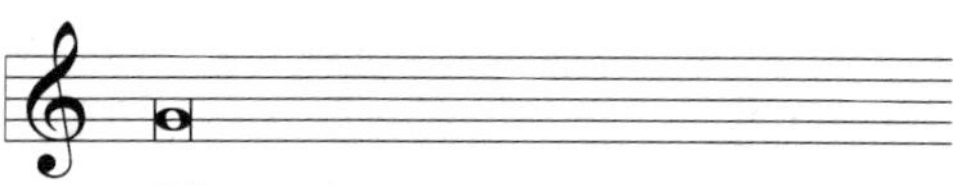

Psalm: **Bless**ed is the **man** who **walks** not . . .

As to the requirement for choral-style reading made under point 2 (a) and (b), the specific accent rules of the Gregorian school now come into consideration here. In the running tone, the *tonus currens*, singing continues until a break or division in the phrase is made by punctuation in the text: by the *distinctio,* or our *comma*; the *semicolon* and the *colon*; the *period*; or the *question mark*; which are made audible in the liturgical performance by a rise or fall of the voice according to a specific rule.

1. The *distinctio*, or what we now call the *comma*, has three kinds of

manner, and for this Luther, in the aforesaid writing, not only established rules for the pericopal lesson tone but also illustrated it with samples of notation. So when he speaks here of *octavo tono*, he does not mean the eighth tone on a music staff, but the eighth mode in the ancient church modes or scales. While the Epistle was to be sung on the pattern of the Ancient Church's eighth mode, as his accompanying example shows, the pitch of the running tone (*unisono*) to be maintained in the process is nevertheless the same as that of the Collect. So despite being sung to two different tones, the Collect and Epistle would have the same tonal pitch.

accents: *accentus immutabilis*, *accentus acutus*, and *accentus moderatus*, depending on the greater or lesser significance of the clause.

In *accentus immutabilis*, no rise or fall occurs in the voice. The observance of the break made by a comma occurs simply by extending the last syllable with a brief pause, perhaps as long as taking a breath:

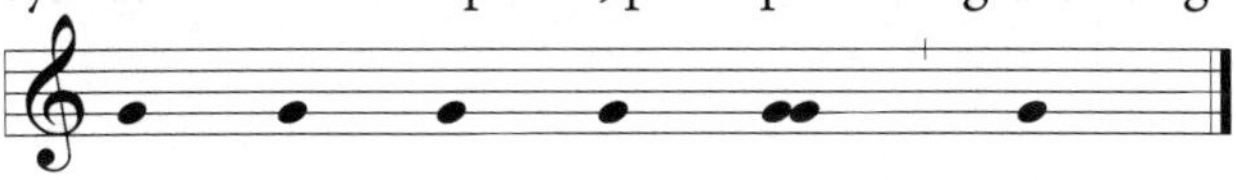

<72>

In *accentus acutus*, the voice returns to the running tone on the last or next to last syllable after first descending two steps:

In *accentus moderatus*, the voice (according to Ornithoparchus) does not return to the running tone on the last syllable of a section as it does in the *acutus*, but comes to a rest on a transitional tone:

2. The *semicolon* and the *colon* (a stronger division) have the *accentus medius*, in which the voice falls a third on the last syllable(s).

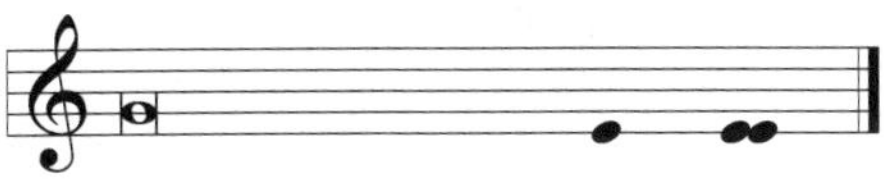

3. The *period* (*colon*) has the *accentus gravis*, that is, the tone falls a fifth:

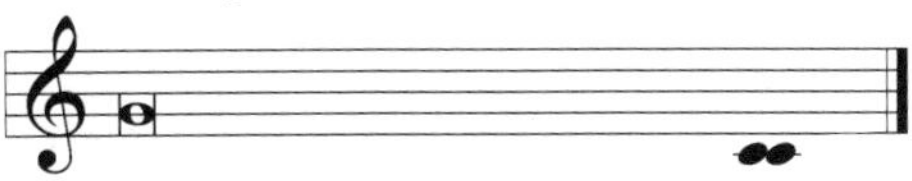

4. The *question mark* or *interrogative clause* has the *accentus interrogativus*, in which the voice rises on the last syllable by one or several steps, or else falls two steps from the running tone and then returns through the intermediate steps:

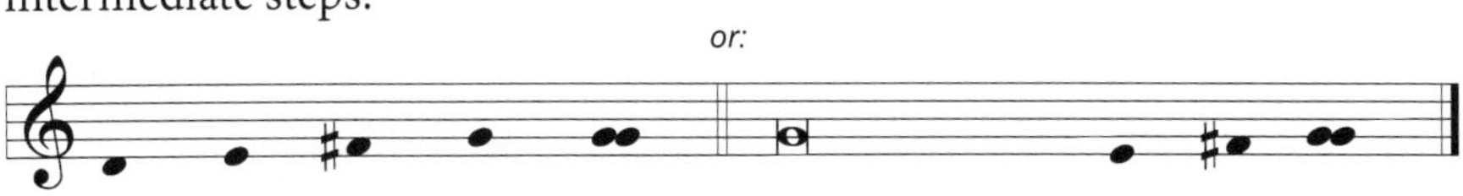

5. Finally, some people also include the *final accent*, the *clausula finalis*,

which according to some involves rising a third through the second and returning, but according to others, falling gradually on the last syllables to a fourth below the running tone:

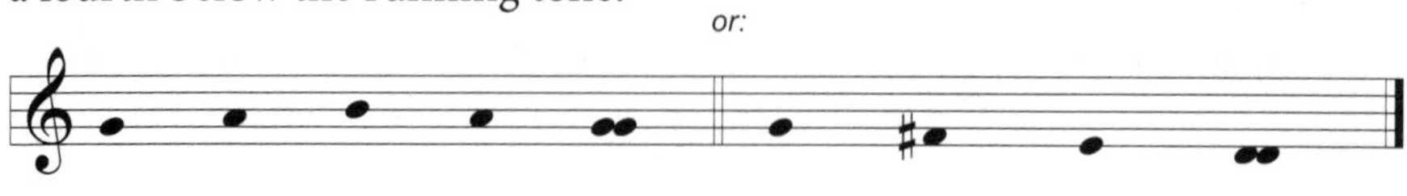

<73>

Using these accents, which are presumably related to the Hebraic accents, every passage of Holy Scripture can be read. Since we still have them in the *tones for the versicle and prayers*—assuming we do not, in our liturgical singing, merely cling to tradition,[122] but rather hold to the more ancient patterns of our singing church—the following examples may illustrate the use of those accents in context:

Accentus immutabilis

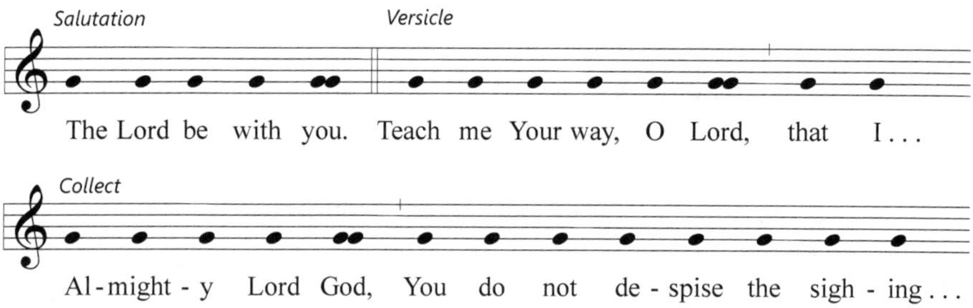

Accentus acutus

[122] *) "Traditional," for instance, is the very widespread formula: *g f e–f# g*. Lyra identifies this as incorrect and calls it "that whining formula . . . which in many places still in effect serves as the first resort for the liturgical recitation of versicles, collects, etc.," and, with the addition of *g – f – e – g*, "completes the process of intentional corruption of our liturgical melodies." No use of these is made in the present work either. [Yet, see below, pages 137–38, "2. With Alleluia."]

Or:

Salutation

Versicle

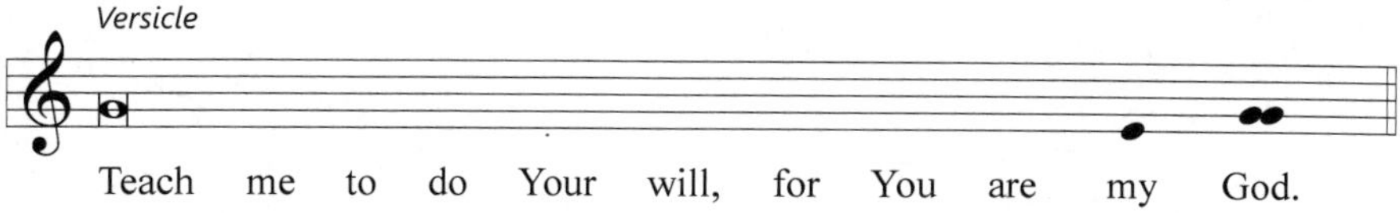

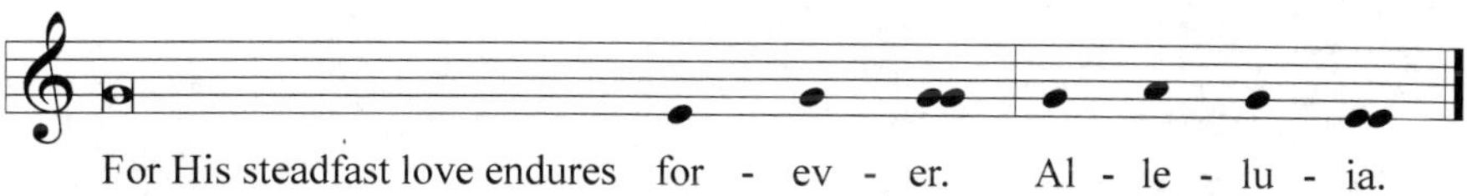

Collect

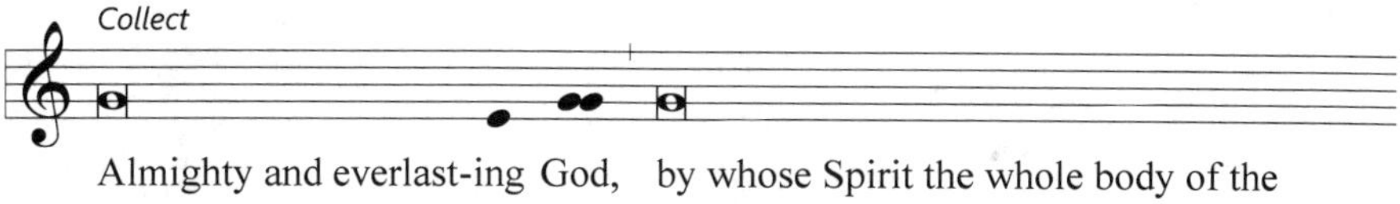

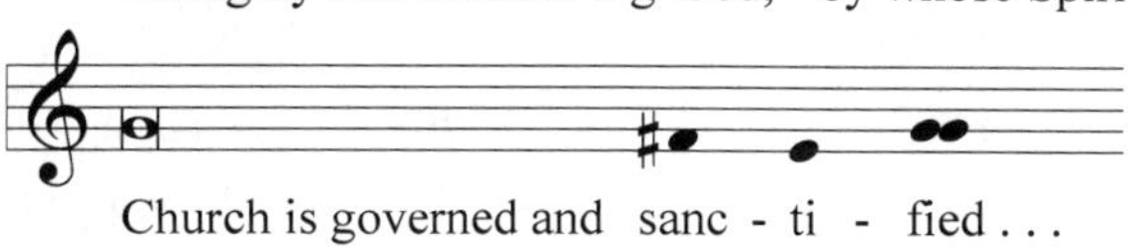

Accentus moderatus

Preface

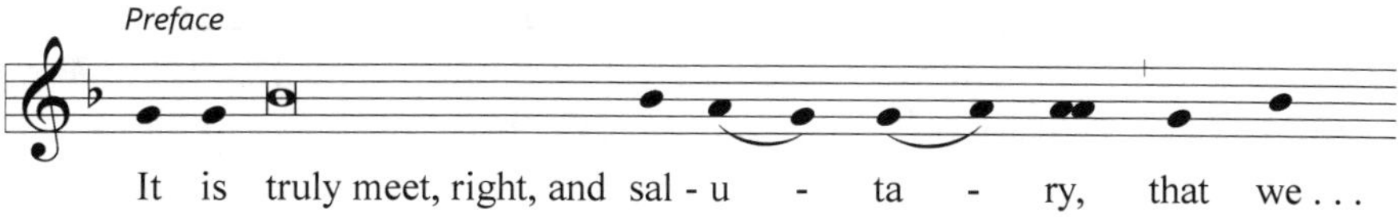

<74>

Accentus medius

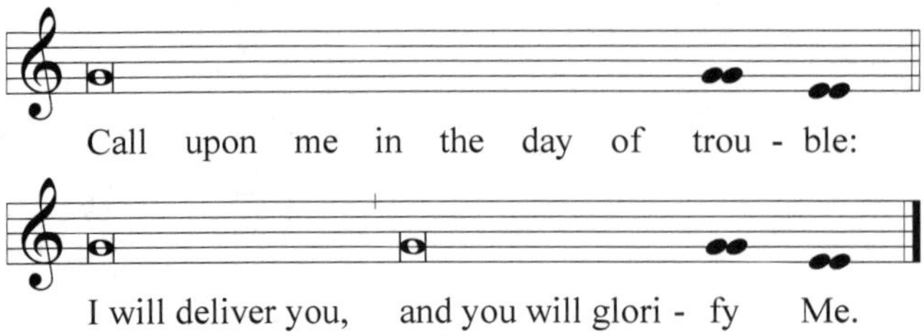

Termination of Collects:

Clausuala finalis

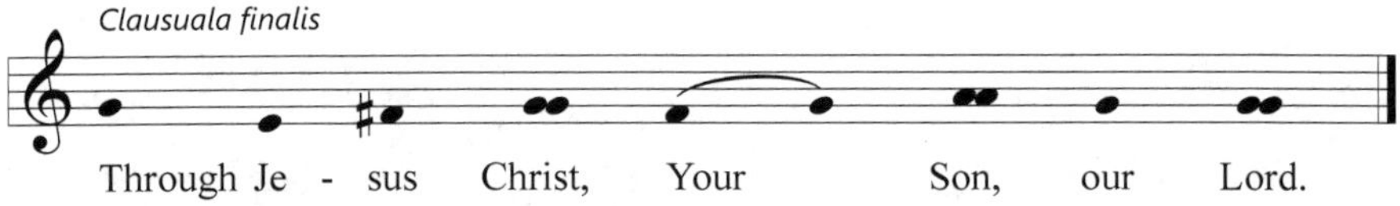

or:

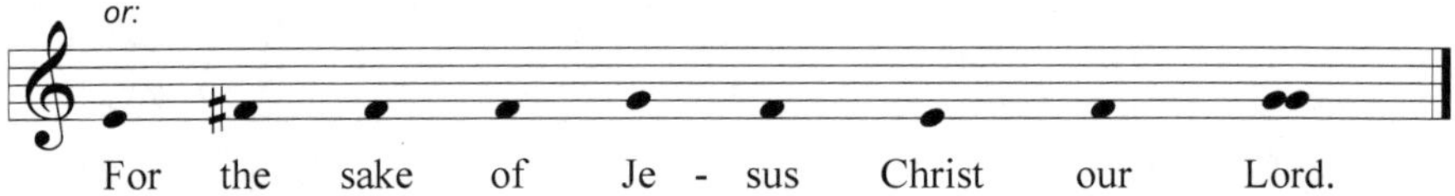

or:

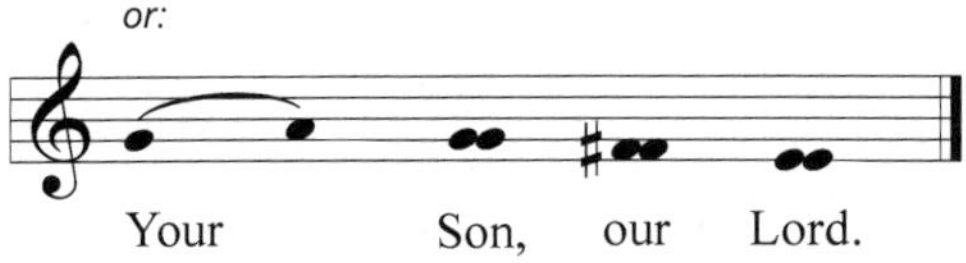

After all this, just a few *suggestions regarding the manner of musical execution*. In order for it to edify the congregation, the following additional points should be observed:

1. *Shouting and droning*, which are not singing, must be strictly avoided, particularly when the melody rises to higher notes. The voice can come out more strongly on low notes, but even then it must not degenerate into bellowing. Unforced singing that flows out without special effort at a steady volume is the most edifying. For that reason, every liturgist should familiarize himself with his vocal range through practice, and so confer with the organist concerning the height or depth of the intonation, <75> whether said organist is to cue the liturgist or simply the responding congregation. Only a natural voice, only the chest voice, and not one such as is squeezed out of a constricted throat!

2. Letters and syllables should be *pronounced cleanly*, and the pronunciation of the *vowels* most especially calls for careful practice. Singing up and down the scales, alternating through the five vowels, is the surest way

to reach that goal. The "a" should sound clear, not like "o" or "oa";[123] the "e" not like "ä"; the "i" not like "e" or "ä"; the "o" not like "a"; and the "u" not like "o." Like so: *Vater*, not *Voater*; *denn*, not *dänn*, *Christum*, not *Chrestum*; *durch*, not *dorch*. Nor should any letters be added to the beginning of a word, e.g., "*N-der Herr segne dich*," etc., nor one syllable split into two, as can likewise be heard sometimes in the Aaronic Benediction: "*Der Her-herr segne dich*," etc.

3. *The posture of the whole body*, including its various parts, should be steady and reverent. The mouth must not be spread too wide nor pulled to the side, nor any part of the face distorted generally.

4. Whenever possible, the liturgist should prepare himself in advance not only for the *selection* of the appropriate liturgical parts, the versicles, collects, etc., but also for the *execution*, and thus, for example, for the collects with respect to accentuation.

§3.

And now one more word concerning *the use of the organ with liturgical singing*.

As already noted, neither Gregorian chant in general nor the priest's altar chant in particular is by origin or nature calculated or designed for harmony, let alone harmonic accompaniment by the organ. For this reason, in fact, the use of the organ with liturgical chant was introduced far later than with the music of the Church in general. Nevertheless, men such as Kraußold, Lyra, Herzog, and Schöberlein believe that, with a judicious selection of stops and an accompaniment in keeping with the style, it might be permitted and defended. Since Kraußold discusses the subject in the greatest detail, the appropriate paragraph from his *Historisch-musikalisches Handbuch für den Kirchen- und Choralgesang* [Musicological Handbook for Church and Choral Music], <76> which simultaneously forms the conclusion to the entirety of that valuable little work, might well be included here with hardly any abbreviation. The passage in question reads:

> The purpose of altar chant would seem to oppose harmonic organ accompaniment, inasmuch as the *modus choraliter legendi* is to be expressed in such a way that the actual musical element, the melody, recedes into the background, whereas in the *choral singing* of

[123] Lochner is naturally addressing German-speakers here, yet applications to English may be drawn from his remarks—for instance: "God," not "Gawd" or "Gad," or in the Benediction, "Lord," not "Lo-hord," etc. A resource for instruction on English diction is M. Alfred Bichsel's *Manual on the Pastor's Chant* (St. Louis: Concordia Publishing House, 1989). —MC.

psalms and hymns, etc., the musical element was more prominent than the singer. However, between the strict *modus choraliter legendi* and the singing of psalms and hymns, there developed in Protestant and Catholic churches alike an intermediate group of distinct altar chants for which organ accompaniment was permitted. Strict chant remained the preferable form appropriate to the reading of the biblical lessons, historical narrative, and Collect prayers. On the other hand, a number of liturgical pieces in which a certain emotion is expressed, which were to be more of an effluence of religious feeling, emerged from the simple lesson tone to specific modulations, to melodic expression. This was the case with the intonation of the Kyrie and the Gloria, then the Our Father, the Words of Institution, and the Preface. As little, then, as the Lessons (Epistle and Gospel) and Collects proper were amenable to organ accompaniment by virtue of their content and purpose, so much, conversely, did the aforesaid melodic pieces lend themselves to it, and only where a true antiphonal song between the clergy and the congregation occurred did the organ accompaniment remain excluded from the former. Thus the traditional practice arose of using organ accompaniment with the *Our Father, the Words of Institution, the Preface,* etc., but not with the *responsories* or the singing of the clergy. When the question, then, is posed whether or not there should be any organ accompaniment at all with altar chant, it must be maintained after all that it is neither essential nor necessary to use it any more than it is to exclude it, and one will be left to weigh the reasons which might make the case for such organ accompaniment. And the first reason usually given is that organ accompaniment has the purpose of supporting and maintaining the ministers in their singing. We will not deny that many ministers may really find in organ accompaniment a crutch for their voice, but wide observation and experience has taught us that this incurs a great limitation. We must exclude this from the outset as a valid reason on its own, since for a musically educated clergyman who has no need of such support, the organ accompaniment <77> would be pointless and have to be omitted, while, conversely, it is precisely with a good, musically-trained voice that organ accompaniment sounds truly purposeful and beneficial. We take it for granted, and demand it as the minister's duty, that he should have a firm grasp of his altar chant and not be led by the organ nor wait for the organ to teach him his notes. He must practice beforehand so that he is as sure and certain of his singing as he is of his preaching. But for this purpose, organ accompaniment would not come to the aid of the singer's voice per se so much as to his ear. Therefore, if the minister has an ear for music, then, as stated, the organ accompaniment can actually do him good. But if we imagine the opposite—and this is certainly not seldom the case—if we imagine a minister with a bad ear for music, then in order for the organ to help him, it must be played so loud that it drowns out the music and the words. And that would be completely contrary to the purpose of the altar chant (the *choraliter* reading), where the *words* of the chant must remain the focus, or else the minister's singing and the organ music are so discordant as to be unendurable. We remember from our early childhood more than one occasion when the organist was forced to change and transpose (as well he should) in the middle of the melody line, for instance, while the minister sang the consecration, so as to be able to *accompany* his singing. If the organist does not do this, but remains in his melody line while the minister goes flat or sharp by a half or whole step—if the organist thinks that his playing is not to *accompany* the minister as much as to *lead* him, keep him in key, and guide him back into key—it results in that ear-splitting discord, which is a shock to all musical sensibility, and elicits from the hearer the unspoken longing, "If only the organ would be quiet!" And we must express this openly so that, in every case where the minister may not trust his ear, he will do better (assuming he wants to sing) to sing without organ accompaniment. His goal should still be "sung reading," and as such it can, even with some musical irregularities, get along far better without organ accompaniment than with it.

But organ accompaniment obviously has yet another purpose: to heighten solemnity and increase reverence. This lies, first, in the undeniable, uncanny effect of organ music in general, <78> as well as in the *harmony* added to the individual voice, which along with the melody is to the human mind the curious, *calming* factor that appeals so soothingly to the mind's religious feeling. But it also lies in the fact that melody and harmony, that is, the minister's voice carrying the melody and the organ providing harmonic accompaniment, must be in agreement in order to prevent the opposite of what was intended with the organ accompaniment.

If the minister does not have a firm and confident grasp of his singing, if he prefers to be led and carried along by the organ, another misfortune can arise, and this brings us to the nature and manner of organ accompaniment with respect to the minister's altar chant. *Namely, it must be categorically distinguished from the accompani-*

ment for the singing of the choir and congregation. The minister's singing is monodic chant—recitative monodic chant, even. The chant should properly be more of a musical speech for the congregation. The congregation should not only hear the melody of the chant, but above all and most importantly the *words* that are sung. So if the organ tried to accompany the minister's every note with a chord, or even play with stronger stops, then, as said before, the main element would be lost. It is better to sing without organ music, or even just to speak, than for the *proper* intent of altar chant to be lost to the organ music. Yet such a thoroughgoing organ accompaniment is not even feasible, since altar chant is not mensural and has no specific meter, but can only move in accordance with *rhetorical* rhythm. The individual notes are delivered not according to their specific measure and form but according to the length or shortness of the syllables, according to the greater or lesser emphasis of the different words as they are stressed. Organ accompaniment must take these things into account if it is to meet its purpose. There are four points which should be given the most consideration in this process, which are here recommended for close observation:

1. When accompanying the minister in liturgical chant, the organist should *never use a strong stop*; the *softer* and *gentler*, the better.

2. The organist should *never play the individual chords for their full duration or in strict time*, but faithfully as the minister recites his chant. We repeat: he should not *lead* him, but *accompany* him. Hence the organist must *hear* <79> the minister while playing. And in order to be able to hear him, in addition to a softer stop as mentioned above, he should especially make sure not to let his chords ring to the full, but to cut them short and leave room for the chant.

3. The minister's singing should never be accompanied *in continuo*. Where there is no change in harmony, where several tones of the melody often have the same chord as their root, *the organ should be completely silent*. Only the ending calls for full harmonic progression.

4. Finally, the organist should avoid the *pedal*. In congregational singing the pedal can be effective, when applicable, at keeping a large group of singers in the right key and tempo, and to make the root (basis) of the song clearly discernible. In the minister's monodic chant, the pedal is *superfluous* and *extremely burdensome*; except, perhaps, at the ending, as above.

It is unbelievable how difficult altar chant is made for the minister by inattention to these points, and (as is self-evident) proportionally so when a larger church is concerned. Verily, if the organist is so inept as to accompany the minister's chant with loud stops and full chords, without breaking, with the great intensity of the pedal bass—a fourfold plague of which one part is enough of a burden!—it will be unendurable in the full sense of the word, both on the part of those listening and on the part of the one chanting. And whoever has any love for his chest and does not wish eventually to be rendered unfit for his office as well as for altar chant should pay attention to these four points. A minister who is to sing the altar liturgy under the pressure of this fourfold burden from the organ has already consumed half his physical energy for the sermon! Away with organ accompaniment if it is going to be a burden! Better to let him sing *without the organ at all!* Then no one will ever again hear the lament that the liturgy is too demanding.[124] <80>

I. INTROIT

The Roman Mass begins with the *Initium missae*, the priest's entrance prayer from Psalm 43, and the *Confiteor*, the public confession, and only then is followed by the *Introit*, the entrance or opening music. With the omission of the entrance prayer, the Chief Divine Service in Brandenburg-Nürnberg (1533), Mark-Brandenburg (1540), and many other agendas based on earlier church orders, begins with the Confiteor, whereas the Saxon Agenda and most of the later ones more or less based on Luther's *Deutsche Messe* place Confession after the Sermon.

This song derives its name Introit, or *Introitus* ("going in, entrance"), from the custom of Christian antiquity according to which everyone entered the church in procession while singing, as is done again today in more ritualistic contexts in the Episcopal Church. This song consisted of a psalm, which the church servers sang alternately with the choir singers, and an antiphon or "answer song" of the congregation between individual psalm verses, and this antiphon was always coordinated with the theme of the Sunday or feast. Accordingly, when this festival entrance later fell out of use, the antiphon was retained along with the first verse of the corresponding psalm, leaving this song with the name "Introit," for which even Luther says, "When singing began in the church, the Psalms were turned into the Introit."[125]

[124] This appears to be mostly Lochner's summary of Kraußold, *Historisch-musikalisches Handbuch,* 189–94. —MC.

[125] Cf. Luther, "An Order of Mass and Communion" (1523), AE 53:21. —MC.

In his *Formula Missae* (1523) no less than in his *Deutsche Messe* (1526), Luther absolutely wished to see the Introit retained as an entrance song. In the former, it says, "We approve the Introits of Sundays and those which are sung on the feasts of Christ, such as Easter, Pentecost, Christmas, and we retain them; *although we prefer the psalms from which they were taken,* as was the observance formerly, yet in this we will yield to common custom." (StL 10:2238; [AE 53:22].) Nevertheless, in the latter work he accomodates his desire: "But to begin, we sing a spiritual hymn or a German psalm *in primo tono,* in manner as follows." (EA 22:237; StL 10:235ff. [AE 53:69].) This is followed by the entire Psalm 34: "I will <81> bless the Lord at all times," with notation according to the first of the church's eight psalm tones. Luther appoints for the Introit "a spiritual hymn *or* a German psalm." After Luther's precedent, the rest also have the Introit precede the Kyrie. Nevertheless, "many lands, many customs." A number of the agendas, particularly those of the post-Reformation era, specifically appoint for the "spiritual hymn" either "Come, Holy Spirit, fill," etc., or "Come, Holy Ghost, God and Lord,"[126] while Braunschweig-Lüneburg (1657) again specifies, "The pastor with the clerk[127] and students, shall begin the Mass or Communion with a German psalm followed by the German Kyrie 'O Vater, allmächtiger Gott'" [O Father, Almighty God].[128] Likewise, according to the Leipzig Agenda (1681), "the *students begin by singing the Introit of the Dominica* (Sunday) *or feast, followed by the* Kyrie eleison," etc.[129]

The Introit consists, as already indicated, of the so-called *antiphona*, the *psalmus* (a verse or two of a psalm), and the *lesser doxology* or *Gloria Patri* ("Glory be to the Father," etc.), that doxological formula of confession stemming from the conflicts with the Arians. For example, the Introit of Christmas Day:

Antiphona: "To us a Child is born, to us a Son is given; and the government shall be upon His shoulder, and His name shall be called Wonderful Counselor, Mighty God, Everlasting Father, Prince of Peace." [Isaiah 9:6]

Psalmus: "Oh sing to the Lord a new song, for He has done marvelous things!" [Psalm 98:1]

Gloria Patri: "Glory be to the Father and to the Son and to the Holy Spirit, as it was in the beginning, is now, and will be forever. Amen."

---

[126] See the Pentecost Antiphon or Luther's versified expansion thereof in Wackernagel 3:14, nos. 19–20. —MC.

[127] *Custos* (or "Küster"), also "sexton, "sacristan," "vestry-keeper," a lay assistant charged with various duties, esp. in rural parishes, usually housed on parish grounds. —MC.

[128] *Agenda Oder: Erster Teyl der Kirchen-Ordnung . . .* (Wolfenbüttel: Sterne, 1657). Quoted is the village order, p. 44; cf. the order for cities, p. 13: "The cantor and all schoolteachers and students begin by singing 'O Vater almächtiger Gott.' —MC.

[129] Cf. *Agenda, Das ist, KirchenOrdnung . . .* (1672), 48. —MC.

The Introit *is to be the herald of the liturgical day, announcing to the assembled congregation from the outset the theme of that Sunday, feast, or festival season*. Its stress therefore falls on the antiphon, inasmuch as this, through a short passage of Scripture, indicates the theme of the day and announces which salvific fact is to be celebrated. Every Sunday and feast has its own Introit, and many Sundays derive their name from its first word(s) in Latin, such as *Estomihi*, *Invocavit*, *Reminiscere*, or *Quasimodogeniti*, *Miscericordias Domini*, *Jubilate*, etc. Congregations which have not succumbed to the current penchant for increasingly shortening the Divine Service, but <82> have rather maintained a tolerance for the duration of the complete Divine Service from earlier times, should be encouraged to readopt the Introit. The best way to implement this, according to church precedent, would be by means of students who are eager and able to sing. Even if they are unable to sing multiple voice parts, singing two parts or even *one part* will suffice, and this sounds especially pleasant with the clear voices of children. And if our abilities are no longer up to the richer custom of singing the festive psalmodic or hymnodic Introit of former days, a few of the psalm tones will do for all the Introits: one for Sundays, one for Passiontide, and one for feasts. In this usage, which is not far removed from church precedent, the singing of psalms which is so lacking in our Divine Service would to some extent be reintroduced. A similar approach is also made in Endlich's *Choralbuch*. And Löhe writes, "It should also be noted that the Introit is best sung according to the eight psalm tones, as long as the ancient melodies of our Church's Introits have not yet been restored." This would also happen in accordance with Luther's precedent. As we know, in his *Deutsche Messe,* he chose Psalm 34 for the Introit, gave it the first psalm tone, and added the notation (StL 10:235ff., or the musical appendix to EA 22 [AE 53:69ff.]).

All the historic Introits are therefore provided below. They have tentatively been set to the melodies of psalm tones I, III, V, and VIII, along with a two-part setting for a *children's choir* appropriate for the organ accompaniment.

Since we are concerned with *a manner of chanting the psalms* which has become so unfamiliar, a little explanation and instruction is in order insofar as it is pertinent to the matter at hand.

1. The beginning of every psalm tone, as chanted on Sundays or feasts, is called the *intonation*; the note on which the constant pitch is continued to be sung, the *dominant*, the ruling or running note; and the notes which follow the dominant in the first half of the verse, the *mediant*; but those which follow it in the second half and end the melody are called the *termination* or *difference*. Here, for instance, an illustration according to Tone I: <83>

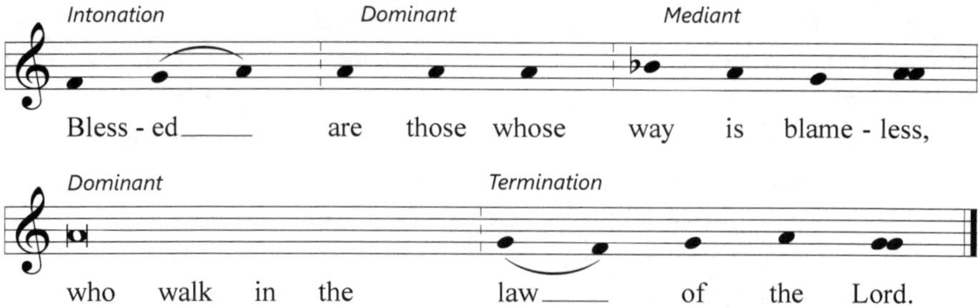

2. Though here, as in other places, the *notes* are of the same value, their *sound* need not be the same. The singing here is not *syllabic* singing, the way a student reads when learning his alphabet, but rather *recitative* chant, an accentuated, sung reading. The rhythm of these psalm melodies (as well as those of the versicles, collects, etc.) conforms to the accent of the text. Here, the general rule is to begin the *intonation* slowly; to chant the *dominant* somewhat more quickly during its frequently repetitive line; and again to chant the ending of either half, the *mediant* and the *termination*, more quietly and drawn out. For example, this is the written form:

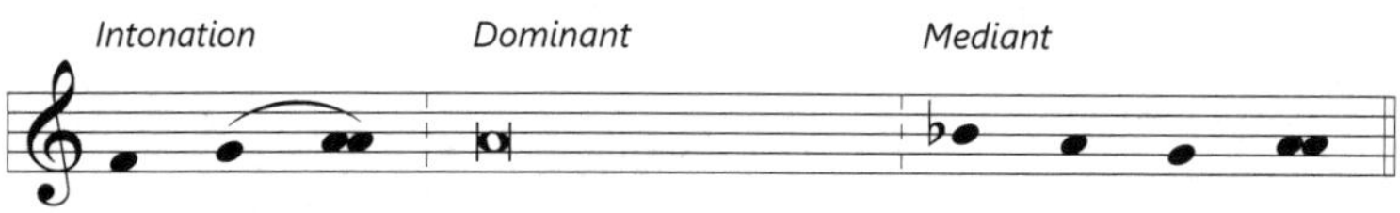

But the execution is something like this:

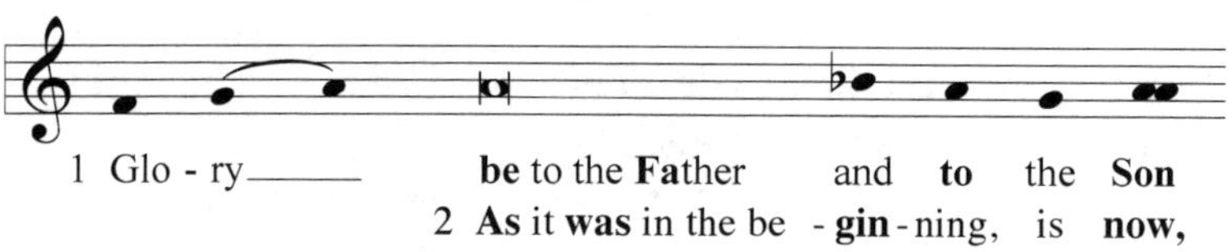

The written form:

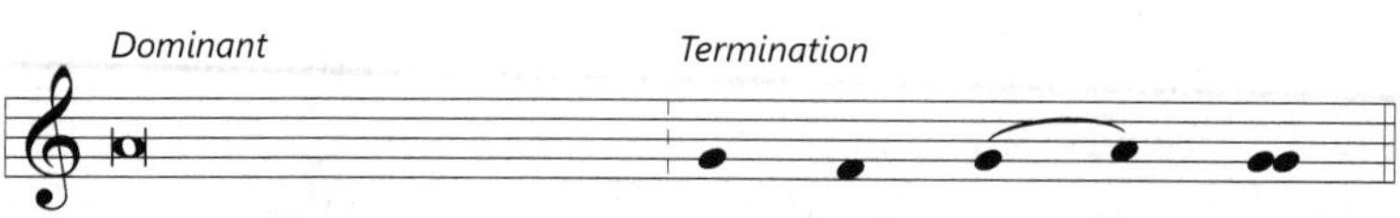

The execution:

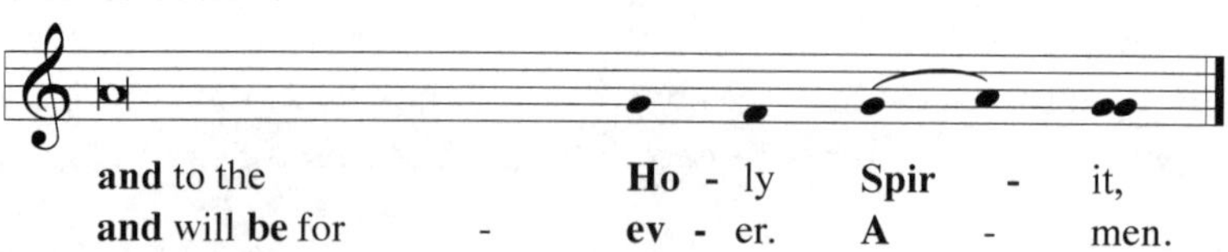

<84>

3. As with every psalm, so with the Introit sung to a psalm tone, only the beginning of the Introit and of the Gloria Patri uses the *intonation*; all other verses are always begun on the *dominant*.

4. The Introit is sung by two choirs in alternation (*antiphonatim*), wherein the second choir is to be occupied with somewhat stronger voices than the first.[130] The Gloria Patri, however, if one should wish not to do the alternation there as well, may *be sung by both choirs together*, which comes off quite nicely. In any case, stronger stops should always be pulled on the organ during the Gloria Patri. It should also be sung *standing* out of reverence (in praise of the Trinity).

5. In the texts of the Introits, the *syllables in bold type* indicate where the mediant and termination begin. The colon (:) indicates where in the singing of the dominant a pause is to be inserted, such as for taking breath, which is often necessary when singing the psalms in the choir.[131]

If an organ is present and it is customary to open the whole Divine Service with an organ prelude, a reminder in respect to this would probably not be out of place here:

1. All the preludes for the *interspersed hymns*, such as the congregational hymn before and after the sermon, *must be as brief as possible*, since they <85> do not form an organic part of the Chief Divine Service, but rather act as a mere transition to the congregational hymn and its accompaniment. The *opening prelude*, however, should not properly be regarded as a prelude to the *entrance hymn*, but a sort of musical introduction to the *Chief Divine Service itself*. As such it *may* be far longer than the transitional preludes which encompass just a few bars. Nor for the same reason *should* it correspond to the character of the entrance hymn as much as to the char-

---

[130] *) In the individual psalm verses, as a rule, a subdivision of the verse in two complementary half-verses is made apparent, as is a parallelism of the thoughts expressed therein. In addition to this, the second half-verse normally represents a heightening in comparison with the one before it. For example:

Bless the Lord, O my soul,
And all that is within me, bless His holy name! [Psalm 103:1]

The first half-verse is merely the *positive* of the sentiment being expressed here; the second is the *comparative*, since now not only the psalmist's *soul*, but *all that is within him*, is to bless the Lord's holy name. This heightening is the reason that the second choir, which sings the second half verse, *is to be filled with stronger voices*, and that a somewhat *stronger stop* may always be pulled on the organ for it.

[131] *) On this also see [Friedrich Lochner,] *Kleines Psalterium. Etliche Psalmen zum Singen in Christenlehren und andern Nebengottesdiensten, wie auch in Jünglings- und Jungfrauenvereinen und im Familienkreise. Ein geringer Beitrag zur Wiederaufnahme und zur Beförderung des altkirchlichen Psalmen-Gesanges in den Gemeinden der lutherischen Kirche von Friedrich Lochner, luth. Pastor.* (Milwaukee: F. Lochner, 1880).

acter of the entire Chief (or even incidental) Divine Service. From the outset, then, this prelude should, by its nature and registration, joyfully and festively prepare the assembled congregation—not only on high feasts but also on common Sundays—for the weekly commemoration of the Lord's resurrection, the "Day of the Lord," on which, as an expression of its joy, the Ancient Church was accustomed to pray standing rather than kneeling. Only on Sundays of Lent or on a special Sunday, such as the Tenth Sunday after Trinity (the remembrance of the Destruction of Jerusalem), should the character of this prelude be somewhat more somber.

2. This, therefore, being the purpose of the prelude which opens the whole Divine Service, it is preferable that an organist lacking in both the gift of invention and expertise in counterpoint should confine himself to a *good prelude collection*, preferably one that accommodates pure church style; for example, besides the works of *Herzog* or the *Präludienbuch* of J. Zahn, Professor Riegel's *Praxis organoedi in ecclesia* ("Church organ music"),[132] which Lyra, like *Siona*, highly recommends to all organists as an "uncommonly pure work of classical organ preludes from past and present," as samples possessed by the present author attest. A now-completed collection published in St. Louis, Missouri should also be pointed out here. It is titled: *Vorspielbuch. Ein Magazin von Orgelvorspielen aus alter und neuer Zeit zu den gebräuchlichen Chorälen der ev.-luth. Kirche* [Prelude book. A Repository of Organ Preludes from Ancient and Modern Times on the Common Chorales of the Evangelical-Lutheran Church], collected and edited by Dietrich Meibohm.[133] <86>

[132] Friedrich Riegel, *Praxis organoedi in ecclesia: Kirchliches Orgelspiel: eine Auswahl von Orgelstücken vorzugsweise der namhaftesten Meister des 16. und 17. Jahrhunderts.* (Brixen: A. Weger, 1869). —MC.

[133] Dietrich Meibohm, *Vorspielbuch: ein Magazin von Orgelvorspielen aus alter und neuer Zeit zu den gebräuchlichen Chorälen der evangelisch-lutherischen Kirche* (St. Louis: D. Meibohm, 1888). —MC.

Psalm Tones for the Introit
First Tone

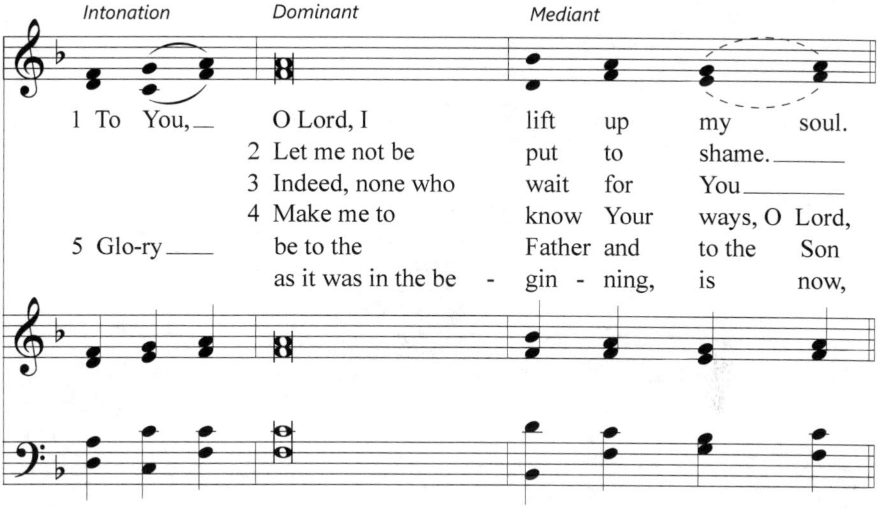

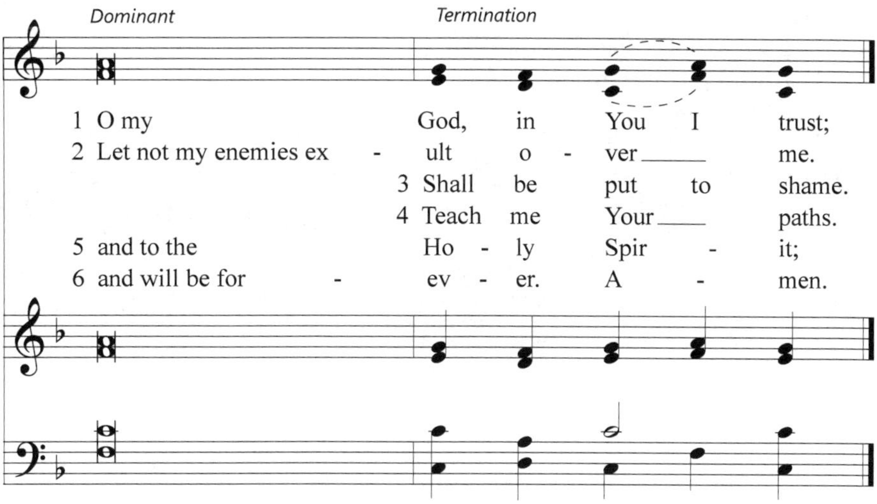

Editorial note: For this and the following examples of introits, Lochner suggests a performance option of one division of the choir singing the first half of each verse, a second division of the choir singing the second half of each verse, and the entire choir singing the Gloria Patri.

<87>

Third Tone

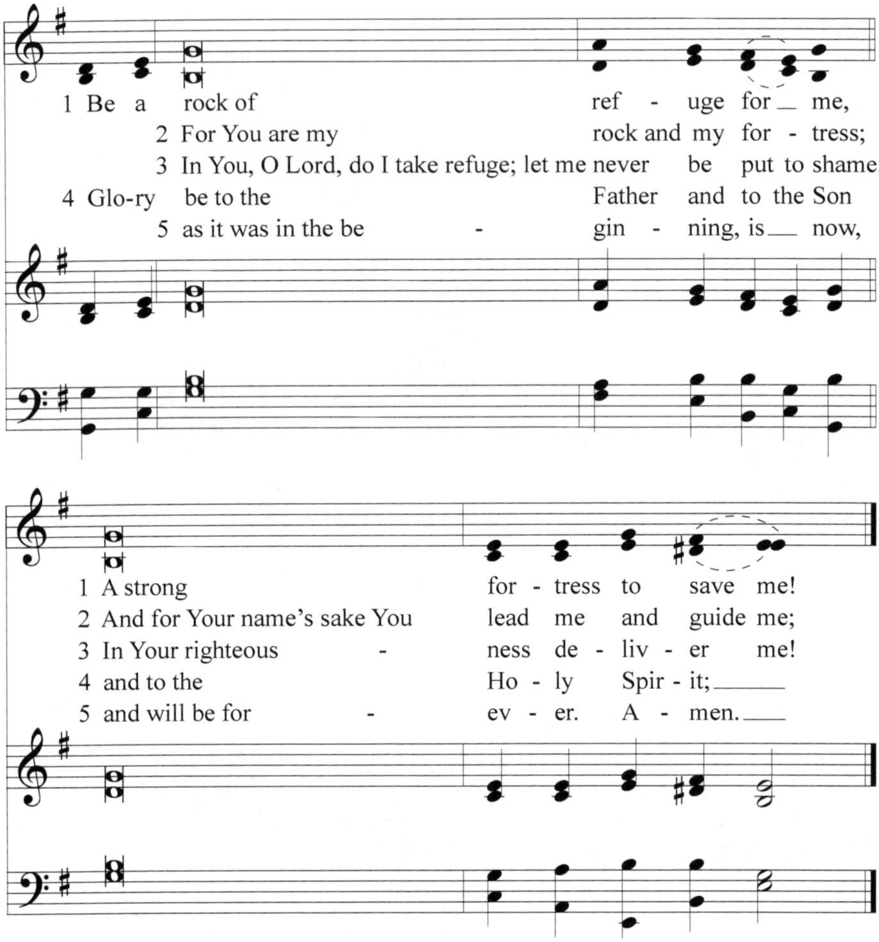

<88>

FIFTH TONE

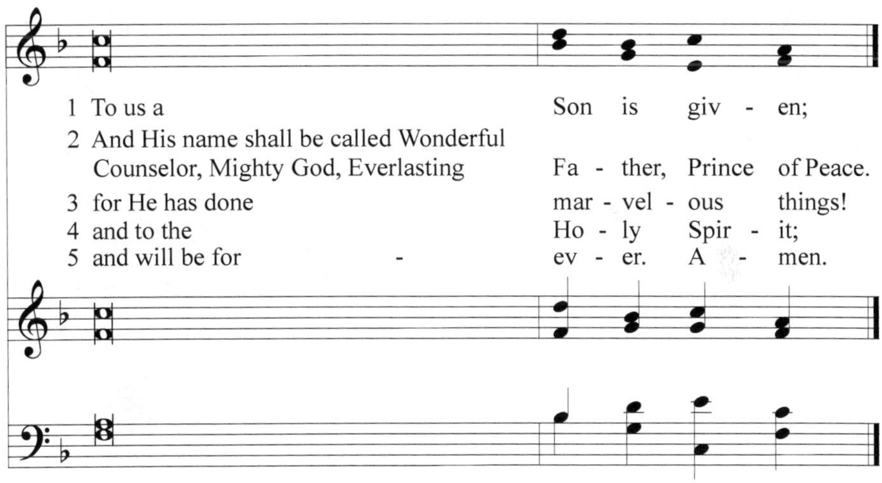

<89>

Eighth Tone

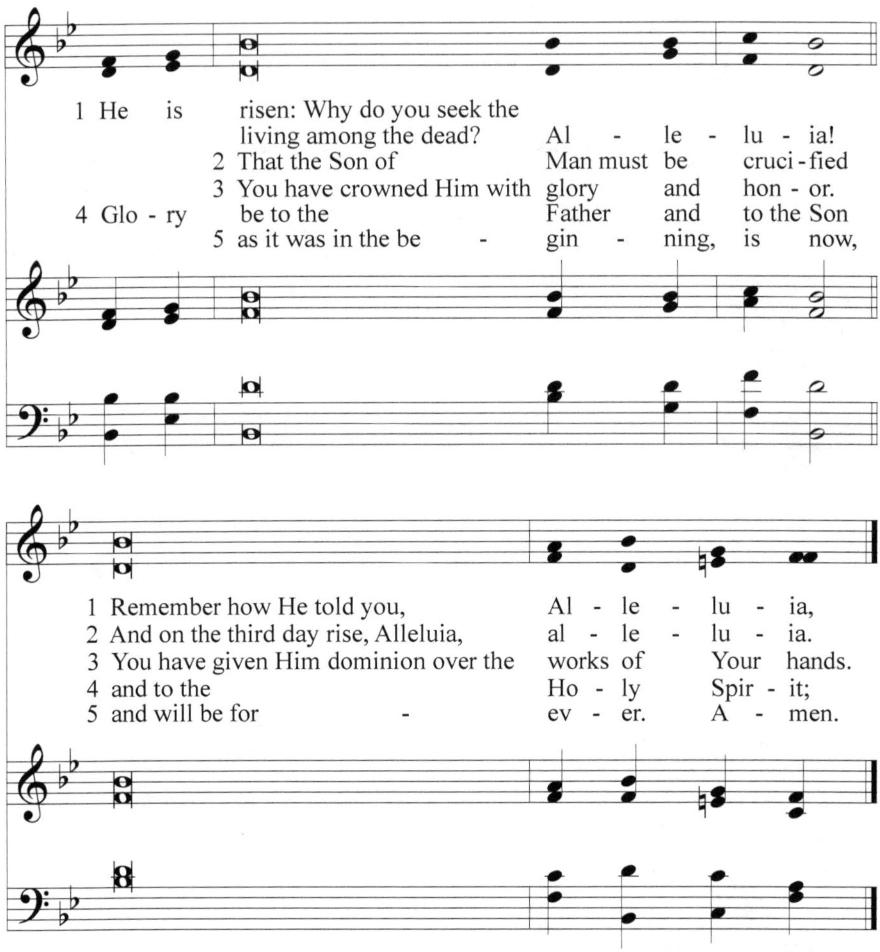

Note: After a few transitional chords, the Introit is immediately followed by the Kyrie, whether it be a Kyrie hymn or an antiphonal Kyrie. <90>

[**Editorial Note:** No single system has prevailed for setting vernacular texts to the Gregorian tones. Luther warns that it must be done carefully with knowledge of the language and the music, not haphazardly in "the manner of the apes" (AE 40:141). What he intends is not known precisely, but he likely means attention to accents in the text as well as in the music. Analysis of Lochner's pointing reveals these insights: 1) he is willing to break melismas for the sake of the text; 2) he is willing to modify his pointing of the termination to preserve the incipit; 3) he usually takes both the ultimate and penultimate accent into account; and 4) he is not always consistent. There also appear to be errors in the text portion of the introits, including whole phrases that are left unpointed.

Lochner's approach is much freer with the music for the sake of the German text. This general approach is evident in other texts from the nineteenth and early twentieth centuries, including those by Luther Reed and Harry Archer[134] (and later, Healey Willan).[135] For a more precise system that attempts to apply the English text to Gregorian plainchant, see *The Brotherhood Prayer Book.*[136] For an accessible overview of various approaches in the twentieth century, with comment on their strengths and weaknesses, see the article by Anthony Ruff.[137] Our approach here attempts to approximate Lochner's application of accents to the tones consistently with the English text, including the use of extra or repeated notes and the breaking or retaining of melismas. The result should be taken as an opportunity to hear how Lochner arranged it in his time, not as a recommendation for pointing and singing Gregorian tones today according to current scholarship or opinion.

Lochner's original only uses three symbols: a **bolded** syllable indicates where the singer leaves the reciting tone and begins the termination; a colon (:) indicates a pause or a breath; and an ellipse (...) indicates where, due to a short verse, the reciting tone is not used. These indications alone make it difficult to identify where extra syllables require repeated notes and where melismas are retained or broken. The original also appears to have errors or inconsistencies in the treatment of similar patterns of speech. Our rendering has attempted to approximate Lochner's fitting of stressed syllables to the tones and apply it to the English consistently. To assist, we have added two additional symbols in our text: an un-der-lined pair of syllables indicates that both are sung on the same pitch (usually the first pitch of the termination); an underscore (_) following a syllable indicates where that syllable must be slurred over a two-note melisma. Note also that in tones V and VIII, it is necessary for the organist to determine how the chords prior to the termination's barline fit to the text, which is not indicated clearly in Lochner's German nor has it been accounted for in our English.]

[134] Harry G. Archer and Luther D. Reed, *The Psalter and Canticles Pointed for Chanting to the Gregorian Psalm Tones: With a Plain Song Setting for the Order of Matins and Vespers, Accompanying Harmonies, and Tables of Proper Psalms for the Use of Evangelical Lutheran Congregations* (Philadelphia: General Council Publication Board, 1901).

[135] Healey Willan, *The Introits and Graduals for the Church Year* (St. Louis: Concordia Publishing House, 1967).

[136] Lutheran Liturgical Prayer Brotherhood, *The Brotherhood Prayer Book,* 2nd ed. (Kansas City, Kan.: Emmanuel Press, 2007).

[137] Anthony Ruff, "Gregorian Psalm Tones with English Texts?," *Custos,* no. 2 (2009): 1–10, https://npm.org/wp-content/uploads/2017/06/Custos-2.pdf.

Introits for the Sundays and Feasts of the Church Year

Note: The first line is sung by Choir I, the second line by Choir II. Finally, both choirs chant the Doxology together, as shown in the musical appendix. To avoid unnecessary repetition, the Doxology is here provided with the first Introit only.

First Sunday in Advent

Psalm 25:1–4

Tone I

To You_, O Lord, I **lift** up my soul.
O my **God**, in You I trust;
Let me not be **put** to shame_;
Let not my enemies ex-**ult** over_ me.
Indeed, none who **wait** for You_
… **Shall** be put to shame;
Make me to **know** Your ways, O Lord;
… **Teach** me Your_ paths.

Both Choirs:

Glory_ be to the **Fa**ther and to the Son,
And to the **Ho**-ly Spir_-it,
As it was in the be-**gin**-ning, is now,
And will be for-**ev**-er. A_-men.

Second Sunday in Advent

Isaiah 62:11; 30:29–30; Psalm 80:1

Tone I

Daughter_ of Zion : behold the **Lord** will come_,
To **save** the na_-tions.
The Lord will cause His majestic **voice** to be heard,*
And you shall have **glad**-ness of_ heart.
Give ear, O **Shep**herd of Isra-el,
You who lead **Jo**-seph like a flock!

THIRD SUNDAY IN ADVENT

PHILIPPIANS 4:4ff. PSALM 85:1

TONE I

Rejoice_ in-**the** Lord always;
A-**gain** I will say, Rejoice. <91>
Let your reasonableness be **known** to every-one.
The **LORD** is at_ hand.
Do not be anxious about anything : **but** in every-thing
By prayer and supplication :
let your re-**quests** be made known to God.
LORD: You were **fav'r**a-ble to Your land;
You restored the **for**tunes of Ja_-cob.

FOURTH SUNDAY IN ADVENT

ISAIAH 45:8; PSALM 19:1

TONE I

Shower_, O **heav**-ens, from a-bove,
And let the clouds **rain** down righteousness;
… **Let** the earth open,
And bring **forth** salva_-tion.
The heavens declare : the **glo**-ry of God,
And the sky above : pro-**claims** His handiwork.

CHRISTMAS (FIRST AND SECOND FEAST DAY)

ISAIAH 9:6; PSALM 98:1

TONE V

To us a **Child** is born,
To us a **Son** is given;
And the government : shall be upon His **shoul**-der,
And His name shall be called : Wonderful Counselor :
Mighty God : Everlasting **Fa**-ther, Prince of Peace.
Oh, sing to the LORD a **new** song,
For He has done **marv**elous things!

SUNDAY AFTER CHRISTMAS
PSALM 93:5, 2, 1
TONE V

Your decrees are very trustworthy : holiness befits Your house, O LORD, for-**ever**-more.
Your throne is established from of old :
You are from **ev**-erlasting.
The LORD reigns : He is robed in **majest**-y;
The LORD is robed : He has put on **strength** as His belt. <92>

CIRCUMCISION, NEW YEAR'S DAY
PSALM 8:1, 4; ISAIAH 63:16
TONE V

O LORD, our Lord : how majestic is Your name in **all** the earth!
You have set Your glory a-**bove** the heavens.
What is man : that You are mindful **of** him,
And the son of man : **that** you care for him?
You, O LORD, are our Father : Our Re-**deem**-er,
From of **old** is Your name.

SUNDAY AFTER NEW YEAR'S DAY
(AS FOR THE SUNDAY AFTER CHRISTMAS)

EPIPHANY
MALACHI 3:1; PSALM 72:1
TONE V

Behold the LORD, the ruler, **has** come,
And the kingdom : and the power :
and the **glory** are in His hand.
Give the king Your justice, **O** God,
And Your righteousness **to** the roy-al Son!

FIRST SUNDAY AFTER EPIPHANY
ISAIAH 6:1; REVELATION 4, 5; PSALM 100:1
TONE I

I saw_ the LORD: sitting upon a throne : **high** and lifted up;
And the train of His robe **filled** the tem_-ple.
The multitudes of angels : worshiped Him : **cry**-ing aloud,
"The glory of His kingdom en-**dures** fore_-ver."
Make a joyful noise : to the **LORD**, all the earth!
Serve the **LORD** with glad_-ness!

SECOND SUNDAY AFTER EPIPHANY

PSALM 66:4, 1–2

TONE I

All the_ earth worships You : and sings **prais**-es to You;
They sing **prais**-es to Your name.
Shout for joy to **God,** all the earth;
Sing the glory of His name : **give** to Him glor'ous praise! <93>

THIRD SUNDAY AFTER EPIPHANY

PSALM 97: 8, 1

TONE I

Worship_ Him, **all** you gods_!
Zion **hears** and is_ glad,
And the daughters of **Ju**-dah rejoice,
Because of Your **judg**-ments, O_ LORD.
The LORD reigns, **let** the earth re-joice;
let the many **coast**-lands be_ glad!

FOURTH AND FIFTH SUNDAY AFTER EPIPHANY

(AS FOR THE THIRD SUNDAY)

SIXTH SUNDAY AFTER EPIPHANY

PSALM 77:19; 84:1–2

TONE I

Your light_-nings **light**-ed up the world;
The earth **trem**-bled and_ shook.
How lovely is Your dwelling place : O **LORD** of hosts_!
My soul longs : yes, faints for the **courts** of the_ LORD.

SEPTUAGESIMA SUNDAY

PSALM 18:4–6, 1, 2

TONE I

The cords_ of **death** en-compassed me;
The torrents of de-**struc**tion as-sailed_ me;
In my distress : I called upon the LORD:
to my **God** I cried for help.
From His **tem**ple He heard my voice.
I love You : O **LORD**, my strength_.
The LORD is my rock and my fortress : and **my** deliv-er-er.

Or: Isaiah 43:22; Jeremiah 31:3.

Thus says_ the Lord, "You did not call upon **Me**, O Jacob;
Nor did you labor about **Me**, O Israel!
I have loved you with an **ev**-er-lasting love;
Therefore I have continued my **faith**-fulness to you."[138] <94>

Sexagesima Sunday

Psalm 44:23–26, 1

Tone III

Awake! Why are You **sleep**ing, O_ Lord?
Rouse Yourself! : Do not re-**ject** us forever!
… **Why** do You hide Your face?
Why do You forget our affliction **and** op-pression_?
For our soul is bowed **down** to the_ dust;
Our belly **clings** to the ground_.
Rise up, O Lord: come to our **help!** Redeem_ us!
O God : we have heard with our ears :
our **fa**thers have told us.

Estomihi Sunday

Psalm 31:2–3, 1

Tone III

Be a rock of **ref**-uge for_ me :
a strong **for**tress to save me!
For You are my **Rock** and my for-_tress
and for Your name's sake : You **lead** me and guide me.
In You, O Lord, do I take refuge :
let me **nev**er be put to shame;
In Your righteous-**ness** de-liver me!

[138] This alternate Introit text from an unnamed source agrees with the series of "Entrance Verses" (*Eingangssprüche*) and is described as "not, generally speaking, historical." See Luther D. Reed, *The Lutheran Liturgy: A Study of the Common Service of the Lutheran Church in America* (Philadelphia: Muhlenberg Press, 1947), 172. It is found in the revised Agenda of the Ministerium of Pennsylvania under the cooperation of the Synods of New York and Ohio and the General Synod. See *Liturgie und Agende: ein Kirchenbuch für die Evangelisch-Lutherische Kirche in den Vereinigten Staaten.* (New York: H. Ludwig, 1855), 35; *Agende für Gemeinden des Evangelisch-Lutherischen Bekenntnisses* (Columbus: Reinhard u. Fieser, 1864), 36. These, in turn, seem to have been derived from a European source; cf. *Allgemeines evangelisches Gesang- und Gebetbuch zum Kirchen- und Hausgebrauch* (Hamburg: das Rauhe Haus, 1846), 585. —MC.

Invocavit Sunday
Psalm 91:15–16, 1
Tone III

When he calls to Me : I will answer him : I will be **with** him in trou_-ble;
I will rescue **him** and honor him.
With long life I will **sat**-isfy_ him
And show him **My** sal-vation_.
He who dwells in the shelter **of** the Most_ High
Will abide in the shadow **of** the Almighty.

Reminiscere Sunday
Psalm 25:6, [22,] 1, 2
Tone VIII

Remember Your mercy, O Lord : and Your **stead**fast love,
For they have **been** from of old. <95>
Let not my enemies exult **o**ver me.
Redeem us, O God of Israel : out of **all** our troubles.
To You, O Lord: I lift up my soul : O my God, in **You** I trust;
Let me **not** be put to shame.

Oculi Sunday
Psalm 25:15–16, 1
Tone VIII

My eyes are ever **t'ward** the Lord,
For He will pluck my feet **out** of the net.
Turn to me and be gracious **to** me,
For I am lonely **and** afflicted.
To You, O Lord: I lift up **my** soul.
O my God : in You I trust : let me **not** be put to shame.

Laetare Sunday
Isaiah 66:10–11; Psalm 122:1
Tone V

Rejoice with Je-**ru**sa-lem,
And be glad for her : all **you** who love her;
Rejoice with her in joy : all you who mourn **o**ver her;
That you may nurse : and be satisfied : **from** her
con-sol-ing breast.
I was glad when they **said** to me,
"Let us go to the **house** of the Lord!"

JUDICA SUNDAY

PSALM 43:1–3

TONE VIII

Vindicate me, O God : and defend my cause : against an ungodly **peo**-ple,
From the deceitful and unjust man deliver me! :
for You are the God in **whom** I take re-fuge.
Send out Your light : and Your truth : let them **lead** me;
Let them bring me to Your holy hill :
and **to** Your dwell-ing! <96>

PALM SUNDAY

PSALM 22:19, 21, 1

TONE III

But You, O LORD: do not be far off! : O You my help, come **quick**-ly to my aid!
Save me from the mouth of the lion :
and rescue me from the horns **of** the wild oxen!
My God, my God, why have **You** forsaken me?*
Why are you so far from saving me,
from the **words** of my groaning?

MAUNDY THURSDAY

PHILIPPIANS 1:10, 8, 11; PSALM 102:2[139]

TONE III

At the name of Jesus : **ev**-'ry knee shall bow,
In heaven : and on earth : and **un**der the earth_.
He became obedient to the point of death :
even **death** on a_ cross.*
Therefore He is Lord : to the glory of **God** the Father_.

[139] Now normally appointed for Holy Wednesday, where Galatians 6:14 and Psalm 67 are sung on Maundy Thursday. —MC.

Good Friday

Isaiah 53:4–6; Psalm 102:1

Tone III

Surely He has **borne** our griefs [d e g g f# e g][140]

And **carried** our sorrows.
He was wounded for **our** transgress_-ions;
He was crushed for **our in**-iquities.
All we like **sheep** have gone astray;
And the LORD has laid on Him the in-**i**-qui-ty of us all.
… **Hear** my pray'r, O LORD;
Let my **cry** come to You_!

Easter Sunday and Monday

Luke 24:6–7; Psalm 8:6–7

Tone VIII

He is risen : Why do you seek the living among the dead? : Alle-**lu**-ia!

Remember how He told you : **Al**-leluia!
That the Son of Man must be **cru**ci-fied
And on the third day rise : Alleluia : **al**-leluia!
You have crowned Him with glory and **hon**-or.
You have given Him dominion over
the **works** of Your hands.

Quasimodogeniti Sunday

1 Peter 2:2; Psalm 81:1

Tone I

Like new_-born infants : **Al**-leluia!

Long for the pure spiritual milk of the Word : Alleluia! : alleluia! : **al**-lelu_ia!
Sing a-**loud** to God our strength;
Shout for joy to the **God** of Ja_-cob!

[140] No examples of such a short opening line exist in Lochner's German, but it is observed that he never omits the incipit. He does spell out notes in this fashion for the Fourth Sunday in Advent in the German.

Misericordias Domini Sunday

Psalm 33:5–6, 1

Tone I

The earth_ is full of the steadfast love of the LORD: **Al**-le-lu-ia!
By the Word of the LORD the heavens were made :
Alleluia : alleluia : **al**-le-lu_-ia!
Shout for joy in the **Lord,** O you righ-teous!
Praise be-**fits** the up_-right.

Jubilate Sunday

Psalm 66:1–3

Tone V

Shout for joy to God, all the earth : Alle-**lu**-ia!
Sing the glo-ry of His name : **Al**-le-lu-ia.
Give to Him **glo**r'ous praise!
Alleluia : alleluia : **Al**-le-luia!
Say to God : "How awesome **are** Your deeds!
So great is Your power : that Your enemies
come **cring**-ing to You."

Cantate Sunday

Psalm 98:1–2

Tone V

Oh sing to the LORD a new song : Alle-**lu**-ia!
For He has done marvelous things : **Al**-le-lu-ia! <97>
He has revealed His righteousness : in the sight of the
nations : Alleluia : alle-**lu**-ia![141]
His right hand and His holy arm :
have worked sal-**va**-tion for Him.

Vocem Jucunditatis *or* Rogate

Isaiah 48:20; Psalm 66:1–2

Tone V

Declare this with a shout of joy, proclaim it : Alle-**lu**-ia.
Send it out to the end of the earth : The LORD has
redeemed His servant Jacob! : Alleluia : **al**-leluia!

---

[141] Lochner has, evidently in error: "He has revealed His righteousness in the sight of the nations : **Al**-le-lu-ia!" without a second Alleluia. The bold type of the first syllable of "Alleluia" indicates a missing half-verse to complete the formula. I have therefore amended it by consultation with other sources cited in the text. —MC.

Shout for joy to God: **all** the earth;*
Sing the **glo**-ry of His name.

Feast of Ascension

Acts 1:11; Psalm 47:1

Tone V

Men of Galilee : why do you stand looking into heaven? : Alle-**lu**-ia.
In the same way as you saw Him go into heaven :
so will He come : **Al**-leluia.
Alle-**lu**-ia.
Alleluia : **al**-leluia!
Clap your hands, all **peo**-ples!
Shout to God **with** loud songs of joy! [142]

Exaudi Sunday

Psalm 27:7–9, 1

Tone I

Hear, O_ Lord: when I cry aloud : **Al**-leluia.
Be gracious to **me** and an-swer me!
You have said : "**Seek** My face_."
My heart says to you : "Your **face**, Lord, do I seek."
Hide not Your face from me : Alleluia : **al**-leluia!
The Lord is my light and my salvation :
whom shall I_ fear? <99>

Feast of Pentecost

Wisdom 1:7; Psalm 68:28–29

Tone VIII

The Spirit of the Lord : has filled the world : Alle-**lu**-ia!
And He who knows what is said : is in all places :
Alleluia : alleluia : **al**-le-lu-ia!
Strengthen, O God : what You have **done** for us.
From Your holy temple **at** Jerusalem.

(Pentecost Monday likewise.)

---

[142] Lochner, although referencing Psalm 47:1, has the text of Psalm 66:1–2 here:
Shout for joy to God, **all** the earth.
Sing the **glo**-ry of his name. —MC.

Feast of Trinity

Tobit 12:6

Tone VIII

Blessed be the Holy Trinity : and the undivided Uni-ty.
Let us give glory to Him : because He has shown
His **mer**-cy to us.
Let us bless the Father, **and** the Son,
And the **Ho**-ly Spir-it.

First Sunday After Trinity

Psalm 13:5–6, 1

Tone I

O Lord_, I have trusted in Your steadfast love :
my heart shall rejoice in **Your** salvation.
I will sing to the Lord: because He has dealt
bounti-**ful**-ly with_ me.
How long, O Lord? : Will You for-**get** me forever?
How long will You **hide** Your face from me?

Second Sunday after Trinity

Psalm 18:18–19, 1–2

Tone V

The Lord was my support : He brought me out into a **broad** place;
He rescued me : because he de-**light**-ed in me.
I love You, O **Lord,** my strength.
The Lord is my **rock** and my fortress. <100>

Third Sunday after Trinity

Psalm 25:16, 18, 1–2

Tone III

Turn to me and be **gra**-cious to_ me,
For I am lonely **and** af-flicted_.
Consider my affliction **and** my trou_-ble,
And for- **give** all my sins_.
To You, O Lord, I **lift** up my_ soul.
O my God, in You I trust : let me **not** be put to shame.

Fourth Sunday After Trinity

Psalm 27:1–3

Tone VIII

The Lord is my light and my salvation : whom shall **I** fear?
The Lord is the stronghold of my life :
of whom **shall** I be afraid?
When evildoers assail me : to eat up my flesh :
my adversaries **and** foes,
It is they who **stum**-ble and fall.
Though an army encamp a-**gainst** me,
My **heart** shall not fear.

Fifth Sunday after Trinity

Psalm 27:7, 9, 1

Tone VIII

Hear, O Lord, when I **cry** a-loud;
O **You** who have been my help,
Cast me not off : forsake me not : O God of my sal-**va**-tion!
The Lord is my light and my salvation: **whom** shall I fear?

Sixth Sunday after Trinity

Psalm 28:8–9, 1

Tone I

The Lord_ is the **strength** of His people;
He is the saving refuge of **His** anoint_-ed. <101>
Save Your people, O Lord: and **bless** Your heri-tage!
Be their shepherd : and carry **them** for-e_-ver.
To You, O Lord, I call : my rock : be not **deaf** to me_,
Lest, if You be silent to me : I become like
those who go **down** to the_ pit.

Seventh Sunday After Trinity

Psalm 47:1–2

Tone I

Oh, clap_ your **hands**, all peoples!
Shout to **God** with loud songs of joy!
For the Lord, the Most **High**, is to be feared,
A great **king** o-ver all the earth.

Eighth Sunday after Trinity

Psalm 48:9–10 [, 1]

Tone VIII

We have thought on Your steadfast **love,** O God,
In the **midst** of Your tem-ple.
As Your name, O God : so Your praise reaches
to the ends of **the** earth.
Your right hand is **filled** with right-eousness.
Great is the Lord : and greatly **to** be praised
In the city of our God! : His **ho**-ly mountain.

Ninth Sunday after Trinity

Psalm 54:4–6 [, 1]

Tone VIII

Behold, God is my **help**-er;
The Lord is the up-**hold**-er of my life.
He will return the evil to my **ene**-mies;
In Your faithfulness : put an end
to **them**, O Lord my strength.
O God : save me **by** Your name,
And vindi-**cate** me by Your might. <102>

Tenth Sunday after Trinity

Psalm 55:16, 18–19, 22, 1

Tone VIII

I call to God, and He **hears** my voice;[143]
He redeems my soul in safety :
from the battle that **was** against me.
God will give ear and humble them :
He who is enthroned from **of** old,
Cast your burden on the Lord: and **He** will sustain you;
Give ear to my **prayer,** O God,
And hide not Yourself from my **plea** for mercy!

[143] Lochner divides this line between two choirs, causing the two consecutive half-verses to be marked for the *finalis*. I have amended this by combining the first two lines into one. —MC.

Eleventh Sunday after Trinity

Psalm 68:5–6, 35, 1

Tone V

God is in His holy habi-**ta**-tion;
God settles the soli-**tar**-y in a home.
The God of Israel : He is the one who gives
power : and strength to His **peo**-ple.
God shall arise : His enemies shall be scattered :
and those who hate Him shall **flee** before Him!

Twelfth Sunday After Trinity

Psalm 70:1–2

Tone VIII

Make haste, O God : to de-**liv**er me!
O Lord : make **haste** to help me!
Let them be put to shame and confusion : who **seek** my life!
Let them be turned back : and brought to
dishonor : **who** desire my hurt!

Thirteenth Sunday after Trinity

Psalm 74:20–23, 1

Tone VIII

Have regard, O Lord, for the **cov**e-nant;
Let not the down-**trod**den turn back in shame.
Arise, O God : de-**fend** Your cause; <103>
Do not forget the **clam**-or of Your foes.
O God : why do You cast us off for-**ev**-er?
Why does Your anger smoke :
against the **sheep** of Your pasture?

Fourteenth Sunday after Trinity

Psalm 84:9–10, 1

Tone I

Behold_ our shield, O God : look on the face of **Your** a-noint-ed!
For a day in Your courts is better
than a **thou**-sand else_-where.
How lovely is Your dwelling **place,** O Lord of hosts!
My soul longs : yes, faints for the **courts** of the_ Lord.

Fifteenth Sunday after Trinity

Psalm 86:1–4

Tone III

Incline Your ear, O **Lord**, and an-swer me,
Save Your servant, who trusts in You : **You** are my God_.
Be gracious to me, O Lord : for to You do I **cry** all the_ day.
Gladden the soul of Your servant : for to You,
O Lord, do I **lift** up my soul_.

Sixteenth Sunday after Trinity

Psalm 86:3, 4, 1

Tone III

Be gracious to me, O Lord : for to You do I **cry** all the_ day.
For You, O Lord : are good and forgiving : abounding in steadfast love : to all who **call** up-on You_.
Incline Your ear, O **Lord**, and answer me,
For I am **poor** and needy_.

Seventeenth Sunday after Trinity

Psalm 119:137, 124, 1

Tone I

Righteous_ are You, O Lord: and right are Your **just** de-crees_.
Deal with Your servant according **to** Your steadfast love.
Blessed are those whose **way** is blameless,
Who walk in the **law** of the_ Lord! <104>

Eighteenth Sunday After Trinity

Sirach 36:17–18; Psalm 122:1

Tone V

Reward those who wait for You, O Lord : and let Your prophets be found **trust**wor-thy.
Hear the prayer of Your servants : and **of** Your people.
I was glad when they **said** to me,
"Let us go to the **house** of the Lord!"

Nineteenth Sunday after Trinity

Psalm 35:3; 34:17; [48:14;] 78:1

Tone III

The LORD has said to His people : I am **your** salva_-tion!
When they cry, I will hear : and save them out of all their troubles : and be their LORD for- **ever** and ever.
Give ear, O my people, **to** My teach_-ing;
Incline your ears to the **words** of My mouth_!

Twentieth Sunday After Trinity

Daniel 9:14 [Aza. 4, 7, 20, 19]; Psalm 119:1

Tone III

The Lord our God is just in **all** that He has done,
For we have not o- **beyed** His commandments.
Bring glory **to** Your name, O Lord;
And deal with us in Your a-**bun**dant mercy_.
Blessed are those whose **way** is blame_-less,
Who walk in the law of the LORD_![144]

Twenty-First Sunday after Trinity

Old Greek Esther 13:9–11; Psalm 119:1

Tone VIII

You are the Lord, the King who rules over **all** things,
For the universe is in Your power : and there is no one who **can** op-pose You. <105>
For You have made heaven and earth : and every wonderful thing in it under **heav**-en,
… **You** are Lord of all;
Blessed are those whose way is **blame**-less,
Who walk in the **law** of the LORD!

[144] Instead of Psalm 119:1 appointed here and, for example, in the *Kirchenbuch* of the General Council, some agendas, like Löhe's, have Psalm 48:1, viz.:
Great is the Lord, and **great**-ly to be praised *
In the city of our God, in His **ho**-ly moun-tain_. —MC.

Twenty-Second Sunday After Trinity

Psalm 130:3–4, 1–2

Tone III

If you, O LORD, should mark iniquities : **O** LORD, who could stand?
But with You there is forgiveness : O **God** of Israel.
Out of the depths : I **cry** to You, O LORD!
… **O** Lord, hear my voice!

Twenty-Third Sunday After Trinity

Jeremiah 29:11–12, 14; Psalm 85:1

Tone I

I know_ the plans I have for **you**, de-clares the LORD,
Plans for wholeness and **not** for e_-vil.
Then you will call upon Me : and come and **pray** to Me_,
And **I** will hear_ you.
And I will re-**store** your fortunes
And gather you from all nations **and** all pla_-ces.
LORD: You were **fav'ra**-ble to Your land;
You restored the **for**tunes of Ja_-cob.

Twenty-Fourth Sunday after Trinity

Psalm 95:6–7, 1

Tone V

Oh come : let us worship and bow down : let us kneel before the LORD, our **Mak**-er!
For **He** is our God,
Oh come, let us sing to **the** LORD;
Let us make a joyful noise to the rock of **our** salvation! <106>

Twenty-Fifth Sunday after Trinity

Psalm 31:9, 15, 17, 1

Tone VIII

Be gracious to me, O LORD: for I am **in** dis-tress;
Rescue me from the hand of my enemies : and from my **per**-secutors!
O LORD : let me not be put to shame : for I call up-**on** You.
In You, O LORD, do I take refuge : let me never be put to shame : in Your righteous-**ness** deliv-er me.

Twenty-Sixth Sunday after Trinity

Psalm 54:3–4, 7

Tone VIII

O God, save me, **by** Your name,
And vindi-**cate** me by Your might.
O God, **hear** my prayer;
Give ear to the **words** of my mouth.
He will return the evil to my **ene**-mies;
In Your faithfulness **put** an end to them.

Twenty-Seventh Sunday after Trinity

(Same as the Feast of the Trinity.)

Purification [Feb. 2]

(Same as the Eighth Sunday after Trinity)

Annunciation [March 25]

(Same as the Fourth Sunday in Advent)

St. John the Baptist [June 24]

Isaiah 49:1–2; Psalm 92:1

Tone V

The Lord called me by name : from the womb of my **moth**-er.
He made my **mouth** like a sharp sword;
In the shadow of His hand He **hid** me;
He made me a **pol**-ished arrow;
It is good to give thanks to **the** Lord,
To sing praises to Your **name**, O Most High. <107>

The Visitation of Mary [July 2]

(Same as the Annunciation of Mary)

Feast of St. Michael [Sept. 29]

Psalm 103:20–21, 1

Tone V

Bless the Lord : O you His **an**-gels,
You mighty ones : who do His commandment,
obeying the **voice** of His Word!

Bless the Lord, **all** His hosts,
His ministers, who **do** His will_!
Bless the Lord : **O** my soul,
And all that is within me : **bless** His ho-ly name!

Feasts of Apostles

2 Timothy 4:8; 1:12; Psalm 139:1–2

Tone V

I know whom I **have** be-lieved,
And I am convinced : that He is able to guard until that Day : what has been en-**trust**-ed to me.
Henceforth there is laid up for me : the crown of **right**eous-ness,
Which the Lord : the righteous judge : will award to **me** on that Day,
O Lord, You have searched me and **known** me!
You know when I sit down and **when** I rise up.

Festival of the Reformation

Psalm 46:7, 2, 1

Tone VIII

The LORD of hosts is **with** us;
The God of Jacob **is** our fortress.
Therefore we will not fear : though the **earth** gives way,
Though the mountains be moved : into the **heart** of the sea.
God is our refuge **and** strength,
A very present **help** in trouble. <108>

Day of Repentance and Prayer

Isaiah 1:2, 4; Psalm 130:3

Tone III

Hear, O heavens : and give ear, O earth : for the **LORD** has spo_-ken:
Children have I reared and brought up : but they have re-**belled** a-gainst me_.
They have for-**sak**-en the_ LORD,
They have despised the Holy One of Israel : they are **ut**ter-ly estranged.
If You, O LORD, should **mark** iniquities,
… **O** Lord, who could stand?

(The *Gloria Patri* is omitted on this day.)

Festival of Harvest and Day of Thanksgiving

Psalm 65:11, 9, 1

Tone V

You crown the year with your **boun**-ty;
Your wagon tracks over-**flow** with abundance.
You visit the earth : and **water** it;
The river of God is **full** of water;
Praise is due to You, O God : in **Zi**-on,
And to You shall **vows** be performed.

Anniversary of a Congregation

Psalm 100:1–2, 4–5

Tone V

Make a joyful noise to the LORD: **all** the earth!
Serve the **LORD** with gladness!
And His **courts** with praise!
Give **thanks** to Him, bless His name!
For the LORD is good : His steadfast love endures for-**ev**-er,
And His faithfulness to all **gen**-erations.

Final Remarks

If it turns out in many places that it is too hard to sing *all* the above Introits, the number of Introits to be rehearsed can be limited by appointing one Introit for every season of the Church Year rather than for every Sunday. For example, that of Advent I could be sung for all of Advent, as is the case currently in the territorial church of Mecklenburg. <109>

II. KYRIE

The **Kyrie eleison** is a *word of Scripture*. The Canaanite woman (Matthew 15:22) makes this cry for divine mercy in Greek, seeking from the incarnate Son of God, the promised Son of David, help for her daughter against the devil's affliction. In order to recall that the Holy Spirit, through the multitude of tongues, has gathered the nations of the whole world together,[145] the Greek Kyrie was given a place in the Divine Service alongside the Hebrew Amen, Alleluia, and Hosanna.

[145] An allusion to the Pentecost Antiphon, *Veni sancte spiritus, reple tuorum corda fidelium.* See *The Liber Usualis, with Introduction and Rubrics in English* (New York: Desclee Company, 1961), 1837–38. —MC.

The first use of the Kyrie in the Divine Service belongs to the third century. It consisted of the people responding to each petition of the intercessory prayer (with which the Mass seems originally to have begun) with a Kyrie, much as in the Litany they now respond with the cry, "Defend us, dear Lord God," and, "Hear us, dear Lord God." Gregory the Great, also called *pater ceremoniarum* on account of his liturgical development of the Roman Mass and the Divine Service generally, left the intercessory prayer of the Mass only for the Church's penitential, mournful seasons of Advent and Passiontide, while eliminating it for other seasons. Yet he made it not only a threefold cry by the addition of the "Christe eleison," but a ninefold cry by the threefold repetition of each of the three parts, just as the ninefold Kyrie is still the usage in the Roman Mass. Since the thirteenth century, the Kyrie has been expanded in many ways. Thus there arose, among others, festival Kyries, some of which found acceptance in the Lutheran Church. But whereas Gregory the Great had made the Kyrie a responsive chant between the clergy and choir, barring the people from participating, the Germans were not content with this and instead began from the tenth century to combine a few German festival hymns to the Kyrie in such a way that it formed the refrain of each stanza. For this reason these hymns came to be known as *Leisen*. Indeed, the most widespread of these *Leisen*, "Christ Is Arisen",[146] had to be included in German missals despite resistance.

In his *Formula Missae,* Luther says, "Next, those are pleasing to me which have added the *Kyrie eleison*; for we <110> read that in the time of Basil, called the Great, the Kyrie eleison *was in common use by all people*" (StL 10:2235 [AE 53:21]). Since it was a quotation of Scripture and was originally used by the people corporately, Luther left the Kyrie in place but limited it to a threefold form. The treasury of the Kyrie which the Lutheran Church found it then further developed after the precedent of the Bohemian Brethren. Thus there arose two kinds of Kyries for Sundays and feasts in respect not only to content but also to form. Concerning the latter, there are (1) *antiphonal* Kyries, and (2) *versified* Kyries. In the following section, examples of both kinds according to form and manner are presented.

The *execution* can accordingly be done in different ways. If the Kyrie is sung *antiphonally*, following Luther, etc., the alternating singing can take place: (1) between the *pastor* and congregation or, as we prefer, between the *cantor* and congregation, in which case the pastor would already have approached the altar at the beginning of the Kyrie in order to intone the "Glory be to God on high" immediately after; (2) between the choir and congrega-

[146] See above, 25, n. 67. —MC.

tion; and (3) between two choirs. But if a *versified* Kyrie is used, such as, for example, in the St. Louis *Gesangbuch*[147] no. 7, "Kyrie, Gott Vater in Ewigkeit" ["Kyrie! God, Father in Heaven Above"],[148] the congregation sings it. And if they want to use it as a festival Kyrie on feast days, in the event that the melody proves too hard for the congregation, the execution can be done antiphonally, for example:

Choir: Kyrie, God, Father, all creation's Author.
Cong.: Eleison.
Choir: Christe, who true God and Man wast born, and borest for us God's great scorn.
Cong.: Eleison.
Choir: Kyrie, God, the Holy Ghost, with Father and with Son one God.
Cong.: Eleison.

The *meaning* of the Kyrie in its place is explained in various ways. Some recent liturgical scholars regard it as a confession of sin by which the congregation draws near to the Lord right at the beginning of the Divine Service, and so the Gloria following it is like the divine Absolution in response to it. Yet in the Roman Mass no less than in the church order of Brandenburg-Nürnberg (agreeing with it in this point) and those agendas which follow it, a *Confiteor* precedes the Kyrie, for which reason this interpretation is not entirely satisfactory. In view of the Kyrie's biblical *origin* as a cry for mercy under <111> the devil's affliction, and of its liturgical *relationship* to the angelic hymn, "Glory be to God," etc., and the further praise of the Triune God ("We praise, we laud, we worship You")[149] to which it leads, we might rather, as already suggested, join others in recognizing in the Kyrie the unanimous and humble *confession of all the misery—the "thousand afflictions and piteous weight of grief which no mouth can express,"*[150]—because of which misery God's only-begotten Son was born a man and hailed by the praises of the heavenly hosts, and by which misery the redeemed of the Lord, though

[147] *Kirchengesangbuch für evangelisch-lutherische Gemeinden ungeänderter Augsburgischer Confession* (St. Louis: Concordia Publishing House, 1862). See Matthew Carver, ed., *Walther's Hymnal* . . . (St. Louis: Concordia Publishing House, 2012) based on the revised, expanded 1892 edition. —MC.

[148] First appears in *Kirchen-Ordnung für die St. Wenzelskirche zu Naumburg von 1537/1538*, Sehling 1:78. Cf. Wackernagel 3:226, no. 250; *LSB* 942. —MC.

[149] "All Ehr und Lob soll Gottes sein," st. 2, line 1. See below, p. 118, n. 157. —MC.

[150] "Wie soll ich dich empfangen, by Paul Gerhardt (1653), st. 5, lines 5–7, the sense of which is not conveyed literally in English translations. Cf. *Walther's Hymnal*, #44; *LSB* 334. —MC.

liberated from the burden of the curse, are still oppressed because of the sin in the flesh, until at last they shall be fully delivered from it. This cry for mercy is also taken by Cardinal Bona (acknowledged even by Lutherans as a master of liturgics) as a confession of the manifold misery that presses upon us from childhood on as a result of the fall.

Since it is with the Kyrie, whether at the beginning or toward the end, that the liturgist approaches the altar in order to begin disposing of the entire office of Communion—inclusive of the sermon—it is well to include here the admirable notice of the Braunschweig-Lüneburg church order from the chapter *Von dem Ornatu Ecclesiastico* [On Church Ornament]: "Let the pastors and ministrants who intend to observe the holy office . . . go before the altar very reverently and with great devotion and invoking the Son of God, considering well what high mysteries they, being sinful men, are nevertheless to conduct there—at which even the holy angels must tremble.[151] Every wise, God-fearing, and conscientious priest will be instructed by his own devotion what and how he ought to pray devoutly, that he may conduct well so high an office."

[151] *Ipsis etiam sanctis angelis tremenda.* —MC.

A. Antiphonal Kyrie

No. 1.

<112>

Tune: Martin Luther, *Deutsche Messe*, 1526.

No. 2

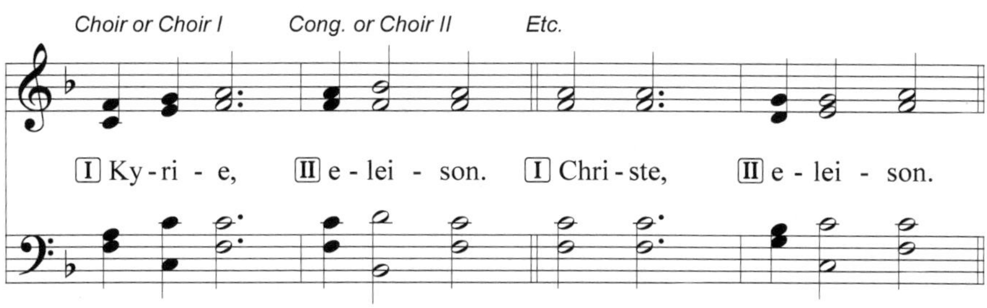

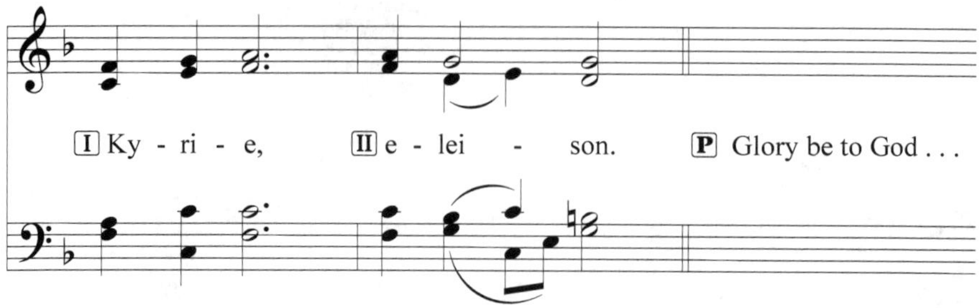

Setting: F. Riegel

No. 3

Tune: *Kirchenordnung*, Strassburg
Setting: F. Riegel

The same, from the Mecklenburg Cantional

Tune: German, 1525; Zweibrückner *Kirchenordnung* 1557, 1570

B. Versified Kyrie

1. In Advent

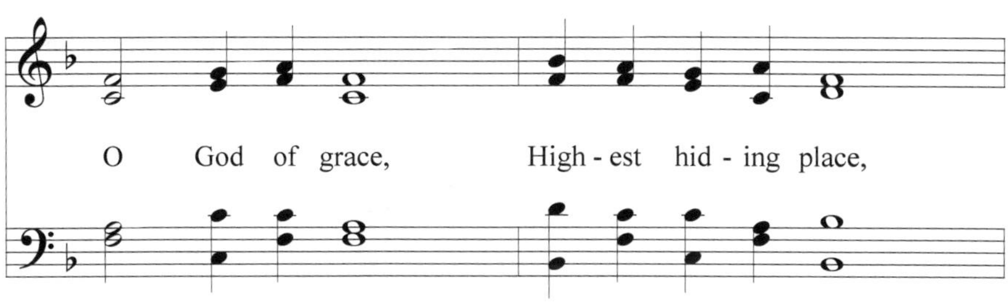

In our need our pray'rs to Thee we raise:
Have mer-cy on us! O Christ, the Son of God,
Our Joy and Crown, Thy name we laud,
Sal - va - tion's boun-teous Flood! Have mer - cy
<115>
on us! O Ho - ly Ghost, true Com-fort -

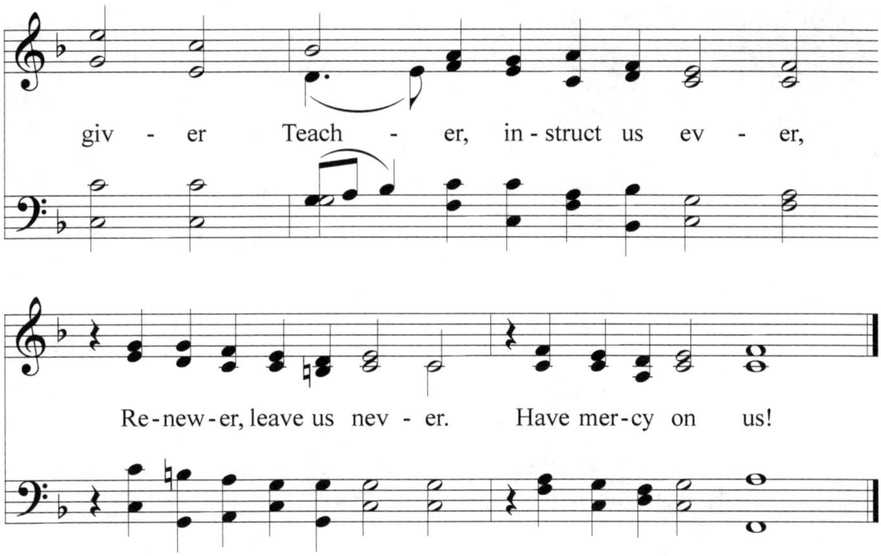

Tune: Bohemian Brethren.
Setting: F. Riegel

2. From Christmas to Easter

<116>

Have mer - cy up - on us! O, Lord Je - sus,
Who, to cheer us, By Mar - y didst draw near us,
Deign to hear us! Have mer - cy up - on us!
Ho - ly Spir - it, by Thy fa - vor, Make Thy
will our sole en - deav - or, And let us love Thee

Tune: Spangenberg, Lossius, etc.
Setting: Michael Praetorius

<117>

3. From Easter to Pentecost

God's great scorn, C E - le - i - son! Choir: Ky - ri - e,
O Ho - ly Ghost, With Fa - ther and Son one God,
<118>
C E - le - i - son! Choir: Ky - ri - e,
Help us to keep this faith in pu - ri - ty,

Tune: Spangenberg, et al.
Setting: F. Riegel

4. For Trinity and Trinity-tide

The *Kyrie Summum*, or "Kyrie Gott Vater in Ewigkeit" [Kyrie! God, Father in Heaven Above"],[152] ([St. Louis] *Gesangbuch* no. 7; or no. 177 in the new *Choralbuch* from St. Louis, MO, 1886.) <119>

III. GLORIA

Like the Kyrie, the *Gloria in Excelsis* also is of biblical origin with respect to content and wording, being quite naturally the hymn sung by the heavenly hosts at the birth of Christ: "*Glory be to God on high, and on earth peace, good will toward men*" (Luke 2:14), for which reason it is called the *hymnus angelicus* [angelic hymn].

Initially, this hymn was sung only on the Vigil of Christmas. From there it passed over into regular use in the Matins service of the Greek Church, the Divine Service of the early morning, "so that in the liturgico-symbolic drama of their worship it might refer to the holy night which brought redemption to humanity from the distress of sin."[153]

---

[152] In English as "Kyrie! God, Father in Heaven Above," *LSB* 942. —MC

[153] Schoeberlein, 1:139. —MC.

The introduction of the Gloria into the Mass is supposed to have occurred at the hands of the Roman bishop Telesphorus around the year 126, where it was later relocated after the Kyrie. In the *Apostolic Constitutions*, the collection of which belongs likely to the fourth century, it is already found expanded by the beautiful, exalted Laudamus, that is, "We praise Thee," etc. In Latin and in the translation used by the Lutheran Church, the hymn runs thus:

> Gloria in excelsis Deo! Et in terra pax hominibus bonae voluntatis. Laudamus te. Benedicimus te. Adoramus te. Glorificamus te. Gratias agimus tibi propter magnam gloriam tuam. Domine Deus, Rex coelestis, Deus Pater omnipotens: Domine fili unigenite, Jesu Christe, Altissime, Domine Deus. Agnus Dei, filius Patris: qui tollis peccata mundi, miserere nostri, qui tollis peccata mundi, suscipe deprecationem nostram. Qui sedes ad dextram Patris, miserere nostri. Quoniam tu solus sanctus. Tu solus Dominus. Tu solus altissimus, Jesu Christe, cum Sancto Spiritu in gloria Dei Patris. Amen.
>
> [Glory be to God on high, and on earth peace, good will toward men. We praise Thee. We bless Thee. We adore Thee. We worship Thee. We give thanks to Thee because of Thy great glory, O Lord God, heavenly King! God, almighty Father! O Lord, the only-begotten Son Jesus Christ, O Most High, and to Thee, O Holy Ghost! O Lord God, Lamb of God, only Son of the Father, who takest away the sin of the world, have mercy upon us! Who takest away the sin of the world, receive our prayer! Who sittest at the right hand of the Father, have mercy upon us! For Thou only art holy, Thou <120> only art the Lord, Thou only art the Highest, Jesus Christ, with the Holy Ghost, in the glory of Thy Father. Amen.][154]

Nevertheless, from the time of Gregory the Great, the Gloria was used with the Laudamus for every Sunday and festival Mass.

"Much of the singing in the Mass," says Luther, "is admirably and gloriously composed of thanksgiving and praise and has remained to this time, such as the *Gloria in excelsis et in terra*, the Alleluia, the Patrem, the Preface, the Sanctus, the Benedictus, the Agnus Dei. In these parts you find nothing sacrificial, but *utter praise and thanksgiving, which is why we keep them in the Mass*" (Jena 5:196b).[155] But whereas the Anglican Church, probably after the precedent of the Eastern Church, in its Book of Com-

[154] The translation here reflects the divergence from the Latin taken by the German translation, which may be found, among other places, in Löhe, *Agende* (1844), 1:33. —MC.

[155] Cf. Luther, "Admonition Concerning the Sacrament" (1530), AE 38:123. —MC.

mon Prayer assigned the Gloria its place after the Consecration, indeed, even after the Distribution, here, too, Luther agreed with the Roman Mass and had it follow the Kyrie.

The *meaning* of the Gloria (with its expansion) in this position and in the Mass generally we have already touched on somewhat in discussing the meaning of how the Chief Divine Service is arranged. We have taken it largely as the doxology to "the mystery which is great indeed: God manifested in the flesh" [1 Timothy 3:16], as a result of which, since redemption has been made, not only is salvation proclaimed to us in Christ, but Christ, in the Chief Divine Service, also gives us His true body and His true blood in sacramental union with bread and wine for oral consumption. Should the incarnation of the eternal Word, then, not itself be the crimson thread on which the individual parts of the Mass are strung like so many pearls, when the Roman Church still has John 1:1–14 read by the priest after the Mass is concluded?

The *treatment* and *execution* of this liturgical element was diverse and variable in the Lutheran Church. Like the Preface, the choir frequently sang it in Latin, in many places into the eighteenth century, though sometimes coupled with the congregation's versified German. Yet a German translation of the Latin text was also in use at an early date, for example, that of the Nürnberg chaplain Andreas Döber in his *Evangelical Mass* (1525).[156] Preference, however, soon came to be given to the versified form, such as that offered to the Church by Decius in his "Allein Gott in der Höh sei Ehr" ["All Glory Be to God on High"] (St. Louis *Gesangbuch*, no. 1), and by Luther in his "All Ehr und Lob soll Gottes sein" ["All Glory Be to God Alone"] (St. Louis *Gesangbuch*, no. 142).[157] <121>

As far as the *execution* in particular is concerned, the liturgist,[158] facing the altar, *intoned* the Gloria: "Glory be to God on high!" whereupon the choir joined with the *Et in terra*, or else the congregation promptly responded with the "Allein Gott in der Höh sei Ehr" ["All Glory Be to God on

[156] *Von der evangelischen meß, wie sie zu Nürnberg im Newen Spital durch Andream Döber gehalten würdt, Caplan daselbst* (Nürnberg: H. Hergot, 1525). This is to be distinguished from *Form und Ordnung . . . im Newen Spital,* (Nürnberg: H. Hergot, 1525) which specifies Latin in accordance with Luther's *Formula Missae*). A reproduction of Döber's German Gloria is included (with the whole order of Mass) in Löhe, *Sammlung,* 3:44. —MC.

[157] Wackernagel 3:565ff., nos. 615–617, and 3:227, no. 252, resp. See *LSB* 947–948. —MC.

[158] *) In the Ancient Church, the bishop intoned the Gloria. In the Lutheran Church, it was referred to the deacon, as was the entire altar service during Communion, wherever a congregation had installed an assistant pastor or second pastor, whereas the first pastor delivered the so-called "office sermon" and assisted during Communion. We find it fitting that wherever more than one pastor is installed in a congregation, in the Chief Divine Service one functions as liturgist and the other as preacher.

High"] or "All Ehr und Lob soll Gottes sein" ["All Glory Be to God Alone"]. In connection to this we find the exhortation that the liturgist should conduct the Gloria "with great reverence" (Prussia, 1525 and 1544), and "stand before the altar with due decency, much devotion, and invoking the Son of God, and after the third Kyrie sing the Gloria" (Oldenburg, 1573). Let it be observed in passing that the liturgist should not wait until the third Kyrie to approach the altar, but already have done so at the *first* Kyrie.

For the *intonation of the Gloria* we find *a variety of melodies*—melodies for Sundays and melodies for the various feasts, but all according to the same *typus*. The intonation for a Sunday is always simpler than that for a feast.

It is therefore much to be wished that, along with Luther's "All Ehr und Lob soll Gottes sein" ["All Glory Be to God Alone"], a translation of the original text might also return to more frequent use, perhaps with both the Gloria hymns being used in alternation on common Sundays and the original form being employed for high feasts and other occasions. This would provide a pleasant variety in which the Gloria might retain its proper place in the liturgy and only change its form, even as happens in most of our local congregations with the so-called "greater" and "lesser" Creed (St. Louis *Gesangbuch*, nos. 183–184).[159]

Now, concerning Luther's Gloria especially—which is a faithful metrical rendering of the *Laudamus*—the custom was frequently to execute it in such a way that the pastor intoned: "Glory be to God on high!" and the choir continued: "All Glory be to God alone, Forevermore the Highest One . . ." <122> and the congregation then completed the hymn from the words: "Who doth our sinful race befriend. . . ." For this hymn we have adopted from Layriz a melody which was originally composed for Luther's hymn on the Our Father, but fits perfectly with his Gloria hymn. It is also included in the St. Louis *Choralbuch* published by Hölter, no. 16, and in the Brauer *Choralbuch*, no. 9.[160]

Regarding the original text in translation, one of the earliest Lutheran melodies is included here as it is found (besides in Hommel) in *Schöber-*

[159] The "greater" being Luther's "Wir glauben all an einen Gott" (Wackernagel 3:16, no. 23) and the "lesser" being the shorter hymn of that name by Tobias Clausnitzer (d. 1684). See *LSB* 954 and 953. —MC.

[160] Friedrich Layritz, ed., *Choralbuch: Eine Sammlung der gangbarsten Choräle der evang.-Lutherischen Kirche* (St. Louis: Lutherischer Concordia-Verlag, 1888); Karl Brauer, ed., *Mehrstimmiges Choralbuch: zu dem Kirchengesangbuch für evangelisch-lutherische Gemeinden ungeänderter Augsburgischer Confession* (St. Louis: Lutherischer Concordia-Verlag, 1888). —MC.

lein, in the musical section of the Bavarian *Agenden-Kern*,[161] in the Mecklenburg Cantional, and in several other more recent liturgical works, and as it also used to be sung in the local Franconian congregations. Should it prove impossible to achieve congregational participation in singing the *Laudamus* as well, the choir would assume that part and the order would then be: Pastor: "Glory be to God on high!" Cong.: "And on earth peace, good will toward men." Choir: "We praise Thee! We bless Thee . . ." etc. In this case, the choir might also make occasional use of the simple and beautiful composition of the *Laudamus* by D. Bortniansky. [See below, page 126 ff.]. Though belonging to the current age, it has a thoroughly churchly character.

Finally, it should also be mentioned that by ancient custom the Gloria was in many places omitted during Lent so that the Kyrie was immediately followed by the Salutation and Collect.

I. Intonations of the Gloria

1. For Sundays (Gloria dominicale)

Magdeburg, 1615

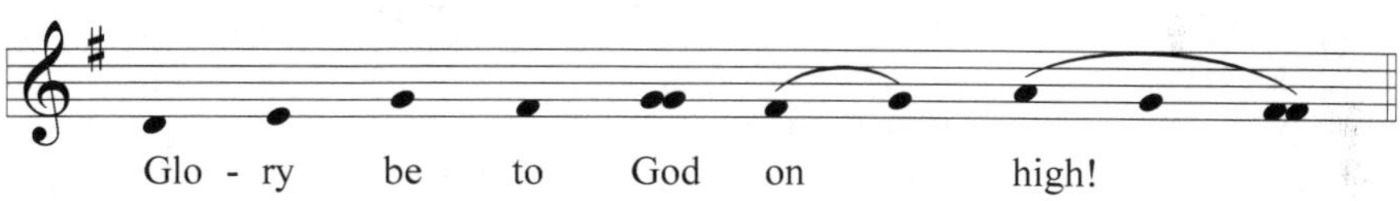

Nürnberg *Agendbüchlein,* 1639

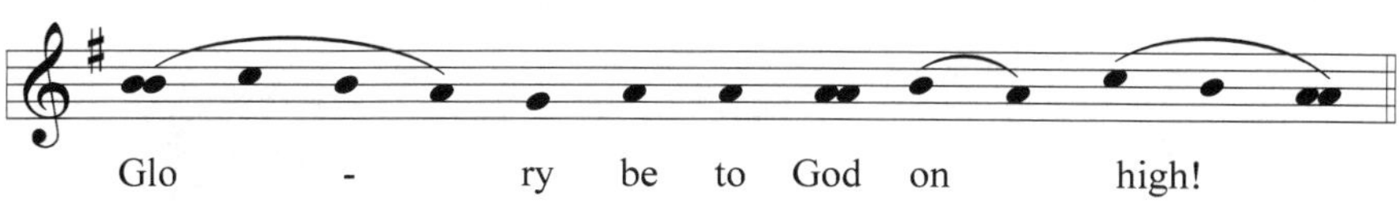

Pomerania, 1563

Spangenberg, 1545

<123>

[161] *Musicalischer Anhang zu dem Agenden-Kern und zu der ihm vorangestellten Gottesdienstordnung für die evangelisch-lutherische Kirche in Bayern.* (Nürnberg: U. E. Sebald, 1856), part 2. —MC.

2. For High Feasts[162]

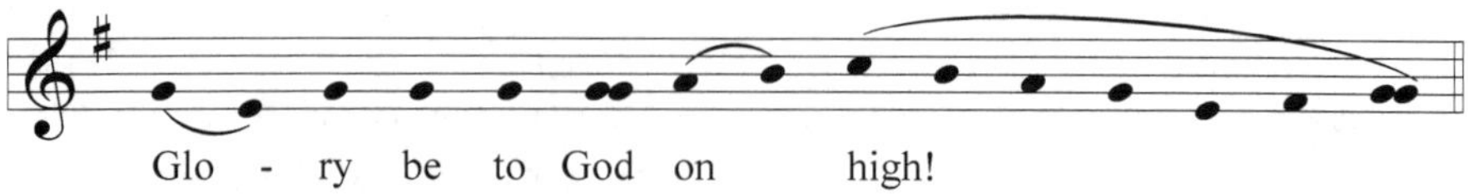

Nürnberg *Agendbüchlein,* 1639; Schwarzburg *Agenda* 1675, et al.

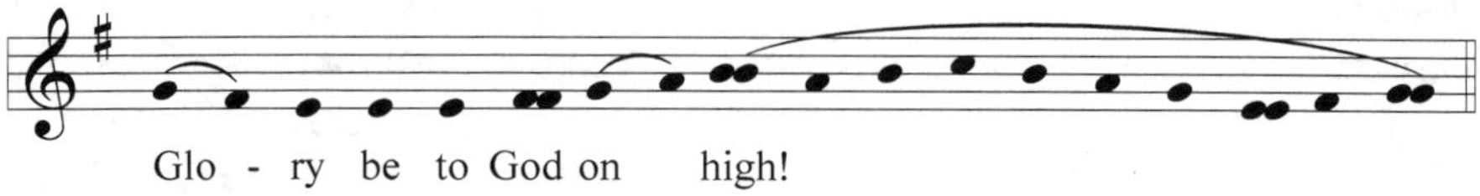

Bayreuth *Chorordnung,* 1755

Easter (Gloria paschale)

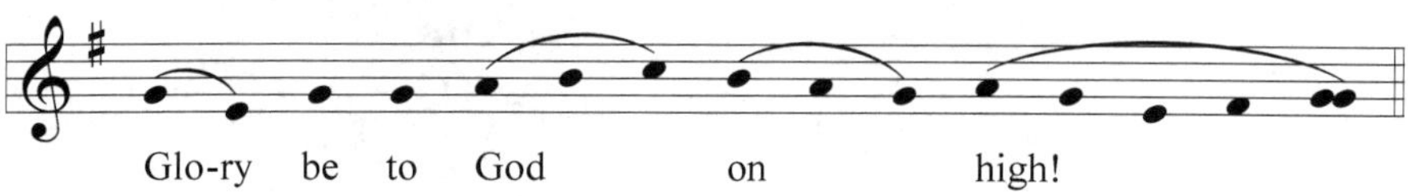

Michael Praetorius, *Liturgodia Sionia,* 1611

Schwarzburg, 1675

3. For other feast days

A. *Advent and St. Michael*

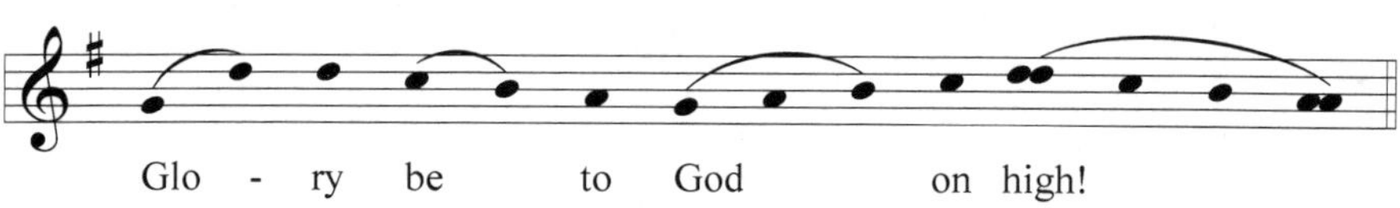

Nürnberg *Agendbüchlein,* 1639

[162] The second example here from 1755 is found in *Chorordunung, wie es mit Intonir- und Absingung derer Collecten, samt denen Antiphonis und Responsoriis, auch andern Hymnis . . . gehalten wird . . .* (Bayreuth: F. E. Dietzel, 1755), 5. Lochner, in reproducing the intonation, omits the rhythmic distinctions, and, perhaps unintentionally, combines into one melisma the two melodic options for "Höhe." —MC.

B. *Feasts of Apostles*

Schwarzburg, 1675

<124>

II. Luther's Gloria Hymn

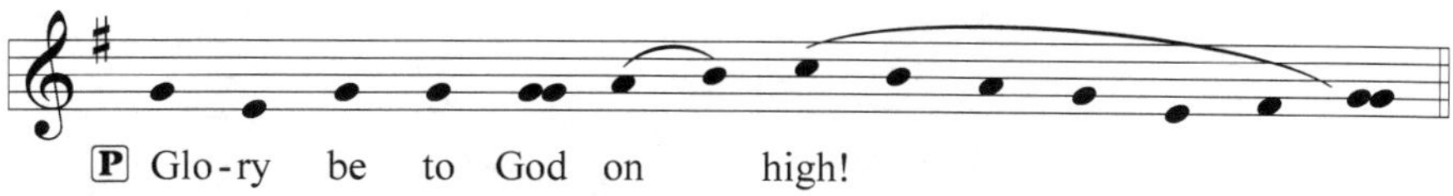

Text: © 1941 Concordia Publishing House.
Tune: Wittenberg, 1544; originally "Vater unser im Himmelreich."

<125>

III. Gloria with Antiphonal
Et in terra and *Laudamus*

* The German here adds ". . . Christ, the most high, and to Thee, Holy Ghost."

Son of the Fa-ther, that tak - est a-way the sin of the world,
have mer - cy up - on us. Thou that tak - est a-way the sin
of the world, re - ceive our pray - er. Thou that sitt - est at the
<127>
right hand of God the Fa - ther, have mer - cy up - on us.

Tune: Strassburg 1525; Pfalz 1570
Setting: Bavarian *Agenda*

<128>

IV. *Laudamus*

Choir

Soloists
p slower
<129>
Je - sus Christ; O Lord God, Lamb of God, Son of the
Fa - ther, that tak - est a - way the sin of the world,
Choir
pp Tempo I
have mer - cy up - on us. Thou that tak - est a - way the sin
of the world, re - ceive our prayer. Thou that sit-test at the right
f
ff

Music: Dimitry Bortniansky, 1751–1825

IV. SALUTATION

The Salutation, with which the liturgist turns to face the congregation following the Gloria, and the *Response* with which it is answered, are quotations of Scripture and have biblical precedent. In an older liturgical work (*Miscellanea,* etc., 1565), it says, "This is a friendly, salutary greeting which the priest bids the people . . . I regard it as coming from the Old Testament, <131> where the angel said to Gideon, 'The Lord be with you!' ('The Lord [is] with you, O mighty man of valor!'; Judges 6:12). Such also is the response: 'And with thy spirit!' from Paul's Epistle to Timothy (2 Timothy 4:22: 'The Lord Jesus be with thy spirit!') This is attested by Pope Soter who instituted its observance." (See Löhe, *Sammlung,* 3:13.) According to its original form it was the Salutation of Peace, and in the time of the *disciplina arcani* could only be used in the *missa fidelium.* As Calvör notes, the current form was availed of after that form ceased.[163]

Whenever the liturgist, as the congregation's spokesman in prayer and praise (whether in the Chief or incidental Divine Services), is to deal with God, he invites the congregation by way of this salutation to join him silently in such dealing. It is for this reason that Gregory the Great assigned to the whole congregation the response, "And with thy spirit." Yet in the twelfth century, the congregation was deprived of this participation, and began to be represented by the Mass servers or ministrants, as is still done today in the Roman Church.

The Lutheran Church, by including this salutation in its Divine Service at all, actually made even more use of it just in the *Chief Divine Service,* as is the case now. It made it precede not only the Preface but also the reading of the Gospel and the Benediction. The dominant *manner* of salutation and response was and remains that of singing. Out of ignorance, "And with *His* (*seinem*) spirit" was sung in some congregations instead of "with *thy* (*deinem*) spirit" as early as the seventeenth century.

The *liturgical meaning* of the beautiful, biblical salutation and its response is obvious. With them, pastor and congregation greet each other in the Lord's house; with them they exhort one another to prayer and praise as well as to the handling and the use of Word and Sacrament as "the presence of the Lord," who was made man and gave the promise, "Where two or three are gathered together in My name, there am I among them" [Matthew 18:20]. Calvör reminds us of the following beautiful exposition by

---

[163] Caspar Calvör, *Ritualis Ecclesiastici Pars Prior* (Jena: Paul Erichius, 1705), 2:468ff. But this observation may be better attributed to a comment in Löhe, *Sammlung,* 3:13, n. 4, from which much of this section is evidently drawn. —MC.

Cardinal Bona: "Through the priest Christ greets us, desiring to make His dwelling in us and unite Himself with us; indeed, to make us His temple by our receiving the Sacrament of the Altar; even as the angel says to the blessed Virgin, 'The Lord [is] with thee!' before the Lord <132> assumed flesh in her womb" (Calvör, *Rituale* [2:470f.]).[164] And of the response, Bona gives us the following explanation from Florus: "The Church has known nothing better to wish the priest than what the priest wishes the Church, which is to say, that the same Lord who deigned to be with the Church might also deign to be with the spirit of the preacher."[165]

Here several *melodies* are provided from various works to be used as desired. It should be noted that it is only at the Preface that the melody for the *Dominus vobiscum* differs from that used with the Collect. If one of the melodies provided here is selected, the same one should be used whenever the Salutation precedes the *Collect*. The melodies set in D major should only serve as an example to indicate that this setting is the one more appropriate for a baritone or tenor voice, for the Salutation as well as the Versicle and Collect.

Naturally, the liturgist sings (or speaks) the Salutation facing the congregation and then, during the response, turns to face the altar so as to intone the Versicle immediately after the Response is ended. The appropriate gesture for the liturgist during the Salutation is to spread the hands a little apart as for the Benediction and then to fold them.

---

[164] *) "Per sacerdotes salutat nos Christus, cupiens in nobis mansionem facere et nos secum unire, ac templum suum eucharistici sacramenti perceptione efficere. Sicut angelus St. virgini dixit: 'Dominus tecum,' antequam in ejus utero carnem susciperet." [From Cardinal Joannis Bona, *Rerum liturgicarum*, book 2, ch. 5. In Calvör, *Ritualis Ecclesiastici*, 2:470, and in Löhe, *Sammlung*, 3:13, it begins: "Salutat nos per sacerdotes Christus . . ." —MC.]

[165] Calvör, *Ritualis Ecclesiastici*, 2:471 attributes these words, in Latin translation, to Chrysostom, Homily 18 on 2 Corinthians: "In tremendis mysteriis ut Sacerdos pro plebe, ita plebs pro Sacerdote vota facit. Haec enim verba: Et cum Spiritu tuo, nihil aliud quam hoc significant: Vovet nimirum populis hac acclamatione, ut idem quod optat Sacerdos Ecclesiae, ipsi vicissim obtingat, quo Domine, qui dignatur esse enim Ecclesia, dignetur etiam esse cum Spiritu Sacerdotis." Cf. NPNF 12:366. —MC.

Salutation

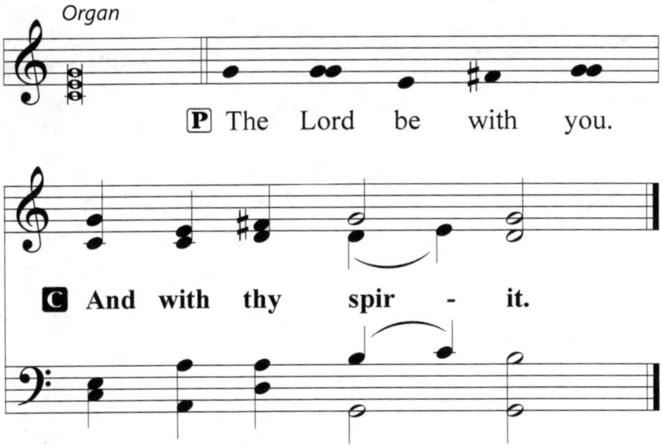

Kirchenordnung, Hannover

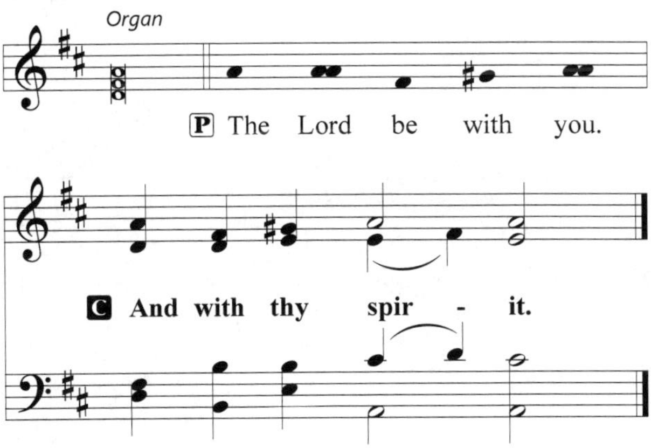

Kirchenordnung, Hannover

<133>

Traditional

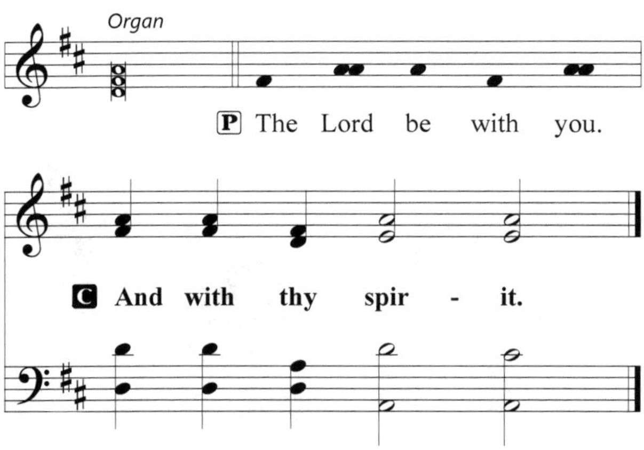

Bayreuth *Chorordnung*, 1755

Note. The Roman form, on which the preceding examples are obviously based, is as follows:

V. VERSICLE

The term *Versicle* (*versiculus*), here and there also referred to as "Antiphon and Intonation," is understood as the antiphonally sung Bible verse or portion of a Bible verse preceding the Collect. Evidently the Versicle has its origin in church psalmody, according to which the two parallel halves of a verse were sung in melodic acclamation and response. It is a singing "back and forth" (Psalm 147:7) or "one to another" [*gegen einander*] (cf. *Gesangbuch* no. 343, st. 2.).[166]

The Roman Church makes use of the Versicle mainly in the incidental Divine Services, and to some extent in the Mass, albeit with a different melody. The Lutheran Church, on the other hand, not only gave the Versicle a place in the incidental <134> Divine Services, but frequently, and in time generally, for the opening and closing Collects of the Mass also. Thus in the Magdeburg church order it says, "Following the hymn 'All Glory Be to God Alone' with the whole congregation and the subsequent salutation: 'The Lord be with you!' given by the deacon, a German collect is sung with the Versicle on feast days, but without a Versicle on Sundays which are not feast days,"[167] etc. While this order intends its use only for a feast day Mass, most church orders of Thuringia also appointed it for Sunday Mass, and this practice was eventually followed almost everywhere. In order, then, to distinguish the feast days, two versicles were sung. Such is the order specified by the St. Louis Agenda also.

In *selecting* the Versicle, one is guided by the occasion of the feast or else by the content of the pertinent Collect. In Passiontide, it is customary to omit the *Alleluia* from a Versicle.

Initially, only the choir chanted the response of the Versicle. However, in order that the congregation might participate in chanting, a collection of versicles was later included in the *Gesangbuch*. This precedent has also been followed by both hymnals of the Synodical Conference as well as the "Church Book" of the General Council. Yet now that, ever since the time of Rationalism's dominance, particularly in this country of Reformed sectarianism, sensibility and taste in liturgical matters has to be nurtured again, it is necessary to highlight a few *improprieties* in chanting the response of the Versicle.

---

[166] That is, "Lobet den Herren, denn er is sehr freundlich." Our translation of this line reads "Sing, voice and chorus." —MC.

[167] Philip Hahn, *Kirchen-Buch* . . . (1615), 462, has a similar rubric. The text here is taken from Schoeberlein, 1:183. —MC.

It is not uncommon to find the Response chanted almost without any rhythm, that is, with every syllable chanted for the same duration. In this way, especially in longer versicles, the Response becomes exceptionally dragging and tedious, and resembles rather the reading of the ABCs in a primer, whereas the liturgist's intonation and chanting of the Collect should be more like sung reading (*choraliter legendi*), or singing with attention to the accents and punctuation of the words. Another impropriety concerns the organ accompaniment often employed during the chanting of the Response. Particularly for those versicles for which the congregation has to chant the running tone somewhat longer, the organist often helps himself to as great a variety of chords as possible. Yet the less familiar the organist is with harmonization, the more unseemly this variation of chords becomes and the more intolerable <135> an up and down rocking motion becomes apparent in the accompaniment. It is no less unseemly, when playing accompaniment, to treat the running tone as the tonic, whereas [in the Versicle and Response] it is always the fifth (as is usually the case in the Collect) and as such calls for the dominant chord. Thus, for example, if the running tone is G, a G chord cannot be chosen; rather, it must be a C chord (c e g). Likewise, at a break, period, or rest, an incorrect modulation has spread among us. We sing:

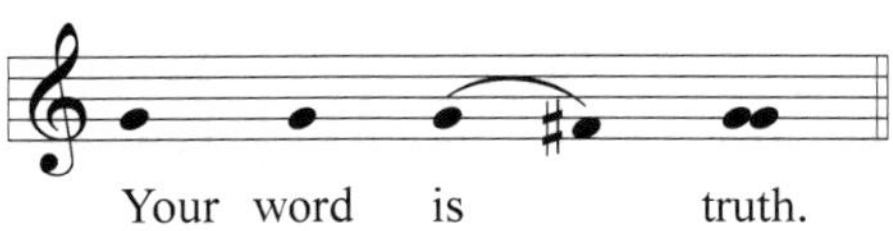

However, it ought to be sung:

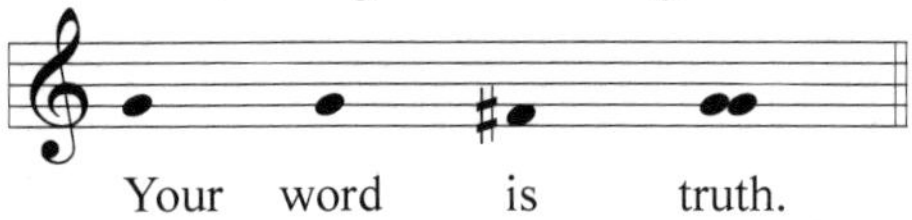

When we discuss the Collect, we will return to the manner of recitative performance also found in the Versicle. Therefore note just a few practical remarks for the musical examples included here.[168] <136>

1. These various examples are intended to show not only how a particular method of *modulation* in the Versicle was used in various localities, but also how attention must be paid to whether the Versicle has one or two parts, and whether the line ends with a monosyllabic or polysyllabic word, with or without an Alleluia. They can thus be used as a system for choosing

[168] *) In the St. Louis Agenda, the following tone is prescribed not only for the conclusion of every versicle with or without Alleluia, but also for the response to the Salutation, the responses before the Preface, and before the corporate Amen.

a standing melody. However, the liturgist and precentor should examine the relevant Versicle a little in advance for the sake of delivery.

2. Since, in the congregational response, the desired goal of a "sung reading" in the accenting of words and syllables is not easily attained, an attempt has been made in these examples to show a simple way to introduce some sense of rhythm into responsive parts, by employing notes of varying values, as informed by practical experience. When chanting is drawn out at natural pauses, especially those words and syllables at the ends of lines, and everything else on the same pitch proceeds more briefly and quickly, and the precentor pronounces the words and syllables very clearly, and the organist (where there is organ accompaniment) meanwhile plays the pedal staccato, then something approaching that goal has already been attained. It would therefore be well worth the trouble for the cantor or organist to set down the collective versicles for feast days, as well as the others that occur most frequently, in alphabetical order with notation, following the method indicated here.

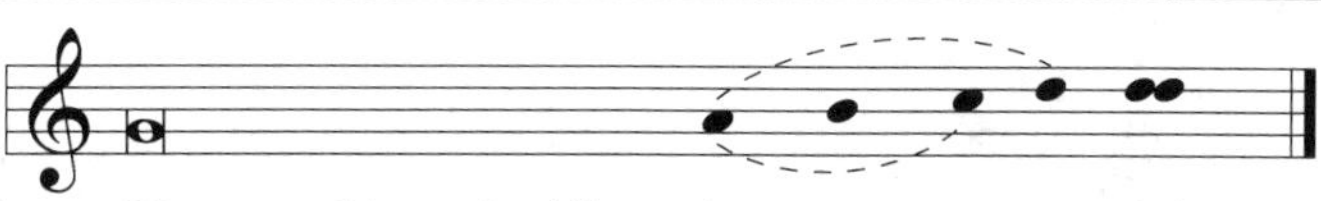

The author could not find this tone, apparently born out of the age of decadence, included in any of the various liturgies at his disposal, nor in Schoeberlein's rich *Schatz*, etc. Only in the muscial agenda published by Schenk in 1851 [*Handagende auf Grund der alten Pommerschen K. O.*] does it appear in a few examples, and even then not for the Versicle for other responsories, much less for the Amen, *but only for the Salutation*, and he also believes he saw it in this position in [J. B. W.] Rußwurm's *Musikalische Altar-Agende* [Musical Agenda] of 1826. Hopefully these will give way more and more to the older, far more beautiful tones, since these have been included by Hölter alongside the others in the new St. Louis *Choralbuch*.

1. Without Alleluia

a. One Part

Wollersheim, *Erlernung des gregorianischen oder Choral-Gesanges*, 1858

<137>

or:

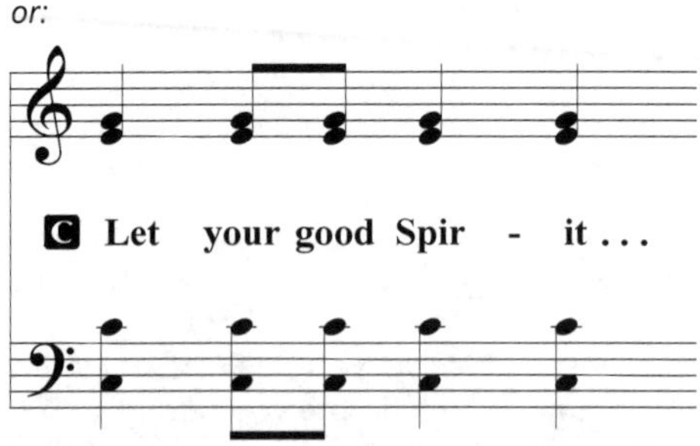

Chorordnung, Bayreuth, 1755

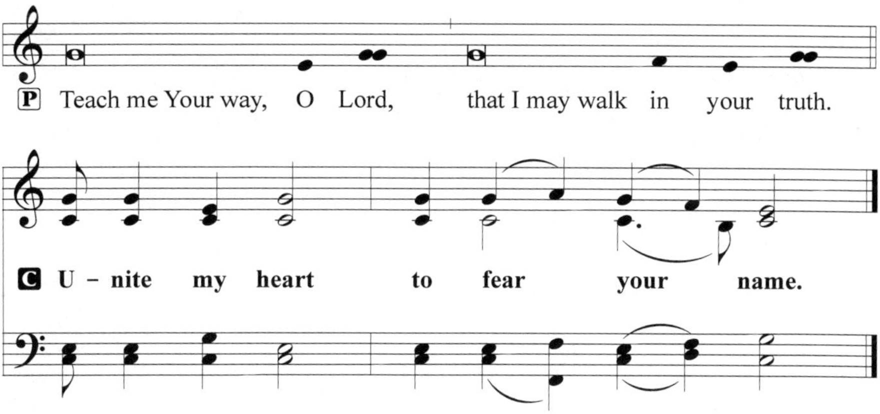

Traditional

2. With Alleluia

Traditional

<138>

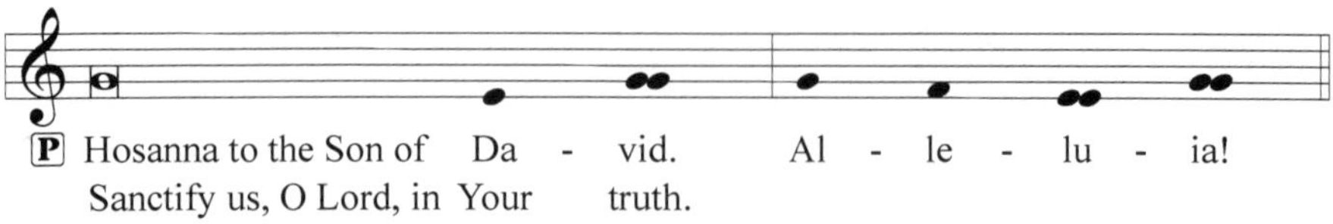

or:

B. Two Parts

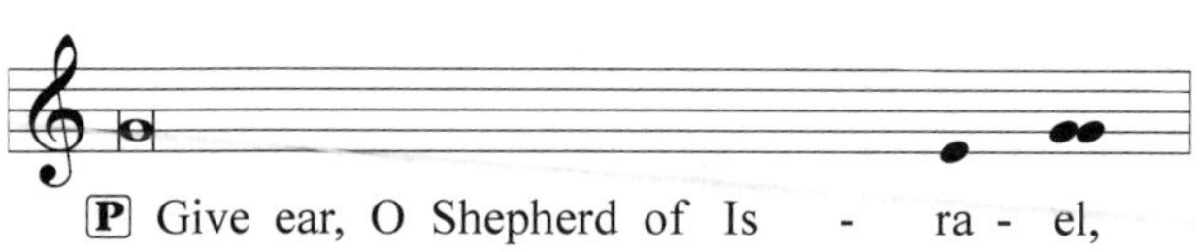

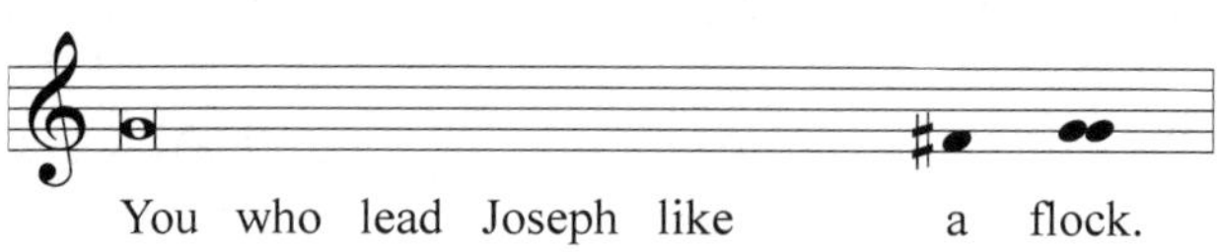

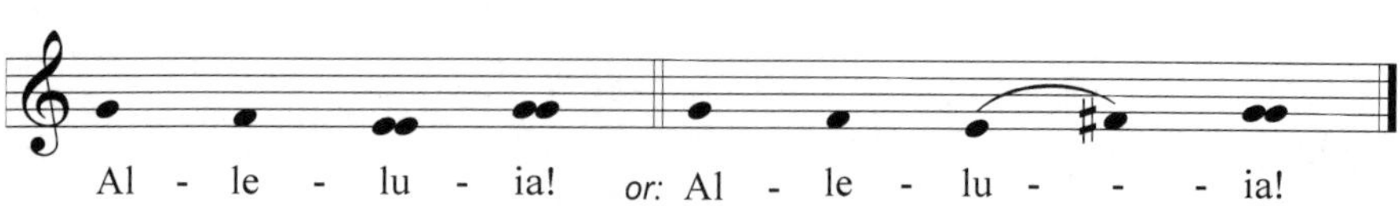

<139>

VI. COLLECT

The origin of this class of church prayers belongs almost to the apostolic age, being mentioned even by Tertullian and Justin. But where the name for this prayer came from—whether because it is a prayer of the gathered assembly, or a summary or collecting together of this assembly's petitions, or because in the oblations of the Ancient Church, the collection of the sacrificial gifts were accompanied by brief prayers—will probably remain a mystery. Luther relates it to the oblations, noting in his treatise, *Against the Heavenly Prophets*: "When the Hebrew language was still common among them, the apostles and first Christians called the bread and wine which they had collected for the Sacrament by the Hebrew term *missa,* according to the Jewish custom, of which one part was then consecrated for the Sacrament, the other distributed among the servants of the congregation and the poor. And for a long time afterward these were still called "collects" because of this collection, as the *Historia Tripartita* attests, *and from this the word* collecta *has still remained in the papist Mass*" (EA 29:181).[169] Using a play on words not replicable in translation, Calvör explains in his *Rituale*: "Collects are without doubt brief prayers of the priest which he prays not for himself but for the whole gathering (*collecta*) and Church, and which the gathered people therefore read together (*collectus collegit*) or at the same time, and pray with the priest for the welfare and needs of

[169] Cf. Luther, "Against the Heavenly Prophets" (1525), AE 40:121. —MC.

the community."[170] Similarly, according to *Cologne Reformation* (1544),[171] it is "a common prayer of the whole congregation, and is therefore called a 'Collect,' a prayer collected from the hearts and prayers of all who are present, or a prayer of the gathered congregation." Suffice it to say, the Collect is *by its very nature* a prayer of the gathered congregation in which it summarizes in the briefest manner and expresses in the most specific way everything in which they united to pray in accordance with the season and occasion. "One prayer—addressed to God the Father—in the name of His only-begotten Son, as the Son Himself commands: one unified sigh of the whole assembly, one word to the heart of the everlasting Father, in which all have been united—such is the Collect, and the more it is so, the more it is what it ought to be. The less it is so, the less it compares with the glorious collects of the primitive age, the more its true shape is distorted" (Löhe, *Agenda* (1853), 1:110). <140>

The Reformation discovered a wealth of ancient collects, among which not a few were still pure. It therefore carried over a number of them, translating them into German but using them in Latin as well. Besides these, a number of collects originated in the Lutheran Church itself. The most exceptional are likely those of *Veit Dietrich* (1541) and *Johann Mathesius* (1568). The collects of Veit Dietrich are Gospel collects, and as such, collects on the *text*. These, however, were only meant to be studied and memorized by the young at school and home,[172] and though entering the Church alongside the Epistle collects composed by [Georg] Major and Andreas Pancratius by way of the latter's *Haus- und Kirchenbuch, oder kurzen Summarien und Gebetlein über Sonn- und Festtagsepisteln und Evangelien* [Brief Summaries and Little Prayer Book over the Sunday and Festival Day Epistles and Gospels], published in 1572, they by no means intended to displace the Collect before the Epistle, since they were meant to be read in conjunction with the summaries *after* the texts. Those of the inventive, "goodly old man" Mathesius were "common prayers of a devout and Christian nature for every distress of the Church,"[173] and found special provision above all in the *Christliche Kirchen-Agenda von*

[170] Calvör, *Ritualis Ecclesiastici*, 2:474. —MC.

[171] *Von Gottes genaden unser Hermans Ertzbischoffs zu Coeln unnd Churfürsten, etc., einfaltigs bedencken, warauff ein Christliche in dem wort Gottes gegrünte Reformation an Lehr brauch der Heyligen Sacramenten vnd Ceremonien, Seelsorg, und anderem Kirchendienst* . . . (Köln: L. von der Mülen, 1544), folio 105, beginning at the bottom of the recto. —MC.

[172] *) For the purpose of domestic use, therefore, these have also been included in the (large) *Gebetsschatz*, pp. 48–70, which was published in St. Louis. [*Evangelisch-Lutherischer Gebets-Schatz* . . . (St. Louis: Concordia Publishing House, 1881). In English, Matthew Carver, trans., *Lutheran Prayer Companion* (St. Louis: Concordia Publishing House, 2018). —MC.]

[173] Printed in Nürnberg, 1568, with preface dated 1563. See Löhe, *Agende* (1853), 1:112. —MC.

Österreich unter der Enns [Christian Church-Agenda of Lower Austria], which was rich in collects.[174] The St. Louis Agenda includes for use at the altar only such collects as have become the common property of the Lutheran Church.

Although many of the earliest church orders, according to the custom of the Roman Mass, specify more than one collect before the Epistle—first a collect *de festo* or *de tempore* and then two collects for common need—the custom of only one collect came to predominate: for feasts a festival collect, for Sundays a common collect as much suited to the day as possible.

The Collect in the Lutheran Church is also preceded by the *Oremus* or "Let us pray!" of the Ancient Church:

Orginally

Later

<141> This exhortation also signals to the congregation that the liturgist brings the prayer to God *on behalf of the congregation*, which therefore acknowledges and confirms it with its *Amen*. This custom of having the prayers of the Divine Service confirmed by the congregation's Amen, shown to be biblical and apostolic by passages such as Nehemiah 8:6 and 1 Corinthians 14:16, was universally observed in the first-century church and maintained in the Roman Church until the twelfth century, and even sporadically after that. How, then, could Luther not reintroduce this custom, since the Collect was thus shown to be a communal prayer not only by liturgist's *Oremus* but also and most importantly by the congregation's *Amen*? Therefore, even when the Collect itself can only be spoken by the liturgist, the Amen should be chanted by the congregation, the most simple manner being best, for example:

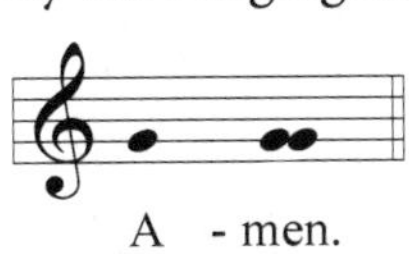

The Collect has its own peculiar *termination formula*. If it is directed to the *Father*—which is most often the case—it goes: "Through Jesus Christ,

[174] The chapter titled "Collects & Litany" comprises a significant portion of Chytraeus's order, fols. CXXVIII r.–CLXXXVI v. —MC.

our Lord," or: "through Jesus Christ, Your Son, our Lord," or: "for the sake of Jesus Christ, Your Son, our Lord," sometimes with the doxological expansion, "who lives and reigns with You and the Holy Spirit (*or* in the unity of the Holy Spirit), ever one God, world without end (*or* forever and ever). If the Collect is addressed to the *Son*, it concludes: "for You live and reign with God the Father and the Holy Spirit, ever one God, world without end," or: "forever and ever." If *the Son is mentioned* in the Collect, the termination is: "through the same Your Son . . ." etc., and if *the Holy Spirit is mentioned*, which occurs seldom, it concludes: "In the unity of the same Holy Spirit, who lives and reigns with the Son . . ." etc.

According to ancient usage this "brief communal prayer" is prayed *facing the altar* and not facing the congregation, which would be counter to all liturgical propriety and reason. Most of the early church orders explicity prescribe this position of the liturgist, and those which do not do so presuppose it as self-evident and common knowledge. Thus in one such church order, that of Braunschweig-Lüneburg, it says, "Thereupon (after the Salutation) let <142> the priest turn again to face the altar and sing a *Collecta de tempore* or *festo* appropriate to the Gospel." How could his posture be any other? When one Bavarian pastor raised an objection (though later retracting it) at the appearance of Löhe's Agenda, seeing a papistic tendency in this posture, Wucherer replied, "We have *altars* in our Lutheran Church, not merely Communion tables. But the concept of a sacrifice to be offered upon the altar is not to be distinguished from the concept of the altar itself. We do not know and never shall know of any unbloody sacrifice in the Supper, yet we know of a sacrifice of the incense of prayer (Revelation 8:3–4), a sacrifice of a repentant heart (Psalm 51:19), and a sacrifice of thanksgiving (Psalm 50:14, 23), and these are the spiritual sacrifices which we present to God on our altars. Therefore, in such sacrifical offerings, *the whole congregation* as a priestly nation (1 Peter 2:9) stands facing the altar. And the pastor, who . . . is speaking the prayer on behalf of the congregation, is supposed to turn his back to the altar?"[175] In confirmation of this response Wucherer appeals to the liturgiologist, Dr. Höfling,[176] and cites from his writing *Von der Composition der christlichen Gemeindegottesdienste* [On the Arrangement of the Christian Divine Service]

[175] Johann Friedrich Wucherer, *Vom Evangelisch-lutherischen Hauptgottesdienste. Eine historisch-liturgische Verständigung mit besonderer Berücksichtigung von Löhe's Agende und Bellfelder's: Gefahr für die Evang. Kirche!* (Nördlingen: C. H. Beck, 1846), 49. —MC.

[176] Johann Wilhelm Friedrich Höfling (1802–1853), Neo-Lutheran theologian in Bavaria, professor at Erlangen, author of *Von der Composition der christlichen Gemeinde-Gottesdienste oder von den zusammengesetzten Akten der Communion. Eine liturgische Abhandlung* (Erlangen: Palm, 1837). —MC.

the following passage: "As pulpit and lectern represent the address of the congregation, the altar, conversely, is the site symbolizing the immediate orientation toward God. . . . And it further lies in the nature of the case that the liturgist, who as the congregation's spokesman and representative before God offers up its prayer and therefore stands in front as one sent by the congregation, has the congregation not in front of him but behind him, speaking not toward congregation but facing the altar. Whenever the opposite is done in church practice, we can never see it as anything better than liturgical indecency."[177]

We now come specifically to the manner of the liturgical delivery of the Collect. It is, as already noted under the Versicle, the manner of the lection tone (*modus choraliter legendi*)—"recitative singing, which occupies a point halfway between genuine speech and genuine singing, and is and should be nothing other than a loftier, solemn elevation of the tone and way of speaking by giving the important word greater resonance."[178] This, too, the Lutheran Church carried over from the Roman Mass, and never to this day was persuaded to reconsider its retention, despite every objection of the Reformed and spiritually agitating enthusiasts, and for good reason. Not only was there a desire <143> to make "no notable change," not only were Christians left free to offer a prayer to God by speaking or chanting, and not only did this *choraliter* reading derive from the chanting of the psalms, but this manner of chant also proved to be perfectly suited to this brief "communal prayer." This manner of reading is solemn, and most importantly, renders all subjectivity in delivery and stress impossible. Here the liturgist is the instrument of the praying congregation; here he is to be the clear, objective voice of the supplicants only, and therefore may not add anything of his own. It is precisely for this reason that, whenever the Collect and other prayers of the Divine Service are *spoken*, all idiosyncrasy and emotion must be eliminated. It is especially necessary during the Collect that, if it is spoken, *it should be performed by the liturgist with a voice free of any emphases, yet with an elevated quality.*

In the Roman Church, the chanting of the Collect can either be *festive* or *ferial*. Collects are sung festively or solemnly during more or less festive, solemn occasions as well as in the Divine Services of Sundays and feasts. At all other times the ferial, simple tone is prescribed, which consists of singing the Collect on the running tone (*tonus currens*) from beginning to end, yet with attention to the punctuation and accentuation of the text. In the festive tone, however, the *accentus ecclesiasticus* comes into use. In his

[177] Ibid.,74f. —MC.

[178] Wucherer, *Ev.-luth. Hauptgottesdienste*, 41. —MC.

Lehre vom römischen Choralgesang [Teaching on Roman Choral Music] (1842), Vilsecker gives the pertinent rules and clarifies them by examples. Though these naturally only deal with the Latin *oratio*, they are still instructive for singing German collects.[179] And even though no one in our Church was strictly bound to this form, it was nevertheless accepted as the model more or less—in fact, connected at times, insofar as the German language permitted, in most of it, as we will see in its place especially in the chanting of the Preface.

The rules in question are:

The beginning of the oration is produced here with an elevated voice holding the beginning note *c* or *f*[180] until the first change comes around the middle of the oration, <144> which is called the *principal point* (*punctum principale*). This is marked by a colon and concludes the first part of the oration.

At the *fourth* or *fifth* syllable before the colon the singing descends by two steps, and for the last two or three syllables returns to the main pitch either by *c b a c* or *f e d f*. If the oration is long enough so as to be able to bear two changes, the half point (*semipunctum*) occurs at the end of the second clause, and this by means of the notes *c b* or *f e*. However, if the oration is too short, only the principal point is used. When both the principal point and half point have been passed, no second principal point or half point is used, nor are multiple conclusions (*clausulae*) to follow. There is a short pause at both points for the sake of breathing. — If two colons appear in an oration, the principal point occurs at the second colon immediately before the half point.

In the conclusions of the festive oration tone, *Per Dominum* and *per eundem Dominum* ("through Jesus . . ." and "through the same Jesus . . ."), there is a half point on the word *tuum*: *c a* or *f e*, and the principal point *b a* | *c c* or *e d* | *f f* on *Sancti Deus*. In the conclusions *Qui tecum* and *Qui vivis*, only the principal point *e d f f* or *b a c c* appears and the half point is absent. The last syllables of each oration must always be held a little longer than the rest of the words. (In the corresponding *German* conclusions, the half point *c c a* would be located on *Sohn* instead of *deinen*, and *e d f* or *b a c* on *wahrer Gott* instead of *sancti Deus*.)[181]

---

[179] And English, too, of course. —MC.

[180] *) *C* for a higher male voice, *f* for a lower one. It was customary even in the Lutheran Church to chant on either pitch. In the present work, as in the St. Louis Agenda, *g* has been adopted as the average pitch.

[181] Thus in English, in the conclusions "through Jesus . . ." or "through the same Jesus . . ." the half point falls on "Son our Lord": *c a a* or *f d d*; in the conclusion "for You live . . ." the principal point falls on "(ev)-er one God": (*c*) *b a c* or (*f*) *e d f*. —MC.

As "repetition of the rule," Vilsecker proceeds to combine everything as in the following example:

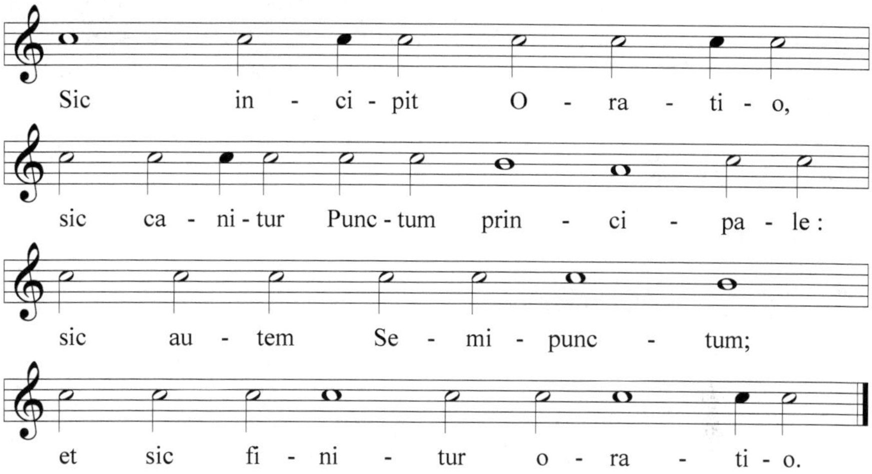

<145>

Yet in order to illustrate this better, the Latin Collect for the Feast of St. Peter and St. Paul [June 29] has also been supplied in notation. Since this tone more or less resembles several of the older German collects, and in fact entirely agrees with one of them (cf. No. 3 of the Collect tones following), it is good to include this example here as well for the sake of orienting the reader, and at the same time to coordinate it with the German text found in the third edition of Löhe's Agenda.

Example of the Solemn Tone

Editorial note: Lochner's intention is to demonstrate a rhythmic equivalence in the chanting of this collect. The English version in particular reflects a closer proximity to the rhythm of speech, without unnatural lengthening of the notes or slowing at the ends of phrases. The note values are always approximate and never strictly metrical. Beams have been added to assist in singing the rhythm of the text in groups of twos and threes.

In the musical appendix to the Bavarian Agenda, Dr. Herzog gives the following *principles* for chanting the *collects according to churchly tradition*:

> He begins on the fifth. A syllable or the word with a particular accent takes the third below; a comma or semicolon falls to the third and returns to the fifth; a period rises from the third through the sharp fourth to the fifth; the termination rises to the sixth and falls stepwise to the third. For example:

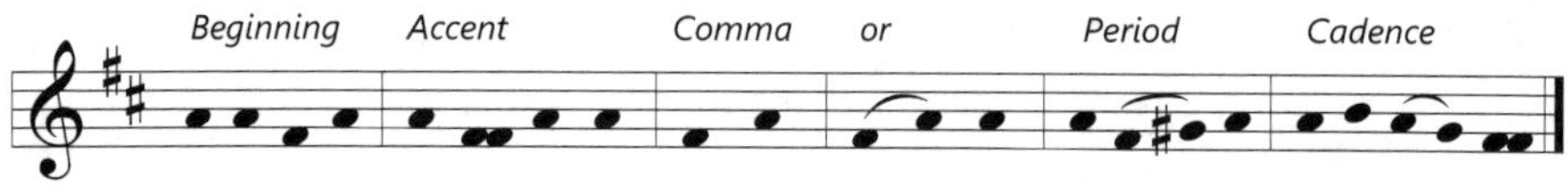

<147>

The monotony which becomes apparent in the chanting of the Collect, particularly in longer collects, can be reduced by using the fourth between the third and fifth.[182]

To clarify this by way of example, refer to no. 5 of the following Collect tones. The fourths, used for reducing monotony, are found in the phrases "that Your word may not be bound but have free course" and "that in steadfast faith we may serve You."

Finally, regarding the following *tones for the Collect and Amen*, these have all been taken from early collections, specifically those of the sixteenth century. There are very simple Collect tones and there are more dynamic ones, but all of similar character. The simplest ones among them not only evince a certain beauty in their simplicity, but for the same reason may also commend themselves to those pastors who encounter difficulty mastering a more dynamic tone.

The Amen for the Collect also has a great number and variety of melodies. Yet whatever the form, simpler or richer, only *a single Amen* is ever appointed for the Collect, not two or three as for the Benediction.

[182] See Johann Georg Herzog, *Musikalischer Anhang zu dem Agende-Kern und zu der ihm vorangestellten Gottesdienstordnung für die evangelisch-lutherische Kirche in Bayern . . .* (Nürnberg, 1856), xi. —MC.

A. Tones for the Collect

No. 1

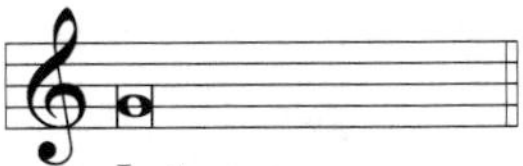

Let us pray.

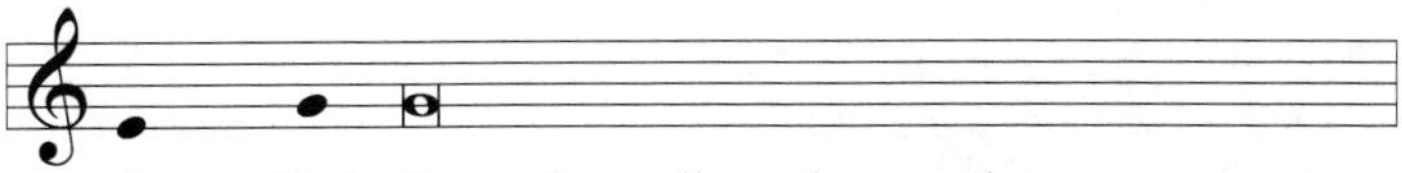

O God, from whom all good proceeds,
grant to us, Your humble servants, Your holy inspiration,
that we may set our minds on the things that are right
and, by Your merciful guiding, accomplish them;
through Je - sus Christ, Your Son, our Lord,
who lives and reigns with You and the Holy Spirit,

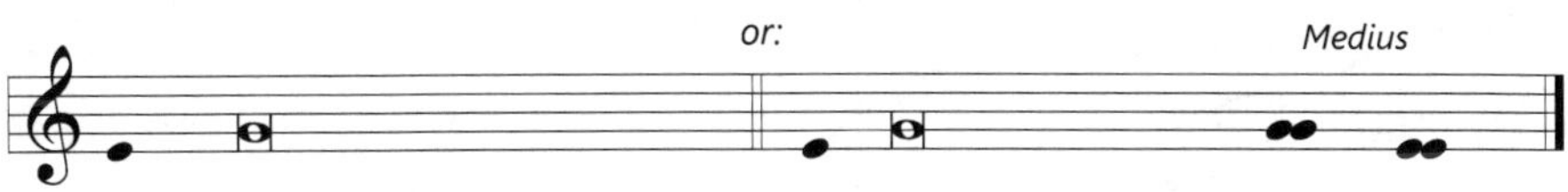

one God, now and forever. one God, now and for - ev - er.

Libellus antiphon. Hof 1605.
Libellus continens Ant. Onolzbach 1627.

<148>

No. 2

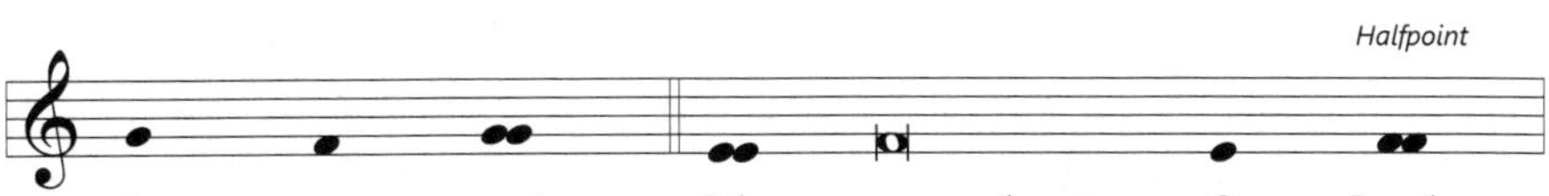

Let us pray! Stir up our hearts, O Lord,

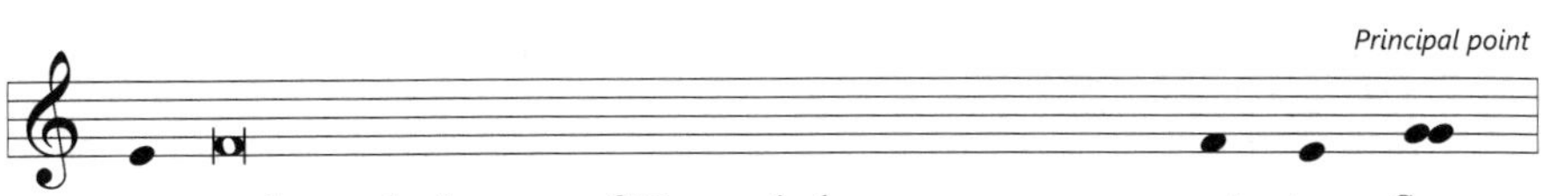

to make ready the way of Your only be - got - ten Son,
that by His coming we may be enabled to serve You with pure minds;

through the same Je - sus Christ, our Lord,

Braunschweig-Lüneburg 1531, 1569, 1657; Oldenburg 1573; Hoya 1531; Ludecus *Missale*, 1589; Verden 1606.

No. 3

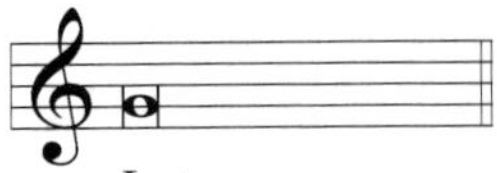

Let us pray.

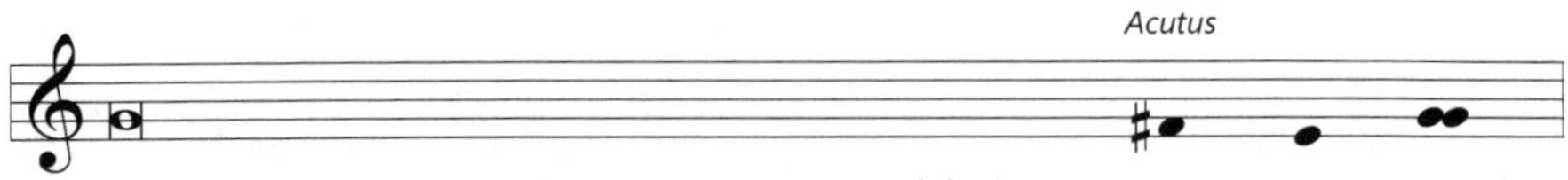

Almighty and everlasting God, by whose Spirit the whole body of the church is governed and sanc - ti - fied,

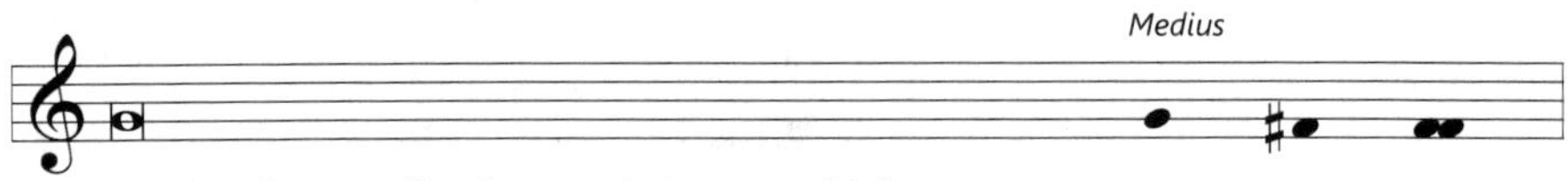

receive the supplications and prayers which we offer before You for all Your servants in Your ho - ly Church

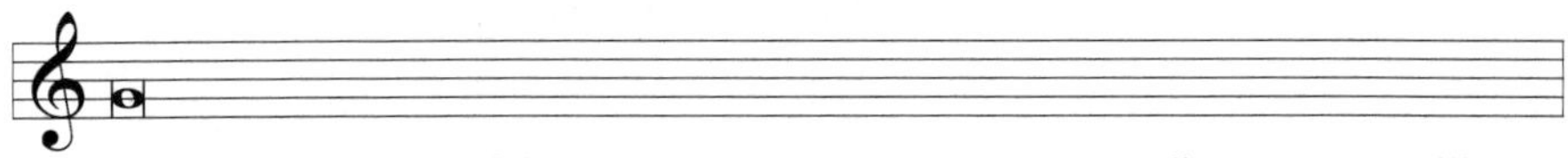

that every member of the same may truly serve You according to Your calling;

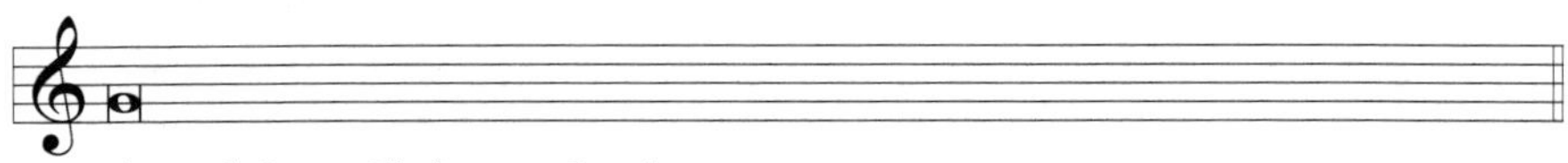

through Jesus Christ, our Lord.

or:

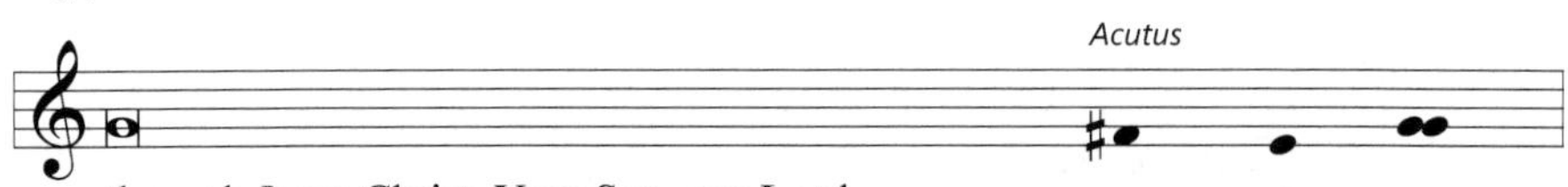

through Jesus Christ, Your Son, our Lord, who lives and reigns with You and the Ho - ly Spirit,

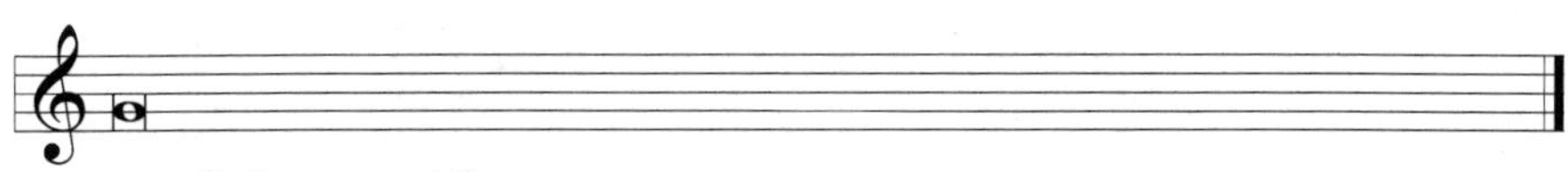

one God, now and forever.

Hommel, *Lit. luth. Gem.-Gottesd.*, 1851.

<149>

No. 4

Hommel, 1851

No. 5

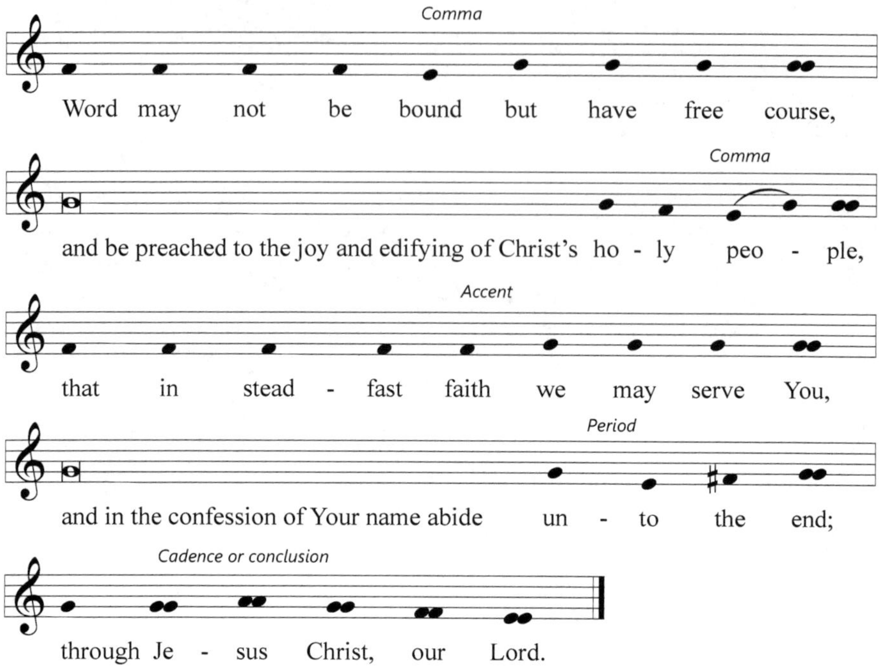

Layriz, *Kern.*, part IV. 1855

<150>

No. 6

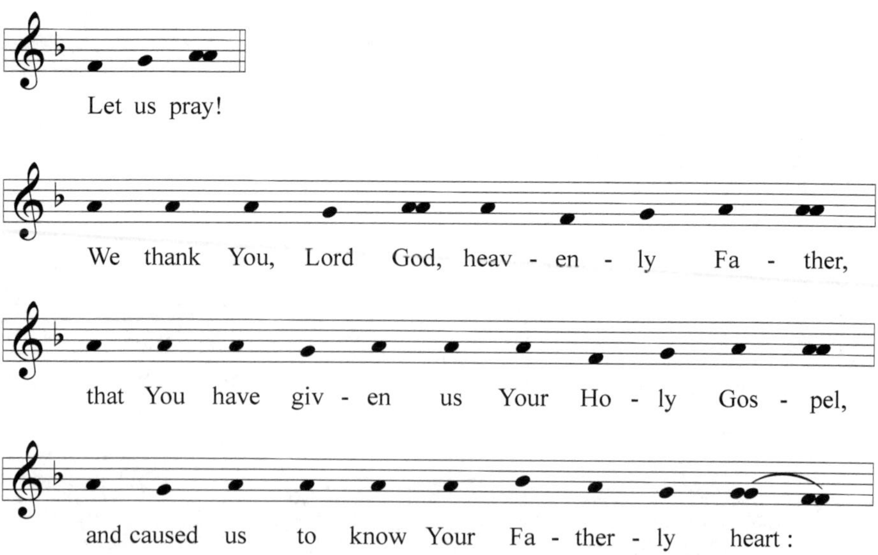

Layriz, *Kern.*, part IV. 1855

<151>

No. 7

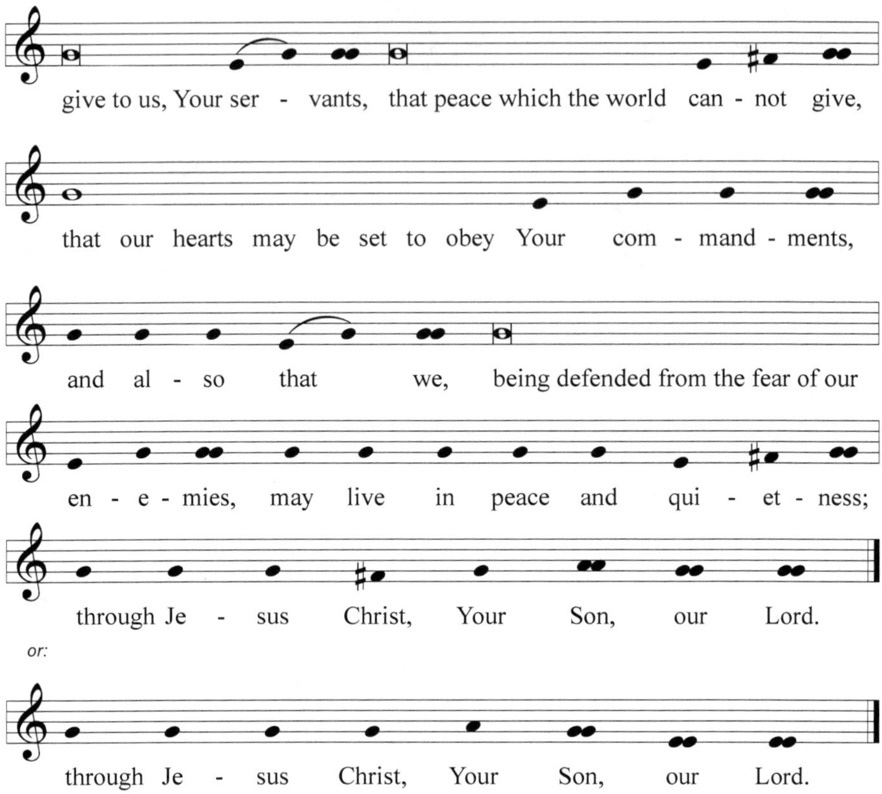

Layriz, *Kern.*, part IV. 1855.

<152>

B. Amen after the Collect

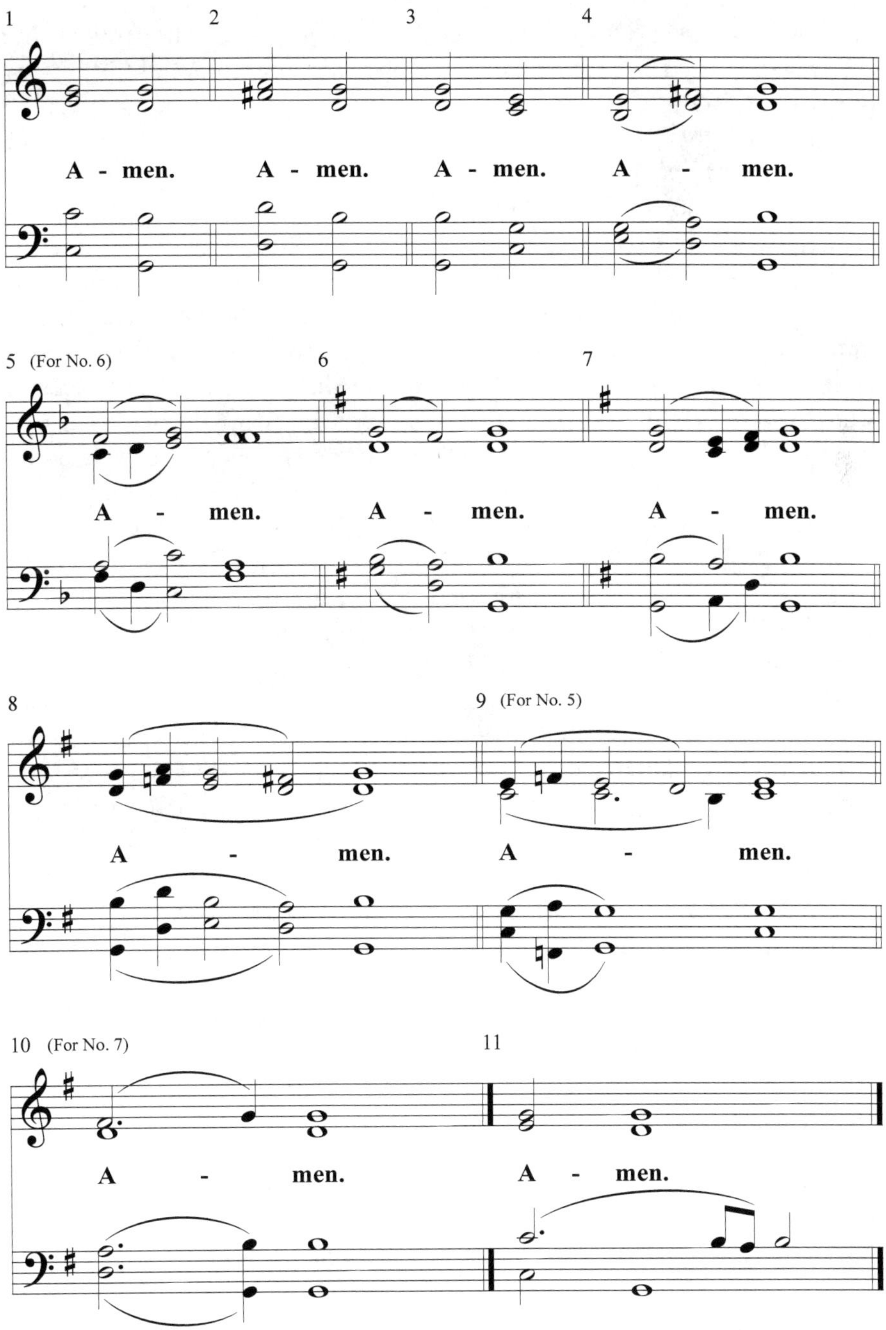

VII. EPISTLE

Having been prepared by the "brief communal prayer," the Collect, the congregation then hears the *Epistle*, and after that the *Gospel*, of the Sunday or feast day. In these Lessons the Lord speaks to the congregation through the mouth of the liturgist. The reason why the Epistle comes first and the Gospel second may be consulted below in the discussion of the latter.

In these Lessons, too, the Lutheran Church has simply retained another feature of the Ancient Church. The custom of reading aloud excerpts of the Law and the Prophets (Luke 4:16–17, Acts 13:14–15; 15:21) in the worship service of the Old Testament was taken by the primitive Church into its cultus at an early date. However, the Church promptly combined with it the reading of both narratives from the life of the Lord and excerpts from the letters of the apostles. Thus Justin Martyr (d. 163) informs us that in Christians' Sunday assemblies, "the memoirs of the apostles, which are called Gospels, and the writings of the prophets"[183] were read, and preaching and prayer followed. Tertullian (d. 220) likewise says that the Church read the Law and the Prophets together with the evangelical and apostolic writings.[184] Continuing on this path, the *Apostolic Constitutions* (2:39, 57) specifically arrange the reading of the Law and the Prophets before that of the New Testament (Acts, the Pauline Epistles, and the Gospels). The Old Testament Lessons were later shifted to the incidental Divine Services, especially Vespers. Soon, however, it became necessary to select for the chief festivals, and then also for the other occasions, those passages of Holy Scripture which contained an account of the day or else had an explicit, intimate connection to them. In the Roman Church, the *pericopal system* was formed.

The Lutheran Church not only assumed this order of pericopes for its Divine Service, but also expanded it further, particularly by assigning to the last Sundays after Trinity Scripture passages on the end of the world. While some churches of the Reformation tried continuous readings, this did not become widespread. There was more of a tendency to follow the practice of Luther, who appointed the continuous Scripture Lessons for the incidental Divine Services and the pericopal Lessons <154> for the Chief Divine Service. Since the sermon in the Chief Divine Service was mainly to address the Gospels, it became the practice here and there to accompany the Epistle with a *summary*, or the reading of a brief synopsis of its contents. An example is the note "an explanation by Pancratius" found in the

[183] *First Apology of Justin,* 67; cf. *ANF* 1:186. —MC.

[184] *Prescription against Heretics,* 36; cf. *ANF* 3:260. —MC.

Officia missae of Hof (1605) and in the Henneberg church order (1582)—a direction that was still found in the 1755 edition of the Nürnberg Agenda. The order still found in the Hannover Agenda to this day, which displaces the Gospel with special continuous Scripture Lessons and relegates the reading of the Gospel to the pulpit, is not earlier than 1769, and has nothing to commend it with respect to the organization of the Chief Divine Service. (No more laudable for the same reason is the practice of some preachers who, in the Lessons, stray from the pericopes and disregard the order of Epistle and Gospel).

Even in places where the Lesson was initially still being done in Latin for the sake of the Latin school, they naturally did not neglect the *German* Lesson for the sake of the people. Emphasis was laid on reading the Lesson "quite loudly, clearly, and slowly, without skipping any words or syllables."[185]

In keeping with Luther's precedent, there is a strong consensus that the Lesson "*be done facing the people*," that the liturgist turn "*to the people*," a thing which did not actually happen during the liturgical Readings in the Roman Mass. In doing so, the liturgist stood for the most part before the altar or on the south side of it, or did the reading from a special stand, the "little pulpit" [or lectern], as is still seen in illustrations from time to time.

It was already mentioned above in Part One, §6 [p. 21], that, following the precedent of the Roman Mass, the *manner* of reading the Epistle and Gospel was a chanted recitation, and that Luther in his *Deutsche Messe* provided rules and examples for it. These are also found in the musical appendix to EA 22 and in StL 10 [:235ff.; AE 53:69ff.], where the notes are provided with the text. So although Luther proceeded cautiously in this matter also, he was nevertheless "moved and driven by the spirit of a churchly German awakened by his Bible translation, to replace the traditional Epistle and Gospel tones—which, though simple, had been variously ornamented from diocese to diocese—with a more fluent, expressive form, or rather *two Reformation forms*, which cannot be explained as the local variation or diachronic development of a scheme traceable to pre-Reformation times, <155> even though they firmly and plainly bear the stamp of certain Gregorian modes. These forms, if necessarily appearing new at that time, were nevertheless suited to supplant their antecedents for all time, as long as the solemnly chanted recitation of the pericopes was not to fall silent at Lutheran altars" (Lyra).[186] And to what extent Luther again demon-

[185] Quoting Schoeberlein, 1:194, who in turn refers to the church orders of Mecklenburg, Wenden, etc. (1540), Ottheinrich (1543), and Duke Augustus of Branunschweig-Lüneburg (1657), etc. —MC.

[186] Lyra, *Ornitho.*, 27. —MC.

strated his expertise here we are shown by the testimony of Johann Walther provided above in Part One, §6 [p. 21].

The liturgical manner of reciting the pericopes was followed uniformly in Saxony; likewise in Pomerania, Mark-Brandenburg, and part of Lower Saxony. In another part of Lower Saxony and in Austria, it was left free whether the pericopes were to be spoken or chanted, while in other areas, speaking was only permitted if the pastor did not have sufficient talent for singing. And so it remained for a long time. Thus Johann Schrader in his *Formular-Buch* (1621) attests that it was still "practiced in larger cities" and that in Magdeburg some years before, a book had been printed in folio "in which all the Epistles and Gospels were set to notation."[187] The Leipzig Agenda (1681),[188] as attested by the present author, likewise contains instruction and examples for the liturgical chanting of the pericopes. Indeed, it was in many places retained into the eighteenth century, and to some extent still endures in the Norwegian Lutheran Church.

Since under the sway of Rationalism in Germany and of Puritanism and Methodism in this country, liturgical chanting has generally lapsed, and as a result of misunderstanding is viewed in a number of congregations as having something Catholic about it, there can perhaps be little talk of reintroducing the chanting of pericopes even in those localities where the liturgical chanting of the other parts of the "Mass" is generally still practiced or is in the process of being reintroduced. But that the *knowledge* of this manner of recitation may be retained among us for liturgical study, as well as for the sake of completeness, one of the three or four chant tones which have come into use for the Epistle may as well be included here, as well as one for the Gospel in its proper place. This is Luther's tone, albeit in a slightly altered form, as it appears most often and as it is found in the above named Leipzig Agenda (1681).

One further thing to note is that, for the unchanted reading of the pericope, a declamatory tone is to be avoided as much as possible, and a more recitative tone should be used. <156>

---

[187] David Ciceler, *Episteln und Evangelia auff alle Sontage, und Fürnembsten Feste durchs gantze Jar* (Magdeburg: J. Weißner, 1604). —MC.

[188] Cf. *Agenda, Das ist: KirchenOrdnung* . . . (1672), 79–84. —MC.

1. Rules for Modulating the Epistle

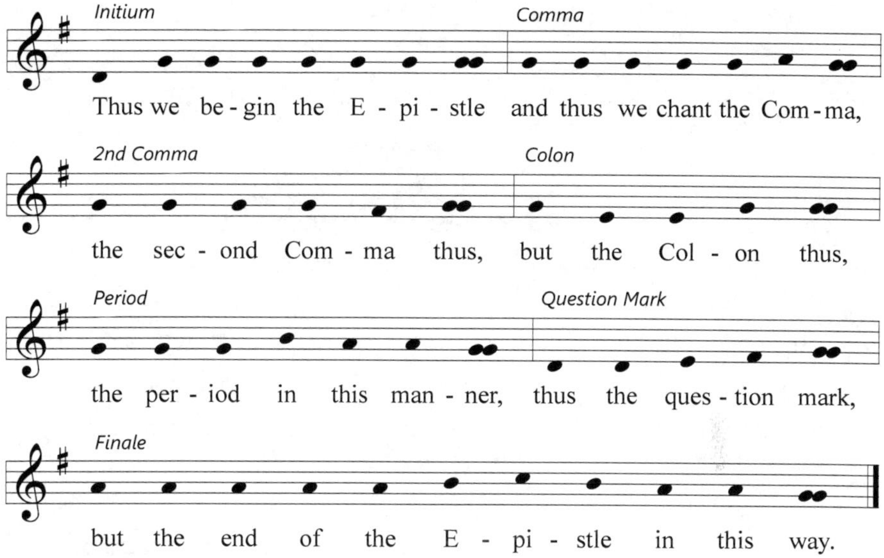

Deutsche Messe, 1526; Braunschweig-Lüneburg, 1542; Magdeburg, 1615; Leipzig, 1611

2. Epistle Tone

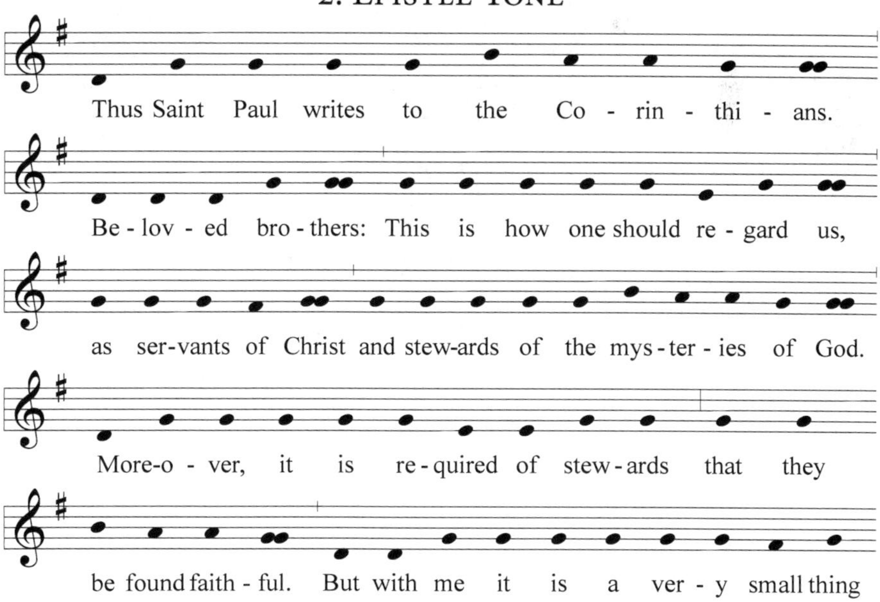

that I should be judged by you or by an - y hu - man court.
In fact, I do not e - ven judge my - self. For I am not a - ware
of an - y - thing a-gainst my - self, but I am not there-by ac - quit - ted.
It is the Lord who judg - es me. There-fore do not pro-nounce
judg-ment be - fore the time, be - fore the Lord comes,
who will bring to light the things now hid - den in dark - ness
and will dis - close the pur - pos - es of the heart.
Then each one will re - ceive his com - men - da - tion from God.

<157>

VIII. GRADUAL

By the term *Gradual*, which is to say, the chant of the step, those chants are indicated which take place between the Epistle and the Gospel. They derive this name from the practice of the Ancient Church according to which the deacon, before ascending the raised area (*ambo*) on which he would read two prescribed lessons of the Old and New Testament and on which the choir singers also stood, intoned from the lowest step a chant which the choir then repeated. Since in the Roman Mass, after the Epistle has been read by the subdeacon on the left side of the altar, certain chants are intoned as the deacon ascends the altar steps to read the Gospel on the right side, the term from the Ancient Church has been applied to these.

In the narrower sense of the word, the Gradual is understood as the chanting of a Scripture passage especially related to the Epistle, being chanted completely or partially by a single voice and then repeated by another voice or the whole choir, and no doubt for that reason is in a special sense called the "*Responsory*." This Reponsory was followed by a simple or lengthier Alleluia in imitation of the Old Testament Hallel (Psalm 113–118, cf. Matthew 26:30), and of the apocalyptic Alleluia <158> (Revelation 19:4), and then a three- or six-line *hymn*, called the *Sequence* or "following song," such as *Grates nunc omnes*, translated: "Let us all give thanks to God," etc., which was sung from Christmas to the Purification. Since the time of Gregory the Great, *proses* and *tracts* have also been sung in this place. When the songs following the Alleluia were prosaic rather than poetic in form, these were called *proses*. As for the Tract, it had the following characteristics: when after the end of the Gradual the lector ascended the ambo, a procession was made to the raised platform from which the Gospel would be read. Since this movement was accompanied by the chanting of psalms, with the congregation's Alleluia between individual verses, this song was called a *tractus* (progression). Later, where the procession disappeared, the Tract was limited to one verse, before and after which multiple Alleluias were sung, and retained its name probably because of the *protracted* notes in which it was sung, replacing the Allelluia during Lent. All these chants were also collectively referred to as the Gradual in the broader sense.

It is true that Dr. Luther (*Deutsche Messe,* 1526 [AE 53:74]) stipulated that, "after the Epistle, a German hymn, such as 'Nun bitten wir den Heiligen Geist' ["To God the Holy Spirit Let Us Pray"], etc., or another, is sung with the whole choir." However, since "the Gradual and Alleluia . . . especially those which are sung according to the season (*de tempore*) or on

Sundays" also belonged to "the ancient purity of the Divine Service,"[189] a number of Gradual chants were carried over, as shown by Spangenberg's glorious *Kirchengesänge* (1545), then by the chants of Wittenberg (1551) and Lossius's cantional ([*Psalmodia,*] 1553).

The Gradual was sung by the *choir*. In this arrangement, individual boys' voices, for the most part, intoned the Alleluia—for which reason they were called the "Alleluia boys."[190] However, the high point of the Gradual was and remained the German congregational hymn. How could it not be the urgent desire of the whole congregation to praise the Lord with their own lips and their own song, as the spiritual gift bestowed on them with the Gospel, and to do so for the gracious gift of His Word, or else for the salvific fact to be commemorated? Therefore the *congregational hymn* at this point in the Chief Divine Service is regarded and identified as the *main piece of singing*, even as it is now called the "Chief Hymn." According to a number of church orders, it was combined in various ways with the choir's chanting of the Gradual. By far and wide the most common method was to have the congregational <159> song immediately follow the choir's song, as for instance in the church orders of Braunschweig-Lüneburg (1544) and Wittenberg (1533, 1599, etc.), and occasionally, according to both church orders, to have the singing of choir and congregation alternate verse by verse. In later times, to some extent as early as the seventeenth century, the "simple Alleluia," or Alleluia with its single verse, and attendant Sequences, etc., came to be replaced by "a piece sung *figuraliter*" in which "accompaniment was provided by the organ." All earlier and later church orders nevertheless show that when the choir took the lead at this point with a special doxology alongside the Chief Hymn of the congregation, our modern "*choir song*" was to have its place after the Epistle, and thus before the Chief Hymn (in which case it would be preferable if the pertinent choir piece were sung without organ accompaniment, yet introduced by a few chords from the organ, lest that ungainly and unpleasant pause occur during which the director is heard indicating the voices while the congregation sits expectantly to see whether it "will not soon begin.")

Now as for the *manner of execution* with respect to the Chief Hymn, the Fathers admittedly had more tolerance than their present-day successors here in prolonging the public Divine Service. While our contemporaries ask for more and more brevity even with respect to the singing, and even in places where circumstances do not call for any shortening of the Divine

[189] These citations from Luther's *Formula Missae* (1523; cf. AE 53:20) are also found in Löhe, *Sammlung*, 2:33. —MC.

[190] As noted, e.g., in the Magdeburg Agenda (1615), 461, under no. 5. —MC.

Service, those in former days were accustomed, as a rule, to sing the Chief Hymn *in its entirety*.

The choice of the Chief Hymn requires special attention. In the church orders, the usual requirement is to the effect that the song fit "with the *occasion* (*de tempore*) or with the *Gospel*." To that end the specific Chief Hymn used to be fixed by means of the agenda. It belonged to a later time to have the Chief Hymn also "suit the *sermon*." Our view is that both are to be considered when making a selection, but primarily the *occasion*—and not merely the relevant feast day but also the Sunday which stands in connection to it. Thus the Chief Hymn for *Sundays in Advent* should be an Advent hymn; for *Sundays after Epiphany* (at least for some of them), an Epiphany hymn; and for *Sundays from Easter to Pentecost*, on the first three an Easter hymn, and on the rest a Pentecost hymn. But if there are no communicants present, the hymn *after* the sermon would then have the content of the sermon primarily in view. <160>

In the following we offer a number of the Alleluia tones immediately following the Epistle and preceding the Chief Hymn.

1. On Common Sundays

(with the exception of Lent, when the Alleluia is entirely absent)

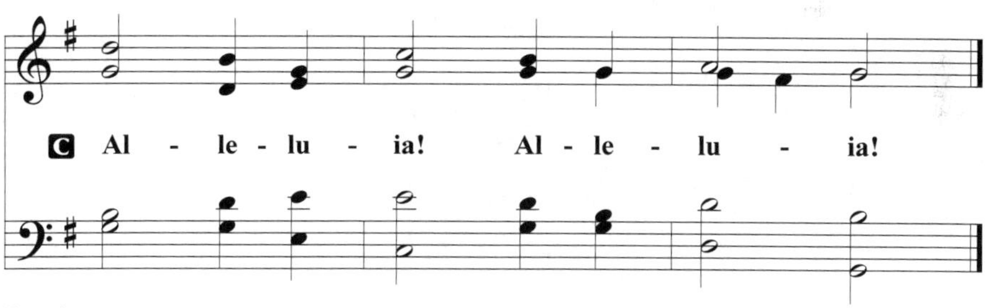

Hommel

2. On Feast Days in general

Tune: L. Lossius, 1553

Tune: Prussian *Kirchenordnung,* 1558

<161>

3. On Easter Day in particular[191]

[191] See Anton Corvinus, *Christliche Kirchen Ordnung, Ceremonien und Gesenge* . . . (Erfurt: Sachse, 1542). Lochner's simplified melody with harmonization is found in Schoeberlein, 1:210. —MC.

Duchess Elisabeth von Braunschweig *Kirchenordnung,* 1542

<162>

IX. GOSPEL

After the precedent of Christian antiquity and in strong agreement with the Roman Mass, the Lutheran Church originally *gave the reading of the Gospel* ***very notable distinction*** *over the Epistle.*

This is already achieved by the *manner of delivery*. While Luther, namely, prescribes for the *choraliter* reading of the Epistle one of the more serious of the eight church tones, he prefers the Gospel to be read in one of the more joyful tones, and in his discussion with the musical director Walther reasons as follows: "Christ is a kind Lord, and His words are pleasant, so let us use the sixth tone (*sextum tonum*) for the Gospel; and because St. Paul is a serious Apostle, let us appoint the eighth tone (*octavum tonum*) for the Epistle."[192] As we know, in the *Deutsche Messe* Luther eventually decided in favor of the fifth tone (*quintum tonum*), and also set the Words of Institution to the same one.

However, this reading is further distinguished *by additional liturgical adornment*. In his *Formula Missae* Luther still wished to see candles and incense retained.[193] And while incense promptly fell out of use, such was not the case with the *candles burning during the reading of the Gospel*, which with the Ancient Church was no doubt regarded as the symbol of the light of the grace proceeding from the Gospel. As in the Roman Mass, the reading of the Gospel was done on the right side of the altar, while that of the Epistle took place on the left side; and the congregation stood to hear the Gospel, whereas they remained seated for the Epistle. First, there was an additional Salutation: "The Lord be with you," etc., this time in a more dynamic tone than the Salutation before the Collect. After the announcement: "Thus writes the holy Evangelist St. __ in the __ chapter" or: "Attend to the Holy Gospel," the choir responded: "Glory be to Thee, O Lord!" whereupon the reading itself followed in the fifth tone (*quinto tono*). In the course of the seventeenth century, the additional practice arose of having a motet ("a figural piece, where one can have it," as it says in the Schwarzburg Agenda, 1675)[194] sung by the choir after the Gospel and before the Creed. *Schoeberlein* construes this as an acclamation of the salvific fact which, as a rule, forms the content of the Scripture readings from the four Evangelists.[195] <163>

---

[192] See above, p. 21, n. 56.

[193] Cf. Luther, "An Order of Mass and Communion" (1523), AE 53:25, the sixth point. —MC.

[194] *Agenda Schwartzburgica: Das ist Verzeichniß* . . . (1675), 5, point 3 under heading "In the afternoon on all feast days.". —MC.

[195] *) This includes the liturgy of those Nestorian congregations which staunchly refused subjection to the Roman antichrist; and among them still today, incidentally, the Mass

Now what is the reason for this liturgical distinction? There was a desire to see in the ascending of the steps from the Epistle to the Gospel a recapitulation of the Jewish Church's practice, according to which an excerpt of the Mosaic Law was heard first, and then one of the prophecies of the prophets, this being the Gospel of the old covenant. But since the content of the Epistle does not always consist of exhortation to holy conduct, and is often partly, sometimes wholly, doctrine—the doctrine of salvation—we might well offer a somewhat different explanation of the gradual progression from the Epistle to the Gospel in the Chief Divine Service. In an assessment of the Ancient Church pericopes, Rudelbach remarks: "As the Old Testament begins with history, so does the New. As the historical material of the Old Testament forms a broad and firm foundation, so does that of the New. As in the Old Testament the didactic material in all places refers back to the historical foundation and can never be wholly understood apart from it, so also in the New. As in the Old Testament the *prophetic* material assumes both the historical and didactic material into a higher order and forms the living capstone of revelation, so also in the New. In a word: everything in Holy Scripture shows us the work of the divine Spirit, in which *act* and *word*, *doctrine* and *history* have become integrally linked and, as it were, intertwined" (*Sacrament-Worte* [Words of the Sacrament], etc., 130). Regarding the main content of the Epistle and Gospel together, we may therefore consider the succession of Epistle and Gospel as one of ascent,[196] and in the following way. The *Epistle* is either apostolic proclamation, sometimes as doctrine "unfolding the full riches of Christ," other times as exhortation occupied with the fruits of faith; or, on occasion, it is also a prophetic word, salvation prophecy (Christmas—Isaiah 9; Epiphany, the Marian feasts, and the feast of St. John). In <164> the Gospel, however, we face the prophetic word in its fulfillment, and behold the incarnate Word in His person and work for our salvation from His conception to His ascension, and hear from His mouth His very words (*ipsissima verba*), and see His signs and miracles. One might also remember here that verse:

---

is to be celebrated not as an unbloody propitiatory sacrifice but strictly as Communion under both forms as the sealing of the forgiveness of sins. This liturgy evinces a progressive increase of solemnity in its three readings of Old Testament Lesson, Epistle, and Gospel—the first by the lector from the south side of the altar access, the Epistle by the subdeacon on the north side of the same, and the Gospel by the priest or the ordained deacon before the altar gate, during which the reader always faces the congregation. In the Eastern Church, whether read or chanted, the Gospel is always attended by ceremonies altogether richer and more festive than in the Roman Church.

[196] *) In the Ancient Church, the reading of the Gospel was even done from a higher level of the chancel than that of the Epistle stand.

"built on the foundation of the apostles and prophets (Epistle), Christ Jesus himself being the cornerstone (Gospel)" [Ephesians 2:20]. That Luther also had a conception of this *ascent* from the Epistle to the Gospel is demonstrated by the quote given at the beginning, when he wished to use the *sextum tonum* for the Gospel as the pleasant voice of Christ, and the *octavum tonum* for the Epistle as the serious voice of the apostle.

The liturgical distinction of the Gospel gradually fell out of use, generally speaking. We know only of a handful of congregations here which have altar candles burning during the reading of the Gospel. In a few others, although no chanting of the Gospel takes place, the reading is introduced with the Salutation and Acclamation according to ancient custom. Even if it should no longer be possible to consider resuming the chanting of the pericope, the reading of the Gospel might nevertheless be distinguished by having candles burning in the manner mentioned above. It would be done as follows:

> Pastor chants (or speaks): "The Lord be with you!"
> Congregation sings: "And with thy spirit."
> Pastor speaks: "This (or The) Holy Gospel on (the first Sunday in Advent, etc.) is written by (St. Matthew, etc.) in the __ chapter, the __ verse. . . ."
> Congregation stands and sings: "Glory be to Thee, O Lord."
> Pastor reads the Gospel.

Immediately after this, the pastor intones the Creed. If a song by the choir is to intervene after the Gospel rather than after the Epistle, it can either come right after the Creed and before the Sermon or else after the Sermon.

As may also be seen from Luther's Works (StL 10 [:235ff.; AE 53:84ff.]), Luther not only composed rules for chanting the Gospel but even offered two melodies as an "*exercitatio,* or exercise, with the melody so that one could learn to use melodies and become accustomed to the colon, commas, and similar pauses." From these rules it may be seen that, at that time, it was chanted not only by one priest but also by three, of which one <165> delivered the narrative words of the evangelist (*vox evangelista*), the second the words of other persons (aside from Christ, *vox personarum*) and the third the words of Christ (*vox Christi*). With omission of these rules, we provide one of the melodies by way of example.

The Introduction

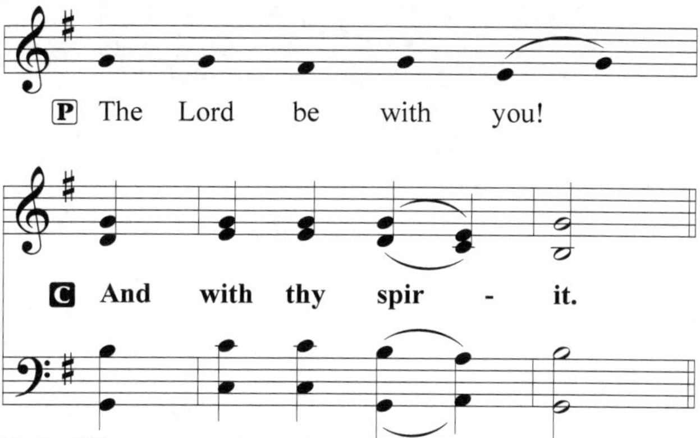

Vopelius, 1682

Or:

Hoya, 1581

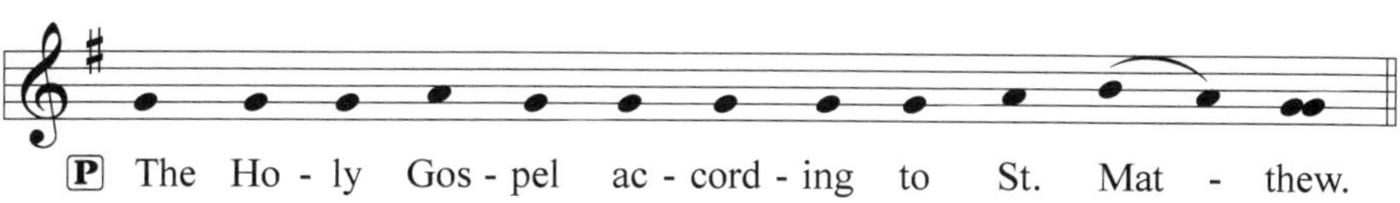

or:

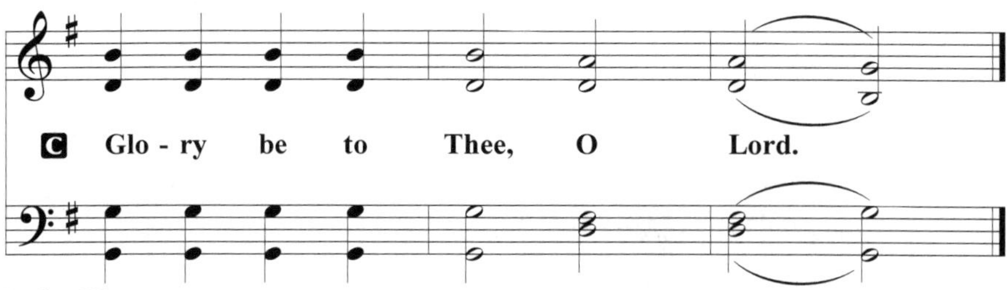

Vopelius, 1682

<166>

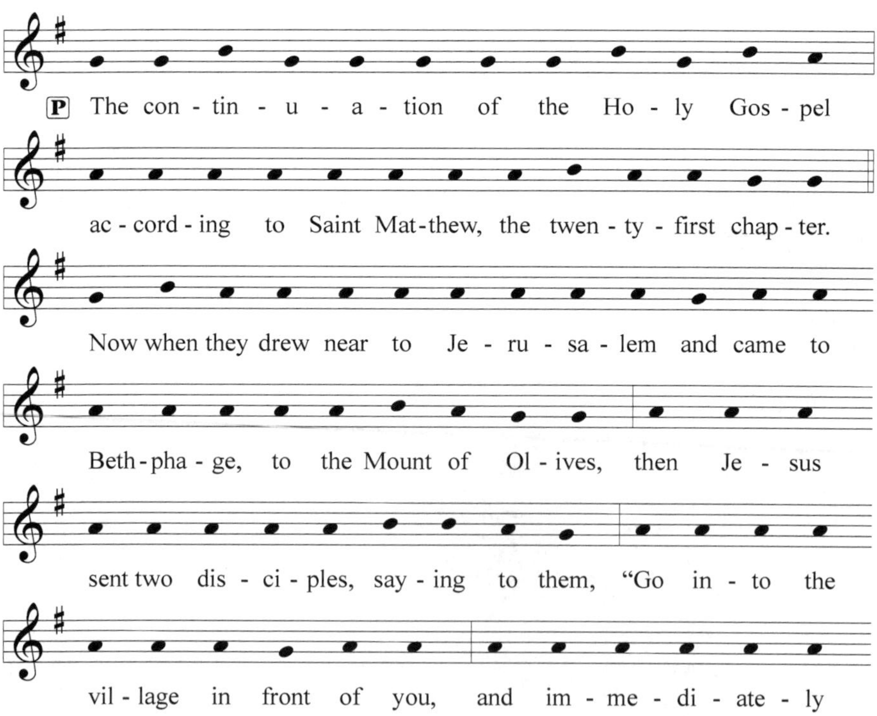

you will find a don - key tied, and a colt with her.
Un - tie them and bring them to me. If an - y - one says
an - y - thing to you, you shall say, ‘The Lord needs them,’
and he will send them at once.” This took place to ful - fill
what was spo - ken by the proph - et, say - ing,
<167>
“Say to the daugh - ter of Zi - on, ‘Be - hold, your king is
com-ing to you, hum - ble, and mount - ed on a don - key,
on a colt, the foal of a beast of bur - den.’”
The dis - ci - ples went and did as Je - sus had di - rect - ed them.
They brought the don - key and the colt and
put on them their cloaks, and he sat on them.
Most of the crowd spread their cloaks on the road,

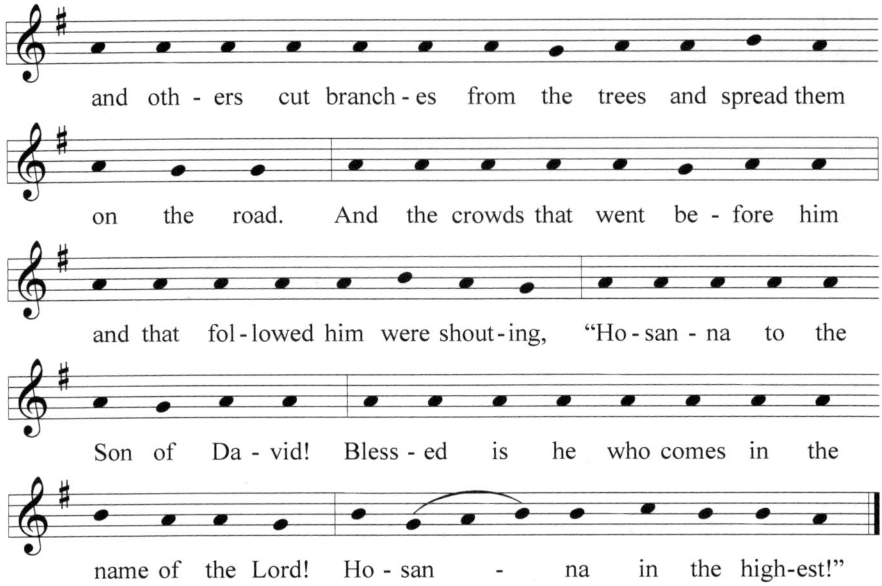

Braunschweig-Lüneburg, 1542

This is followed by the transition to the intonation of the Credo.[197] <168>

X. CREDO

In the aftermath of the Arian controversy, the Apostles' Creed was followed by the formation of the Nicene Creed, the second ecumenical confession. As early as the fifth century it found its use in the Chief Divine Service of the Eastern Church, but it was not until the end of the eighth century that the Western Church followed suit, and initially only in the Gallican Church when, at Emperor Henry's urging, Pope Benedict VIII incorporated it into the Mass.

After the reading of the Gospel, the priest, standing at the center of the altar, either speaks the whole Nicene Creed, or, if the Mass is festive in nature, intones, "Credo in unum Deum." Then the choir sings from "Patrem omnipotentem" (hence the name "Patrem") to the end. And as Luther implies in a sermon,[198] it was (as it still is) tradition at the words, "Et incarnatus est de Spiritu Sancto, ex Maria virgine: et homo factus est" [And was incarnate by the Holy Spirit of the virgin Mary and was made man], for priest and peo-

[197] *) For a different Gospel tone [than above], see StL 10:243ff., 253ff.

[198] Cf. Luther, *Sermons on John* (1537), AE 22:102–3. —MC.

ple to genuflect as a sign of adoration of the "indeed great mystery" [1 Timothy 3:16] of the incarnation of the Son. This custom was also followed to a certain extent in the Lutheran Church, in which a tradition appeared in the Austrian territories during the Reformation era, and afterward spread in part to Saxony, for the whole congregation to stand up at these words—as well as for those of Luther's *Patrem*: "Born of Mary, Virgin mother / By the power of the Spirit / Made true Man, our elder Brother, / That the lost might life inherit."[199]

In his *Deutsche Messe* (1526), Luther directs: "After the Gospel, the whole church sings the Creed in German: 'Wir glauben all an einen Gott' [We All Believe in One True God]. After that comes the sermon on the Gospel of the Sunday or feast day" [AE 53:78]. According to this, Luther follows the received practice of having the Credo come after the Gospel Lesson, while he introduces a change by making the sermon after the Credo an organic part of the Mass. In the Roman Mass, the sermon may even be omitted here, and often is, so that the Preface comes immediately after the Credo, the priest already saying the *secreta* during the Credo, whereby the Sermon seems more like an interjection. Originally, the Credo, too, belonged to the Service of the Sacrament (*missa fidelium*), and as such stands at the front of the Communion rite. <169> Since only believers are to approach the table of the Lord, everyone is to testify publicly through the Creed that he is a believer. This is the intent of the original placement of the Credo. Therefore in his *Formula Missae*, Luther says, "Concerning the German sermon, we do not think it is important whether it be held after the Patrem [Creed] or before the Introit, although reason might be shown why it would be better for it to be done before the Mass, since the Gospel is 'a voice crying in the wilderness' which is to invite unbelieving hearts to faith. *But the Mass is to be the use or enjoyment of the Gospel and distribution of the Sacrament, to which only believers are entitled,* and ought to be held in another place to the exception of unbelievers. Yet since we are free, this manner should not bind us or hold us captive" [AE 53:25]. Now since Luther in Christian freedom justly departed from this, the original practice and placed the sermon not before the Introit but after the Credo, it must be asked what *significance the latter has in this position.* It might well be this: *Following the Gospel,* the Creed is to be construed as oral confession of what the Church believes in her heart concerning God's nature and will according to the Gospel and through it, while *preceding the Sermon,* it simultaneously stands as a rule of faith (*regula fidei*) according to which the preacher is to expound the Word which has been read, in keeping with the apostle's instruction: "If anyone has prophecy, let it be in proportion to the faith" (Romans 12:6).

---

[199] See Luther's hymn, "Wir glauben all an einen Gott" (1524). Cf. *LSB* 954, stanza 2. —MC.

Even in the early days of the Lutheran Church, not only was Luther's *Patrem* sung, but so was the *Nicene Creed*, in some places in Latin, in some places in German, too. Yet it was always followed by Luther's hymn sung by the congregation, or else the recommendation was made that both be used in alternation "so that each might be practiced" (Veit Dietrich, *Agendbüchlein,* 1548). Frequently, however, there was a limitation of one Creed, the preferred version being that of Luther's sung by choir and congregation together, until in time it came to be used everywhere as a rule. Around 1680, Tobias Clausnitzer penned the so-called "*lesser*" Creed (see the St. Louis *Gesangbuch,* no. 184), which was then used in Divine Services in addition to the "greater" Creed, and was used on those occasions when a lengthier Chief Hymn was sung, or the number of communicants was large, or the circumstances otherwise called for some abbreviation. Master among them, however, remained the "greater" Creed, the Nicene Creed put into German verse. <170>

And such it remained together with its *majestic melody* with which it first appeared in Walther's *Chorgesangbüchlein* (1524), and then also in the Strassburg *Kirchenamt* (1525). Then, in the year 1790, Johann Christian Kittel [1732–1809], Bach's last pupil, devised his C major melody: *c c b-a g a d g e* (see also the 1886 St. Louis *Choralbuch,* no. 297), and so it was that this child of an age scarcely able to produce a church *hymn* or a church *melody* anymore suddenly and almost universally supplanted this tune of Luther's,[200] one of the most magnificent tunes in the Lutheran melodic treasury. With respect to this and many other superseded tunes of the Reformation, Palmer, in his response to the "new *Choralbuch*" (*Süddeutscher Schulbote,* 1845, no. 5), expresses the sigh: "Would to God we might sing such majestic chorales with our congregations! Perhaps when it becomes literally true again that we all believe in God, we will also learn to sing it better again." In our local churches and schools those majestic chorales of the Reformation period have (God be praised!) become familiar once more, and Luther's Credo is sung every Sunday and feast day in every place. It is even sung with *Luther's tune*, no less, in some places even from the beginning, in others alternating with Kittel's melody, the latter being used first. Unfortunately, however, a reverse tendency has already gained new ground here and there—not because learning Luther's tune

[200] *) Johann Walther, music director, ascribes this melody, like that of the German Sanctus ("Jesaia dem Propheten," etc.) to Luther, as does [Carl] von Winterfeld. However, since a versified German rendering of the Nicene Creed was already available to Luther, and a melody for it by Nicolaus von Kosel (1417) is to be found in manuscript form in the library of Bratislava, the melody, like the text, is probably a reworking, albeit a masterful one, by Luther.

became too difficult, but because the more ariatic melody of Kittel's is more agreeable to poor taste than that noble churchly tone free from all sentimentality. May this disadvantageous tendency gain no more ground, and Luther's tune rather retain supremacy in the Chief Divine Service!

Concerning *execution*, a few more points to remember:

1. As in the Roman Mass, so also in the Lutheran Chief Divine Service, the Credo was first **intoned** in Latin or German by the liturgist "facing the altar," standing at its center. Not only does intoning in this way correspond to the "Glory be to God on high!" of the Gloria, but by it the unsuitably *long* prelude <171> between the Gospel Lesson and the congregation's Credo naturally disappears, since the Gospel is followed either by the Responsory with the Credo intonation or the latter alone. Even where this is not the usual practice, only a few appropriate chords on the organ should introduce it. A lengthier organ prelude between the reading of the Gospel and the "We all believe," etc., is completely unacceptable.

In the hopes that intoning the Credo, which has long been practiced in several of our congregations, may gain wider acceptance, several intonations have been included here. The melody under "A," for Luther's Credo, is found consistently with that for the Gloria in the old agendas. That under "B" is taken from the Nürnberg *Agendbüchlein*, where it is found with Luther's Credo, while here it has been transposed for the "lesser" Creed (a.); the alternate form (b.) is used in a few of our local congregations. The melody under "C" is the festival form for a very beautiful Nicene Creed in German, set in D major and found in L. Lossius, *Psalmodia sacra* (1553, 1579), the Pomeranian church order (1563), Keuchenthal (Wittenberg, 1573), Ludecus's *Missale* (1589), the Nürnberg *Agendbüchlein* (1639), and from the latter in Hommel.[201]

2. Since the confession of the faith is to be done in a generally vigorous, forthright, and clear manner, Luther's powerful melody in particular must be sung **without sluggishness** of any kind, yet all the words must also be **enunciated with proper clarity**. To this end the organist can accomplish a great deal himself if, while playing, he keeps to the melody more as a staccato. It may be noted here that in many earlier works, the four slurred notes following the first note belong to the "We," by which, it is reported, Luther wished to indicate that the peoples scattered to the four corners were gathered into unity of the faith. The incipit of Luther's Credo accordingly went thus:

[201] Hommel, 13–16. —MC.

3. At the words: "Who the Church, His own creation," it is customary to ascend the pulpit.[202] <172>

4. It has been customary for the sake of variety, and particularly for feasts, not only to sing the Nicene Creed, but sometimes also to substitute for it the *Apostles'* Creed. Therefore the beautiful melody which appeared early on in the Strassburg *Kirchenamt* (1525), and then in several church orders of the sixteenth century, and was recently included by Hommel and Layriz, has been reproduced here. For the intonation, the pastor may also use the beginning of the melody with organ accompaniment by singing, "I believe in God the Father Almighty." Then the congregation continues, "Maker of heaven and earth." The author, in his previous congregation, experienced first-hand how a congregation, being familiar with the text, can be quickly taught to sing this melody after the choir.

5. Since the congregation stands during the reading of the Gospel, it is fitting that it remain standing during the intonation and first line of the Credo.

[202] *) An older Silesian pastor, whose trusty assistant used to remind him to ascend the pulpit by saying, "Pastor, sir, now 'all Christendom' [*die ganze Christenheit*] is coming," observes: "This phrase always fills my heart with wonder; it reminds me of my mighty ministry within the great host of all Christendom on behalf of the great host of all Christendom. All Christendom comes along with my congregation, even those who are now in triumph at the throne of the Lamb—they come to meet me—me, a lowly child of man with a faint heart and dull lips. And then I sigh from the depths of my heart: 'Oh, may that host of all Christendom not come in vain! Lord, help! Lord, be with me, that she may find You in me and through me.'" [This account, which for its effect depends on the phrase from Luther's creedal hymn, is also found in Eduard Emil Koch, et al., *Geschichte des Kirchenlieds und Kirchengesangs* . . . 8 vols., 2nd ed. (Stuttgart: Belser, 1853), 4:793f. —MC.]

1. Credo Intonations

A.

B.

or:

<173>

C.

2. A. The Apostles' Creed

<174>

C I be-lieve in God, the Fa - ther Al - might - y,
mak - er of heav-en and earth.
And in Je - sus Christ, His on - ly Son, our Lord,
who was con-ceived by the Ho - ly Spir - it,
born of the vir - gin Mar - y, suf-fered un - der

Pon - tius Pi - late, was cru - ci - fied, died
<175>
and was bur - ied. He de - scend-ed in - to hell. The
third day He rose a - gain from the dead. He a -
scend - ed in - to heav - en and sits at the
right hand of God the Fa - ther Al - might - y. From
<176>

Braunschweig-Lüneburg *Kirchenordenung,* 1542
Setting: F. Jubitz

B. The Nicene Creed

on - ly - be - got - ten Son of God, be - got - ten
of His Fa - ther be - fore all worlds. God of
God, Light of Light, ver - y God of ver - y
God, be - got - ten, not made, be - ing of one
sub - stance with the Fa - ther, by whom all

<179>

things were made; who for us men and for our sal-
va - tion came down from heav - en
and was in - car-nate by the Ho - ly Spir - it
of the vir - gin Mar - y and was made
man; and was cru-ci-fied al - so for us

<180>

un-der Pon-tius Pi - late. He suf-fered and was bur - ied.
And the third day He rose a - gain ac - cording to the
Scrip-tures and as-cend-ed in - to heav - en and
sits at the right hand of the Fa - ther. And He will

<181>

come a - gain with glo - ry to judge both the liv - ing
and the dead, whose king - dom will have no end.
And I be - lieve in the Ho - ly Spir - it, the Lord and
giv-er of life, who pro - ceeds from the Fa - ther

and the Son, who with the Fa - ther and the Son to -
geth - er is wor - shiped and glo - ri - fied, who
spoke by the proph - ets. And I be - lieve in one
<182>
ho - ly Chris - tian and ap - os - tol - ic Church, I ac -

Music: Lucas Lossius, 1553. Pomeranian C. O. 1563. Wittenberg *Kirchengeseng* 1573. Ludecus *Missale* 1589, etc.
Setting: Dr. Herzog.

XI. THE SERMON
AND ITS RELATED & ADJACENT CEREMONIES

A.
1. THE SERMON

Of the three great abuses of the papistic Divine Service generally, Luther, in his writing, "Concerning the Order of Public Worship" (1523), characterizes as the first and worst abuse the fact "that God's Word has been silenced, and is only read and sung in the churches." For this reason he desires "that *the Christian congregation should never come together unless God's Word is preached and prayed there,* though it be in the briefest manner." Indeed, "the whole of Scripture shows this, and Christ Himself says in Luke 10 [:42]: '*One thing is needful,' i.e., that Mary sit at Christ's feet and hear His Word daily. That is the best portion which is to be chosen and will never be taken away. It is an eternal Word. Everything else must pass away, no matter how much work it makes for Martha.'* God grant it to us. Amen." (EA 22:154, 156; StL 10:220, 225.)[203]

And thus he appointed the sermon to be a *chief part* of the purified Mass. And although he was at first inclined in his *Formula Missae* to place the sermon *before* the entire Mass for the sake of its evangelizing character,[204] nevertheless, he eventually inserted it in his *Deutsche Messe* (1526) in the position <184> where it is now found in every Lutheran Chief Divine Service in the world. In this position, however, it becomes a sort of *caesura* (resting point) in the progress of the liturgy, where Mary sits at the Lord's feet, as well as a *crescendo* (high point), from which the celebrating congregation proceeds to the second crescendo, the Sacrament, as the seal of that Word.

The *text* for the sermon of the Chief Divine Service was the Gospel of the day or feast, while in one of the incidental Divine Services preceding or following the Chief Divine Service—Sunday Matins or Sunday Vespers—the Epistle was preached. Only later was any variation between the Gospel and the Epistle permitted with respect to the sermon of the Chief Divine Service. Though previously read at the altar, the Gospel was read again from the pulpit, especially if it had been read *choraliter* at the altar.

---

[203] Cf. Luther, "Concerning the Order of Public Worship" (1523), AE 53:11, 14.

[204] Cf. Luther, "An Order of Mass and Communion" (1523), AE 53:25, the seventh point. —MC.

Now, where variation occurred was in the *introduction* to the sermon. According to Luther's precedent in the House Postils, a standard opening was used for the reading of the text and for the sermon.[205] It was an exhortation to prayer for the fruitful handling of the Word, this prayer consisting of an Our Father, which in some places the preacher said aloud, and in some places the preacher was joined by all in praying silently—a directive that was likely made with reference to Revelation 8:1, Habakkuk 2:20, and Isaiah 14:7. Later, a short hymn *de tempore* was inserted between the audible or silent Our Father and the reading of the text, or else before the Our Father, while other contemporaneous church orders prescribe for the opening, along with the Our Father, an invariable opening prayer, as may be seen from the formularies included below. Still other church orders of the post-Reformation period provide for a free opening to the sermon—this being, however, not an introduction to the theme of the sermon, but only further exhortation to prayer. For example, it says in the Braunschweig-Lüneburg church order of Duke August (1657):

> Before the sermon, the preacher is to speak the usual *votum*: "The grace, peace, and mercy of God the heavenly Father, His only-begotten Son, Jesus Christ, and the Holy Spirit, be and abide with us henceforth and forever. Amen." Then let him exhort the people to Christian prayer, that God would grant them His Holy Spirit to handle His Holy Word profitably, and to take it to heart, that they may amend their sinful life, find consolation and strengthening of their faith, and henceforth live a Christian life, and finally die a blessed death. Immediately after that, let him join with the congregation in praying <185> the Our Father silently, the whole congregation kneeling with him.[206] But before this let the hymn "To God the Holy Spirit Let Us Pray," etc., be sung at certain times; likewise at Christmas: "Ein Kindelein so löbelich" ["A Little Child so Praiseworthy"], etc.; and on Pentecost: "Komm, Heiliger Geist, Herre Gott" ["Come, Holy Ghost, God and Lord"], etc. When the prayer is finished, let the text of the Sunday or festival Gospel be read according to blessed Luther's version, and then let the sermon begin."[207]

[205] See, for example, WA 52:10, lines 1–8. Cf. Eugene Klug, ed., *Sermons of Martin Luther: The House Postils,* 3 vols. (Grand Rapids: Baker Books, 1996); reprinted as vols. 5–7 of *The Complete Sermons of Martin Luther* (Grand Rapids: Baker Books, 2000). A new translation of Luther's House Postils is projected for future volumes of AE. —MC.

[206] *) Of the preacher's kneeling *upon entering the pulpit,* as is now the practice here and there, there is nothing to my knowledge in the earlier church orders.

[207] *Agenda oder: Erster Teyl der Kirchen-Ordnung* . . . (1657), 15f. —MC.

The hymns identified here are also indicated as pulpit hymns in the Schwarzburg Agenda (1675).[208]

Regarding the *duration* of the sermon in the Chief Divine Service, the Braunschweig-Lüneburg church order (1657) specifies "that all preachers in cities and rural areas should avoid and refrain from long sermons and should not preach *more than three quarters of an hour, or a scant hour at most.*"[209] Thus at that time, a sermon of three-quarters of an hour was not considered lengthy.

2. The Ceremonies Related and Adjacent to the Sermon

(a) The Confiteor, or Corporate Confession

In close parallel with the Roman Mass (see the table above in Part One [pp. 46–51]), a number of old church orders and agendas place the *Confiteor or General Confession at the beginning* of the Chief Divine Service. Among these we find in Löhe's *Sammlung liturgischer Formulare* [Collection of Liturgical Formulas] (1839) reference to Andreas Döber's *Evangelische Meß im neuen Spital zu Nürnberg* [Evangelical Mass in the New Hospice at Nürnberg] (1525), the *Straßburgisches deutsches Kirchenamt* [Strassburg German Church Office] (1525); Brandenburg (-Ansbach) and Nürnberg (1533); Wittenberg (1559, 1563); Mecklenburg (1552, 1650); Frankfurt am Main (1565); Lüneburg (1564, 1569); Lippe (1571); Oldenburg (1573); Liegnitz (1594), etc.

The form and manner of the Confiteor in this position is as follows:

Standing at the steps of the altar, the liturgist says: "In the name of the Father and of the Son and of the Holy Spirit. Amen. Dearly beloved in God, open your hearts and let us confess our sins to God, beseeching Him in the name of our Lord Jesus Christ to grant us forgiveness. Speak after me with sincere desire to God, in faith in the Lord Jesus Christ, through the Holy

---

[208] *Agenda Schwartzburgica* (1675), 37ff. The full list includes for Advent:" "Gott durch deine Güte" or "Herr Christ, der einig Gotts Sohn." Christmas: "Ein Kindelein so löbelich." New Year: "Ein Kindelein . . ." or "Jesu nun sei gepreiset." Purification: "Herr nun lässest du deinen Diener" or the German Magnificat. Annunciation: "Herr Christ, der einig . . ." or the German Magnificat. Lent: "O Lamm Gottes unschuldig" or "Ehre sei dir Christe." Easter: "Also heilig ist der Tag." Ascension: "Christ fuhr gen Himmel." Pentecost: "O heiliger Geist, du Göttliches Feuer" or "Nun bitten wir den heiligen Geist." Trinity and Sundays following: "Die heilig Dreifaltigkeit wohn uns bei" or "Nun bitten wir . . ." or (as on other Sundays also) "Herr Jesu Christ, dich zu uns wend." St. John and Visitation: "Herr Christ der einig . . ." or the Benedictus or the Magnificat in German. Michael: "Gelobet sei der ewige Gott" or "Es stehn für Gottes Throne." —MC.

[209] *Agende Oder: Erster Teyl der Kirchen-Ordnung* . . . (Wolfenbüttel: Sterne, 1657), 18. —MC.

Spirit." Hereupon the pastor kneels down with the congregation, speaks responsively with them: "Our help is in the name," etc. <186> "I said, I will confess," etc., and then continues by himself: "I, a poor, miserable sinner, confess to Almighty God, my Maker and Redeemer, that I have not only sinned in thought, word, and deed, but am also conceived and born in sin, and my whole nature and being is worthy of punishment and condemnation before His righteousness. Wherefore I flee for refuge to His infinite mercy, seeking and imploring His grace. O Lord, be merciful to me, a poor sinner." The congregation says: "May our gracious God have mercy upon us, pardon our sins, and give us the Holy Spirit, that through Him we may accomplish His godly will and receive eternal life. Amen." The liturgist now ascends the altar and says to the congregation as they remain kneeling: "Incline your hearts to God. The almighty and merciful God has had mercy upon us, and has given His only Son into death for our sins, and for His sake has granted us pardon. And to all who believe in His holy name He has given the power to become the children of God, and promised them the Holy Spirit. Whoever believes and is baptized shall be saved. God grant it to us all. Amen." (Yet some church orders also use in this place the rite of Confession and Absolution which elsewhere has become the general practice after the sermon.)

After Luther's precedent, however, many other church orders and agendas assign to the Confiteor its place *after the sermon*. In his *Deutsche Messe* (1526), Luther adds a remark to the paraphrase of the Our Father and the exhortation to communicants, between the Sermon and the Consecration (see the St. Louis Agenda, 93ff.), saying: "Whether this paraphrase and exhortation should be done *from the pulpit directly after the sermon* or in front of the altar I leave free to each man according to his discretion. It seems as though the ancients used to do it from the pulpit; hence the speaking of the general prayer or recitation of the Our Father has continued to be done from the pulpit, but *the exhortation has become a public confession*. The Our Father, with a short explanation, would thus remain among the people, and there would be a remembrance of the Lord, even as He commanded at the Supper."[210] In full agreement with this, Bugenhagen, as the "pastor of Wittenberg," soon published *Ein Ordnung Christlicher Meß* [An Order of Christian Mass] (1524),[211] which says: "Then (namely, after delivering the sermon) he (the pastor), returning to the altar or remaining in the pulpit, may address those in attendance with these or other words:

[210] Cf. Luther, "The German Mass and Order of Service" (1526), AE 53:80. —MC.

[211] Contained in the book *Von der Evangelischen Meß, was die Meß sey . . .* (Wittenberg, 1524) and "translated from the Latin." This passage is found on the verso of folio B3v. —MC.

'Dearly beloved in Christ! That you may with a glad and <187> eager heart receive the tender body and crimson blood of our Redeemer Jesus Christ, humble your hearts to God, confess your sins and transgressions to Him with sincere desire and longing for His divine grace and assistance, and I, your chosen priest, will presently administer to you the Holy Absolution." While a formula for Confession is not then indicated, there follows not only a formula of Absolution but also after this "the Confession of the priest." And it continues: "The almighty and merciful God forgive you your sins. And at the command of our Lord Jesus Christ and in the stead of the Holy Church I declare you free, released, and absolved from all your sins in the name of the Father and of the Son and of the Holy Spirit. Amen. And because I also am burdened with many trespasses, therefore implore God faithfully on my behalf, that I may diligently carry out and accomplish this His service to His glory and to our comfort and salvation; as it is written in Psalm 123: 'Our help is in the name of the Lord, who made heaven and earth.'" In close parallel with Luther and Bugenhagen, then, Confession and Absolution are also found as the conclusion to the beautiful Communion exhortation by the Augustinian Prior from Nürnberg, Johann [Wolfgang] Volprecht, similarly dating to the year 1524. This Communion exhortation passed over into a number of agendas, and thus into the St. Louis Agenda, pp. 223–235. After the words: "for we are all one bread and one body, inasmuch as we are all partakers of one bread and drink of one cup," the words continue: "And since we all have sinned and are in need of God's grace, humble your hearts before Almighty God, confess your sins and trespasses, and with that public sinner say: 'God, be merciful to me, a poor sinner!' with sincere love and desire for His divine grace and assistance, with firm faith and trust in His gracious promise, forgiving everyone his neighbor from his heart, that your heavenly Father may also forgive your sins and iniquities. Upon your doing so, therefore, in the stead of the Holy Christian Church by the command and promise of our Lord Jesus Christ, when He said, 'Whose sins you forgive, they are forgiven him,' I release you from all your sins in the name of the Father and of the Son and of the Holy Spirit. Amen."[212] How often the present author heard <188> the exhortation with this conclusion in the churches of Nürnberg! In the same manner, a Divine Service order from Wittenberg (1559) contains an admirable formula in which Confession, Absolution, exhortation to prayer, and a general prayer are united in a beautiful whole so that Confession is given all the more preference *after* the sermon, while the

[212] *) Was it perhaps this corporate confession of sins before the Supper which Osiander refused to see practiced alongside private confession and because of which the disputes around confession arose in Nürnberg?

Wittenberg form has the advantage of making clear the connection between the Confiteor and the preceding sermon and the following Supper. Only a lack of space prevents the author from sharing this form.[213]

Meanwhile, in the church order of Duke Erich II (1544), we find another form of the Confiteor following the sermon. This begins, first of all, with an exhortation to prayer which is discharged in the Our Father. Then, with a brief introductory exhortation, come the Apostles' Creed and the Ten Commandments, and then with reference to these, confessional formulas and Absolution. But from about 1569 or so, as far as the author is able to determine, the form of the Confiteor became usual in the place where we have it now, and was increasingly adopted in that position anywhere it had not already had its place at the beginning of the Divine Service; the only distinction being that the Absolution still included a Retention. Such was the form in Erich's church order, where it says after the Absolution: "But

[213] *Kirchenordnung: Wie es mit Christlicher Lere, reichung der Sacrament, Ordination der Diener des Evangelii, ordentlichen Ceremonien in den Kirchen, Visitation, Consistorio und Schulen . . . gehalten wird* (Wittenberg: Lufft, 1559), beginning on the verso of folio 89v. It is important to note that in the original church order, this Confession is placed before the Introit and is not connected to the General Prayer, so that it seems Lochner is thinking of another order: "Mass, or Communion. As instituted and practiced in several territories, it shall begin with general or public confession, prayer, and absolution, initiated by the priest as follows. Let the priest turn from the altar to the people and say: 'My dearly beloved in God, open your hearts. Let us confess our sins to God and pray for forgiveness in the name of our Lord Jesus Christ. Repeat after me with sincere desire to God, in faith in the Lord Jesus Christ, through the Holy Spirit." Then the priest kneels before the altar, and a ministrant or clerk with him, and the priest says with a loud voice, "Our help is in the name of the Lord." The choir responds: "Who made heaven and earth." The priest: "I, a poor sinner, confess to You, O Almighty God, my Maker and Redeemer, that I have sinned, not only in thought, word, and deed, but also that I am by nature sinful and unclean, conceived and born in sin. Yet I flee for refuge to Your infinite mercy, seeking and desiring grace for the sake of the Lord Jesus Christ. O Lord, be merciful to me, a poor sinner." The other ministrant responds to this prayer: "O Almighty, merciful God, who gave Your only begotten Son into death for us, have mercy on us, and for the sake of the same Your beloved Son forgive us all our sins; and give us Your Holy Spirit, to kindle and increase in us true knowledge of Your godly ways and will, and true obedience toward You, that by Your grace we may obtain eternal life for the sake of the Lord Jesus Christ. Amen." After this, the priest speaks this Absolution: "The Almighty and merciful God has had mercy on us, truly forgives us all our sins for the sake of His Son whom He gave into death for us, and has given us power to become the children of God to all who believe in His name; and gives us His Holy Spirit to that end. Whoever believes and is baptized shall be saved. God grant it to us all. Amen." While this Confession, prayer, and Absolution is spoken, the whole church shall be quiet and hear it, and with the priest likewise confess, pray, and take the Absolution to heart, learn it well, and often speak in like manner before God. Afterward the choir sings the Introit . . ." The unremarkable rubric for the General Prayer, however, is found after the sermon, beginning on folio 93r. —MC.

as for those who have not heartily confessed their sins nor set the confidence of their heart upon the merits of Christ, the wrath of God remains on them." [214] We find Absolution *with* Retention in the church orders of Braunschweig-Lüneburg (1657)[215] and Magdeburg (1663);[216] likewise, in those of Pomerania, Silesia, and others, in which the *Retention* usually appears in this form: "But on the basis of God's Word and in the name of Jesus Christ I say to all unrepentant, unbelieving, self-secure despisers of God, of His Word, and of the most Holy Sacraments, that God has retained their sins and will surely punish them in time and eternity, if they do not cease and repent in the season of grace. And such repentance we heartily wish for them, desiring that they be admonished to the same." An Absolution *without* this special *Retention* is contained, for example, in the various Saxon agendas.

In the event that the Confiteor *follows* the sermon, it serves in connection with the sermon as the *exercise and application of the Law and Gospel proclaimed in the sermon;* while in connection with the subsequent *General Prayer*, it serves as an instruction to draw near to God in the General Prayer, boldly and confidently, being all the more assured of God's grace in the forgiveness of sins. <189> This is also what the introductory words express to every person, in the form in which they appear in their respective agendas. The introduction to Confession runs: "Having heard God's Word, let us now also humble ourselves before God's high Majesty, and begin by confessing and saying thus: . . ." And the transition to the prayer as, for example, in the Leipzig Agenda (1681): "Forasmuch as our gracious and merciful God has forgiven our sins and iniquities, let us also lay before Him the needs of all Christendom, and so join one another in prayer." This connection of the Confiteor with the Sermon, and especially with the "General Prayer" is at the front of Luther's mind as already in 1520 he writes in his *Sermon on Good Works*:

> A vestige of this General Prayer has remained from ancient custom, *when at the end of the sermon, in the pulpit, the confession of sins is recited and prayer is made for all Christendom.* But that should not be the end of the matter, as is now the custom and practice. Rather,

[214] *Christliche Kirchen Ordnung, Ceremonien und Gesenge* . . . (Erfurt: Sachse, 1542), folio 103v. —MC.

[215] *Agenda Oder: Erster Teyl der Kirchen-Ordnung* . . . (1657), 25f. —MC.

[216] *Ertz Stifftische Magdeburgische Kirchen Agenda* . . . (Halle: C. Salfeld, 1663). While conditions for absolution are found here, e.g., in the instruction of a catechumen prior to the Absolution (p. 36f.), a Retention of Sins, as such, seems to be absent from the absolution formula proper. —MC.

> there should be an exhortation to pray throughout the whole Mass for such needs as the preacher urges. *And that we may pray worthily, he first admonishes us of our sins and thereby humbles us; which should be done as briefly as possible, so that then the people may together lament their own sins before God, and pray for everyone with earnestness and faith.* Oh, if only (please God!) some congregation still heard Mass and prayed in this way, so that a collective and earnest cry from the heart of the whole people might ascend to God—what immeasurable virtue and help would follow from such prayer! What greater work could be done on earth, by which so many godly people would be sustained and so many sinners converted? For surely, the Christian Church on earth has no greater power or work than this collective supplication against all that may befall her. The evil one knows it well, which is why he does all that he can to hinder this prayer (EA 20:241–42).[217]

Regarding the Confiteor's relationship to prayer, a similar sentiment is expressed by the church order of Hesse, printed in Marburg in 1566:

> What greater and more excellent thing could we desire of God than that our sins should be forgiven us for the sake of Christ? For this alone we ought to be heartily careful and attentive. For how will we pray for others or do something fruitful in the Christian assembly if we are not earnestly reconciled with God? Yet if we seek <190> forgiveness of sins from God, it is necessary that we earnestly humble ourselves before Him and acknowledge and confess that we are poor sinners. For this reason these three things—true humility, confession or admission with remorse and sorrow for sins, and faithful prayer for the forgiveness of sins for the sake of Christ—ought to be done after the singing in the Christian congregation.[218]

And however much this last idea may be cited in favor of placing the Confiteor *at the beginning* of the Chief Divine Service, nevertheless, taking everything into consideration, *the placement of the Confiteor after the sermon and before the Prayer of the Church deserves precedence.*

The practice of the whole assembly kneeling during this Confession, based on ancient custom in agreement with the church orders, is still found in the congregations of the separated Free Church of Germany and

[217] Cf. Luther, "Treatise on Good Works" (1520), AE 44:65–66. —MC.

[218] *Kirchen Ordnung: Wie sich die Pfarherrn und Seelsorger in irem beruff mit leren und predigen, allerley Ceremonien und guter Christlicher Disciplin unnd Kirchenzucht halten sollen: Für die Kirchen inn dem Fürstenthumb Hessen . . .* (Marburg: A. Kolbe & heirs, 1566), folio 69r. —MC.

in many of our local congregations which have immigrated, namely, out of the separated Lutheran Church of Prussia. Remaining seated in any event is inappropriate.

(B) The Prayer of the Church with Intercessions, etc.

Since the corporate prayer of the faithful gathered in the name of Jesus has a glorious promise in Matthew 18:19, and Paul exhorts in 1 Timothy 2:1–4 regarding assemblies of the Divine Service, "First of all . . . that supplications, prayers, intercessions, and thanksgivings be made for all people, for kings and all who are in high positions . . . ," the *"General Prayer for various necessities"* received its liturgical position as early as the second century. In this place it stood largely as a transition from the Mass of the catechumens to the Mass of the faithful. In the third century, it was brought more explicitly into connection with Communion, in some places preceding, in other places following, the Consecration. In the Roman Mass, in keeping with the whole idea of the Mass as sacrifice, it surrounds the Consecration.[219]

For the Lutheran Chief Divine Service, certain church orders of the Reformation period insert the General Prayer of the Church earlier with the Lessons, which is to say, *before* the Sermon. Nevertheless, most church orders have it in our position.

Where there is variation, it is in the *form*. After Luther's precedent in his *Deutsche Messe,* [AE 53:78ff.] as well as in his *House Postils* ("Eine gemeine Form, wie zum Beschluß <191> der Predigt das Volk zum gemeinen Gebet soll vermahnet werden") [A General Form, Whereby at the Conclusion of the Sermon, the People Should Be Exhorted to Common Prayer; WA 52:732f.], the Prayer consisted, according to one group of church orders, of the *Our Father* with a preceding *Exhortation*, in which the things to be prayed for collectively in the Our Father are announced, and at the same time those specially requested intercessions and thanksgivings are identified explicitly. This is the case in the agendas of Breslau (1526), Lüneburg (1569 and 1598), Oldenburg (1573), Nürnberg, etc. Frequently the Our Father was followed by the invariable hymn, "Lord, Keep Us Steadfast in Thy Word" with "Grant Peace, We Pray, in Mercy Lord,"[220] which were viewed as belonging to the Prayer of the Church. It was nevertheless the *direct form of prayer*, of which other agendas make use from an early period, that became the dominant one. The most widely disseminated form of the

[219] That is, in the form of litanies and prayers said secretly, as discussed above, p. 42 f. —MC.

[220] Wackernagel 3:26, no. 45; cf. 3:21, no. 35; 3:26, no. 43; *LSB* 777/778. —MC.

General Prayer of this kind originates in the middle of the sixteenth century and was already included in the Baden Agenda (1556)[221] and in that of Duke Wolfgang (1557).[222] It existed with different openings in many different expansions and variations. Besides that, traces of it are also found in many other independent forms of the General Prayer, and here and there one part or another of this primitive form of the General Prayer is encountered unexpectedly. Its first paragraph, for example—the petition for the teaching estate—is reproduced exactly in the St. Louis Agenda's "Prayer of the Church," as is the petition for the afflicted and persecuted.[223]

Additionally, the use of special *festival prayers* in the Chief Divine Service does not belong to a later period, but is dated to the end of the sixteenth century.

Among the *special intercessions* and *thanksgivings* following the General Prayer of the Church, the intercession for the communicants is everywhere placed first.[224] Any public deprecation or an excommunication to be made is inserted in the proper place. <192>

According to the Braunschweig-Lüneburg order, the *Our Father* is to follow these intercessions, etc., immediately, which is to say, *before* prayers are made for the rest of the church announcements "so that the whole congregation may be left undisturbed in their devotion until the end of the prayer." [225] The invitation to pray the Our Father is made, according to the church order of Oels (1592), with approximately these words: "*This need and every other in Christendom, and whatsoever need and concern each*

[221] *Kirchenordnung, Wie die inn der Marggraveschafft Baden . . . soll angericht und gehalten werden* (Tübingen, 1556), beginning on p. lxxviii. —MC.

[222] *Kirchenordnung wie es mit der Christenlichen Leer, Raichunge der heiligen Sacramenten, . . . gehalten werden soll.* (Nürnberg: Johann von Berg & Ulrich Neuber, 1557). Preliminary notes are found on p. ciiii, with the opening and prayer proper on p. cv. —MC.

[223] *Kirchen-Agende für evangelisch-lutherischen Gemeinden* (1856), 44–46. —MC.

[224] *) Formularies for the special intercessions and thanksgivings in this location using the direct-prayer form could not be found by the author. The indirect form was probably used beforehand as briefly as possible. Thus, for example, in the Braunschweig-Lüneburg Church Order (1657) it reads: "Prayer or thanksgiving for the sick, those with child, or others, etc., is to be made briefly in this place." In the Schwarzburg church order (1657 [1675]), only the following "Formula of Intercession for Communicants" is found: "In our prayer let us also include those persons who now intend to go to the Holy Supper of the Lord, numbering __. The Almighty God, who has given them the desire, work in them the fulfilment also, and mercifully grant that they may receive this holy food not to their judgment but to the salvation and blessedness of their soul for the sake of Jesus Christ. Amen." Other intercessions, etc., would then no doubt have been made according to this form.

[225] *Agenda oder Erster Teyl . . .*, 30. —MC.

man has and is aware of, let us bring before God in the name of Christ His Son, in our devout, faithful, and humble prayer and Our Father."[226]

A remark not irrelevant even for today's preacher is also found in the Braunschweig-Lüneburg church order first mentioned, and runs: "Then he reads the General Prayer to the congregation in a *relatively slow, loud, and distinct* manner." With the weakness of the flesh and the necessary use every Sunday of the same formula, the preacher can easily fall prey to the danger of a hurried and irreverent recitation.[227] The same church order also recommends that the whole congregation *kneel* during the Our Father.[228] Yet the congregation ought to remain *standing* not only during the Our Father but also during the Prayer of the Church, as was always the custom from ancient times, especially on Sundays and feasts.

The rest of the *church announcements*, for which it seems the congregation was seated, closed in many places with an "*Exhortation to make an offering for the poor.*" Thus it reads in the Frankfurt *Agendbüchlein* (1688): "Be always faithful and diligent to assist the poor and sick with your prayers and contributions for the Lord's sake." Likewise in the Oels Agenda (1592): "In conclusion, assist the poor, and remember the charity fund, the almshouse, and those without means who have a good reputation."[229] Here, then, would be the appropriate place for the announcement of the collects for special purposes of the Church.

The *closing votum: "The peace of God, which surpasses,"* etc. is found everywhere. <193>

B.

1. Opening Formulas for the Sermon

(a)

That we may render service this day to our dear Lord God, and hallow the day of rest according to His command by spending it in the Word of God, which alone is holy and makes all things holy, let us now listen to

[226] See Friedrich Lochner, *Liturgische Formulare für etliche Handlungen und Acte, nebst Gebeten, Collecten und einem Anhang* (St. Louis: Concordia Publishing House, 1895), 195. —MC.

[227] *) It is for this reason unacceptable that many a preacher arbitrarily permits himself all manner of abbreviations in the Prayer of the Church. He is the mouth of the congregation, and it is precisely those who pray along devoutly, and on whom the words have thus been impressed, that find this whim of the pastor's painful and offensive.

[228] *Agenda oder Erster Teyl . . .*, 30. —MC.

[229] See Lochner, *Liturgische Formulare*, 195. —MC.

the Holy Gospel, and ask God for grace so to hear it that He may be glorified, our faith be strengthened, and our life be amended. Pray an Our Father. (Luther, *Hauspostille*: "Eine gemeine Vorrede auf die Hauspredigten" [WA 52:10].)

(B)

Dear devout friends in Christ! Let us ask God for the Holy Spirit to be with His divine Word, that He may lead us into all truth and sanctify our hearts in the true knowledge and fear of God, that we may hear His divine Word for our divine instruction, consolation, and amendment, and by virtue of it live eternally in the faith of Jesus Christ; in whose name say: "Our Father," etc.

Reminder: "In this prayer, the preachers may also refer to the text which they intend to preach, and the occasion of the feasts, and draw from them reasons and conclusions by which to exhort the Christian congregation to pray for the grace of the Holy Spirit to be with the Word of God." (Pomerania, 1568, 1691.)

(C)

Grace, peace, and mercy be with us all from God our dear heavenly Father, through Jesus Christ His beloved Son, our Lord, with the Holy Spirit, now and unto all ages. Amen.

Beloved in the Lord! Let us together call heartily upon the almighty, eternal, merciful God, our faithful Father in heaven, imploring the grace, help, and assistance of the Holy Spirit, that we may so listen to and dispose of His holy, divine Word, that by it His glorious name may be honored, our weak faith be strengthened, and our sinful life be truly amended. For the obtaining of these and all good things from God Almighty, pray to the Lord and sing together from your heart: "To God the Holy Spirit Let Us Pray . . ."[230]

Next, also say a holy *Our Father*. (Frankfurt am Main, 1688.) <194>

2. Opening Prayers for the Sermon

(A)

Almighty God, dear heavenly Father, forasmuch as all our salvation depends on our having a right understanding of Your Holy Word, grant to us all who are gathered in the name of Your Son that, our hearts being freed from all worldly affairs, we may hear and lay hold of Your Holy

[230] *) According to the Schwarzburg Agenda (1650), the so-called pulpit hymn is to vary according to the occasion of the feast.

Word with all diligence and earnest desire, that from it we may rightly discern Your fatherly will and live according to it, for the honor and praise of Yourself, the fruitful amendment of our neighbor, and the eternal salvation of us all; through Your Son, our Lord and Savior Jesus Christ. Amen. (Hanau, 1659.)[231]

(B)

O Almighty God, heavenly Father, at Your bidding we have come into Your house to pray and to hear Your saving Word, that we may obtain instruction, consolation, and refreshment for our souls. But because, alas, our hearts and understanding are darkened, and by nature powerless, sluggish, and drowsy to hear it, and our mind is weak to observe and keep it; therefore we humbly implore You to open our mouth, ears, heart, and mind by Your Holy Spirit, that we may rightly learn Your Holy Word, and with hearty desire, eagerness, and devotion attend to it, and from it learn to know You, and be strengthened in faith and godliness; that, in the midst of all trials and needs, we may have powerful comfort thereof in the face of sin, death, and the devil, until our last breath, and so attain to life everlasting; through Jesus Christ, our Lord. Amen. (Limburg, 1666.)[232]

(C)

Christ, Truth and Life, we implore You / that unto us who adore You
Your Spirit from heaven, / With all His gifts may be given,
That Your Word on earth may surely / Be preached and taught purely.
Grant that the Scripture here sounded / Be rightly grasped and expounded.
Let it spread and flourish / Our heart so to pierce and nourish,
Yours be the glory. In common / Now answer we "Amen." Amen.[233]
(This hymn from the year 1550 which was presented for singing might also lend itself to the opening prayer.) <195>

---

231 *Hanawische vermehrte Kirchen unndt Schul-Ordnung* (Strassburg: J. Pickel, 1659), 51. —MC.

232 *Limpurgische Kirchen-Ordnung: Wie es beedes mit der Lehr, und Ceremonien . . . soll gehalten werden* (Schwäbisch Hall: Laidig, 1666), 337, where it is curiously titled "Festival Prayer: a common Sunday and Festival Prayer, before the sermon." —MC.

233 This two-stanza hymn by Michael Weisse is first found in the Bohemian Brethren *Kirchengeseng* (1531), with the superscription: "Sung when the Gospel has been read, before it is expounded; to the tune '*Begeren wir*.'" A literal rendering of the German is: "O Christ, truth and life, we implore You to give us Your Spirit from above with His sacred gifts, that Your Word may be proclaimed in purity here on earth. O grant that the words before us may be rightly explained and understood. Let them prosper and pierce our heart to the praise and glory of Your name. Now let us say, Amen. Amen." —MC.

XII. THE OFFERTORY

In the apostolic age, the celebration of the Holy Supper was clearly preceded by a love-feast (*agape*) to which wealthier Christians brought food and drink, namely bread and wine, and shared these with those less fortunate. From this was set aside whatever bread and wine was needed for the subsequent Supper. When in the first half of the second century, for compelling reasons, the agapes were brought to an end and the celebration of the Supper was joined to the mid-morning preaching service, the tradition of offering the elements of bread and wine necessary for the celebration of the Supper, as voluntary offerings of the congregants, was carried over from this connection with the agape, and the receiving of these gifts by the clergy was counted as a formal affirmation of the church community (no gifts for church purposes being accepted from gross, impenitent sinners, the excommunicated, etc.). Whatever was left over from these gifts after the Supper was used, along with other gifts offered then, for the support of church ministers and the assistance of the poor.

These contributions of bread and wine, as well as the other charitable gifts, were called *sacrifices* [*Opfer*], the offering of them *sacrificing* [*Opferung*] (*oblatio*) and the table or place on which they were deposited, the *altar*. But inasmuch as these charitable gifts thus offered counted as *primitiae creaturarum* (firstfruits of creation), they were simultaneously the symbolic expression of the assembled faithful showing their inner self-offering to the Lord, as those who joyfully gave themselves and all that they had to the service of God. But above all, the elements standing ready for the celebration of the Supper were, as *primitiae creaturarum*, offered not only with a lofty prayer of thanksgiving (the Preface) but also with the adjoined prayer that God would receive these gifts of bread and wine for their sacramental purpose, and through the sending of the Holy Spirit sanctify the bread and wine for the communion of Christ's body and blood, and the recipients for worthy participation.

All these things were thus in origin the sacrifice offered by the congregation, and this tradition was initially retained even in the Church of Rome, "in that the faithful, first the men, then the women, offered their gifts of bread and wine in white <196> cloths, then the priests and deacons simply in bread, and finally the singers in water,[234] while the choir sang the Offertory, consisting of antiphonal passages of psalms and other books

[234] *) In the East, it was generally customary, on account of the wine's strength, to mix it with water for consumption. It was strictly for this reason that water was originally used [with wine] in the Holy Supper.

(*versus offertorii*), which varied for each Divine Service. At the beginning of the Middle Ages, those gifts began to be replaced by money, through which these oblations must have lost their proper significance and wholly disappeared" (Schöberlein, [1:300f.]).

From the middle of the third century, however, the unevangelical concept of a *clerical Christian priesthood* gradually gained acceptance. As a result, the notion of the Supper as a *sacrificial action of the Christian priest* also was increasingly cultivated, and the prayers associated with the Supper (especially those for the dead), now immediately following the completed Consecration, were gradually invested with such high significance that, already at this stage, the Supper began to be regarded as a sacrifice for the dead (*oblatio pro mortuis*). And thus it eventually led to the abomination of the papistic sacrifice of the Mass. What was at first a simple offering of the bread and wine, referred to as a sacrifice in a good sense and designated as "unbloody" in contrast with the bloody sacrifice of the Old Testament, was now a so-called sacrifice of the body and blood of Christ Himself, designated "unbloody" to distinguish it from His bloody sacrifice on the cross and repeated perpetually as a propitiatory sacrifice for the living and the dead. Indeed, in the sacrificial prayers, the alleged power of propitiation was extended even to the yet-unconsecrated elements.

And thus the place in the liturgy formerly occupied by the congregational oblations was taken over by those ceremonies of the priest's which prepare for the effectual offering of the propitiatory sacrifice. Next, in a soft whispering tone, the priest says the *versus offertorii* [Offertory Verse] itself, varying according to season and circumstance. Then he takes the host, deposits it on the paten, and likewise in a whispering tone calls upon God mercifully to accept this "immaculate sacrifice" which he offers for his own sins, for the sins of all present and all believers, and for the living and the dead, and to let it avail unto salvation.[235] This prayer is then joined by four

[235] *) This first of the sacrificial prayers reads: *Suscipe, sancte Pater, omnipotens, aeterne Deus, hanc immaculatam hostiam, quam ego indignus famulus tuus offero tibi, Deo meo vivo et vero, pro innumeris peccatis et offensionibus et negligentiis meis, et pro* <197> *omnibus circumstantibus, sed et pro omnibus fidelibus christianis, vivis atque defunctis: ut mihi et illis proficiat ad salutem in vitam aeternam. Amen.* [Receive, Holy Father, Almighty, Everlasting God, this immaculate host which I, Your unworthy servant, offer to You, my living and true God, for my countless sins and offenses and omissions, and for all those present, and also for all believing Christians, living and dead: that it may avail to me and to them for salvation in life everlasting. Amen]. In his treatise, "The Abomination of the Secret Mass" [1525], in which he glosses the individual parts of the canon, Luther remarks concerning this and the following prayer relating to the chalice: "Behold, there stands the priest with a host or wafer of mere bread and a chalice with wine in front of him, and tells God to look at it, and that it is supposed to be so excellent and worth so much that it is in God's sight a

more sacrificial <197> prayers, which are likewise spoken softly, whereas the priest speaks or sings aloud the Preface which follows them, and which are therefore called *secreta*, yet it is in conjunction with the first one that the *offertorium* of the Roman Mass is composed.

How Luther stood with respect to this portion of the received Mass, as well as to the Preface following, the sacrifical prayers surrounding the Words of the Testament, the *canon missae*, also spoken softly with the Words of the Testament, he expresses among other things in his first liturgical treatise, the *Formula Missae* [1523] in this way: "Then, what follows it"—namely, what follows the offering chant, or the *versus offertorii*, which is to say, the Psalmody—"sounds and smells altogether like utter sacrifice, while the holy words of salvation and life"—the Words of the Testament—"are embedded in the midst of (this abominable sacrificial activity), just as the ark of the Lord stood in the idolatrous temple next to the false god Dagon. . . . Therefore let us drop all that has the sound of sacrifice, together with the whole canon, and keep only what is pure and holy."[236]

Accordingly, the *Psalmody*, the *versus offertorii*, of the Early Church, being "pure and holy," has been retained. "In Protestant churches, the *Psalmody* has been restored in place of the Offertory,"[237] says Calvör in his *Rituale* I, c. I [ch. xlvii], 565). While at first this was in some places a fitting hymn for transitioning from the Sermon to the Supper, in other places it was a specific Offertory chant of the choir varying with the festivals, "the chant which was formerly observed in place of the Offertory," as it says in the Mark-Brandenburg church order.[238] Often Psalm 111 was used for the Psalmody, to which end [Johann] Spangenberg, in 1545, composed a melody modeled on a psalm-tone.[239] Or else in praise of the Lord's goodness,

sacrifice for the whole of Christendom. Is this not blasphemy against the blood of Christ, that bread and wine are regarded equal to Him? No one notes or sees what a blasphemy it is" (EA 29:118 [AE 36:314]). In another place, Luther remarks: "What is evil in the Mass is of sacrifice and works, which God wondrously arranges so that the priest reads everything secretly and calls it the silent Mass." [See AE 38:123.]

[236] Cf. Luther, "An Order of Mass and Communion" (1523), AE 53:26. —MC.

[237] *In protestantium ecclesiis restituta est loco offertorii Psalmodia.* —MC.

[238] *Kirchen-Ordnung im Churfurstenthum der Marcken zu Brandenburg, wie man sich beide mit der Leer und Ceremonien halten sol* (Berlin, 1540), folio J4v (unmarked). —MC.

[239] *Cantiones ecclesiasticae latinae . . . / Kirchengesenge Deudtsch, auff die Sontage und fürnemliche Feste durchs gantze Jar . . .* (Magdeburg: M. Lotther, 1545), vol. 2, folio 22r ff. The first appearance of this tone, however, is in Joseph Klug's *Geistliche lieder auffs new gebessert zu Wittenberg* (Wittenberg: Joseph Klug, 1533), and the authorship of Luther is otherwise generally posited. See Luther, "The Communio" (1533), AE 53:181ff.; WA 31^1:393; and Markus Jenny, ed., *Luthers Geistliche Lieder und Kirchengesänge* (Köln: Böhlau, 1985), 124. —MC.

Psalm 34:8 was used; or as an expression of brotherhood, Psalm 133; and so on. From the middle of the seventeenth century, however, "Create in me a clean heart, O God," taken from Psalm 51, <198> spread more and more, and at last nearly became *the* Psalmody generally. And indeed, this choice might well appear to be the most thoughtful and thus the most fitting, since this Psalmody is the finest expression of the offering of those sacrifices which are most pleasing to God and which pertain to the worthy reception of the Holy Supper. For of such it says in verse 17: "The sacrifices of God are a broken spirit; a broken and contrite heart, O God, You will not despise." The beautiful melody, which passed into all choral-books, is first found in the Gotha Cantional (1646) and is [elsewhere] ascribed to G. Winer "pastor at Henrici Henneberg."[240] There is also an alternate setting for it, which, being no less beautiful, has likewise been included in the St. Louis *Choralbuch* published by H. F. Hölter (no. 335). Hommel's *Musikalische Liturgie* [Musical Liturgy] adds to the beginning of this Psalmody verses 18–19 of Psalm 51: "Lord, do good in Thy good pleasure unto Zion," etc. Because the melody provided is so beautiful, it is included here. This Psalmody could be sung by the choir, and the other, "Create in me a clean heart," etc., could be sung by the congregation immediately following it.

However, while Luther desired (and rightly so) to omit everything that even smacked or sounded of papistic sacrifice, he was nevertheless inclined from the beginning, after the custom of the Early Church, to connect *the liturgical presentation of the charitable offering with the celebration of the Supper*. In his *Deutsche Messe* (1526), while discussing the *missa fidelium* with the words, "If there are such people and individuals as longed in earnest to be Christians," he continues: "Here a common collection could be solicited from Christians, to be voluntarily given and distributed among the poor, according to the example of St. Paul in 2 Corinthians 9 (:1–2, 12)" (StL 10:229; EA 22:231 [AE 53:64]). And in the "Treatise on the New Testament" (1520), he writes:

> Of this custom (namely, of "waving" the food offering in the Old Testament) three vestiges still survive. *The first is that the first and last prayers of the Mass are both called 'collects,'* that is, collections. By this it is testified that these prayers were spoken as a "blessing" and "thanksgiving" over this collected food, to bless it and thank God for it, and in accordance with St. Paul's teaching (1 Corinthians 10:30–31; [1 Timothy 4:4–5]). The second *is that the people, after the Gospel,*

[240] *Cantionale sacrum, das ist, Geistliche Lieder von Christlichen und Trostreichen Texten . . .* (Gotha, 1646), 2:460ff. For more information on the origins of this tune, see *LSB: Companion to the Hymns,* 1:1563. —MC.

> *still go to the offering;* from which the *chant* that is sung there is called the *Offertory*, that is, offering. <199> The third is that the priest lifts up the paten and offers to God the unconsecrated host at the very same time that the *Offertory* is being sung and the people are making their offerings. By this it is shown that what is being offered to God by us is not the Sacrament but only these *collects and offerings of the collected food and goods,* and that God is being thanked for them and blessing them for *distribution to all the needy* (EA 27:157–58).[241]

This presentation or collection of the charity offerings for the needs of the Divine Service, the poor, or other benevolent or church-related purposes, also became and has remained a general usage. But while it became the predominant custom among the Reformed to have this collection taken after the close of the Divine Service by means of basins set out before the church doors, there was a general preference among Lutherans to set a place for it within the Divine Service and to have it administered by circulating a so-called bell-purse,[242] coffer, or other receptacle. For the most part, the collection took place during the [Offertory] Psalmody or, if that did not allow enough time, earlier during the singing of the Creed. With what keen awareness this institution reflected the intimate connection between the congregation's offerings of praise and charity, is illustrated by the following passage of the *Cologne Reformation* (1544): "In this way, while the Creed is being sung, the faithful are to present their freewill offerings, each according to the blessing bestowed on him by the generous hand of God. To this end all preachers shall diligently exhort them, showing how these offerings always begin with the true confession of the faith and with prayer made in faith."[243] Here we have a distinct reminder of the Old Testament practice according to which the presentation of the burnt offering was accompanied by the singing of the singers and the sounding of the cymbals, harps, and lyres of the Levites and the trumpets of the priests (2 Chronicles 29:25–28). This was no doubt meant to show even then that a

---

[241] Cf. Luther, "Treatise on the New Testament" (1520), AE 35:95. —MC.

[242] *) Concerning the circulation of the bell-purse, which many today consider inappropriate even after the elimination of the bell, Dr. Slevogt writes: "This *modus collectandi* [procedure for collecting] without doubt derives from the old oblations, for the manner of collecting the oblations into a sack in the church was prescribed already in the Ordo Romanus [primus, cap. 19]: 'Et accedentes subdiaconi sequentes cum acolythis, qui sacculum portant a dextris et sinistris altaris'" [And the subdeacons, with the acolytes following carrying little sacks, draw near to the right and left of the altar] etc. (*Rechte der Altäre, Taufsteine,* etc. 1732, 458.) [Gottlieb Slevogt, *Gründliche Untersuchung von denen Rechten der Altäre, Tauf-Steine . . .* (Jena: Joh. Friederich Ritter, 1732), 458. —MC.

[243] *Von Gottes genaden unser Hermans . . .* folio 108r. —MC.

gift was to be presented to the Lord voluntarily and joyfully; concerning which David also prophetically pointed to the time of the Messiah, whose people, after His victory, would offer Him willing sacrifices in holy adornment (Psalm 110:3). <200>

To what extent the collection of the charitable donations in the Divine Service was conceived of as a component of the spiritual priesthood is demonstrated by the term *oblation* [*Opfer*], which is the term still used in many places for any church collection, whether for the poor, parish needs, schools, mission, etc. Those who collect them are called *oblationers* [*Opfermänner*]. The receptacle installed in the church for other gifts of alms is called the *oblation-post* or *oblation-box* [*Opferstock, Opferbüchse*]. In some of the local congregations of Lutherans who immigrated from Prussia, the author witnessed a special charitable donation being laid on the altar during Communion. And during a church dedication of immigrant Norwegian Lutherans, after the sermon, the whole congregation passed by the altar and deposited their gift on the right side of it as they sang. In the Episcopal Church's *Book of Common Prayer,* the following beautiful procedure is prescribed: "After the sermon, the priest returns to the Altar and begins the Offertory, saying one or more of the following Sentences at his discretion."[244] These Sentences, to be read by the "priest," are all references to giving, such as Matthew 5:16; 6:19–20; Luke 19:8; 1 Corinthians 9:7, 11, 13–14; 2 Corinthians 9:6–7; Galatians 6:6; 7:10; 1 Timothy 6:17–18; Hebrews 6:10; 13:16; and the like. Then after a note that, during the collection of the offering (Oblation), a "Hymn of oblation and thanksgiving" may be sung, it further instructs: "Whilst these Sentences are in reading, the Deacons or other men appointed for that purpose shall receive the Alms for the Poor, and other Oblations of the congregation, in a decent Basin to be provided by the Parish for that purpose, and reverently deliver it to the Clergyman, who shall humbly present and place it upon the Altar."

In accordance with this, the Offertory (or whatever it may be called) of the Lutheran Chief Divine Service is entirely different from that of the papistic Mass. It is the Church's term for the spiritual priesthood's collective

[244] Here and through the rest of this paragraph, Lochner quotes from a German translation of the *Book of Common Prayer:* Karl E. G. Oppen, trans., *Das Allgemeine Gebetbuch der Protestantischen Episkopal Kirche in den Vereinigten Staaten von Amerika*... (Milwaukee, 1891), 86–88. In a contemporary printing of the *Book of Common Prayer* (New York: James Pott & Co., 1892), it says: "a Hymn, or an Offertory Anthem in the words of Holy Scripture or of the Book of Common Prayer ..." In my translation, I have supplied the word "Oblations" for *Opfer* ("sacrifice" or "offering"), according to its traditional use in the English version of the *Book of Common Prayer.* I have generally kept the language of the English edition, except where significant variation occurs, e.g., "Altar" instead of "Holy Table." —MC.

offering of oblations—of the repentant heart through the Psalmody, "Create in me a clean heart," etc., and of grateful love through the collection of charitable gifts connected with, or in certain circumstances preceding or following, the Psalmody. However, in the preface to the second edition of his Agenda (1853) [p. vii], Löhe feels that this form of the Offertory is not complete. He regards as the "high point of the Offertory" the Ancient Church's "offering of the *primitiae creaturarum*, that is, the prayerful presentation of the elements in order that the Lord may unite His holy body and precious blood with them." Nevertheless, he is hesitant to include it in a Lutheran agenda <201> without further ado, though only on account of "the proclivity which exists in the agenda for innocent words and actions to be misunderstood and interpreted in a manner disturbing to the peace." At the same time, while noting, "It was not unknown to the early days of Lutheranism either, though it did not penetrate," he was no doubt thinking especially of a passage in Bugenhagen's German Mass[245] which he gives in his *Sammlung liturgischer Formulare* [Collection of Liturgical Formulas, vol. 4], published in 1839, where, after preparing the elements, "the priest, with the people," prays: "O most gracious Father, merciful God! Grant that this bread and wine may become for us the true body and the innocent blood of Your all-beloved Son, our Lord Jesus Christ. Amen."[246] That this presentation, despite its harmless language "did not penetrate" and come into common use is explained when we remember that Luther very decisively desires that everything that even smacks or sounds of sacrifice be omitted. It is also good that this "did not penetrate" and pass over into the Lutheran Divine Service orders of the sixteenth and seventeenth centuries, since (especially in our day) it might have once again turned the harmless presentation of the *primitiae creaturarum* into the blasphemous offering of an "immaculate sacrifice" for the living and the dead, as before. It may be noted here in passing that a similar presentation of the elements is also found in the Episcopal *Book of Common Prayer*, and as an "Oblation" no less, combined with an "Invocation." It is characteristic here that these do not precede the Consecration but immediately follow it.[247]

---

[245] *) *Ain ordnung Christlicher Messen wie gehalten wirdt, von dem Gewirdigen herren Johann Bugenhagen auß Pommern, Pfarrherr zu Wittenberg 1524.* [Also known as "Pseudo-Bugenhagen," the order resembles that of Kaspar Kantz (ca. 1483–1544) published in 1522. —MC.]

[246] Cf. Schoeberlein, 1:303. —MC.

[247] *) *The Oblation:* Wherefore, O Lord and heavenly Father, according to the institution of thy dearly beloved Son our Saviour Jesus Christ, we, thy humble servants, do celebrate and make here before thy divine Majesty, with these thy holy gifts, which we now offer unto thee, the memorial thy son hath commanded us to make; having in remembrance

It was customary during the Offertory not only for the pastor to approach the altar to uncover the holy vessels and by praying to prepare to celebrate the Sacrament,[248] but also for the communicants <202> to go to the chancel and, if it was sufficiently large, to arrange themselves therein, male communicants on the right side of the altar, females on the left. On this last point, Schöberlein brings together the following provisions from different church orders. The communicants should "enter the chancel not with ostentatious and pompous clothing or reckless behavior, but in clean and decent church attire, namely, black formal wear, etc., in a good, modest manner, with great reverence and devotion, and not leave the chancel again until the blessing," since "chancels are made in churches for the purpose of celebrating Communion in them, and while Communion is being celebrated, from beginning to end, only communicants are to stand, sit, and kneel in them, so that they may more devoutly and better perceive and pay attention to all the things that are done in this holy Divine Service with reading, singing, and prayer."[249] Luther, too, finds it fitting for the communicants to stand in a place set apart. In his *Formula Missae* (1523), he writes,

> When Communion is celebrated, it well becomes those who wish to go to the most worthy Sacrament to gather together and stand in a separate place by themselves, since both altar and chancel were made for that purpose. Not as though it were anything in God's sight whether a man stands here or there, or that it added anything to faith. But it is necessary *that those persons be publicly seen and recognized* as much by those who receive the Sacrament as by those who do not go up, *in order that their life might be better observed, examined, and made known afterwards*. For the use of this Sacrament in the congregation is a part of Christian confession by which those who go up confess in the sight of God, angels, and men that they are Christians. For this reason, close attention should be paid lest any persons secretly steal the Sacrament and afterward, being mixed among other Christians, it cannot be discovered whether they lead a good or bad life. Nevertheless, I do not wish to set up any law here,

---

his blessed Passion, etc. — *The Invocation:* And we most humbly beseech thee, O merciful Father, to hear us, and, of thy Almighty goodness, vouchsafe to bless and sanctify, with thy Word and Holy Spirit, these thy gifts and creatures of bread and wine; that we, receiving them according to thy Son our Saviour Jesus Christ's holy institution, in remembrance of his Death and Passion, may be partakers of his most blessed Body and Blood, etc.

[248] *) If the pastor is being assisted, the assistant stands before the steps of the altar either in the middle or to the side during the Consecration.

[249] Schoeberlein, 1:301. —MC.

> but simply to indicate this so that all that is decent and in good order (1 Corinthians 14:40) may be done freely without compulsion by Christians, who are indeed free.[250]

This admirable practice can of course only take place when the chancel is of sufficient size. If this is not the case, or if the congregation is very large, it is better for the communicants to remain in their pews and to rise at the beginning of the Consecration. <203>

For the Offertory

[250] Cf. Luther, "An Order of Mass and Communion," AE 53:34. —MC.

Music: Hommel

<204>

XIII. PREFACE WITH SANCTUS

1. The Preface

The ceremony of the Consecration is preceded by a solemn prayer of thanksgiving and praise which gave the name *Eucharist* to the whole Communion rite which now follows it. This is the *Preface* (foreword, prelude, or introduction to the thanksgiving). While the term *Preface* was understood in the Ancient Church as the collective prayers preceding the Consecration, the centerpiece was the prayer of praise and thanksgiving introduced by the rousing *Sursum corda!* ("Your hearts on high!"), concluding with the *Trisagion* ("Thrice Holy" or "Seraphic Hymn").

The testimony from Justin and the *Apostolic Constitutions*, quoted above in Part One, §2 [p. 7], the first note, has already alluded to the great antiquity of the Preface. From one of the oldest recorded liturgies, called the "Liturgy of St. James," and verifiably still in use in fourth century Jerusalem, it appears here in one of its earliest Eastern forms, originally composed in Greek:

> Then he (the priest) says aloud: The love of the Lord and Father, the grace of the Lord and Son, and the fellowship and the gift of the Holy Spirit, be with us all.
>
> The people: And with thy spirit.
>
> The priest: Let us lift up our minds and our hearts.
>
> The people: It is becoming and right.
>
> Then the priest prays: Verily it is becoming and right, proper and due to praise Thee, to sing to Thee, to bless Thee, to worship Thee, to glorify Thee, to give Thee thanks, Maker of every creature visible and invisible, the treasure of eternal good things, the fountain of life and immortality, God and Lord of all:
>
> Whom the heavens of heavens praise, and all the host of them; the sun, and the moon, and all the choir of the stars; earth, sea, and all that is in them; Jerusalem, the heavenly assembly, and Church of the first-born that are written in heaven; spirits of just men and of prophets; souls of martyrs and of apostles; angels, archangels, thrones, dominions, principalities, and authorities, and dread powers; and the many-eyed cherubim, and the six-winged seraphim, which cover their faces with two wings, <205> their feet with two, and with two they fly, crying one to another with unresting lips, with unceasing praises:

(Aloud.) With loud voice singing the victorious hymn of Thy majestic glory, crying aloud, praising, shouting, and saying:—

The people: Holy, holy, holy, O Lord of Sabaoth, the heaven and the earth are full of Thy glory. Hosanna in the highest; blessed is He that cometh in the name of the Lord. Hosanna in the highest.[251]

From the Eastern Church the use of the Preface passed early into the Western Church. There, however, not only did it retain the simpler form in which it is still found in the Mass at Rome, but in the fourth century there arose in the same use the composition of *festival prefaces*, in which the common form was augmented by a passage relating to the respective feast. Naturally, with the proliferation of feasts in the papacy, the number of these special prefaces, called *propriae*, increased, even though the predecessor of Gregory I reduced their number.

The Preface was also immediately received in the Lutheran Church in the Chief Divine Service, and not only the common (*quotidiana*) but also the special prefaces—those for the most notable feasts (*propria*). On the one hand, Luther, in his *Deutsche Messe* (1526), replaced the Ancient Church's Preface with the Exhortation to Communicants and its preceding paraphrase of the Our Father, and retained only the Sanctus, appointing "Jesaia dem Propheten," etc., written and set to music by himself, as the German Sanctus and assigning it a place after the Consecration.[252] On the other hand, he had included the Preface, at least in part, in his *Formula Missae* (1523), namely, up to the words *per Christum Dominum nostrum* ("through Christ our Lord . . ."), and after ancient precedent inserted the Consecration there.[253] One group of church orders conformed to the 1526 system, another group to the 1523 system—except that the whole Preface was incorporated, to which the Communion Exhortation was also connected, as follows below.

Since the Preface of the Roman Mass was generally taken up unchanged into the Lutheran Chief Divine Service, it was used for the most part in Latin, or else the Latin <206> Preface was appointed for cities and the German for villages. In other places, however, the Preface was sung or spoken in German from the outset, as seen in the church orders of A. Döber (Nürnberg, 1525),[254]

[251] *) König, 146f. [English translation from *ANF* 7:543f. —MC.]

[252] Cf. Luther, "The German Mass" (1525), AE 53:78ff.; see also "An Exhortation to the Communicants" (1525), AE 53:104f. —MC.

[253] Cf. Luther, "An Order of Mass and Communion" (1523), AE 53:27f. —MC.

[254] *Von der evangelischen meß, wie zie zu Nürnberg . . .* See Löhe, *Sammlung,* 3:46. —MC.

Riga (1530),[255] Braunschweig-Lüneburg (1542),[256] the *Cologne Reformation* (1544),[257] and others.

In the eighteenth century, prefaces began gradually to disappear from church books. They lasted longest in Saxony. Much to be lamented was the substitute suggested by Rationalism, for example: "Let every one of us now lift up mind, heart, and spirit to the invisible world according to his power of comprehension," etc. But in every recent move to recover the ancient order of the Divine Service, the Preface is not disregarded. Examples include Löhe's Agenda (initially used so much in this country), the Missouri Synod Agenda, and the *Kirchenbuch* of the General Council. It forms an essential feature of all liturgies of the first centuries, and indeed, it is a jewel among the prayers of the Divine Service, the placement of which is at the same time altogether appropriate. As it was the custom in Israel during a meal to partake of the bread and wine with a special thanksgiving,[258] and as we Christians are to give thanks to the Father of light and mercy for every gift, so it is truly *worthy*, or *meet*, and *right*, as the Ancient Church put it, that we should first give thanks to God for the unspeakable gift of our Lord Jesus Christ's body and blood given to us under bread and wine, and worship and praise His name with all the angels and the elect.

As a rule the Preface was not and is not spoken but *chanted* by the liturgist. However, the original tones are justly more dynamic than those of the collects. The melodies for all the prefaces are reproduced here after Hommel[259] and are found in the *Directorium chori* (1589) of Guidetti, friend and pupil of Palaestrina.[260] The melody available to the author for a Sunday Preface in the church order of Braunschweig-Lüneburg (1657)[261] is

[255] *Kurtze Ordnung des Kirchendiensts samt einer Vorrede von Ceremonien* . . . (1530). See Sehling, 5:16, where the rubric occurs: "The sermon is followed by the Preface, which the priest sings in German up through *per Christum*." —MC.

[256] *Kirchenordnung des Herzogs Ernst von Braunschweig-Lüneburg* (1544). See Sehling, 2:55. —MC.

[257] *Von Gottes genaden unser Hermans* . . . folio 109v. —MC.

[258] *) Covering the bread with both hands, the Jewish father says: "Blessed are You, Lord our God, King of the world, who have brought forth this bread from the earth." And he blesses the wine in similar fashion.

[259] Hommel, 19ff. —MC.

[260] The book indicated, *Directorium chori ad usum omnium ecclesiarum cathedralium, et collegiaturum* (Rome: S. Paulinus, 1589) contains no Preface tones, which are rather in *Prefationes in cantu firmo juxta ritum Sanctae Romanae Ecclesiae* (Rome: A. Gardano, 1588). Pertinent are the *ferial* prefaces, beginning on p. 19. —MC.

[261] *Agenda Oder: Erster Teyl der Kirchen-Ordnung* . . . (Wolfenbüttel: Sterne, 1657). While the melody of the Preface (p. 33f.) generally agrees with Guidetti's ferial tone, the Salutation and versicles on p. 32 are simpler, being based in part on the melody of the Te Deum. —MC.

plainly modeled on Guidetti's setting of the Latin text. Since the melody by Guidetti is not only beautiful but also easy to sing, it may well be that in recovering the old liturgy, it will be preferred to the other tone which, though more difficult for many, is more dynamic, and is found with minor variation in a number of older agendas, including Spangenberg's Cantional, *Kirchengesänge lateinisch und deutsch* [Church Music Latin and German] (Magdeburg, 1545). <207> This is followed by the chant setting of one of the prefaces for the three high feasts from the Schwarzburg Agenda (1675), by way of example, only that it is underlaid by the author with the text of the St. Louis Agenda, which was very easy to do.

2. The Sanctus

Having made reference to our joining with the hymns of the heavenly hosts, the Preface leads us to the Sanctus, the *hymnus seraphicus* [seraphic hymn] from Isaiah 6:3. Its inclusion in the Divine Service seems to belong to the earliest period, since it is ascribed to Ignatius (d. 116). It is supposed to have been made a feature of the Roman Mass quite early by Sixtus I (d. 130).

In the fourth century, the Sanctus was augmented by the addition of the *Benedictus* ("Blessed be," etc.) along with the *Hosanna*. An ingenious connection! Just as once on His entry into Jerusalem the incarnate Son of God was, with the Benedictus and Hosanna, hailed by Israel as the Son of David; so here He is hailed by the celebrating Church as the Son of Mary and the Paschal Lamb,[262] who has truly come to her, the daughter of Zion, in His body and blood under the bread and wine, to seal all the grace declared and presented in the Word and to unite Himself with her in the most intimate manner.

Up to the time of Gregory I and Charlemagne and even after that, *the people* still sang the whole Sanctus (in Latin) with the clergy. Gradually, however, it ceased to be a congregational song. The Reformation found it only as a song of the choir.

Wherever the Chief Divine Service stood in closer agreement with the Roman Mass by inclusion of the Preface, such as in the church orders of

[262] Especially in mind here are the optional phrases (*versus vagans*, or *passus*) used in the old Saxon agenda's Sanctus-Benedictus: "Blessed is the Son of Mary" or ". . . the Paschal Lamb"; see *Kirchen-Agende für ev.-Luth. Gemeinden . . .* (1856), 55. These options were not retained by the Common Service (1888). A translation is given below, p. 235. —MC.

Strassburg (1525),[263] Erfurt (1526),[264] Wittenberg (1559),[265] Mecklenburg (1552),[266] Frankfurt am Main (1565),[267] etc., it was typically concluded with the Sanctus. But where, following the precedent of Luther's *Deutsche Messe* (1526), the Preface was replaced with the Exhortation, the Sanctus (namely, the German Sanctus, "Jesaia dem Propheten,"[268] etc.) came immediately after the Consecration. How varied the delivery of the Thrice Holy was and what special distinctions were generally given to it is shown by *Schöberlein* [1:334] in the following composite from various church orders and cantionals: Thus it says: "*The congregation shall sing the line 'Holy [is God the Lord of Sabaoth]' three times* ***slowly****, with devotion* <208> *and great reverence.*"[269] (Pomerania, 1563).[270] Likewise: "But in cities with schools, three boys shall sing the line *slowly* whilst kneeling before the altar, and the choir with the congregation shall respond to it" (or: "it shall be sung by the boys twice with a loud voice") (Ludecus, *Missale,* 1589). When the boys have sung the line for the third time, the choir concludes with the following line: "His glory fills the heavens and the earth,"[271] etc. (Pomerania, 1563). There also seems to have been some attempt in the threefold "Holy is God, the Lord of Sabaoth" to impose a gradual increase of solemnity by having it sung first in two voices, then in three voices, and the third time in four voices, but the rest of the Sanctus sung by the whole

[263] *Teutsch Kirchenampt mit lobgsengen . . .* folio B2r (Straßburg: W. Köpphel, 1525), from which the pertinent *Ordnung der meß, so die Kirch zu Straßburg yetz noch haltet* is reproduced in Löhe, *Sammlung,* 3:54f. —MC.

[264] *Teutsch Kirchenampt So man itzt (Got zu lob) ynn der Kirchen singt . . .* (1526), partly quoted, without prefaces, in Löhe, *Sammlung,* 3:60ff., note on p. 65.

[265] *Kirchenordnung. Wie es mit der Christenlichen Lere, reichung der Sacrament . . .* (Wittenberg: Lufft, 1559), with the rite on folio 93v, and dominical (complex) preface tones beginning on folio 105r. —MC.

[266] *Kirchenordnung: Wie es mit Christlicher Lere, reichung der Sacrament . . .* (Mecklenburg: Lufft, 1552), essentially the same as Wittenberg (1559) above, with preface tones beginning here on folio 95v. —MC.

[267] *Kirchenordnung, das ist, Form und Weise nach welcher die reyne Christlicher Lere, Sacramenten, und allerley nötige Ceremonien . . .* (1565), similar to the two previous orders, with mention of prefaces on folio 82r and dominical preface tones beginning on folio 93r. —MC.

[268] Wackernagel 3:18, no. 30; see *LSB* 960 "Isaiah, Mighty Seer in Days of Old." —MC.

[269] *) The present author emphasizes this because he has heard so many organists in this country play this part so fast that it prevented reflection on the fact that the Thrice Holy was here being sung with the Seraphs.

[270] Reproduced in *Die pommersche Kirchen-Ordnung und Agenda: nebst den Legibus praepositum . . .* (Greifswald, 1854), 355. —MC.

[271] That is, the next line of the hymn "Jesaia dem Propheten das geschah." —MC.

choir or the congregation (Michael Praetorius, *Missodia Sionia,* 1606); or by singing the "Holy is," etc., first in monodic chant, then in four, five, and six parts, and then "His glory," etc., in seven parts, and for the last line ("The beams and lintels," etc.) returning to the simpler setting (M. Vulpius, *Kirchengesänge,* 1604).

Introduction to all Prefaces

<209>

A. The Common Preface[272]

To be used on ordinary Sundays

<210>

[272] *) For comparison, an excerpt of the *Quotidiana* from the *Directorium chori* [=*Praefationes . . .*] by Guidetti (1589) is included here:

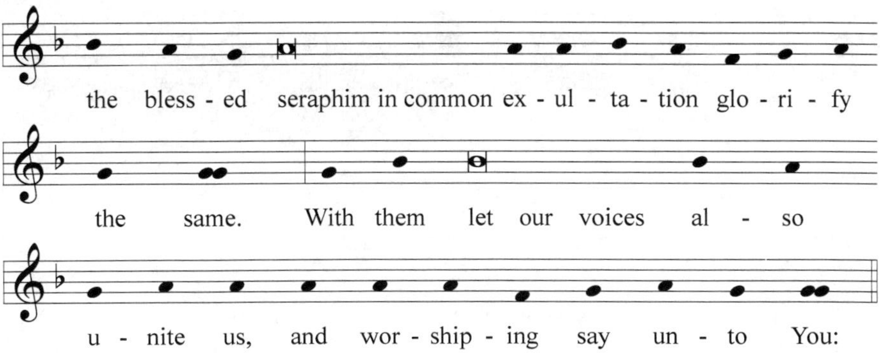

B. The Proper Prefaces
On Christmas Day

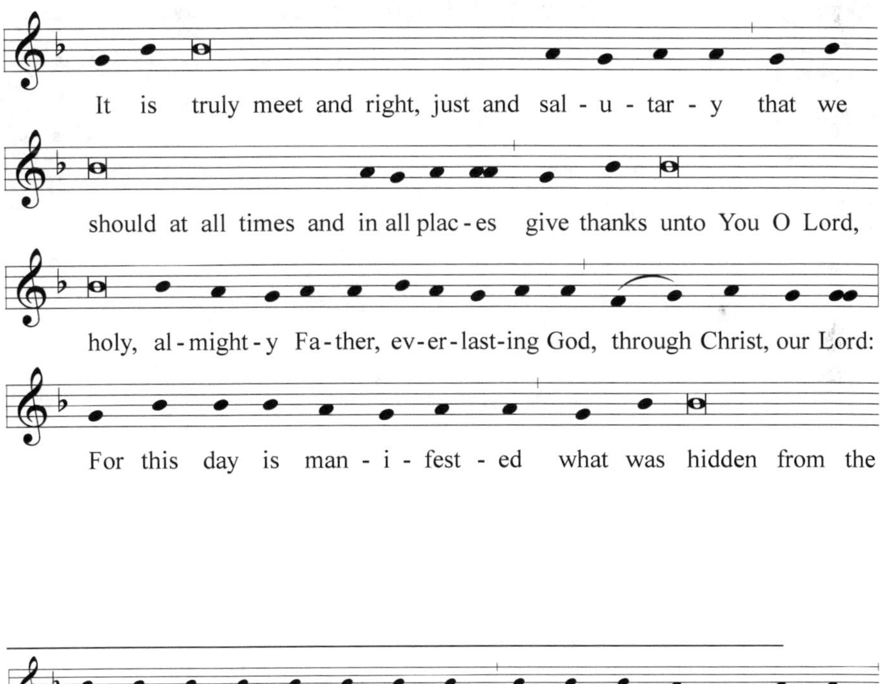

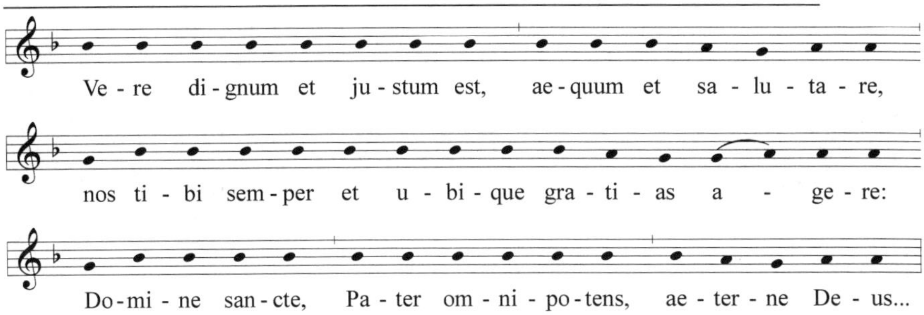

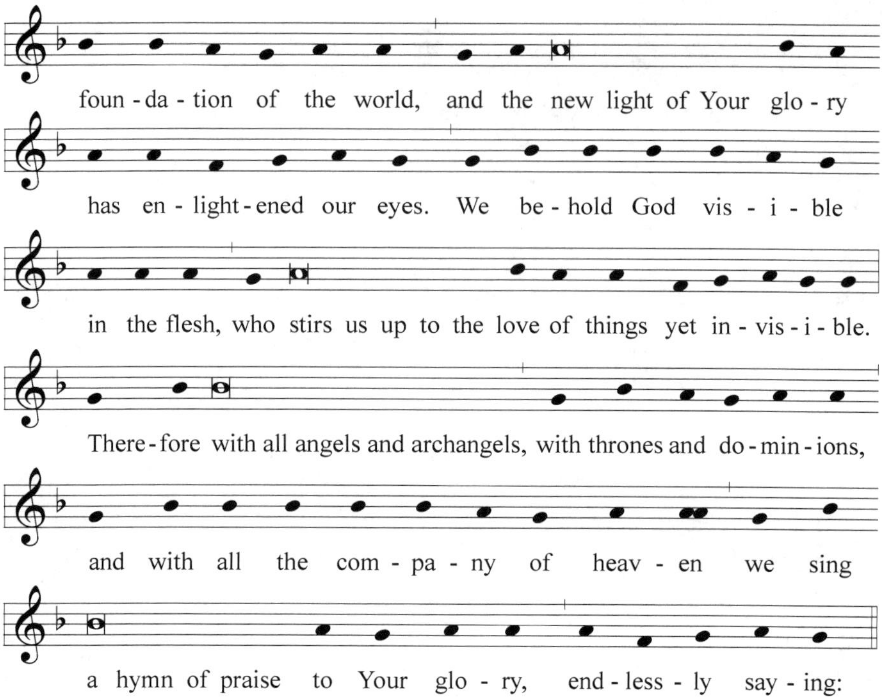

<211>

On the Feast of Epiphany
or in Epiphany-tide

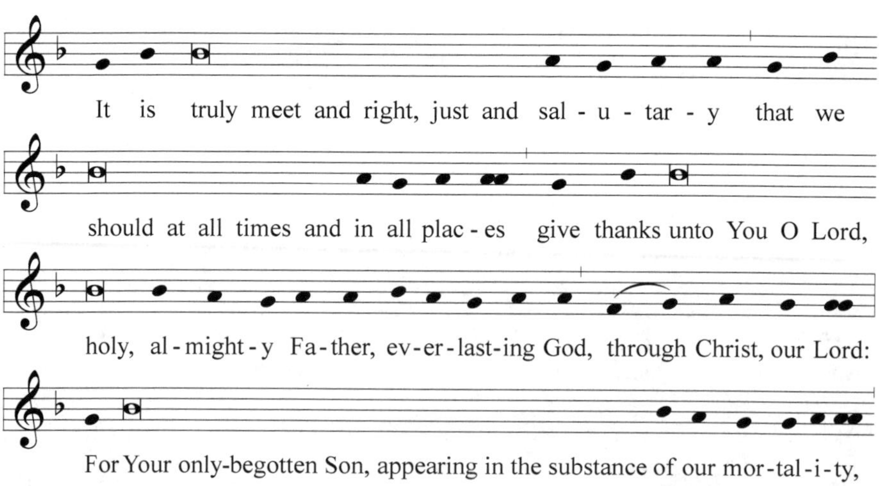

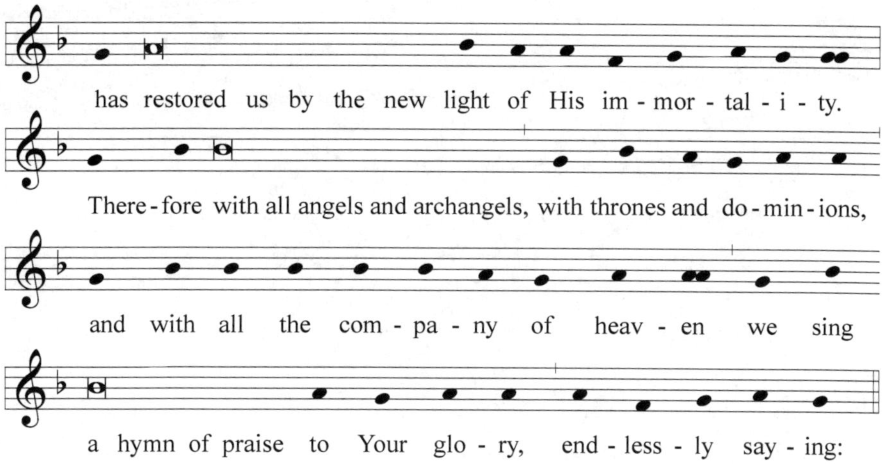

<212>

In Passiontide

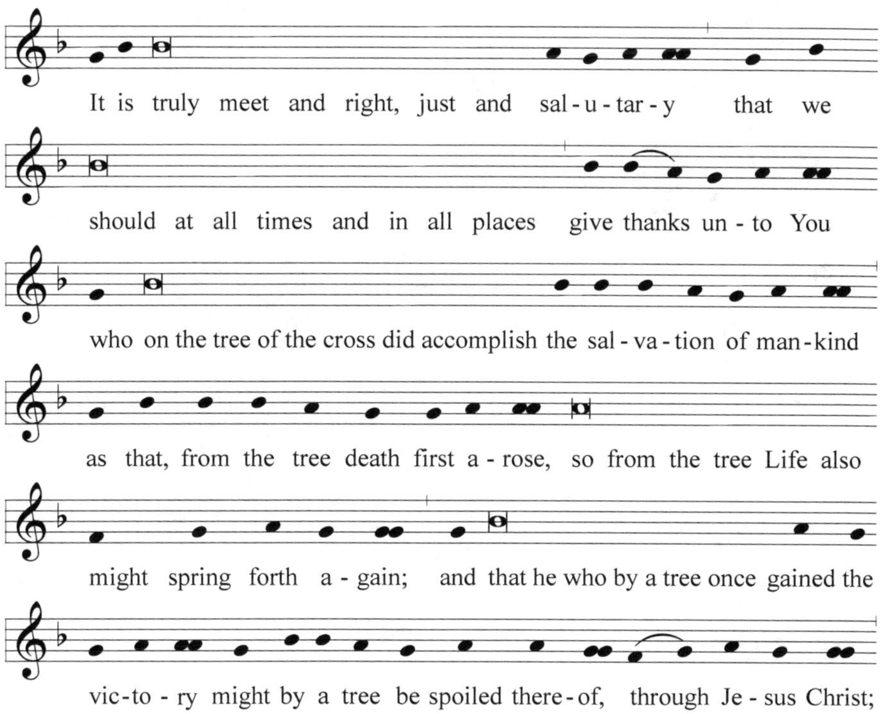

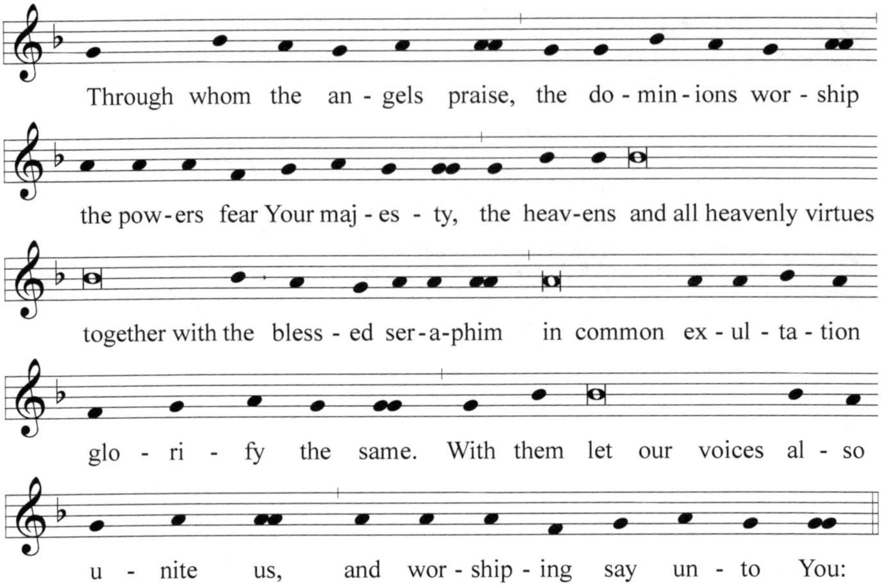

<213>

On the Feast of Easter

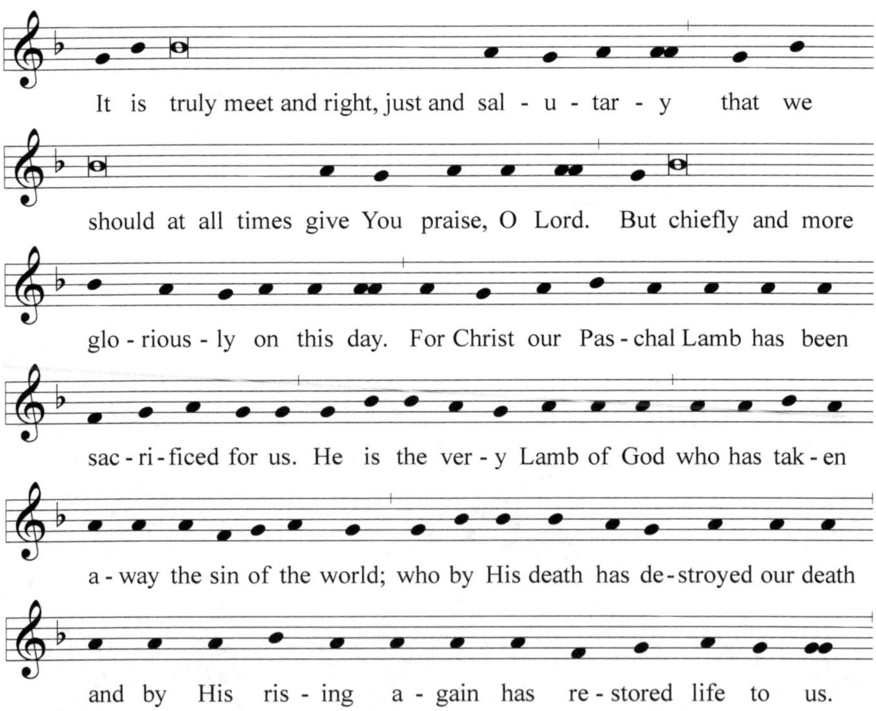

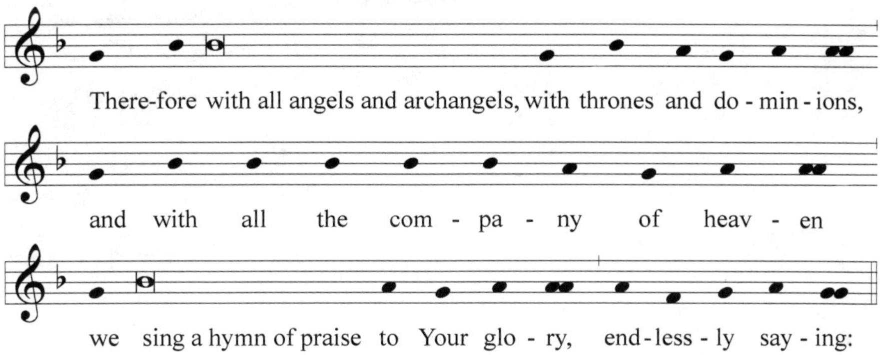

<214>

On the Feast of the Ascension

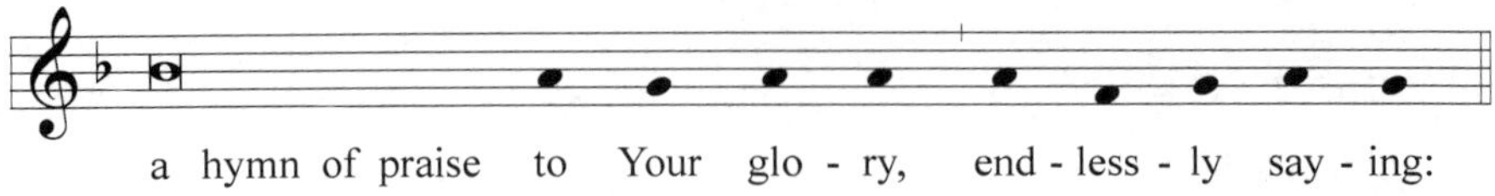

<215>

On the Feast of Pentecost

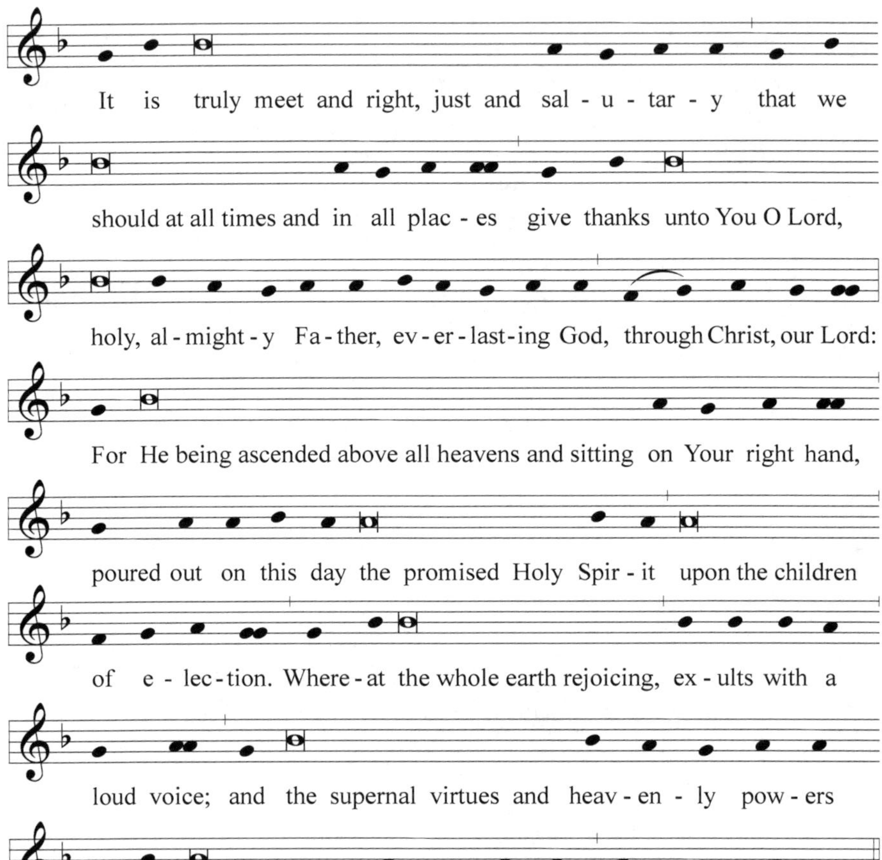

<216>

On the Feast of the Trinity

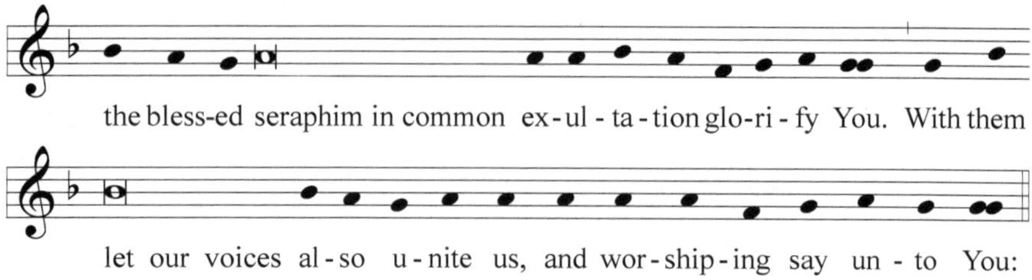

<217>

Another Tone for Chanting the Preface
On Christmas

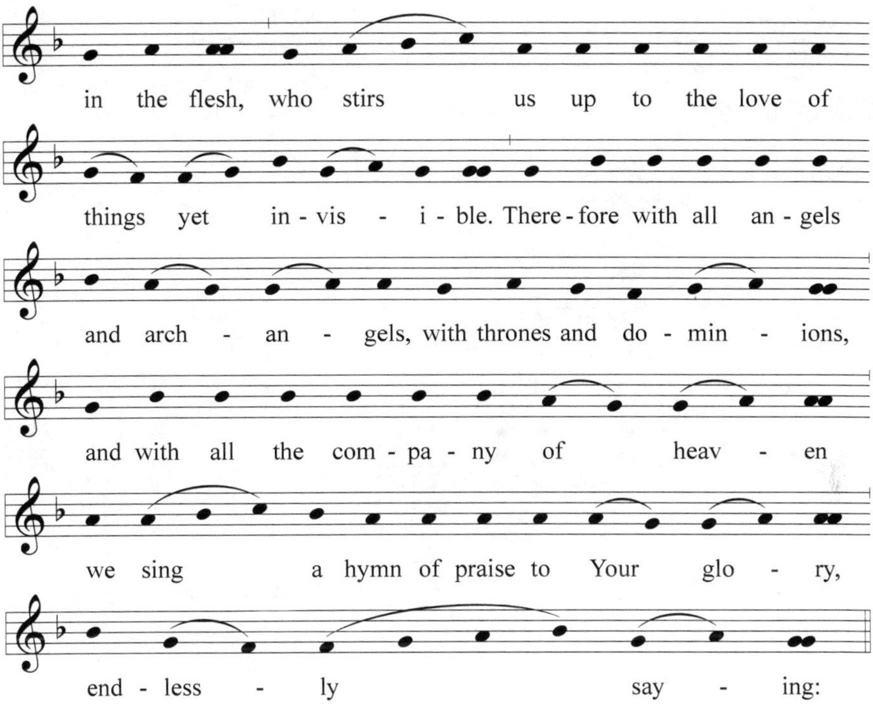

Spangenberg 1545, Mansfeld 1580, Schwarzburg 1675

<218>

I. Sanctus

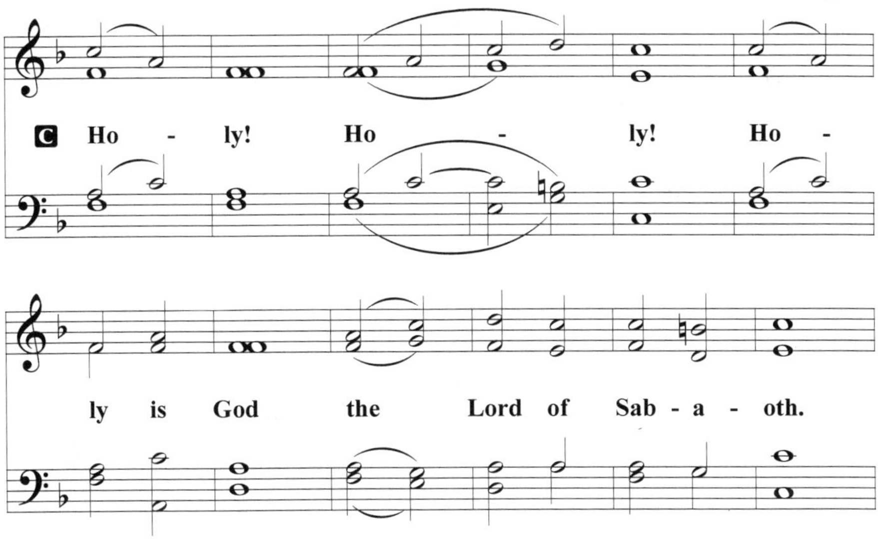

All the heav-ens and all the earth are
full, are full of Thy glo - ry. Ho -
san - na ho - san-na in the high - est!
Bless - ed is the Vir-gin's Son, that com -
Pas-chal Lamb,
<219>
eth in the name of the Lord. Ho - san - na

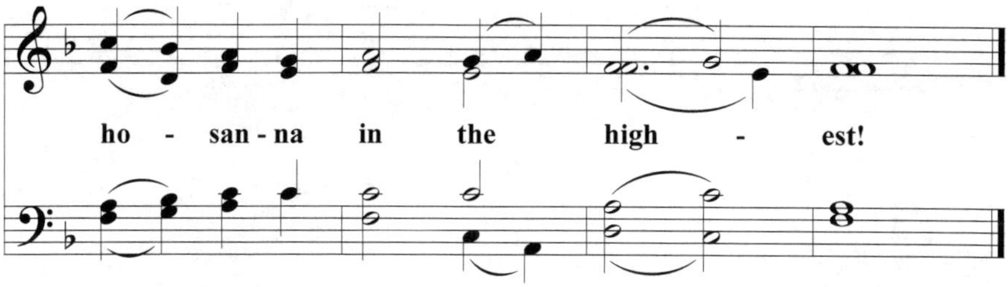

Text: tr. *Lutheran Worship,* 1982, alt.
Tune: L. Lossius, *Psalmodia,* 1551
Setting: F. Jubitz and G. von Tucher

II. Sanctus minus summum[273]

<220>

[273] "Less high," i.e., festivals ranking between feasts of Christ and ordinary Sundays. There is a note here in the original, which translated reads: "The words supplied by the author under the bass notes of [this] Sanctus are to show how the wording of the Sanctus in use among us may fit." These suggested changes in order to adapt a slightly different rendering of the Sanctus (including "Holy art Thou . . ." and "Praised be He . . .") from Riegel's version, rendered superfluous by our adaptation, have been omitted. —MC.

glo - ry. Choir: Ho -
san - na in the high - est!
C Bless - ed is He that com - eth in the name of the
Lord. Ho - san - na

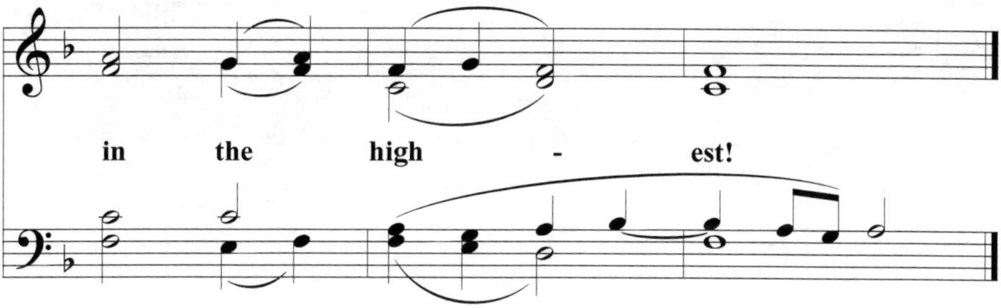

Music: Lucas Lossius, 1553; Palsgrave Wolfg. Church Order, 1557; Ludecus, 1589
Setting: F. Riegel, 1865

<221>

III. Sanctus

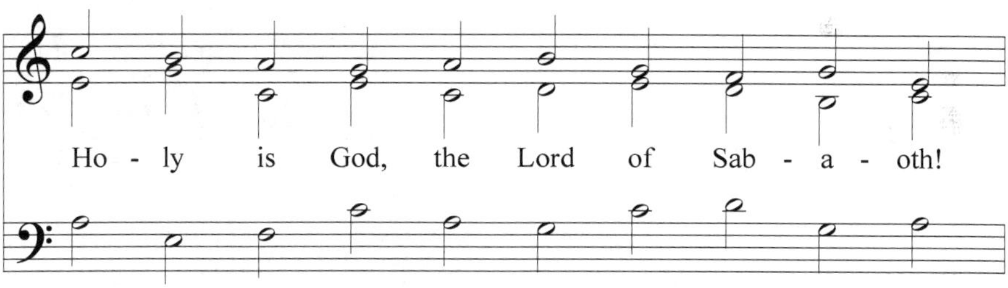

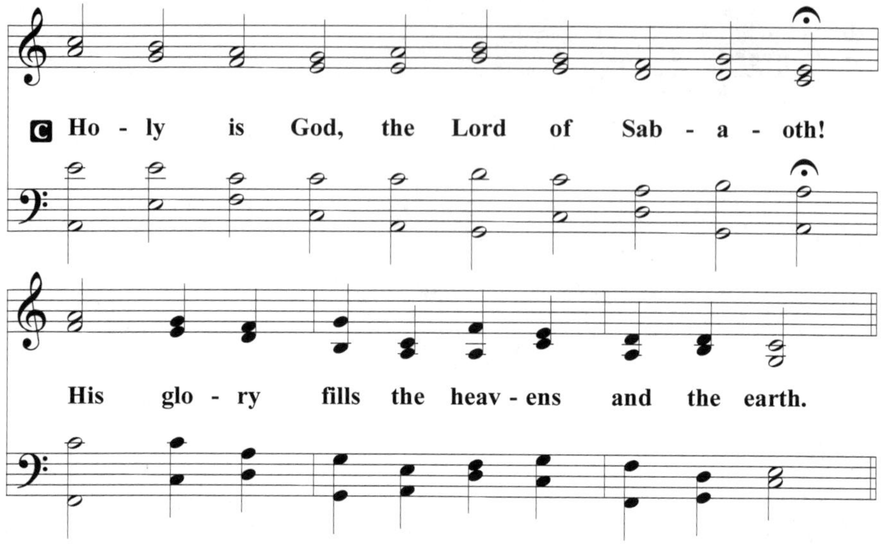

Music and text: Martin Luther, "Isaiah, Mighty Seer."

<222>

IV. Sanctus[274]

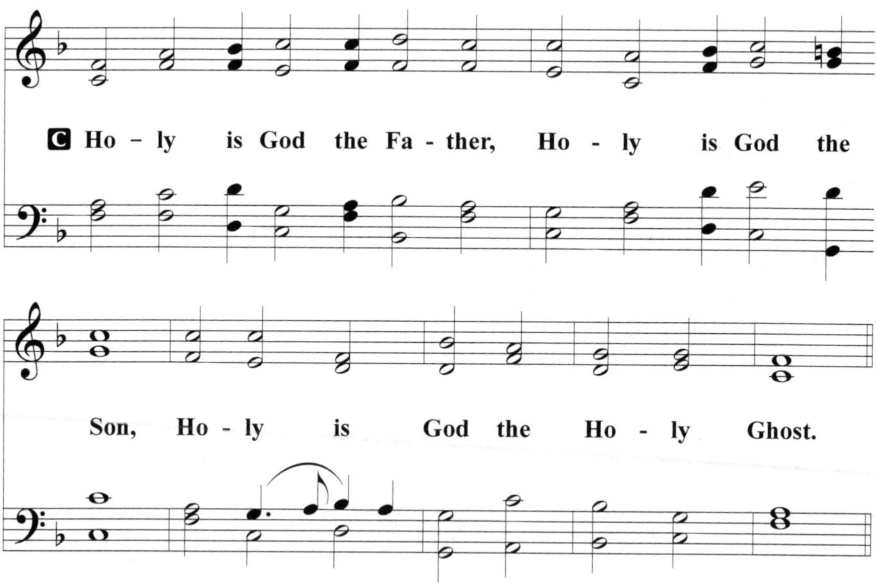

---

[274] This setting may be traced to *Christlike Kerken-Ordeninge im lande Brunschwig-Wulffenbüttels deles* (Wittenberg, 1543), folio O4r. The trope or interpolated reference to the persons of the Trinity in the three Holies is later removed—e.g., in Layriz, 32f., where it is included as an optional variant. —MC.

He is the Lord of Sab - a - oth.
All the world is full of His glo - ry.
Ho - san - na in the high - est.
Bless - ed is He that com - eth

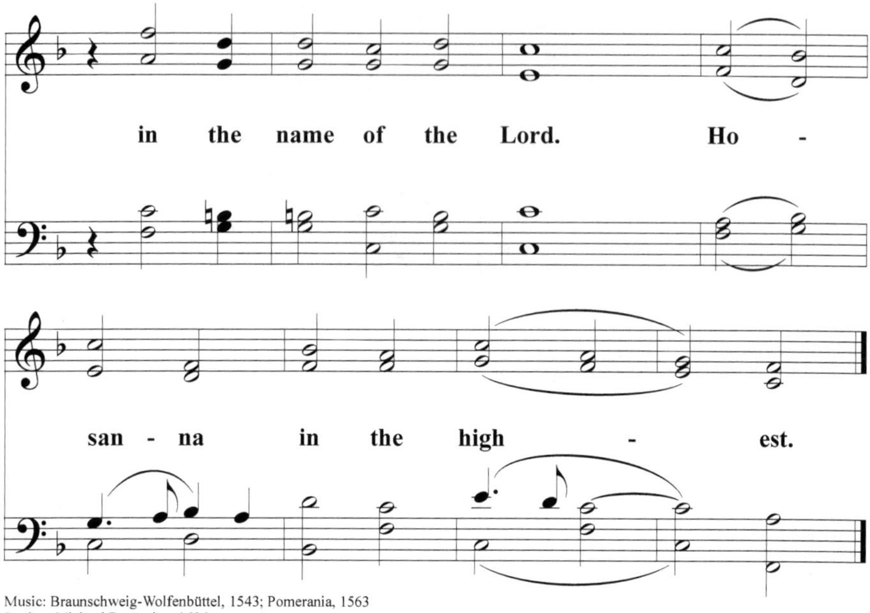

Music: Braunschweig-Wolfenbüttel, 1543; Pomerania, 1563
Setting: Michael Praetorius, 1606

<223>

V. Sanctus[275]

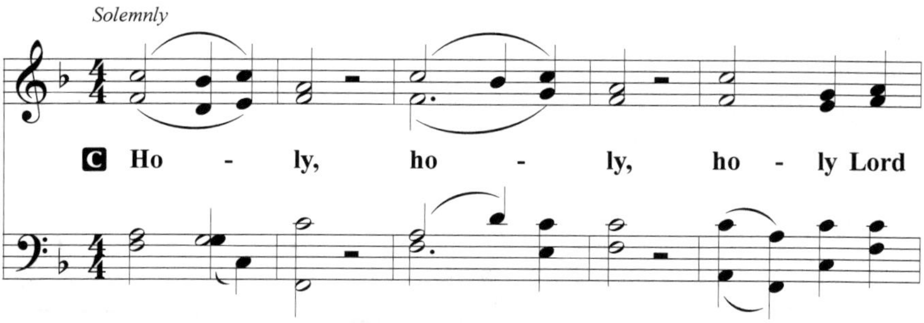

[275] This setting may be a development of the old Gregorian ferial (weekday) Sanctus. Hölter, *Choralbuch* (1902), 207, says of the German version: "Prevalent here since ca. 1848." Musicologist James L. Brauer, traces the musical sources of the Communion setting in the *Evangelical Lutheran Hymn-Book* (1912), the Missouri Synod's first official English-language hymnal in "Trusty Steed or Trojan Horse? The Common Service in the *Evangelical Lutheran Hymn-Book*," *Logia* 14, no. 3 (2005): 21–30. Brauer notes that unlike most of his *opus magnum,* Lochner provides no source for this musical setting. Brauer suggests it may be of nineteenth-century origin, but is otherwise inconclusive. —MC.

God of Sab - a - oth; heav'n and earth are
full of Thy glo - ry.
Choir boys or soloists
Ho - san - na,
Choir
ho - san - na, C ho - san - na in the high - est.
Solo
Bless-ed is He, C bless - ed is He, born the Vir-gin's Son, that
Christ, the Pas-chal Lamb,

<224>

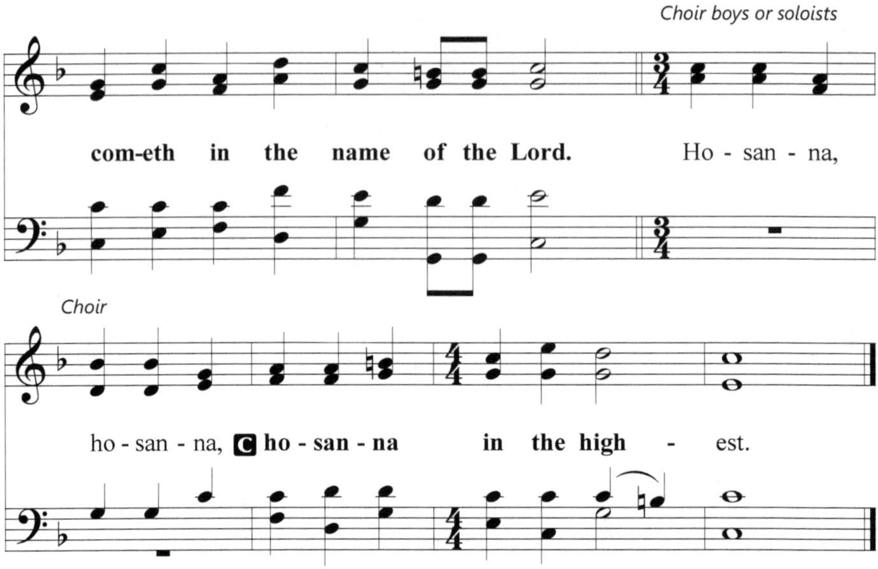

XIV. COMMUNION EXHORTATION

The Communion Exhortation has no precedent in the Roman Mass. It is a peculiar *product of the Reformation*. It even states in the Augsburg Confession, Article XXIV: Of the Mass: "Likewise, the utmost care is taken to instruct the people why the Holy Sacrament was instituted and how it is to be used."[276] This, then, was the purpose which a special Exhortation before the Supper was to serve.

A move toward inserting the Exhortation into the Communion liturgy was made by Luther, for his part, as early as 1525. In a letter to Nikolaus Hausmann dated March 26, with which he sends back some of the liturgical music which he had shared with him, he includes an Exhortation to the Supper which he composed, with the title "The Preface."[277] In 1524, a Communion Exhortation also appeared in Nürnberg in the German order of Mass by the provosts of St. Sebald and St. Lawrence, [Georg] *Besler* and [Hektor] *Böhmer*,[278] and in 1525 in that of *Andreas Döber*, chaplain of the

[276] AC XIV 1 (German). —MC.

[277] Cf. Luther, "An Exhortation to the Communicants" (1525), AE 53:104f. —MC.

[278] *Ordnunge so zu Nurmberg angefanngen ist mit denn Ampten der Meße unnd Vesper* . . . reproduced in *Monatschrift für Gottesdienst und kirchliche Kunst* 1, no. 10 (1897): 325. —MC.

Neues Spital.[279] <225> This is the well-known Exhortation by W. Volprecht,[280] apparently in its original form. It begins with the familiar words: "Dearly beloved in God, forasmuch as we now purpose to remember and keep the Holy Supper of our Lord Jesus Christ," etc. As we know, Luther, in his *Deutsche Messe* (1526) set in place of the Preface the paraphrase of the Our Father with its prefatory Communion Exhortation, which the Consecration then immediately followed.[281] On account of its beauty and brevity (yet frequently with the omission of the Our Father paraphrase) it received the greatest acceptance next to Volprecht's equally admirable, if longer, Exhortation.

In what high regard an Exhortation of this kind was held is shown by the Pomeranian church order, among others, which states: "These Exhortations shall not be lightly omitted, if time allows for it, but rather the hymnody shall be curtailed or adjusted."[282] As in the church order of Braunschweig-Lüneburg[283] and elsewhere, several formulas were provided for discretionary use. The church orders of the sixteenth, seventeenth, and to some extent the eighteenth century, all contain a number of Exhortations differing widely in form, yet agreeing in sentiment.

Yet one point of difference is the place which this Exhortation occupies in the liturgy. Some church orders, such as Brandenburg-Nürnberg,[284] put it *instead of* the Preface. Some, such as Erfurt (1526) and Austria (1571),[285] put it *before* the Preface; while others, such as Mecklenburg (1552),[286] Wittenberg

---

[279] *Von der Evangelischen Meß, wie sie zu Nürmberg* . . . , in Löhe, *Sammlung,* 3:47f. —MC.

[280] *) Wolfgang Volprecht, prior of the Augustinian cloister in Nürnberg, friend of Staupitz and Luther, as early as 1518 published in Nürnberg a treatise of Luther's against indulgences, and belonged to the truest and staunchest friends of the Reformation. He was also the first who in 1523, yielding to some degree to the desire of Nürnbergers, distributed the Supper under both forms to his converted monks and a few burghers. He died in 1528, being greatly mourned by Luther.

[281] Cf. Luther, "The German Mass" (1525), AE 53:78–81. —MC.

[282] *Die pommersche Kirchen-Ordnung und Agenda* . . . (1854), 79. —MC.

[283] *Kirchenordnung unnser von Gottes genaden Julii* . . . (Wolfenbüttel: C. Horn, 1569), 23ff., has the following: (1) "My dearly beloved in God, forasmuch as we now purpose . . ." (2) "My dearest friends, through preaching of the Gospel . . ." (3) "Whereas, through the Fall and transgression . . ." the third of which, being rather lengthy, is not included by Lochner. —MC.

[284] *Kirchen Ordnung in meiner gnedigen herrn der Marggraven* . . . (1533), folio 48r–v, followed immediately by the Verba on folio 49r. —MC.

[285] *Christliche Kirchen Agenda: Wie die von den zweyen Ständen* . . . (1571), folio 104v–105v, followed by rubric on 106r: "Hereupon he shall begin to sing the Preface . . ." —MC.

[286] *Kirchenordnung, wie es mit christlicher Lere* . . . (Mecklenburg, 1552), folio 84v: "If there is time, the priest may also recite an Exhortation and instruction on the most worthy Sacrament, as indicated after the prefaces." —MC.

(1559),[287] Pomerania (1563),[288] Braunschweig-Lüneburg (1594),[289] Schwarzburg (1675),[290] Leipzig (1681),[291] etc., put it *after* the Preface, which is to say, between the Preface and the Consecration. A few, such as Döber (1525)[292] and Mark-Brandenburg (1540),[293] even place it after the Consecration before the Distribution. *Most frequently it had its place between the Preface and the Consecration.* It would be difficult to decide which position—immediately *before* or *after* the Preface—deserves preference. If the Exhortation is put before the Preface, the momentum of the liturgy, at any rate, is not interrupted by the prose of the Exhortation. Volprecht's Exhortation, for example, in view of its content and length, (as with each of Luther's older Exhortations, in view of its content and form) <226> would, in our view, find its proper place *before* the Preface. However, even if most of the church orders which have retained the Preface put Luther's briefer Exhortation after the Preface, that is, between the Preface and the Consecration, this must have been done not only because it was so brief and therefore regarded as having more momentum, but also because it refers particularly to "the words in which Christ gives us His body and blood for forgiveness," and through its conclusion forms a direct connection with the Consecration. The author, who found Luther's Exhortation in this place in his former parish and used it that way for many years, must also admit that he did not, in doing so, sense any interruption caused by the prose. On the contrary, it was always a poignant moment for himself and others when, following the Sanctus, this Exhortation was read, after which a few chords from the organ led into the liturgical recitation of the Our Father.

There was no intention to consider a *free* exhortation in the Communion liturgy. Persuasive in this regard was Luther's note on his Paraphrase and Ex-

---

[287] *Kirchenordnung, wie es mit christlicher Lere* . . . (Wittenberg, 1559), folio 95r., as above. —MC.

[288] *Die pommersche Kirchen-Ordnung und Agenda* . . . (1854), 70: "[after the Sanctus] shall follow the Exhortation to the communicants, according to the various forms included below in the Agenda." —MC.

[289] Cf. *Agenda. Das ist. Kirchenordnung, wie es mit Teuffen* . . . (Eisleben: U. Gaubisch, 1581), folio O4v f. According to Sehling 2:456, the referenced 1594 edition, printed by Paul Donat at the press of Ambrosius Kirchner, was "entirely unchanged." —MC.

[290] *Agenda Schwartzburgica* (Rudolstadt, 1675). The Exhortation, p. 113, follows the prefaces without rubric. —MC.

[291] Cf. *Agenda, Das ist: KirchenOrdnung* . . . (1672), 109: "Then [after the Preface] let the priest read the Paraphrase of the Our Father, as follows. Exhortation to Prayer before Communion. . . ." —MC.

[292] Reproduced in Löhe, *Sammlung*, 3:47, where it is shown to fall after the Sanctus and before the corporate pre-Communion Collect . —MC.

[293] *Kirchen Ordnung im Churfurstenthum der Marcken zu Brandenburg* . . . (Berlin, 1540), folio 50v, following the Agnus Dei and three collects said by the priest. —MC.

hortation: "I would request, however, that this Paraphrase and Exhortation be put in *conceptis seu praescriptis verbis* [set or prescribed words], or in a particular way, for the sake of the people, lest someone do it one way today and another way tomorrow, and each man display his skill in confusing the people so that they cannot learn or retain a thing. The purpose of this all is to teach and guide the people. Thus it is necessary here to break our freedom and use a single form for this Paraphrase and Exhortation, especially within every church or congregation, if in their freedom they decide not to follow someone else."[294]

For the sake of information and for use accordingly, a few of the old exhortations follow here. They are:

(1) *Luther's Exhortation in the Deutsche Messe* (1526). Whenever this *replaces* the Preface, it always includes the Paraphrase of the Our Father, as is very fittingly done in the St. Louis Agenda's "Form of Early Communion."[295] When it is *used with* the Preface, it always appears without the Paraphrase. It is given here in this latter form.

(2) *Luther's alternate Exhortation* from his letter to Nikolaus Hausmann (1525).[296] Even if this one was not, to our knowledge, disseminated more broadly than in the church order of Coburg (1626)[297] and Gotha,[298] <227> it is nevertheless included here as a German-Lutheran echo of the Ancient Church's saying, "Holy things for holy people." Should there be a desire now and then to make use of it, it could be followed by the prayer attached in parentheses or the one connected to Volprecht's Exhortation.

(3) *Wolfgang Volprecht's Exhortation* (1524). This originally extended only to the point indicated by us. The subsequent passage was added, according to Löhe, in the Baden church order (1556).[299] Because of its beauty, the addition then found wide acceptance. Whether the beautiful and fitting prayer following the Exhortation (as in the St. Louis Agenda) originates with that Baden church order, the author cannot say at this time.[300] Despite being also found in

---

[294] Cf. Luther, "The German Mass" (1526), AE 53:80. —MC.

[295] *Kirchen-Agende für ev.-Luth. Gemeinden*, 93. —MC.

[296] Cf. Luther, "An Exhortation to the Communicants" (1525), AE 53:104f. —MC.

[297] *Ordnung Wie es in deß Durchleuchtigen Hochgebornen Fürsten und Herrn Herrn Johann Casimiri . . . gehalten werden solle* (Coburg: P. Ilseburg, 1626), 30f. —MC.

[298] *Kirchen-Agenda: Das ist, Ordnung, Wie es von Pfarrern und Seel-Sorgern . . .* (Gotha, 1647), 47. —MC.

[299] *Kirchenordnung wie die inn der Marggraveschafft Baden . . .* (Baden, 1556). Exhortation begins on p. xlvi with some changes: "Most beloved in Christ Jesus, forasmuch as we now purpose to celebrate and keep the gracious Supper of our dearest Savior, in which . . ."; the addition begins on p. lxix without special distinction. —MC.

[300] Ibid., lxx, after the Exhortation, the rubric: "Then shall the public Confession and Ab-

the St. Louis Agenda,[301] the General Council's *Kirchenbuch*, and other agendas,[302] it is included here for the sake of thoroughness.

(4) *Exhortation from the Hamburg Agenda* (1538 [1529] and 1788).[303] This was widely disseminated in northern Germany and to some extent in central Germany. It is worth noting that the Exhortation is followed here by the singing of "Holy is God the Lord of Sabaoth" from Luther's Sanctus, "Isaiah, Mighty Seer," etc., and then by the Consecration. This may be seen as an indication that, when the Preface is entirely omitted and Volprecht's Exhortation or another is used instead of Luther's 1526 version, the singing of the whole German Sanctus ("Isaiah, Mighty Seer") should come after this Exhortation and before the Consecration. This, then, would likely be the most appropriate place for it, in the event that one does not wish to sing it during the Distribution as Luther directs in the *Deutsche Messe*.[304]

(5) *Exhortation and Prayer from the Braunschweig-Wolfenbüttel Church Order* (1657). Regarding the Exhortation there is included in the church order the following note: "Since in many places there is a worthy tradition of encouraging the congregation in their devotion, particularly those who wish to go to the Sacrament, by way of a German Exhortation either *before* or *after* the Preface; and whereas we regard it conducive to greater devotion that the ceremony to which the congregation is exhorted be preferably put into action itself than that the Exhortation to said ceremony be greatly prolonged; therefore, to this end, we have caused a form of prayer to be composed which shall be read aloud to the congregation in place of the

---

solution follow ['I a poor sinner . . . Almighty God has had mercy . . .'], as indicated hereinabove in the foregoing chapter 'On Penance' [p. lxf.]. After the public Confession, another corporate, public prayer shall follow thus: 'Let us pray. Almighty God, heavenly Father,'" etc., which accompanies Luther's alternate Exhortation (2) here. Regarding the prayer attached to (3), cf. Löhe, *Agende* (1844), 161f., and the somewhat loose translation found in Johannes Deinzer, ed., *Liturgy for Christian Congregations of the Lutheran Faith*, trans. F. C. Longaker, 3rd ed. (Newport, Kentucky: 1902), 31f., where it is called the *oratio fractionis* ("prayer of the breaking [=Distribution]"). —MC.

301 *Kirchen-Agende für ev.-Luth. Gemeinden* . . ., 233f. —MC.

302 Notably Löhe, *Agende* (1844), 159, with the prayer on p. 161. That the prayer is not in view here is shown by the reference to the *Kirchenbuch* of the General Council, which omits the prayer. —MC.

303 *Der Erbarn Stadt Hamborch Christlike Ordeninge* . . . (Hamburg, 1529), reproduced in *Johannes Bugenhagen's Kirchenordnung für die Stadt Hamburg vom Jahre 1529* (Hamburg, 1885), 142f.; and *Ordnung des Gottesdienstes in den Hamburgischen Kirchen* (Hamburg, 1788), 58. The Exhortation is also found as an option in church orders of Braunschweig and Lüneburg, e.g., *Kirchenordnung Unnser von Gottes Genaden Julii* . . . (Wolfenbüttel: C. Horn, 1569), 25f.; *Chur-Braunschweig-Lüneburgische Landes-Ordnungen und Gesetze* . . . (Göttingen, 1739). —MC.

304 Cf. Luther, "The German Mass" (1526), AE 53:81f. —MC.

Exhortation."[305] It will be apparent at first glance that this special form is modeled on Volprecht's Exhortation. <228>

Various Forms

1.

Dear friends of Christ, since we are gathered here in the name of the Lord to receive His holy testament, I exhort you in Christ to apprehend the testament of Christ in true faith, and above all to embrace firmly in your heart the words in which Christ gives us His body and blood for forgiveness, that you may remember and give thanks for His boundless love which He showed us when by His blood He delivered us from the wrath of God and from sin, death, and hell; and to take the bread and wine, that is, His body and blood, as a guarantee and pledge of this. Let us therefore celebrate and receive the testament in His name, at His command, and through His own words:

2.

Dearest friends in Christ, you know that our Lord Jesus Christ, out of unspeakable love, instituted at the last this, His Supper, as a memorial and proclamation of His death suffered for our sins. This memorial calls for steadfast faith, which will make every conscience and heart that wishes to use and partake of the Supper assured and certain that Christ suffered death for all his sins.

But whoever doubts this and does not in some manner feel such faith in him, he should know that this Supper is of no benefit, but rather harmful to him, and should refrain from it. Since we do not see this faith, and it is known only to God, we will leave to the conscience of everyone who comes forward, and admit him at his request and petition.

But those who still live in open sins, such as coveting, hatred, wrath, envy, usury, unchastity, and the like, and have no intention of renouncing them, are hereby refused, and admonished faithfully not to take judgment and harm upon their own soul, as St. Paul says.[306] Yet if anyone has stumbled out of weakness, and proves by his deeds that he earnestly wishes to amend his ways, he shall not be refused this grace and Communion of Christ's body and blood. Let everyone be able and informed to act accordingly and proceed with caution. For our God is not mocked, nor will He have what is holy given to dogs, nor pearls cast before the swine.[307] Amen.

---

[305] *Agenda Oder: Erster Teyl der Kirchen-Ordnung* . . . (Wolfenbüttel: Sterne, 1657), 12. —MC.

[306] 1 Corinthians 11:29. —MC.

[307] Galatians 6:7; Matthew 7:6. —MC.

(Therefore let us pray: Almighty God, heavenly Father, since we cannot please You except in Your beloved Son, our Lord, <229> sanctify our body and our soul, and grant us with true desire and gratitude to partake of His blessed Communion in the Holy Supper, that we being comforted again by Your everlasting mercy and love toward us, and strengthened in newness of life, may more diligently and fearfully live and serve You for the glory of Your holy name and for the good of Your people; through the same Jesus Christ, our Lord. Amen.)

3.

Dearly beloved in God, forasmuch as we now purpose to remember and keep the Holy Supper of our Lord Jesus Christ, in which He has given us His flesh for food and His blood for drink for the strengthening of our faith, it becomes every one of us with great diligence and fervent devotion to examine himself, as St. Paul says, and then to eat of this bread and drink of this cup. For this Holy Sacrament has been given for the special comfort and strengthening of poor, afflicted consciences who confess their sins, fear God's wrath, are afraid of death, and hunger and thirst after righteousness.

But if we examine ourselves, and each of us enters into his own conscience, as St. Paul teaches us, we shall certainly find nothing in us but all manner of detestable sins, and death which we have merited by our sins, from which we can in no wise deliver ourselves. Therefore, our Lord Jesus Christ has had mercy on us, and because of our sins was made Man, that so He might fulfill for us and in our behalf the Law and whole will of God, and for us and for our deliverance take upon Himself and suffer death and all that we deserve for our sins.

And so that we may more confidently believe this, and by believing live cheerfully in His will, after He had supped He took bread, and when He had given thanks, He broke it and said, "Take, eat, this is My body which is given for you." That is, "I was made man, and all that I do and suffer is your own, accomplished for you and for your good. As a certain token and testimony of this, I give you My body to eat." In the same manner also He took the cup and said, "Take, drink of it, all of you; this is the cup of the new testament in My blood, which is shed for you and for many for the forgiveness of sins; do so, as often as you do it, in remembrance of Me." That is, "Having taken your sins upon Myself, I will give Myself into death for those sins, <230> shed My Blood, obtain grace and forgiveness of sins, and so establish a new testament in which sin is forgiven and never accounted to you. As a certain token and testimony of this, I give you my blood to drink.

Therefore, whoever so eats this bread and drinks this cup, confidently believing these words which he hears from Christ and these signs which he receives from Christ, dwells in the Lord Christ and Christ in him, and has eternal life.

We should also do this in remembrance of Him, showing His death—that He died for our sins and rose again for our justification; and giving Him our most heartfelt thanks for the same, we should each of us take up his cross and follow Him, and love one another even as He has loved us.[308] For we are all one bread and one body, even as we all partake of one bread and drink from one cup. For just as from many grapes being trodden one wine and one drink flows forth and is mingled together, and from many grains of wheat one meal is ground and one bread and one loaf is baked: so all of us who by faith are incorporated into Christ are by brotherly love on account of Christ, our Savior, made one body and bread and drink, and faithfully and without guile demonstrate the same to one another, not only in word, but in deed and in truth, as St. John teaches (1 John 3 [:18]).

The almighty and merciful God and Father of our Lord Jesus Christ, by His Holy Spirit, grant this to us! Amen. Now that we may the obtain this all, let us pray:

O my Lord Jesus Christ, almighty and everlasting Son of God! According to the will and counsel of Your heavenly Father, and through the single, holy, and perfect sacrifice of Your body and blood, You have forever <230> perfected those who are being sanctified, and have ordained this Your true and precious body and blood in the Holy Supper for us to eat and to drink. With what earnest and heartfelt contrition and sorrow for sin and with what eagerness and reverence of a strong faith it therefore behooves us to observe and partake of Your Holy Supper! But because of the sin which clings to us, we men are too little, weak, and unworthy to keep this according to Your will and command, profitably in the beauty of holiness. Sanctify us, therefore, O faithful Lord and Savior, in our soul and body by Your Holy Spirit, and make us ready and fit to come worthily to this heavenly benefit. And whatever we through such weakness lack in true repentance,

---

308 *) Thus far the widely disseminated Exhortation of Nürnberg Abbot Volprecht, originating in the year 1524. That which follows the asterisk was added by the Baden church order (1556), while the Brandenburg-Nürnberg church order ([*Kirchenordnung in meiner gnedigen Herrn* . . .] 1592 [folio 50v] and 1639) has the following addition: "And since we have all sinned, therefore humble your hearts before Almighty God, confess your sins and iniquities with a heartfelt love and desire for His divine grace and help and with firm trust in His gracious pledge, and sincerely forgive every man his neighbor, that your heavenly Father may also forgive you your sins and trespasses. If you do so, then once more in the stead of the holy Christian Church and by the command and promise of our Lord Jesus Christ, when He said, 'Whose sins soever you forgive, they are forgiven him,' I absolve you of all your sins in the name of God the Father and of the Son and of the Holy Spirit. Amen."

contrition, and sorrow for sin, in firm and childlike confidence and faith in Your merits, and in the earnest and genuine purpose to amend our life, mercifully fulfill and perfect with the riches and merits of Your bitter sufferings, anguish, and death which You suffered and endured for us all on the tree of the cross, so that we who on the pilgrimage of this world intend to partake of You, our only comfort and Savior, now under the form of the Holy Sacrament, may at last behold You face to face hereafter, and stand in Your presence in the eternal and true fatherland; for You live and reign with the Father and the Holy Spirit, true God, most blessed forever. Amen.

4.

My dearly beloved! Through the preaching of the Gospel we are continually reminded that, on our own, we are ignorant, wretched sinners and lost. And since we are of ourselves nothing more than flesh and blood, and so cannot by our own reason and strength free ourselves from the strict judgment of God and from the power of the devil under which we have fallen by transgressing the commandments and will of God: therefore God, knowing better than we our weakness, has as a gracious Father given His only-begotten Son, Jesus Christ, for us, that by His death we might be delivered from our sins and by Him become the children of God, having eternal salvation, if so we believe. He causes this to be preached to us continually; whoever believes it surely has eternal life.

On the basis of this faith and for this salvation we are also baptized; therein we are to remain continually. In this way we remain in Christ and Christ in us, and <232> continually and without ceasing we eat the body of Christ and drink His blood in a spiritual manner by faith. That is, we are incorporated into Christ and united with Him by believing that He delivered up His body for us into death and shed His blood for us on the cross. In this we confide unto salvation against all false doctrine, all sin, tribulation, and distress.

Out of this benefit of Christ we also learn what love and forbearance we ought to have toward our neighbor, even toward our enemies. What more should we desire?

Yet lest we grow forgetful or weary (as, alas, we do) of believing in the incarnation and death of Christ, He has committed to us a special memorial or declaration of His death, as often as we desire; that, in the outward Sacrament concealed to reason and known only to faith from the words of Christ, we should eat His body and drink His blood, that we may not doubt that His death and the shedding of His blood on the cross is our sure salvation, which it becomes us to sing, read, hear proclaimed, even as we do now (in this our congregation). Afterwards, moreover, we ought to speak of it and *declare* it to one another for our mutual consolation and for the salvation of many, according to the command of Christ: "This do in remembrance of Me!"

Therefore, whoever would eat and drink this Sacrament worthily should do two things: he should believe what Christ says and do what He commands. He says, "This is My body, which is given for you. This is My blood, which is shed for you for the forgiveness of sins." This is what you are to believe. And He commands, "Take, eat; take, drink it, all of you in remembrance of Me!" This is what you are to do, according to His gracious word and command. Amen.

5.

(These—the Hymn, Preface, and Sanctus—being done, let the priest face the communicants and the whole congregation, addressing them with the following words:)

My dearly beloved in God, forasmuch as we purpose to keep the Supper of our Lord Jesus Christ, in which His body is given to us for food and His blood for drink, that in so doing we may remember His death and heartily thank Him, let us therefore call upon God the Father in the name of Jesus Christ, praying from our inmost heart as follows:

(Here let the priest pray with a clear voice, intelligibly, and slowly, so that the whole congregation may hear it and every man say it with him in his heart.)

Lord God, heavenly Father, we heartily thank You that, because of our sin and for our salvation, You have caused Your only beloved Son, our Lord and Savior, Jesus Christ, <233> to be made man, to suffer so many unspeakable agonies, and to die a bitter death upon the cross; who, lest we should forget what He endured for us, also commanded us to keep this present remembrance of His agony and death in the Holy Supper, in which He, out of His unspeakable love, truly gives us in and with this bread and wine the very body which died for us upon the cross and the very blood which was shed for us upon the cross, to eat and to drink, that we may not doubt, but the more confidently believe that His death and the shedding of His blood upon the cross is our certain salvation.

By the same Your dear Son, the only Mediator between You, the righteous God, and us poor sinners, and by His bloody merit, we beseech You, O heavenly Father, to have mercy upon us all. Look upon the face of this our faithful Mediator, Your beloved Son, Jesus Christ, who intercedes for us and is our Advocate at Your right hand. Regard His holy, innocent bloodshed, suffering, and death, which He endured for our trespasses with all patience, out of unspeakable love for us lost men. Forgive us our sins, and give us Your Holy Spirit, that renouncing ungodliness and worldly lusts, we may live in this world moderately toward ourselves, justly toward our neighbors, and in constant, childlike fear toward You, O God, our heavenly Father, as we await the blessed hope and appearing of the glory of our mighty God, Your Son, our Savior Jesus Christ. Let each of us take up his cross, follow Your dear Son, and love one another even as Your dear Son has loved us. For this Holy Sacrament is one bread, and we are all one body, since we partake of one bread and all drink of one cup. Grant to us also, and to all believing Christians, as is profitable and good for us, that we may conduct and conclude this life in fear of You, and obtain eternal salvation. Whereupon let us say from our heart, Amen.

(Note from the author: An Amen subsequently sung by the congregation would not only best express this collective Amen, but also form a transition to the chanting of the Our Father, etc.) <234>

XV. CONSECRATION

Since, according to the records of the evangelists Matthew, Mark, and Luke, and of the apostle Paul, our Lord Jesus Christ, "after He took the elements, *gave thanks*, and then, with specific words of presentation *distributed* them, it is therefore clear that the *Consecration* and *Distribution*, in specified form no less, form the essence of the Holy Supper—that without which it is no Supper . . . since the other part—the preceding Preface and, if need be, the 'Invocation of the Holy Spirit' as in the Greek Church—are to be numbered among those things which constitute ecclesial fullness" (Rudelbach, *Sacrament-Worte* [Words of the Sacrament], 56f.). When in 1 Corinthians 10:16, the bread and cup over which thanks have been given according to the Lord's actions and command are referred to by the apostle as the "consecrated" bread, the "consecrated" cup and so designated as the "*Communion*" of Christ's body and blood, it is an expression not only of the sacramental union of the heavenly good with the elements, but also of the setting apart of the latter for the purpose of that union and its corresponding use, which consists of eating and drinking.

The *ritual* of the Consecration consists of speaking the Words of Institution (*verba testamenti*) over the elements. In every age, the Church has used these words to perform the Consecration. By doing so, she has expressed the conviction "that she cannot more fully or comprehensively fulfill the Lord's command than by joining the Word of Life with the documentarily attested act, and thus doing in every point what Christ did, or rather, representing Christ Himself as still continuing to effect, produce, and sanctify by His Word" (Rudelbach [p. 63]). By the mouth of the minister He repeats the once-spoken Words of Institution and sets them apart from common use. And just as the words of creation, "Be fruitful and multiply and fill the earth," being spoken once, are continually efficacious in nature, so the words of this testament ("This is My body; this is My blood") are efficacious and effectual whenever His institution is kept, so that when the elements are received, they are no longer mere bread and wine but the agency, vehicles, and means for the oral participation of the true body and blood of Christ. <235>

To the Words of Institution, however, the Church joins the holy *Our Father* (*oratio dominica*). Admittedly, a liturgical disparity between the Eastern and Western Church has existed on this point since the fifth century. The former opted for a special consecratory prayer, the aforesaid "*Invocation of the Holy Spirit*," as it is found in various forms in the liturgies which have come to be known by the names of Clement, James, Mark, Basil, Chrysostom, etc. The Western Church opted for the *Lord's Prayer*, and the Lutheran Church followed her in this regard. As in the *Words of Institution*, *here too* the *ipsissima verba* [very words themselves] are to be used. It is not insignificant that *Gregory the Great* says, "It would seem to me most unfitting to speak over the oblation a prayer composed by a church scholar (*scholasticus*) and, on the contrary, not speak over the body and blood of the Redeemer the prayer which He Himself composed."[309] Nevertheless, the fact that the Our Father was used with the Consecration from earliest

[309] *) It is good to include here by way of example a form of the "Invocation of the Holy Spirit" [e.g., *epiclesis*] found in the Liturgy of Clement (itself contained in the *Apostolic Constitutions*, bk. 8), one of the oldest of the liturgies committed to writing. After beginning with the Words of the Sacrament, albeit interpolated (as in all those liturgies) it reads thus: "Being mindful, therefore, of His passion, and death, and resurrection from the dead, etc., we offer to You, our King and our God, according to His constitution, this bread and this cup, giving You thanks, through Him, that You have thought us worthy to stand before You, and to do You service; and we beseech You that You would regard with a good will these gifts which are here set before You, O God, who stand in need of none of our offerings. Accept them to the honor of Your Christ, and send down upon this sacrifice Your Holy Spirit, the Witness of the Lord Jesus' sufferings, that He may make this bread to be the body of Your Christ, and this cup to be the blood of Your Christ, that those who are partakers thereof may be strengthened in godliness, obtain the remission of their sins, be delivered from the devil and his deceit, be filled with the Holy Spirit, be made worthy of Your Christ, and obtain eternal life, according as You are reconciled to them, O Lord Almighty." (König, 114 [Gregory, *Epist. XII. Ad Joannem Syracusanum Ep.* Cf. Jacques P. Migne, ed., *Patrologia cursus completus, series Latina,* 221 vols. (Paris: Garnier Fratres, 1841–55): 77:957a. English translation adapted from *ANF* 7:489. Note here that in the original context, the "prayer" referred to by St. Gregory is the *prex* or *canon.* —MC.]).

times is made clear by the sayings of Justin, Cyril, Jerome, Augustine, and Gregory the Great which Rudelbach cites (*Sacrament-Worte* [Words of the Sacrament], 64, 67, 70). <236>

A point of difference among Lutheran communion liturgies is the *placement* of the Our Father. In agreement with the Roman Mass, some of them let it come *after* the Words of Institution, while the others place it immediately *before*. This difference is found even in Luther's two orders for Divine Service. In the *Formula Missae* (1523), the Our Father *follows* the Words of Institution, and in the *Deutsche Messe* (1526) it *precedes*, albeit in the form of the Paraphrase. The orders which, after the precedent of the *Formula Missae*, left it in place include those of Mark-Brandenburg, Brandenburg-Nürnberg, and Otto Henry [Pfalz-Neuburg]. Meanwhile, the other church orders in northern, central, and southwestern Germany, especially in Saxony, Lower Saxony, Mecklenburg, Schleswig-Holstein, Pomerania, Silesia, Württemberg, etc., follow Luther's second system and insert the Lord's Prayer *before* the Words of Consecration. Yet in so doing, they not only move it to the altar—since Luther himself left it free "whether this Paraphrase and Exhortation should be done *from the pulpit directly after the sermon* or in front of the altar"[310]—but also prescribe it to be used *without* the Paraphrase, accompanied by Luther's brief Communion Exhortation proper, which introduces the Consecration connected to the Our Father, and indeed, with Luther's closing words: "Let us therefore celebrate and receive the Testament in His name, at His command, *and through His own words*." It is only just, then (as noted before), that the *ipsissima verba* be heard in the Our Father as well.[311]

What then is the *meaning* of the Our Father within the Communion rite? Since, on the basis of its initial words and its nature as the Lord's prayer, it was regarded from the beginning as *"the prayer of the faithful,"* by which we "as children of God may come into God's presence and make supplication for every good thing by virtue of our right of sonship," and since it originally had its place in the Communion rite *after* the Words of Institution, *Schöberlein* rejects as erroneous the theory that it has the meaning of a consecratory prayer, and construes it in this position only as a prayer of the faithful "before approaching the holy meal" [Schoeberlein, 1:371], which was spoken by them <237> here (long ago in unison, no less) "to reinforce themselves in the

---

[310] Cf. Luther, "The German Mass" (1526), AE 53:80. —MC.

[311] *) It is very fitting that the "Form for Early Communion" in the St. Louis Agenda, consisting only of Confession and the Supper, nevertheless retains the rich and beautiful Paraphrase of the Our Father which encompasses all the needs of the whole Church, and by which it becomes an Exhortation to the Lord's Prayer.

awareness of their adoption as sons, which guaranteed them the right to that Meal." Here, however, it should not be ignored that a consecratory prayer for the elements nevertheless passed into the liturgy of the West from the Communion liturgies of the Ancient Church; and, as already noted, even some of the Lutheran church orders, conforming to the *Formula Missae*, contain such a prayer, yet orthodox both in sense and form. A different view, however, is offered by *Rudelbach* in his writing, *Die Sacrament-Worte* [The Words of the Sacrament]. Here it says (p. 67): "She (the Ancient Church), we answered, joined to the Consecration the Lord's Prayer as the sum of all that we can pray and therefore as the true *eulogia*. And thus our Church, summarizing the whole matter, teaches that through the *Lord's Prayer* the elements are *destined* for the holy rite; this rite itself, the Consecration, is performed with the Words of Institution; and with the connected Distribution the Mystery is completed, and Christ's body and blood are given to us in, with, and under the bread and wine." This reading, which we for our part regard as more satisfactory, is likewise more consistent with the placement of the Our Father before the Words of Institution. And in fact this was the position which later became the predominant choice in the Lutheran Church.

Now let us turn our attention to the **liturgical execution** of the Consecration, beginning with the *delivery* of the Words of Institution and the Our Father.

In the Roman Canon of the Mass, the Words of Institution are partly interpolated from the liturgies of Clement and James—partly, because the phrase "which is given for you" is simply omitted. Luther *restored for the Consecration the ipsissima verba Domini* [very words of the Lord] *without admixture or abbreviation*, and since that time they have been heard without variation at every Lutheran altar.

In Christian antiquity, the Consecration was done with *a loud, intelligible voice*. Divergence from this practice eventually arose in the papacy when the Mass was turned into a so-called unbloody sacrifice for the living and the dead, resulting in the "abomination of the silent Mass," namely, the *canon missae* <238> narrowly conceived, which begins immediately after the Preface. By this term is understood those five to six subsequent sacrificial prayers which make reference to the Consecration. In the *Formula Missae* Luther calls it "the tattered, ragged, abominable canon or silent Mass, which was composed and concocted from many stinking cesspools."[312] These prayers are said "privately," with a soft voice, by the priest while the choir sings the Sanctus—a lucky thing for the Church, indeed. But after these prayers have been murmured and the Words of Institution come, the

[312] Cf. Luther, "An Order of Mass and Communion" (1523), AE 53:21. —MC.

[choir's] singing stops and a deep silence ensues, the entrance of which is announced by the bell of the ministrant; except that with the *Qui pridie* ("who in the night when He was betrayed" etc.), the priest's voice becomes a full whisper, and after the Elevation which accompanies the Consecration, he prays the few remaining sacrificial prayers with a soft voice while the choir continues singing, and his voice does not resume normal volume until the Our Father, which, in the event that the Mass in question has music, is chanted by him. Thus Luther, by mercilessly purging the whole abomination of sacrifice along with whatever tasted like it, also eliminated the abuse of *speaking softly*, especially with respect to the words of the Consecration. Right in his first liturgical treatise, the *Formula Missae*, he arranges for the *chanting* of the Words of Institution—in the *German* language, no less, while leaving the Preface and many other parts still in Latin. And although out of deference here he places the loud or soft delivery in the freedom of the individual, yet ten years later in his treatise, "The Private Mass and the Consecration of Priests," he is able to proclaim without hesitation, "There our pastor approaches the altar . . . *He publicly and plainly chants* the ordinance of Christ instituted in the Supper."[313] Thus the old church orders contain prescriptions for the liturgist to chant the Words of Institution "with *special vigor* and slowly with good intelligibility";[314] "with *loud, intelligible* words";[315] "with an *elevated and distinct* voice and with special vigor."

While this plainly suggests that the Consecration was done *in a chanted manner*, at the same time, some of the orthodox church orders of the Reformation period explicitly directed the Words of Institution, and the Our Father with them, to be "*spoken* and not chanted." These include the church orders of Augsburg, Ulm, and Schwäbisch Hall, and the Württemberg church order composed by Brenz.[316] Likewise, there was no singing in Alsace, the Palatinate, Frakfurt am Main, Nassau, or Hesse—in short, southwestern <239> Germany, where the influence of Reformed neighbors, namely as a result of Bucer's attempts at a union, if perhaps unable to assert itself in doctrine, certainly did so in liturgy. Otherwise, however, the chant-

[313] Cf. Luther, "The Private Mass and the Consecration of Priests" (1533), AE 38:208. —MC.

[314] In Schoeberlein, 1:357, attributed to the *Cologne Reformation*, i.e., *Von Gottes gnaden unser Hermans* (1544), folio 109v. —MC.

[315] Ibid., attributed to Rothenburg, i.e., *Ordnung Der Kirchen in eines Erbaren Rahts der Statt Rotenburg auff der Tauber Oberkeit unnd Gebiet gelegen* (Frankfurt am Main: N. Hoffman, 1611). The phrase "with loud and intelligible words" can be found, e.g., on p. 229, in the rite of ordination. —MC.

[316] Ibid., attributed to the Württemberg order, i.e., *Gemein Kirchenordnung, wie die dieser Zeit im Fürstenthumb Württemberg gehalten werden soll* (1536), reproduced in *Sammlung der Württembergischen Kirchen-Gesetze* (Tübingen: L. F. Fues, 1834), 8:48. —MC.

ed treatment of this part was prevalent throughout northern and central Germany and even gained entrance in scattered parts of southern Germany. And why not? *Schöberlein* justly observes, "Even if the clergy's chanting is not regarded with favor, it cannot be denied him in this place. For what is to be solemnly recited here is not an act of prayer which is performed, but the Words of the Lord, which compose the sacred foundation of the whole ritual. *And if sacred chant is in place anywhere, it is here.*"[317] Therefore, even if it is impossible, in spite of this, to persuade a congregation to accept the chanting even of the Words of Institution themselves—and even this salutary custom of the orthodox Church remains an adiaphoron—the liturgist should make a concerted effort always to speak these words with an *elevated voice!*

Since in the Roman Mass the Words of Institution were whispered, Luther found no melody for them as he had for the Our Father. In the *Formula Missae*, then, while he says, "I would prefer the Words of Christ—with a brief pause after the Preface—to be chanted in the same tone in which the Our Father used to be sung in the canon,"[318] yet in the *Deutsche Messe* he provided his own melody, one of the beautiful aspects of which includes its making a bold step down to *f* at the beginning of the Lord's words ("Take, eat" etc.). With a few changes it found acceptance particularly in Saxony and Thuringia, and to some extent in Lower Saxony. *In addition to Luther's tone,* a few more tones then appeared. These include that of *Bugenhagen* (1528) and of *Brandenburg-Nürnberg* (1533). The former spread, with a few negligible variants, across north Germany and Pomerania, and even reached Saxony and into Lusatia, and after 1662 was adopted even in Hesse. Over the course of time, Bugenhagen's tone was probably used the most, and for this reason it is also included in the St. Louis Agenda.[319] The other tone, that of Brandenburg-Nürnberg, which was more faithful to the Preface tone, was well received in Franconia, where it is still used today almost everywhere, and was also transported to Austria and even to the Lutheran Palatinate—likewise a majestic melody! So even though it was customary to introduce one of these chant tones into each territorial church, <240> the older church orders frequently offered the option of the other tone also, and several more as time progressed; one example being the Leipzig Agenda (1681) which we have in our possession. In this way "each priest may take the one best suited to himself and his voice," as it says in another agenda.[320]

[317] Schoeberlein, 1:359. —MC.

[318] Cf. Luther, "An Order of Mass and Communion" (1523), AE 53:28. —MC.

[319] *Kirchen-Agende*, 246. —MC.

[320] Oldenburg (1573), i.e., *Kirchenordnung, Wie es mit der Reinen Lere Göttliches Worts . . .*

Partly for the purpose of study, partly for discretionary use, the *three liturgical chant tones* for the Words of Institution and the Our Father referred to follow here. *"Since in these melodies the liturgical delivery approximates actual singing more closely than in others and is for this reason more tolerant of organ accompaniment"* (Schöberlein),[321] therefore, referring the reader to what was said above in Part Two, §3 [pp. 69 ff.], we have included for discretionary use an organ accompaniment based, with only a few exceptions, on Riegel's harmonization in *Schöberlein*'s work. However, an accompaniment *in continuo* was avoided on the basis of many years of experience and of a testimony, made the firmer thereby, that if any organ accompaniment is to be used here, *the accompaniment should come in only at the conclusion, or now and then during the change of the harmony, and conversely be entirely silent wherever several notes of the melody are based on the same chord, so that only the liturgist may be perceived.*

It should also be observed that the *melody for the Our Father* included here with *Luther's tone* originates in Thuringia. Since, on account of the paraphrastic form of the Our Father in Luther's *Deutsche Messe*, the melody is found only for the Words of Institution, a corresponding melody for the Our Father appeared in Thuringia, where Luther's tone was predominantly in use and probably still is. The author, who used it for over twenty-five years in his previous congregation, reproduces it here in the form and harmonization in which he became familiar with it.

Finally, a few words on *decorum*.

As a matter of course, the Consecration is executed *facing the altar*.

At the words "*took bread*" and "*took the cup*," the paten and chalice are *taken* or *touched*, and at the words "*This is My body*" and "*This is My blood*" or "*This cup is the new testament in My blood*," a *cross* is made over the elements. Some agendas, such as the Schwarzburg Agenda (1675),[322] put the sign of the cross at the word <241> "is"; others, such as the St. Louis Agenda,[323] at the words "body" and "blood."

(Jena: D. Richtzenhan, 1573), folio DD3v. The line in full, "Of these melodies, each priest may take the one which is best suited to himself and his voice," forms the title of the page immediately following the consecration chants. —MC.

[321] Schoeberlein, 1:360. —MC.

[322] *Agenda Schwartzburgica* (1675). A cross is printed in the pertinent chants between the words "is" and "My body" on p. 115, but "in" and "My blood" on p. 116. This would seem to indicate that they are oriented toward the body and blood rather than to "is," though additionally including the word "My" in both cases. —MC.

[323] *Kirchen-Agende* . . . A cross is printed between "My" and "body" and again between "My" and "blood" on p. 247. —MC.

It is an Ancient Church custom for either the whole congregation or the assembled communicants to kneel during the Consecration. Luther: "There our pastor approaches the altar . . . And we, in particular those of us who wish to take the Sacrament, kneel beside, behind, and around him," etc.[324] (In the author's former parish, the communicants, having entered the chancel and aisles during "Create in me a clean heart," then knelt at the beginning of the Consecration.)

[324] Cf. Luther, "The Private Mass and the Consecration of Priests" (1533), AE 38:208. —MC.

The Our Father & the Words of the Testament

A. Luther's Tone

(a) Our Father (*Oratio dominica*)

<242>

on earth as it is in heav - en; give us this day our
dai - ly bread; and forgive us our tres - pass - es
as we forgive those who tres - pass a - gainst us; and lead us

not in - to temp - ta - tion, but de - liv - er us from e - vil.
<243>
C For Thine is the king - dom and the pow - er and the
glo - ry for - ev - er and ev - er. A - men.

Or:

Thuringia

Note. In place of these two doxologies, the first one following may also be used.[325] <244>

[325] See the Bugenhagen tone, p. 264. —MC.

(B) Words of the Testament (*Verba Testamenti*)

†) This parenthetical clause from the original may also be omitted.

<245>

††) *Deutsche Messe:* "after the Supper, and said" — a a a c b b a.

†††) *Deutsche Messe:* "This is the cup, a new testament," etc. f f e f | f f f f f, etc.

<246>

In some places also:

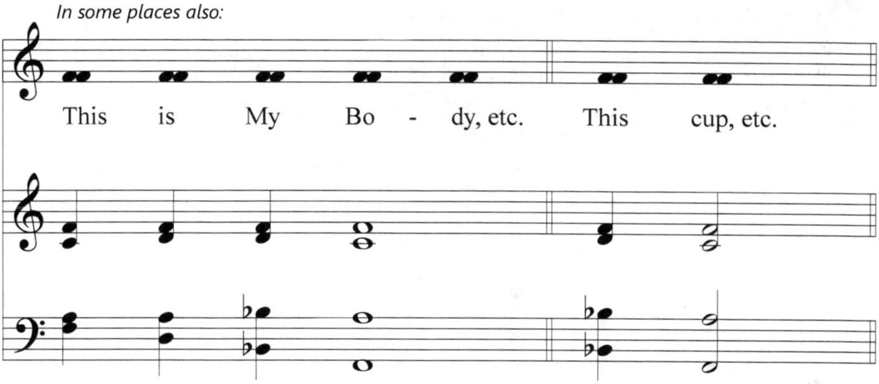

B. Bugenhagen's Tone (1528)

(a) Our Father

<247>

is in heav - en; give us this day our dai - ly bread;
and for - give us our tres - pass - es as we for - give those who
tres - pass a - gainst us; and lead us not in - to temp - ta - tion,

but de - liv - er us from e - vil.
<248>
C For Thine is the kingdom and the power and the
glo - ry for - ev - er and ev - er. A - men.

(B) Words of the Testament

<249>

you. This do in re - mem - brance of Me.” In the same way al - so
He took the cup af - ter supper, and when He had giv - en thanks, He gave it
to them, say - ing: “Drink of it, all of you; this cup is the new

<250>

tes-ta-ment in My ☩ blood, which is shed for you for the for-give-ness
of sins. This do, as often as you drink it, in re-mem-brance of Me."

C. Brandenburg-Nürnberg Melody

(a) Our Father

<251>

is in heav - en; give us this day our dai - ly bread;
and for - give us our tres - pass - es as we for - give those who
tres - pass a - gainst us; and lead us not in - to

<252>

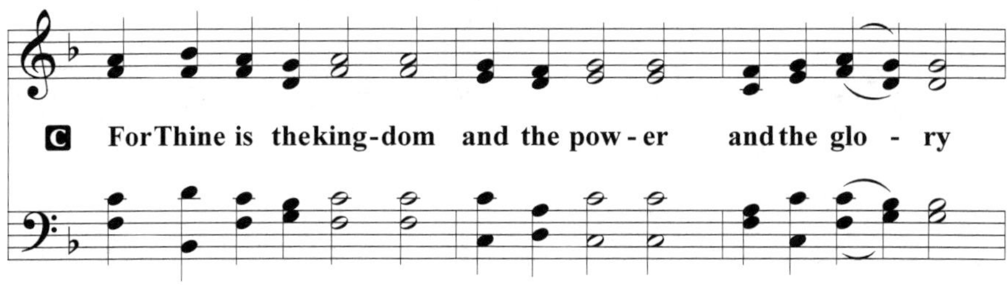

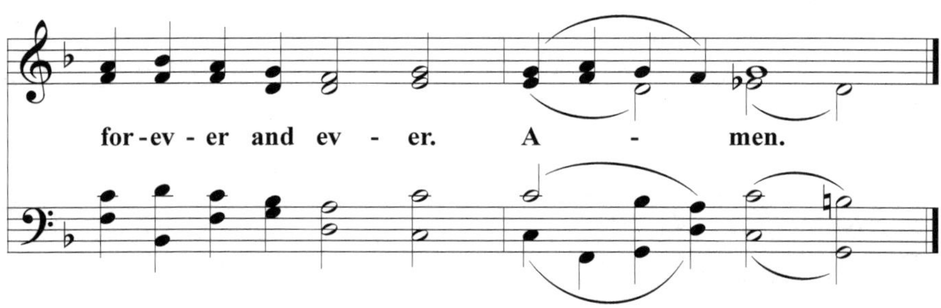

When the doxology ("For Thine is the kingdom...") is omitted, one of the following Amens are sung.

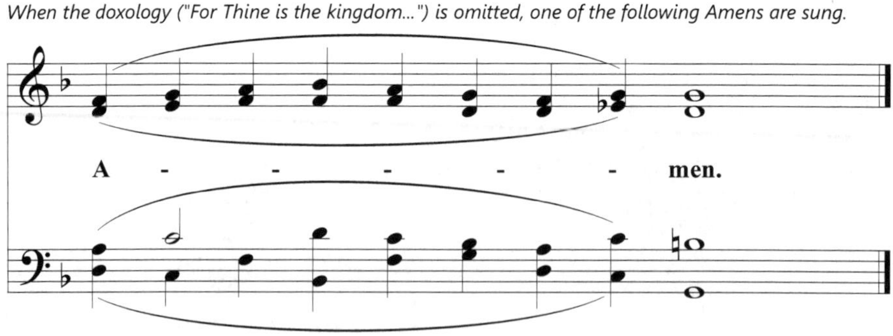

or:

(B) Words of the Testament

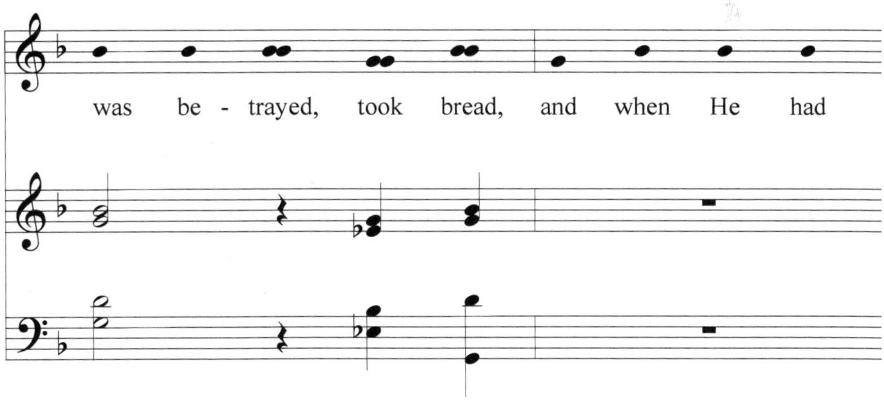

<253>

giv - en thanks, He broke it and gave it to
the dis - ci - ples and said: "Take, eat; this is My ✠ bod-y,
which is giv - en for you. This do in re - mem - brance of Me."

In the same way also He took the cup after supper,
<254>
and when He had given thanks, He gave it to them,
saying: "Drink of it, all of you; this is My ✠ blood of the new

tes - ta - ment, which is shed for you and for man - y
for the for - give - ness of sins. This do, as of - ten
as you drink it, in re - mem - brance of Me.

<255>

XVI. AGNUS DEI AND PAX DOMINI

In his *Formula Missae* (1523), Luther writes:

> Next, the Paternoster shall be read or sung, but with omission of the subsequent prayer: 'Deliver us, we beseech You,' etc. with all the hand motions which used to be made over the host and with the host over the chalice; and the host shall not be broken nor a part of it mixed (with the wine) in the cup.[326] Rather, immediately after the Paternoster the words '*Pax Domini,*' etc., shall be read. This is *a public absolution of the sins of all who are going to the Sacrament,* and is indeed a true word of Gospel which proclaims the forgiveness of sins, and is the only and worthiest preparation for the Lord's Table, provided it be grasped with faith just as if Christ had spoken it with His own lips. For this reason I would like the priest to turn to face the people when he says these words, just as bishops are accustomed to do (which is the only point in which current bishops imitate the old ones). Then, while the Agnus Dei is being sung, let him administer the Sacrament both to himself and to the people. But in the event that the priest wishes to say the prayer: "Lord Jesus Christ, Son of the living God, who according to the will of the Father," etc.,[327] before the Communion, <256> it is not wrong for him to do so as long as he reads "our" and "us" for the words "my" and "me." He may also say this prayer: "The body of our Lord," etc., "preserve my (or your) soul unto life everlasting; and the blood of our Lord preserve," etc.[328]

[326] *) [In the Roman rite], this hand movement, or making the sign of the cross, consists in the priest's breaking off a piece of the consecrated host, crossing the cup three times with said fragment, and then singing: "Pax domini sit semper vobiscum," upon which he then inserts the fragment into the cup.

[327] The whole prayer from the medieval rite following the Pax, reads: "O Lord Jesus Christ, Son of the living God, who, according to the will of the Father, the Holy Spirit cooperating, through Your death, have given life to the world: deliver *me*, I beseech You, by this holy body and this Your blood from all *my* iniquities and from all evils: and so make *me* always to obey Your commandments, and never permit *me* to be separated from You forever; who live and reign with God the Father and the same Holy Spirit, one God forever and ever. Amen." Emphasis added to show where Luther intended the words to be changed. —MC.

[328] Cf. Luther, "An Order of Mass and Communion" (1523), AE 53:28f. —MC.

Agnus Dei

Now concerning the *Agnus Dei* taken from John 1:29, its use extends far back into Christian antiquity, and in the Eastern Church it was primarily a *morning chant*. Then in the sixth century, Gregory the Great brought it by way of translation into the Latin Church. However, it received its inclusion in the Mass and its placement between the Consecration and Distribution from Pope Sergius I (in 687), with the specification that it should be "chanted by the priesthood *and the people*,"[329] which Pope Adrian I [†795] revised a hundred years later so that *only the choir* could sing it, as is the case today. The threefold repetition first appeared around 1120, with the third phrase exchanging "miserere nobis" (have mercy upon us) for "dona nobis pacem" (grant us Your peace), specifically referring to the kiss of peace (*osculum pacis*) which was the congregants' customary way to greet each other in that period. In both his *Geschichte des Kirchenlieds und Kirchengesangs* [History of Church Song and Church Music] (4:191)[330] and in Herzog's *Real-Encyclopaedia* (1:179), Koch, quoting an older translation of a passage from Bishop Durandus's (†1270) work, *Rationale officiorum divinorum*, gives as the reasoning behind the threefold repetition the following: "No one exhibited greater patience in the greatest of sorrows, temptations, and trials than the Redeemer. Therefore the Christian Church stands in awe of this and intentionally sings three times: '*Agnus Dei, qui tollis*,' etc. During the threefold repetition we consider how the Lord Jesus (1) took away our sin, (2) personally bore the punishment for it, and (3) has conveyed His merits into our heart in the preaching of the Gospel and in the most Holy Supper."

In view of the fact that, when Christ institutes the Holy Supper, He says, "*This do in remembrance of Me*," and Paul accordingly writes, "*As often as you eat of this bread and drink of the cup of the Lord, you shall proclaim the Lord's death until He comes*" [1 Corinthians 11:26], Luther found the use of the Agnus Dei during Communion all the more appropriate <257> and sensible. He writes: "The *Agnus* especially, more than any song, is of service to the Sacrament, since it clearly sings about and praises Christ as the one who bore our sins, and *powerfully and gracefully urges* ***the remembrance of Christ*** *with a few, beautiful words*" (EA 23:191; StL 10:2195 [AE 38:123]).[331]

[329] See Louis Duchesne, ed., *Liber Pontificalis: Texte, Introduction et Commentaire*, 2 vols. (Paris: 1886–92): 1:381; and Theodor Mommsen, ed., *Gestorum Pontificum Romanorum pars I: Liber Pontificalis* (Berlin, 1898), 1:381: *Hic statuit, ut tempore confractionis Dominici corporis Agnus Dei qui tollis peccata mundi, miserere nobis, a clero et populo decantetur.* —MC.

[330] Koch, *Geschichte des Kirchenlieds und Kirchengesangs*, 4:191, and also 8:30. —MC.

[331] Also quoted in Löhe, *Sammlung*, 3:33. —MC.

In his *Formula Missae*, on the one hand, he adheres more closely to the structure of the Roman Mass in this regard, specifying, "The Consecration, the Our Father, the Peace, the Agnus with the prayer 'O Lord Jesus Christ,' etc."[332] On the other hand, in his *Deutsche Messe*, he has the Our Father precede the Words of Institution, as we have already seen.[333] Because Luther here separates the consecration and distribution of the bread and wine, he appoints for the distribution of the bread the singing of hymns such as "Isaiah, Mighty Seer" or "O Lord, We Praise Thee," or "Jesus Christ, Our Blessed Savior," but after the consecration of the chalice, while it is being administered, "whatever remains of the aforesaid hymns, or else the German Agnus Dei" (EA 22:241; StL 10:249 [AE 53:81f.]). Accordingly, those church orders which, following Luther's precedent, place the Our Father before the Words of Institution, while at the same time rejecting Luther's suggestion to separate the Consecration and Distribution, frequently place the Agnus at the close of the Distribution; the others, however, at the beginning of it, that is, right after the Words of the Testament. For example, in the Braunschweig-Lüneburg church order[334] it reads: "As soon as Communion is begun, without any prelude on the organ or any other music, the whole congregation shall immediately sing '*Lamb of God, Pure and Holy*,'[335] slowly and with devotion. If, when it is finished, there are still communicants present, the hymn on Christ's Passion, '*Christ, Who Saves Us by His Cross*,'[336] etc., shall be sung. And after that, depending on the number of communicants: '*Lord Jesus Christ, Thou Highest Good*,' '*Jesus Christ, Our Blessed Savior*.'"[337] Thus *immediately* after Christ's words, "This do in remembrance of Me," comes the specific proclamation of Christ's death through the Agnus Dei! Whenever people in our day return to the earlier form of the Divine Service, they find it preferable to place the Agnus right after the Words of the Testament, as most of the Saxon agendas prescribe. A case in point is the Missouri Synod Agenda. As evident from

[332] Cf. Luther, "An Order of Mass and Communion" (1523), AE 53:29. —MC.

[333] That is, the "Paraphrase of the Our Father." Cf. Luther, "The German Mass" (1526), AE 53:78ff. —MC.

[334] *Agenda Oder: Erster Teyl* . . . (Wolfenbüttel: Sterne, 1657), 42. —MC.

[335] "O Lamm Gottes unschuldig" (N. Decius, 1531). Wackernagel 3:568f, nos. 619ff. See *LSB* 434. —MC.

[336] "Christus, der uns selig macht" (M. Weiße, 1533). Wackernagel 3:259, no. 289. The English translation is found in John C. Kunze, ed., *A Hymn and Prayer-Book* . . . (New York: Hurtin & Commardinger, 1795), 46f., no. 35. —MC.

[337] "Herr Jesu Christ du höchstes Gut" (B. Ringwald, 1588), Wackernagel 4:1028, no. 1523. "Jesus Christus, unser Heiland" (M. Luther, 1524), Wackernagel 3:9f., no. 10. Cf. Luther, "Jesus Christ, Our Savior True" (1524), AE 53:258–59. —MC.

the materials referenced, the versified reworking of the Agnus by Decius ("Lamb of God, Pure and Holy") was also used in some places.

The Agnus Dei boasts a number of *melodies*. That which is now in use almost everywhere is the familiar, simple, graceful melody <258> found in all good choir books, including the St. Louis *Choralbuch*. Its inclusion here is therefore superfluous. For the sake of *organists*, however, it should just be noted that, when in the Roman Mass the Agnus "is sung accompanied by gentle sounds, frequently with soft flute music and delicate strings,"[338] the corresponding registers in the organ accompaniment would be Rohrflöte with Gamba or Salicional.

Pax Domini

Regarding the Salutation of Peace (John 20:21), its relationship to that in the Roman Mass is as follows. As already mentioned, after the Our Father, the priest fractures the consecrated host in two halves and one of those again in two parts. With the smallest of these he makes the sign of the cross over the chalice and sings, "Pax Domini sit semper vobiscum." ("The peace of the Lord be with you always.") Hereupon he drops this particle of the host into the chalice with the words, "Haec commixtio et consecratio Corporis et Sanguinis Domini nostri Jesu Christi fiat accipientibus nobis in vitam aeternam. Amen." ("May this mixture and consecration of the body and blood of our Lord Jesus Christ attain unto everlasting life for us who receive it. Amen.")[339]

However relentless Luther was, then, in abolishing this latter ceremony in view of the fact that, although stemming from antiquity,[340] it was nevertheless blasphemous, yet in his *Formula Missae* he did not "throw out the baby with the bathwater," but retained the Salutation of Peace, beautifully interpreting it as "a public absolution of the sins of all who are going to the Sacrament," and as "a true word of Gospel which proclaims the forgiveness of sins, and is the only and worthiest preparation for the Lord's Table,

[338] Herzog, *Real-Enzyklopädie*, 1:179. The source which Lochner has relied on here and there throughout this chapter he now quotes directly. —MC.

[339] *) In his writing, "The Abomination of the Secret Mass" (1523), Luther gives the following gloss: "Here the fool speaks of many who receive, yet receives it alone. And it is a further slander when he says that he mixes the body and blood of Christ together. I would like to know how the body and blood could be mixed when it is one Christ! He may well mix bread and wine. However, it is far worse when he calls it a hallowing of the body and blood, as though there were anything in Christ that needed hallowing. And he says in addition that that mixing helps those who take it attain to everlasting life, that is, that the work does it. What becomes of the words in which life consists? It is all placed solely upon us and the sacrifice!" (EA 29:128ff. [AE 36:324]).

[340] *) Cf. König, [n.p.].

provided it be <259> grasped with faith, just as if Christ had spoken it with His own lips."[341] For this reason he desires this salutation to be spoken or chanted not over the altar, as in the Roman Mass, but facing the people.

The Salutation of Peace is found only in those Lutheran liturgies which adhered more to the *Formula Missae*, such as, for example, those of Strassburg, Erfurt, and Brandenburg-Nürnberg. Because of its admirable interpretation, good liturgies of more recent times have mostly adopted the Salutation of Peace and rightly appointed its place after the Agnus, immediately before the Distribution: for example, the *Kirchenbuch* of the General Council, which, although agreeing closely with the Brandenburg-Nürnberg church order on the model of Löhe's, nevertheless has the Our Father precede the Words of Institution. For those who are able or willing to use the Salutation of Peace before the Distribution, a few melodies are included below.

In the Roman Mass, after the Agnus and before the consumption, there are a few *Prayers of Preparation*. One of these ("Lord Jesus Christ, Son of the living God, who according to the will of the Father," etc.) Luther, in the *Formula Missae*, regards as good, yet leaves its use to individual discretion.[342] Clearly the fine Prayer of Preparation which was later appended to Volprecht's Communion (and is included in the St. Louis Agenda, p. 235ff.), is an expansion of it, and for that reason also to be used in this place. Thus in the new edition of Löhe's Agenda (1884)[343] it is also in this place, at first abbreviated, then word for word from the point, "Therefore sanctify us," etc. The Breslau Agenda contains the following Prayer of Preparation, used, as far as we know, in most Silesian Lutheran churches:

> Devout and chosen people, that God may grant you grace to partake of the Holy Supper unto your salvation, let us call upon Him with lips and heart, praying thusly:
>
> O Lord, although I am not worthy that You should enter under my roof, yet I am in need of Your help and desirous of Your grace that I may attain to godliness and salvation. Thus I come, trusting in nothing but Your Word, with which You have invited me to this Table, promising me, unworthy though I am, that I shall have forgiveness of my sins through Your body and blood, which I eat and drink in this Sacrament. O dear Lord, I know that Your divine promise and Your words are true; I do not doubt them, <260> and on this basis I eat and drink; be it unto me according to Your Word. Amen. (Luther.)

[341] Cf. Luther, "An Order of Mass and Communion" (1523), AE 53:28f. —MC.

[342] Ibid., AE 53:29. —MC.

[343] Löhe, *Agende* (1884). Cf. Deinzer, *Liturgy for Christian Congregations*, 31f. —MC.

O Lord Jesus, unite Yourself to me, that I may abide in You and You in me, nor I be parted from You here in time or hereafter in eternity.

Lord Jesus Christ, Your holy body feed me, Your precious blood be drink to me, Your bitter suffering and death strengthen me. In Your holy wounds I hide me. Let me nevermore depart from You. From the evil foe deliver me, and in true faith sustain me, that with all the elect I may praise and worship You, here in time and hereafter in eternity. Amen.[344]

Pax Domini

(For the Words of the Testament settings A–B)

Braunschweig, 1531

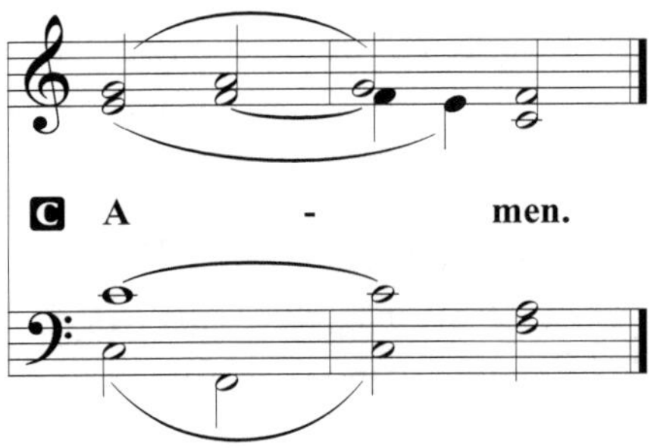

[344] Cf. Wilhelm Löhe, *Seed-Grains of Prayer: A manual for Evangelical Christians,* trans. H. A. Welle (Chicago: Wartburg Publishing House, 1912), 157f. (no. 90). A similar prayer at this point in the liturgy is found in the *Agenda, oder Ordnung derer Evangelischen Kirchen im Oelßnischen Fürstenthum* . . . (1664), folio 100r: "O Lord Jesus Christ, although I am not worthy that You should enter under my roof, yet I need and desire, hunger and thirst for Your grace, refreshment, comfort, and strength in the most worthy Sacrament of Your true body and precious blood. Therefore I implore You, my only Redeemer and Savior, grant me Your bountiful grace, that I may receive the most worthy Sacrament in a repentant, believing, and God-fearing heart for the strengthening of my faith, the forgiveness of all my sins, and life everlasting; for You live and reign with the Father and the Holy Spirit, one God, now and forever. Amen." Luther's prayer by itself is also found in the Missouri Synod's *Kirchengesangbuch*. Cf. *Walther's Hymnal*, 367, no. 20b. —MC.

(For the Words of the Testament, setting C)

or:

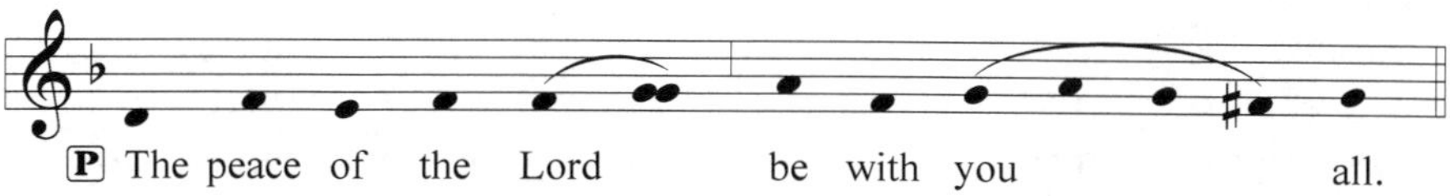

Brandenburg-Nürnberg, 1533

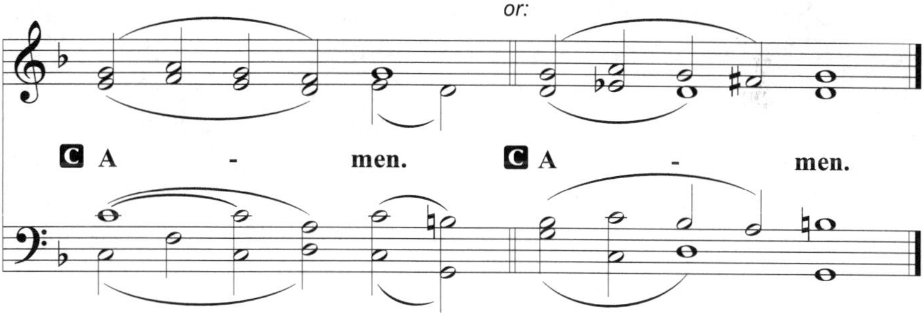

<261>

XVII. DISTRIBUTION

"The *Distribution* of the Holy Supper (with administration formula) is so intimately connected to the Consecration that our Church regards both properly as a *continuum*. The Distribution can no more be omitted than the Consecration, when the subject of discussion is the administration of the Sacrament" (Rudelbach).[345] It is quite otherwise with the Roman Mass. Although in that rite the Consecration is followed by the *sumptio* (self-communion) of the priest, and after that comes the communion of the laity under one kind, yet the Roman Church especially considers the Distribution a mere inessential addendum to the Mass, and speaks more of a spiritual co-participation of the congregation, while it regards the *sumptio* of the priest as essential to the Mass, or belonging to the sacrifice of the Mass, and in so doing asserts that the people in attendance derive benefit from the *sumptio* of the sacrificing priest.

[345] Rudelbach, 73. —MC.

That in the Lutheran Chief Divine Service the *sumptio* was not simply abolished is demonstrated in the previous section with the words cited from Luther's *Formula Missae*: "Then, while the Agnus Dei is being sung, let him administer the Sacrament both to himself and to the people."[346] In accordance with this, the *sumptio* is found with the Distribution in the church order of Wittenberg by Bugenhagen, [347] in that of Strassburg,[348] and in that of Andreas Döber in Nürnberg (1525).[349] But it has long since been demonstrated that the Smalcald Articles [II II 8], in those famous words, is not speaking *against the priest's self-communion where the congregation also communes*, but only against the priest's self-communion when it is done *to the exclusion of the congregation* in the so-called silent or sacrifical Mass. It is only viewed as the irregular form of dispensing inasmuch as it is declared permissible only as a matter of necessity: "when, as is often the case here, preachers are so solitary and separated from their brethren in the office that, if they were not willing to administer the Holy Supper to themselves, they would in many cases have to abstain from it for years and years." (For further details generally, see Dr. Walther's *Americanisch-lutherische Pastoraltheologie*, §18, comment 8.)[350]

With the Distribution of the Holy Supper under both kinds, the Lutheran Church returned to the Lord's institution and so to the practice of the Ancient Church. But whether, according to ancient usage the *joint* <262> consecration of both kinds should be made to precede the Distribution, or whether the bread should be distributed right after being blessed, and so for the chalice as well, Luther, in his *Formula Missae* as well as in his *Deutsche Messe*, leaves it entirely to the discretion of the individual pastor. In the former he writes:

> Here the method by which both kinds are received or administered is to be left to the choice of the bishop or pastor. He may bless both the bread and the wine together before he partakes of the bread or,

[346] Cf. Luther, "An Order of Mass and Communion" (1523), AE 53:29. —MC.

[347] *Ain ordnung Christlicher Messen* . . . (Wittenberg, 1524) in Löhe, *Sammlung*, 3:40: "After this prayer [O Lord Jesus Christ . . .] the priest feeds himself, then the people." —MC.

[348] *Ordnung der Meß so die kirch* . . . (Straßburg, 1525), in Löhe, *Sammlung*, 3:57, regarding Distribution: "Then he takes the host in hand and says, 'Our Lord Jesus said to His dear disciples, Take, eat; this is My body which is given for you.' Likewise with the cup, as written in the Evangelists and Paul. Then the priest may also partake of the Sacrament, which he might have done previously as well, before he distributed it to the people." —MC.

[349] *Von der Evangelischen Meß* . . . (Nürnberg, 1525), in Löhe, *Sammlung*, 3:47–48, after the Exhortation and Prayer of Preparation: "Now he communes the people . . ."; ". . . When he has taken, he covers the chalice . . ." —MC.

[350] C. F. W. Walther, *American-Lutheran Pastoral Theology*, ed. David W. Loy, trans. Christian C. Tiews (St. Louis: Concordia Publishing House, 2017), 230–32. —MC.

> between the blessing of the bread and wine, feed the bread to himself and as many others as desire it, and after that bless the wine, and then give it to all to drink. This is the practice Christ used, I believe, as is apparent form the words of the Gospel, since He invited the disciples to eat the bread before he blessed the cup. Afterwards the evangelist says more plainly, "In the same manner also He took the cup after supper," etc., so that it may certainly be perceived that the cup was blessed only after the partaking of the bread. But this practice is all too new and will not allow all for those things which until now we have said after the blessing, unless someone wished to change them, too. (StL 10:2245 [AE 53:30].)

And in the *Deutsche Messe*, in which he simultaneously also takes up the corresponding change of the form and practice, he writes, "But it seems to me that it would accord with the Supper to administer and give the Sacrament directly after the consecration of the bread, before the cup is blessed (for both Luke and Paul say, 'In the same manner also the cup, after they had supped,' etc. [Luke 22:20; 1 Corinthians 11:25]), and meanwhile to sing the German Sanctus or the hymn, 'O Lord, We Praise Thee,' or John Huss's hymn, 'Jesus Christ, Our Blessed Savior.' Then let the cup be blessed and given, and whatever is left of the aforementioned hymns be sung, or else the German Agnus Dei" (EA 22:241, StL 10:249 [AE 53:81–82]). Nevertheless, the joint Consecration of both kinds became the dominant practice, and the other method was used only here and there for Communion of the sick, as for instance in the Nürnberg *Agendbüchlein* (1755), to which rite it may be best suited.

After the precedent of the Ancient Church, the Lutheran Church also has a *distribution formula*. In the *Formula Missae*, Luther retains that of the Roman Church: *"The body of our Lord Jesus Christ preserve your soul unto life everlasting."*[351] In the Agenda of Duke Henry of Saxony (1536),[352] it says somewhat more explicitly, "The *body of our Lord Jesus Christ, given into death for you, strengthen and preserve you in the true faith unto life everlasting.*" Veit Dietrich's *Agendbüchlein* <263> (1543)[353] has the formula: *"Take, eat, this is the body of Christ which was given for you. Take, drink,"* etc. In opposition to the Sacramentarians, however, it was considered necessary in later times to make the confession of the true presence of Christ's body and blood under the bread and wine even more definitive, and thus there arose the administration formula still everywhere in use in the Lutheran

---

[351] Cf. Luther, "An Order of Mass and Communion" (1523), AE 53:29. —MC.

[352] Cf. *Agenda: das ist Kirchenordnung* . . . (1540), folio 20v, in the rite of Communion of the Sick; but "true (faith)" is only in the formula for the blood. —MC.

[353] *Agend Büchlein* . . . (1565), folio G2v. —MC.

Church: "*Take, eat, this is the true body,*" etc. And rightly so, for if "preserving the purity of the Word was the main concern in the Consecration, then in the Distribution (and the better to rule out every personal whim) it will be no less than what is required in order to encompass in those few words of *appropriation* the sum of all that comes before." (Rudelbach.)[354] However, when the pastor communes himself, he receives the bread alone with the benediction: "*The body of our Lord Jesus Christ preserve my soul unto life everlasting. Amen*"; likewise the cup with the words: "*The blood of our Lord Jesus Christ preserve my soul unto life everlasting. Amen.*"

Concerning the order of reception, as in the Early Church, the Holy Supper is administered first to the men and then to the women. In many places it was, and still is, observed as follows: "adult males and young men go up first, then young women along with married women and mothers" (Brandenburg-Magdeburg),[355] while in other locations the young men lead the males and young women the females. If the preacher communes, then according to Ancient Church practice he receives the Sacrament *first*. Yet there does appear, albeit somewhat less frequently, the provision, "When everyone has received the Holy Sacrament, then shall the priest also receive it" (Otto Henry).[356] In any case, it is generally assumed that the preacher is the most diligent companion at the Lord's Table, and therefore, if possible, communes with the people on every occasion. One may note, among other things, the exhortation in the Austrian Agenda: "Church ministers and pastors shall also habituate themselves (as has always been the practice of the Church since apostolic times) *to communing with the people*, and shall do so as a good example to the Church and the congregation."[357]

While the Sacrament was, here and there, received standing, this represented rather the exception. As a rule, it was, and still is, received kneeling, preceded by a profound bow of obeisance. For this reason, "a low bench" was to be fixed before the altar "on which the communicants <264> could kneel, as fitting, when they receive the Supper"[358] (Höya, 1571, etc.).[359] Kneeling while receiving the Sacrament is also more fitting because of the

[354] Rudelbach, 73f.

[355] *Chur-Fürstliche Brandenburgische Im Hertzogthum Magdeburg publicirte Kirchenordnung Anno 1685* (Halle, 1708), 44, no. 24. —MC.

[356] *Kirchen ordnung: Wie es mit der Christlichen Lehre* . . . (Nürnberg: 1543), part 2, p. 30. —MC.

[357] *Christliche Kirchen-Agenda, wie die bey den zweyen Ständen* . . . (Austria, 1571), folio 109r. —MC.

[358] *) In the Roman Church, only the celebrant receives the Sacrament at the altar. It is normally administered to all others at the screen which divides the chancel from the nave.

[359] *Kirchen Ordnung, Wie es in Religions* . . . (Leipzig, 1580), 46. —MC.

administration of the chalice. If *processing around the altar* is usual and feasible, as it was in most cases, three people at a time approach to receive the consecrated bread on the left side, or north side when the altar faces east. If they kneel or stand around the altar so that the Distribution takes place in shifts, it is possible even to omit the *votum* [blessing] from the administration formula during the reception of the holy body under the consecrated bread, and then, when the table has received the holy blood, the blessing may be said by the celebrant with the words: "*The body of our Lord Jesus Christ, and His precious blood, strengthen and preserve you in the true faith unto life everlasting. Amen.*" Yet the administration formula may also be used in combination with the *votum* as during the communicants' procession around the altar.

If the consecrated bread or the consecrated wine run out, the organ and singing stop and *consecration is performed anew*, whether it be the bread or the wine or both. According to the Ulm church order, they were "by no means to break any host" in order to make enough, but "to bring such hosts as were wanting."[360] This church order also called for the Our Father as well as the pertinent Words of the Testament to be repeated in the new Consecration,[361] while others only required the latter.

Accordingly, when it says further in Luther's *Deutsche Messe*, with respect to the reception: "so that *it is done with good order and decency,*"[362] isolated provisions for this are found here and there in the church orders. Thus, for example, we read in the Magdeburg church order (1685): "And all communicants shall go to the Lord's Table with dutiful obeisance, devotion, decency, and humility, without any regard for any sort of privileged order, and by their clothing, actions, and all things shall permit no flippancy, vanity, or arrogance to be detectable in them, but rather true Christian beauty, which consists not of braiding the hair, wearing gold, etc. . . . In particuar, as at all other times no less than while receiving the Holy Supper, women shall not expose themselves, but shall remove <265> any apparel *which serves as a hindrance or otherwise causes offense during distribution.*"[363] And in the *Corpus of Saxon Church Law* of 1735, it says, according to Augusti's *Denkwürdigkeiten* [Augusti's Memorabilia from Christian Archaeology],[364]

[360] *Kirchenordnung wie es in der Stadt Ulm* . . . (1747), 334. —MC.

[361] Ibid., 334–5. —MC.

[362] Cf. Luther, "An Order of Mass and Communion" (1523), AE 53:34. —MC.

[363] *) It was not long ago that women's hats became a hindrance when it comes to distribution, especially the chalice. [*Chur-Fürstliche Brandenburgische* . . . (1685), 43, no. 22. —MC.]

[364] J. C. W. Augusti, *Denkwürdigkeiten aus der christlichen Archäologie,* 12 vols. (Leipzig: Dyk, 1817–31), 5:249. —MC.

"But especially, men (shall) not offensively put their whiskers in the chalice and thereby give double offense. Likewise also the women shall not have veils in front of their mouth or caps over their eyes. Likewise, communicants shall open their mouth so that the Sacrament can be put into their mouth, and not, as might possibly happen, drink nothing at all from the chalice."[365] (Even in some of our local congregations there was formerly the admirable custom not only of women going to the Lord's Table in dark, simple garments, but also of young women having their heads bared and married women wearing a white bonnet when approaching. Unfortunately this custom has increasingly disappeared.)

As long as the Distribution lasts, the rest of the congregation (whose presence is thereby presupposed—and to this end the Braunschweig-Lüneburg church order specified that "the priest make earnest exhortations several times a year for the congregation to stay during Communion")[366] is edified by singing Communion hymns; namely, the hymns "Jesus Christ, Our Blessed Savior" and "O Lord We Praise Thee, Bless Thee, and Adore Thee," as well as the German Sanctus, "Isaiah, Mighty Seer," etc. When the number of communicants is large, *antiphonal music* would be preferably employed to sustain and increase devotion. For example, "the choir and the people would sing [responsively] stanza by stanza" (Pomerania).[367] On high feasts, it was here and there accompanied by instrumental music.[368] However, for the use of instrumental music there is the explicit limitation "that the singing of the choir be not completely overshadowed." And for <266> organists there is the note that interluding on the organ should be done "with moderation"—a needful note for our day as well. How seldom does it not arise that an organist believes that perfectly long organ playing is required between individual stanzas of the Communion hymn, either because he fears that the Communion hymn may not be long enough, or even more, the congregation might be wearied by too much singing, while he does not notice that his immoderate interluding wearies the congrega-

[365] *Corpus Juris Ecclesiastici Saxonici* . . . (Dresden / Leipzig: R. Sauereßig, 1735), 34. —MC.

[366] See *Kirchenordnung Vnnser von Gottes Genaden Julii* . . . (Wolfenbüttel: C. Horn, 1569), 22: "And the preacher shall at times exhort the people to remain in the church during the General Prayer and during Communion." —MC.

[367] Reproduced in *Die Pommersche Kirchen-Ordnung und Agenda* . . . (1854), 80. —MC.

[368] *) Thus, for example, in the Communion hymn by Sigismund Schererz [1584–1639]: "Mein Seel, dich freu," stanzas 21–23:

"My violas pure, resound freely for joy! Now sing ye in harmony from the heart with good courage! And according to old custom, let the organ ring with beauty in God's temple, and the sound of trumpets adorn the singing with delightful tones, so that the guests rejoice for this feast, and sorrow may well vanish from their spirit."

tion and makes them reluctant to sing further, especially when the musician is not a master on the organ. Therefore let moderation be kept here in playing between individual stanzas, remembering that the congregation does not exist for the organist but the organist for the congregation. If the selected Communion hymn is not long enough, let another hymn number simply be added, or take the first two stanzas of "O Lord, We Praise Thee," and use the third as the concluding stanza [following the Benediction].[369]

XVIII. POST-COMMUNION

In the *Formula Missae*, it reads: "If there is a desire to sing the *communio*, let it be sung. But instead of the *complenda*, or final collect—since this commonly refers to sacrifice—one may say, in the same tone, the prayer, 'What we[370] have by mouth received, O Lord,' etc. Also, one might say the prayer, 'May Your Body, O Lord, which we[371] have taken,' etc., and conclude with the words, "for You live and reign," etc. Then let the priest sing, '*Dominus vobiscum*'" (StL 10:2244 [AE 53:29]). After the reception, the Roman priest, standing on the Epistle side, sings or speaks a verse, normally Tobit 12:6 ("Bless and give thanks to the God of heaven in the sight of all, because He has shown such mercy to you"), or another Bible verse according to the occasion. This is the *communio* of the Roman Mass. Then <267> he lets some of the unconsecrated wine to be poured into the chalice by the ministrants in order to ablute it,[372] at which he says the first prayer mentioned by Luther ("What we have taken with our lips, O Lord," etc.). Then he wipes out the chalice with a napkin, holds his thumb and forefinger over the chalice, has water poured over them to wash them, and says the second prayer ("May Your Body, O Lord," etc.).

[369] *) I experienced this *non plus ultra* years ago on the occasion of a gathering of representatives of several synods, when, during the Distribution of the Holy Supper, they only got as far as the second stanza of the hymn "Soul, Adorn Thyself with Gladness," whereas the whole hymn could have been sung if *Herr* Organist had used due moderation in his stanzaic interludes, which on top of it all sounded a good deal operatic. I can still picture blessed Wd[alther] sitting in front of me, repeatedly shaking his gray head and casting angry glances at the man on the organ bench. [For more on the closing stanza, see below, p. 293. —MC.]

[370] *) "We" — what a self-testimony on the part of the celebrant against his private Mass!

[371] Note that a change to the plural "we" is intentionally indicated here. Cf. Luther, "An Order of Mass and Communion" (1523), AE 53:29.

[372] *) On occasion this abluted wine is also offered to the laity, and then those poor people believe they have received the Sacrament under *both* kinds.

What follows this, then, is what is referred to as the *Postcommunio*. This consists of yet another prayer that the reception of the Sacrament which has just taken place may be a blessed one for the participants. The congregation's dismissal, "Ite, missa est," is followed by the "Post-Communion Collect," or *complenda*, beginning with the words "Placeat tibi, sancta Trinitas," etc.[373] Luther eliminates this final prayer (which returns to the idea of sacrifice and therefore asks that it may be "Deo acceptabile," and "propitiabile" for the priest and those for whom he offered it) and in its place sets the previous two Post-Communion collects of the *Formula Missae*. In his *Deutsche Messe*, however, he replaces these prayers with a "Thanksgiving Collect," which begins with the cue, "Let us thank the Lord and pray."[374] This, along with a similar collect, was adopted universally, and since that time has formed the Post-Communion of the Lutheran Chief Divine Service.

And justly so! It is the *gratias* ["returning of thanks"] after the heavenly feast. As the celebration of the Supper is begun by the Preface with its thanksgiving, so it is concluded by the Post-Communion with its thanksgiving. Chrysostom very beautifully expresses the scriptural reason for this when, writing on Matthew 26:30 ("*And when they had said the hymn, they went out over the Mount of Olives*"), he says to those who were accustomed to leave the church before the conclusion of the Divine Service: "Hear this, you who do not wait for the final prayer of the Sacrament, for this is the significance <268> of it. The Lord gave thanks before he gave it to the disciples, that we also should begin with thanksgiving. He gave thanks after He gave it to them, and sang a hymn, that we too might do in like manner"[375] (Rudelbach, *Sacrament-Worte* [Words of the Sacrament], 81.)

[373] *) In his treatise, "The Abomination of the Secret Mass" (1525) [AE 36:327], Luther translated this *complenda* as follows: "May our service be pleasing to You, O Holy Trinity; and grant that the sacrifice which I, though unworthy, have offered up in the sight of Your Majesty may be acceptable to You; and, through Your mercy, propitiatory for me and all on those for whom I have offered it; through Christ, our Lord. Amen." On this Luther makes the gloss: "As he began, so he concludes, continually offering and praying that it may be acceptable," etc.

[374] This cue is not in the *Deutsche Messe* itself, but as it is found in church orders, e.g., Duke Henry of Saxony (1580). —MC.

[375] Jacques P. Migne, ed., *Patrologiae cursus completus, series Graeca,* 161 vols. (Paris: J. P. Migne, 1857–66), 58:740. —MC.

A Form of the Thanksgiving Collect[376]

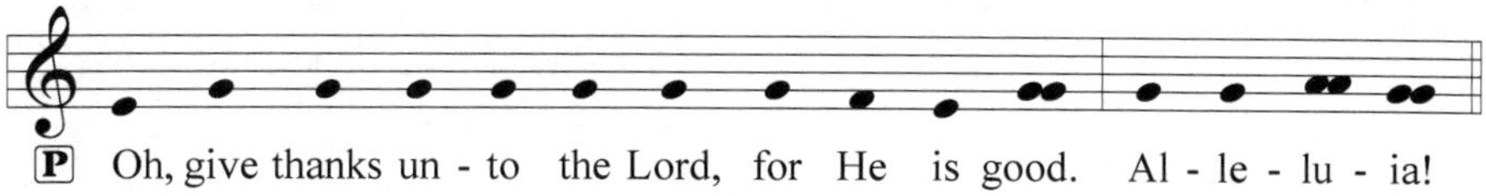

or:

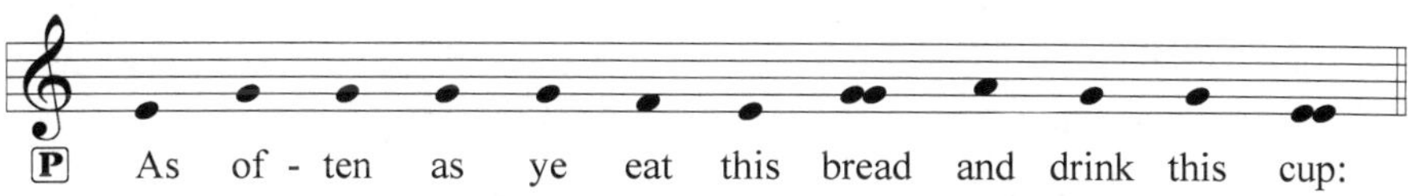

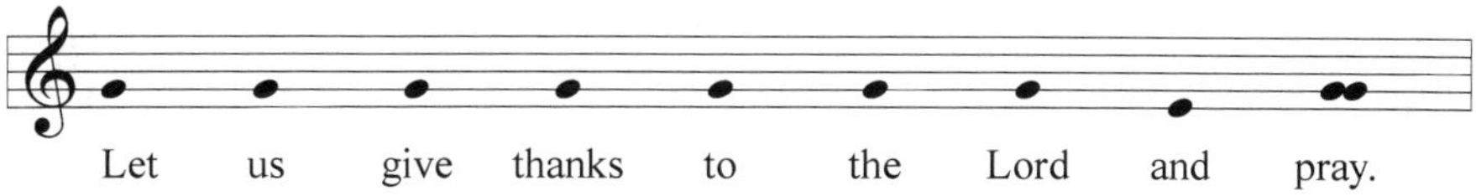

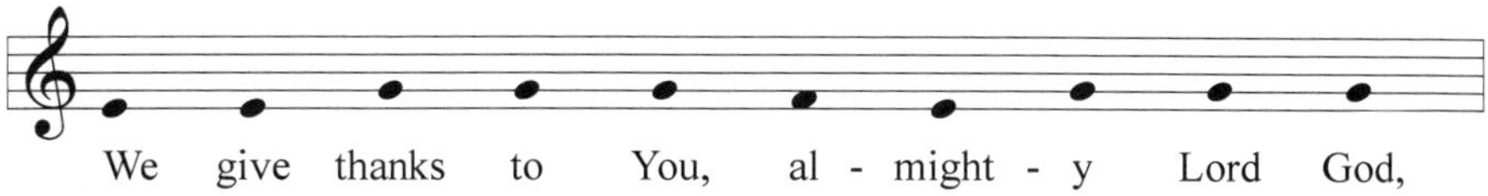

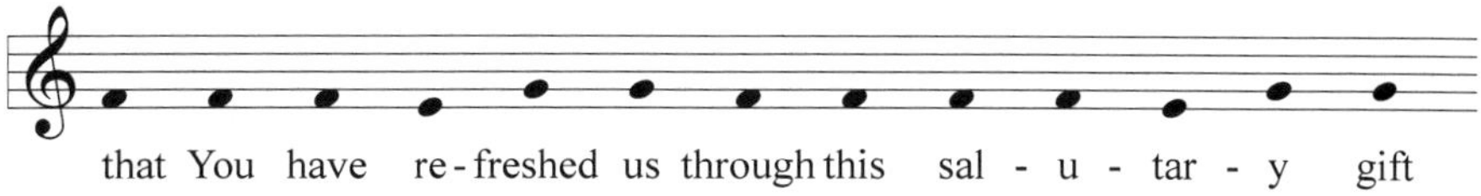

<269>

[376] See Layriz, 41. —MC.

of the bod - y and blood of Your dear Son, Je - sus Christ,
and we im - plore You that of Your mer - cy You would
strength - en us through the same in faith toward You
and in fer - vent love toward one an - oth - er;
through Je - sus Christ, Your Son, our Lord,
who lives and reigns with You and the Ho - ly Spir - it,
one God, now and for - ev - er.
or:
or:
A - men. A - men. A - men.

Layritz

<270>

XIX. CONCLUDING CEREMONIES

In the *Formula Missae*, Luther structured the *Conclusion* of the Chief Divine Service as follows: "Then (after the Communion Collect) the priest shall sing: *Dominus vobiscum*, etc. And instead of the *Ite, missa est*, let the *Benedicamus Domino* be sung with the Alleluia in the usual melody, where and when it pleases, or take the Benedicamus which is used at Vespers. Lastly, let the priest say the usual *Benediction* over the people, using the one from Numbers 6:24–26, which the Lord Himself appointed ("The Lord bless you," etc.), or else the one from Psalm 67:8 ("God, even our own God, bless us," etc.). And I believe that Christ said a similar benediction over His disciples when He ascended into heaven."[377] Accordingly, the Conclusion comprises two ceremonies: the *Benedicamus* tied to the *Salutation*, and the *Aaronic Benediction*.

1. First, concerning the *Benedicamus Domino* ("Let us bless the Lord"), it is true that Luther omitted it (as he did the Preface) from the *Deutsche Messe*, at the same time appointing it for the daily *Matins* and *Vespers* (EA 22:236; StL 10:235 [AE 53:68]) to which it originally belonged and from which it was taken for the Chief Divine Service and used in the *Formula Missae* to replace the "Ite, missa est" and its reponse, "Deo gratias." Nevertheless, this application to the Chief Divine Service found approval at the time. It is found in the church orders of [Pseudo-] Bugenhagen (1524),[378] Andreas Döber (1525),[379] Strassburg (1525),[380] Erfurt (1526), and Brandenburg-Nürnberg (1533).[381] Being an antiphonal expression of praise endowed with peculiar beauty, it is also being reinserted by more recent liturgiologists into the Chief Divine Service.

What then is its meaning in this position? Since Luther sets it in place of the Roman Mass's closing "Ite, missa est" ("Go, the Mass is ended!"), it forms the actual conclusion of the Chief Divine Service, just as it forms the conclusion of Matins and Vespers. Furthermore, since the Post-Communion Collect is the thanksgiving, particularly of the communicants for the gift of the body and blood of Christ, the *Benedicamus* is, in our view, the thanksgiving not only for the gift of Christ's body and blood but also for the gift

[377] Cf. Luther, "An Order of Mass and Communion" (1523), AE 53:30. —MC.

[378] *Von der Euangelischen Meß: was die Meß sey* . . . (Wittenberg, 1524), folio C2r; (1525), folio D3r. —MC.

[379] *Von der Evangelischen Meß, wie sie zu Nürmberg* . . . (1525), in Löhe, *Sammlung*, 3:49. —MC.

[380] *Ordnung der Mesß so die kirch zu Straßburg* . . . (1525), in Löhe, *Sammlung*, 3:58. —MC.

[381] *Kirchen Ordnung in meiner gnedigen herrn der Marggraven* . . . (Wittenberg, 1533), folio 51v. —MC.

of the Word which has been heard; and therefore the thanksgiving not only of <271> the communicants on any particular occasion but also of the whole assembled congregation, among whom the Lord has again opened His gracious presence through Word and Sacrament in accordance with His promise (Matthew 18:20).

A glance at the agendas and rituals of the Lutheran Church shows how richly endowed, *musically* speaking, the Benedicamus is in such sources. For each one there is a threefold Alleluia for the individual feasts as well as for Sundays in general, indeed, even for certain particular Sundays; and without an Alleluia for Matins and Vespers on weekdays. Yet since the execution of these various melodies, especially of the Alleluias, presents unseasoned singers with too much difficulty, and may be unfamiliar to the ear, we join Hommel, Löhe, and Layriz, etc., in choosing one of the *simple* melodies.

2. The *Benedicamus* is thus followed by the *Aaronic Benediction*, the second ceremony of the Conclusion. By this the assembled congregation is dismissed. In the Roman Mass, the Benediction formula for dismissal runs: *Benedicat vos omnipotens Deus, Pater et Filius et Spiritus sanctus. Amen.* ("The Almighty God, the Father, the Son, and the Holy Spirit, bless you. Amen"). Despite the simultaneous inclusion of Luther's suggested Psalm 67 [:6–7] and two other options[382] in the Brandenburg-Nürnberg Agenda[383] and Veit Dietrich's *Agendbüchlein*,[384] it was the Aaronic Benediction (Numbers 6 [:24–26]) which found the most universal distribution and became *the* Benediction formula for dismissing the congregation at every Divine Service or separate rite.[385] It is the form of Benediction most suitable for "confirming and sealing all the gifts of grace received in the Word and Sacrament, by one last impartation of grace."[386]

The Benediction formula, spoken or chanted, is accompanied by symbolic *movement of the hands*. During the Benediction, the pastor raises his

---

[382] The two other options are: (1) "God the Father and the Son and the Holy Spirit bless and preserve us." (2) "The blessing of God the Father and the Son and the Holy Spirit be with you, and abide with us all continually. Amen." —MC.

[383] *KirchenOrdnung in meiner Gnädigen Herrn der Marggrafen* . . . (1591), 145f.; *Kirchenordnung in Brandenburg und der Stadt Nürnberg* (Nürnberg: Gerlach, 1592), folio K3v. —MC.

[384] *Agend-Büchlein für die Pfar-Herren* . . . (Franfurt/Main: Gülfferich, 1546), folio H2r–v; (1565), folio F4r–v. —MC.

[385] *) Luther is also known to have written an excellent explanation of the Benediction "which is spoken over the people after Mass." See EA 36:156ff. Cf. Luther, "The Blessing Spoken over the People after the Mass, from Numbers 6 [:22–26], Expounded by Dr. Martin Luther" (December 8, 1527/1532), AE 56:233–39.

[386] Uncited source, ultimately from Gaupp, *Praktische Theologie*, 1:294. —MC.

hands, or at least the right hand, but at the conclusion, at the word "peace," makes the sign of the cross. The *raising of the hands* over the congregation is the biblical gesture of blessing, while the *making of the sign of the cross* over the congregation at the conclusion "imprints the symbol with its specifically Christian character, and here, as everywhere, serves as a reminder that all grace and all <272> blessing flow from the merits of the Crucified One."[387] The sign of the cross, according to historic prescription, is to be made in the following form and sequence:

1
4 2 5
3

and it may be formed with the whole hand or with the thumb and first two fingers, in such a way that the little finger faces the recipient of the blessing, with hand pointing upward and slow, moderate movement of the arm. In other words, it should not be done with the palm facing the congregation or with a hasty motion, which rather than being a remembrance of Christ's cross instead has the appearance of a signal for the standing congregation *to be seated*, or of "wiping away the cross," as a simple farmer once supposed—and not altogether unjustly!

And although in the church orders, a single Amen is for the most part prescribed with collects as well as the Benediction, in later times the use of a *twofold*, occasionally even a *threefold*, Amen eventually came to be preferred.

3. There is also a third concluding ceremony which we should discuss at this point, namely, the so-called *closing stanza*. While in the Roman Mass, after the *Ite, missa est* and subsequent Benediction, the assembly leaves the church, the priest remains standing on the Gospel side of the altar to read or chant, after a final Salutation, the Gospel of the Incarnate Word (John 1:1–14). This was justly eliminated throughout the Lutheran Chief Divine Service from the very start. But whereas in Luther's *Formula Missae* and *Deutsche Messe*, and in the church orders of Bugenhagen, Döber, Strassburg, Erfurt, and Brandenburg-Nürnberg, nothing further follows the Benediction, other, somewhat later church orders replace the Johannine Gospel of the Roman Mass with yet another closing hymn, the so-called *closing stanza*, for the most part an *invariable* song. Thus Wittenberg (1559, 1565),[388] Mecklenburg (1562, 1650),[389] Frankfurt am Main

[387] Schoeberlein, 1:474. —MC.

[388] *Kirchenordnung: Wie es mit Christlicher Lere* . . . (Wittenberg: Lufft, 1559), 97. —MC.

[389] *Kirchenordnung, wie es mit christlicher Lere* . . . (Wittenberg: Lufft, 1552), folio 87v. *Revidirte Kirchenordnung wie es mit christlicher Lere* . . . (Lüneburg: M. Lamprecht, 1650), folio 159v. —MC.

(1565),[390] Lüneburg (1564, 1569),[391] Liegnitz (1594),[392] and others appoint the hymn "Lord, Keep Us Steadfast in Thy Word," but Westphalia (1585):[393] "Grant Peace, We Pray, in Mercy, Lord," etc., and Magdeburg (1692):[394] "O Lord, We Praise Thee, Bless Thee, and Adore Thee." But in <273> Augustus's Braunschweig-Lüneburg church order (1657), it says after the Benediction, "Then let the whole congregation sing *choraliter*: Lord, now lettest Thou Thy servant depart in peace . . . And then: 'O Lord, We Praise Thee,' etc., to the end."[395] Both, it must be granted, would by today's standards too greatly prolong the Divine Service, since people are accustomed to singing only one stanza, or at most a few brief stanzas, after the Benediction. Yet how easily both closing hymns might be used if they were alternated, and the whole hymn "O Lord We Praise Thee, Bless Thee, and Adore Thee," were appointed to be sung during the Distribution, and then the Canticle of Simeon were made the closing stanza, as has been done by Layriz.[396] Löhe also, who in the editions of his Agenda places the Nunc Dimittis before the Thanksgiving Collect, finds it very suitable as a closing hymn as well. He remarks: "When everything is concluded, it is certainly quite beautiful to sing the Canticle of Simeon before going home."[397] Concerning this canticle, Calvör (I, 715) shares a beautiful passage by Casaubonus which might as well be included here in translation. It runs:

> When the sacred rite is completed and the celebration of the Supper concluded, then, after the closing prayer said by the deacon, the people are dismissed, which in the liturgy of Chrysostom is implied by the words, 'The priest completes the dismissal [ἀπόλυσιν], the

[390] *Kirchenordnung: das ist Form und Weise* . . . (Frankfurt am Main, 1565), folio 85v. —MC.

[391] *Kirchenordnung Vnnser von Gottes Genaden Julii* . . . (Wolfenbüttel: Horn, 1569), 54. —MC.

[392] *Kirchenordnung. Wie es mit Christlicher Lehre* . . . (Liegnitz: Schneider, 1594). A verbatim duplicate of Wittenberg (1557) with two additional exhortations inserted. —MC.

[393] *Kirchen Ordnung, Unser von Gottes gnaden, Frantzen* . . . (Lübeck: Balhorn, 1585), 132. Not "Grant Peace, We Pray," etc., but the second stanza later appended to it, beginning, "Gott gib unserm Fürsten und aller Obrigkeit . . ." ("God, grant to our prince and all rulers . . ."). —MC.

[394] *Consilia, sive Judicia Theologica et Requisita Ministerii, totius Ecclesiae: New verbessert und vollständig KirchenBuch D. Philip. Hanen* . . . (Magdeburg/Braunschweig: Kirchner/Duncker, 1647), pt. 2, p. 226: "Finally, when the communicants return from the altar and exit the chancel, one or two stanzas of the German "O Lord We Praise Thee, Bless Thee, and Adore Thee," etc., is sung in the choir as a conclusion." Cf. *Ertz Stifftische Magdeburgische Kirchen Agenda* . . . (Hall/Saxony: C. Salfelden, 1663), 30. —MC.

[395] *Agenda Oder: Erster Teyl der Kirchen-Ordnung* . . . (Wolfenbüttel: Sterne, 1657), 43. —MC.

[396] Layriz, 42f. —MC.

[397] Löhe, *Agende* (1853), 1:53. —MC.

> *missa*, which means, he dismisses the people.' The Conclusion rite [ἀπόλυσις] is itself the *missa* or *missio*, a word drawn from the Canticle of Simeon: 'Lord, now *lettest* Thou [*dimittis*, ἀπολύεις] Thy servant depart in peace'; which is quoted there. In many Protestant churches, the whole ceremony of celebrating the Holy Supper of the Lord concludes with this hymn, which the people sing *while kneeling*, which is a very beautiful and very holy tradition.[398]

Löhe[399] adds to this: 'The *plerisque* ('in many') might perhaps be doubted; the evaluation of the song is certainly correct."[400] <274>

But whether the final concluding ceremony is done with this hymn or another, it should be noted that, while it is being done, the consecrating *minister stays at the altar so as to put it in order* in the event that it was not possible to do so after the Distribution and before the Thanksgiving Collect. It is unseemly *for the pastor, immediately after the Benediction, to leave the altar when the holy vessels are still standing* ***open*** *and* ***disorderly*** *on the altar.* Therefore, during the closing hymn, he closes the flagon, chalice, and pyx and sets them in their places. The chalice is covered with the paten, and the paten with the pall (small, square-shaped protective cover of white linen). Then the veil, used in the Early Church and early Lutheranism, being a cloth of white or dyed silk, is spread over the whole. After a silent prayer, the pastor leaves the altar. It should also be noted that, in order to maintain the admirable custom of the assembly praying after the conclusion of the Divine Service and before dispersing, and to prevent people from exiting noisily after the hymn, the custom has arisen in many of our local Lutheran congregations for the pastor to remain standing at the altar throughout the closing hymn, in order to follow it by praying another audible Our Father.

---

[398] Calvör, *Ritualis ecclesiastici*, 1:715, with note: "Exercit. 16, no. 58, conf. supr. h. sect. C, 1. De Missae vocab." —MC.

[399] Ibid. This selection of Calvör is copied from Löhe's note. —MC.

[400] *) There is a Closing Hymn in Layriz titled "Ite, benedicti et electi," reproduced from the Hymns of the Bohemian Brethren ([*Kirchengeseng*] 1566), which was clearly used in their congregations in place of the "ite, missa est." It runs:

> Go forth, ye who are blessed and elect in Christ,
> Go forth with joy in peace, God direct your every step.
> Blessed is your going out, blessed is your going in,
> Blessed is all that you do through Christ, the Son of God.
> The same our Lord and Savior bring us into the true Fatherland
> To the praise and glory of His name forever. Amen.

1. Benedicamus

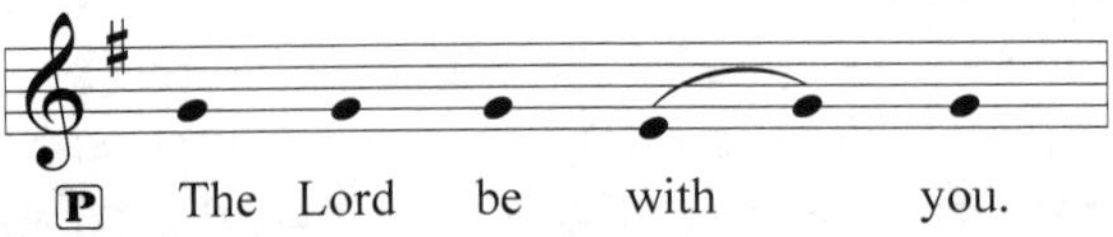

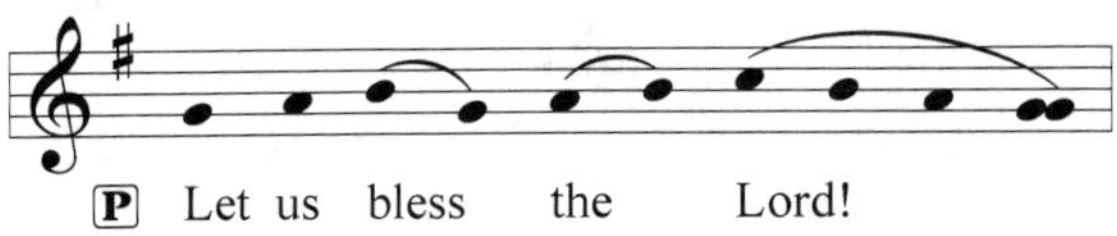

<275>

or:

2. BENEDICTION (*BENEDICTIO*)

CONGREGATION:

Layritz

<276>

2. Closing Song (*Nunc Dimittis*)

(To be used in alternation with "O Lord, We Praise Thee," etc.)

<277>

- - ra - el. Glo - ry be to the Fa - ther and
to the Son and to the Ho-ly Ghost; as it was in the be - gin -
ning, is now, and ev - er shall be, world with - out end.
* optional
A - - - - men. Is - ra - el.

<278>

Appendix

The Liturgical Stations

Introductory remarks. The Reformed Church, as we know, in opposing the abuse of art in the Roman Church (with respect also to the places in the church where Word and Sacraments are adminstered and prayer is made), at first entirely rejected the service of art, and later limited it to very modest dimensions.[401] In this regard also the Lutheran Church differed, following the words of Luther, who was not of the opinion "that all the arts were to be cast down and disappear through the Gospel, as some pseudo-spiritual people propose."[402] Accordingly, it undertook "no substantial change" in this regard, least of all a conspicuous one, but only eliminated the abuse and other impure practices. It left the altar in place, as it did the baptismal font and the pulpit also, and not only in the church buildings inherited from the papacy but also in those which they built themselves. And although the so-called Age of Enlightenment brought with it a puritanical purge and the introduction of secular design, it was only temporary.

Thus, while the Lutheran Church, free from any unevangelical servitude or legalistic anxiety, hardly made any deliberate attempt to keep the church building <280> on the level of an unadorned prayer hall, its distinction from the papistic church became equally apparent here. Rejecting for the church building the profane brightness of a workshop or school, it likewise avoided mystical dimness, and chose a softly subdued light. Although for the Lutheran Church the gathering-place, through Word and Sacrament, certainly becomes the site where God's gracious presence is revealed, it is nevertheless not the site of the continually present Christ of the Roman Mass. For this reason, the Lutheran altar has a completely

[401] *) The local, fashionable, Puritan congregations, growing increasingly more secular, have fallen to the other extreme. Their churches, though outwardly and inwardly constructed more or less in the Gothic style, boasting even a cross on the spire, have the appearance more of a painted concert hall, since an organ has been installed above the speaker's podium in a niche in place of an altar, and the choristers, both men and women, face the whole assembly. At the same time, instead of a side-chapel, there may even be, in addition to a "lecture-room," a special hall for holding social events, fairs, etc., and next to it a kitchen with its accoutrements!

[402] Cf. Luther, "Preface to the Wittenberg Hymnal" (1524), AE 53:316. —MC.

different meaning, a completely different use. On the one hand, it is that on which the Holy Supper is conducted with a distinct and definite confession of the true presence of Christ's body and blood under the forms of bread and wine. On the other hand, because the Lutheran Church knows nothing of transubstantiation nor of a sacramental presence outside of the use [*Genuß*] of the Supper, the altar does not become for her a sacred shrine in which the monstrance with the consecrated host is enclosed, and toward which priests and laity bow or nod the head in adoration as they pass by.[403] The Lutheran Church, in Christian freedom, certainly makes the altar a site of sacrifice in that it is particularly there, as the most appropriate site, that the church, through the called minister, causes the sacrificial incense of prayer and thanksgiving to be offered up and solemn vows (of confirmation, marriage, and ordination) to be made. At the same time, however, it turns in horror from the pompously consecrated altar of the sacrifice of the Mass, for which some bones of saints are required, hidden inside the altar as in a sepulcher, through which it can even evince miraculous power. For this reason, in the Lutheran Church only *one* altar is built or needed for the purposes indicated, while in the Roman Church the high altar has at least two side-altars, of which one is dedicated to Mary, the other to Joseph. <281>

We see that, with regard also to God's house and its interior furnishings, the Lutheran Church is the true middle between the false faith of papists and the false spirituality of enthusiasts.

Because the sacred ceremonies are always to be performed in plain sight of the gathered people, in accordance with the public character and communal principle of the Lutheran Divine Service generally, an *architectural layout* is demanded in which pulpit, altar, and font can be *seen* by the majority of those gathered. Likewise, because the Lutheran Church is the Church of the Word, the Word forms the central focus of the public Divine Service, "the greatest and chiefest part of every Divine Service is the preaching of God's Word," indeed, "even the Sacrament itself is made and blessed and sanctified by God's Word" (Luther),[404] therefore, not only must God's house

---

[403] *) How far toward Rome the ritualists of the Anglican Church have already gone, including with respect to the altar, is shown by "The Parish Annual of St. Paul's Church, Springfield, Ills., 1884," which explicitly designates the altar as God's "earthly" throne, and gives hearers the following instruction for their conduct: "I. On entering the Church do not stop to chat at the door, but make your obeisance toward the Altar. It is the throne of the King of kings, Who sanctifies it by His Presence, especially in the Holy Eucharist. 'Ye shall reverence my sanctuary. I am the Lord.' IX. Leave the Church with the same reverence with which you entered it. It is always God's house: the shelter of His Altar, whether service is in progress or not."

[404] Quoted in Schultze, 23. WA 10^3:70, lines 29–30. Cf. Luther, "The German Mass" (1526), AE 53:68; and "The Chief Article concerning the Eternal and New Testament, Preached

be constructed *with acoustics in mind*, but pulpit, altar, and font must be so placed within it that the Word is *heard* and *understood* everywhere.

Having made our introductory remarks, let us now examine in greater detail the *altar* and *pulpit*, as well as the *font*, with regard to their *placement, form, and features.*

I. The Altar

1. This most ancient (according to Genesis 8:20; 12:7ff.) monument of the public Divine Service has retained the name "altar" (from *altus* and *ara*) throughout the Western Church, signifying in a general sense an elevated site of consecration [*Weihestätte*]. Since Western Christians were from earliest times accustomed to pray facing east, recalling that it was from thence that salvation came, the custom therefore developed, circa AD 420, of setting up the altar on the *eastern* end of the church building. Because of this cogent symbolism (which so beautifully expresses the ancient saying "Ex oriente lux") in which the praying and worshiping congregation, with its mouthpiece before it, faces the altar, the Lutheran altar also has its **placement** to the *east*.

Customarily, the altar, elevated by two or three steps, is located in a distinct area called a "**chancel**" or "*high chancel*" [*Chor, hohe Chor*].[405] This is approached by ascending again from the church's nave, the area for the hearers, by two or three steps, the purpose of which is to keep the altar <282> from sitting too low. Similarly, the chancel *must not be too small*, so that the requisite area is available for those approaching for Communion or confirmation, and for assistants and witnesses at an ordination, wedding, and other ceremonies to be conducted at the altar.

It is telling that in the Catholic Church a *screen* is erected between the chancel and the nave. It is from there that all communicants except for the celebrating priest receive the Supper (under one kind); the chancel belongs exclusively to the clergy. In keeping with the doctrine of the ministry and the spiritual priesthood of all Christians, it is customary in the Lutheran Church not to install such a screen, or else, if for other reasons a screen has been installed, to interrupt it and make a broad, open gate in the middle leading from the nave into the sanctuary.

Now since the Supper is received in the Lutheran Church not *in front of* the chancel but *within* the chancel, the people either kneel in a semicircle around the altar or else walk around it, receiving the bread on the north

---

on Maundy Thursday, Matthew 26:26–28" (April 17, 1522), AE 56:11. —MC.

[405] The chancel or sanctuary, the latter meaning the area just around the altar, also *Altarchor* or *Altarraum*. The "high chancel" is the chancel containing the high altar as opposed to a side-altar —MC.

side and the wine on the south side. In the latter and predominant method of reception, the altar must, for the sake of passing around it, stand sufficiently far from the chancel wall.

2. While the Reformed Church for the celebration of its supper uses exclusively the bare form of a table, the Lutheran Church retains the Ancient Church's form. It is the oblong block—with or without the *reredos*.[406]

> While the most important part of the altar is the altar base, conflicts have arisen over the permissibility of a *reredos*. If the sanctuary window is obstructed by the reredos, its painted panels being thereby deprived of the powerful east light, it is obviously to be avoided. Otherwise, an altar should not be without this beautiful adornment. It is more than a mere decoration, for it simultaneously marks the location for symbolic and typological enactments and offers a welcome opportunity to put before people's eyes medieval, sacramental typology (Abel, Melchizedek, Abraham and Isaac, the bronze serpent, et al.) and symbolism (Lamb of God, vine, cluster of grapes, chalice, et al.). But the reredos should always have an organic connection with the altar base, and not be exchanged for something like a painting in a gilt frame (Schultze).[407]

Therefore, if one wishes to use a reredos, it calls for a rosette window rather than a full window on the rear wall, located high enough to be seen above the reredos from the nave. If a painting is integrated into a reredos— <283> if there is a crucifix on the altar, the depiction of the Resurrection or the Ascension is most fitting, or else the Institution of the Holy Supper—greater care should be taken so that the necessary light falls on the altar, whether by a narrow side-window being set on the right and left between the altar and the chancel arch, or else by a skylight.

As already noted, the altar base itself stands in the sanctuary elevated by a few steps. In many places, on the north and south sides of the upper level, rails are installed over which the communicants receive the Sacrament. The rails are of low height so as to allow the chalice to be administered without hindrance. It hardly needs to be mentioned that a kneeler should not be absent here. Since it is necessary for weddings, confirmations, and ordinations to have a kneeler in front of the steps, it is appropriate here to use a *portable* kneeler of such length as will leave enough room for unhindered ascent to the altar.

3. "I wish," exclaims Scriver in his *Seelen-Schatz* [Soul's Treasure] "that the whole church, and especially the altar, might be adorned as a miniature

[406] That is, the super-altar, including any structure placed on or above the altar, such as an altarpiece, gradine, retable, etc. —MC.

[407] Schultze, 77. —MC.

heaven, in honor of the most worthy Supper and as a reminder to godly hearts."[408] More than that, it is to be wished that the adornment of the altar might be devoid of all that is unseemly, foreign, and mundane! For the **furnishing** of a decent, decorous, and well-appointed altar of a Lutheran Church, the following items are called for.

(a) The *altar dressing*, consisting of the altar parament, the altar cloth, and the carpet. If the material or exterior of the altar cannot be shown uncovered, or if it is simply *able* to be covered, a full covering by means of the *altar parament* is appropriate. But even where this not a consideration, that is, where the altar base is monumental, the altar parament should be present in some form or in a reduced capacity. In this case, the hanging may consist of a narrow frontal running along the lip and decorated with an appropriate symbol or ornamental embroidery, approximately one third of the altar's breadth and the full length of the altar's height.

The altar parament is best spread around the altar base with complete smoothness; "hanging *in folds* is too reminiscent of worldly decoration."[409]

To mark progress in the cycle of the Church Year, the historic Church also retains the **liturgical colors** to a greater or lesser degree. These <284> were in ancient time *violet* in Advent and Lent (beginning with Septuagesima); *white* from Christmas to Epiphany, on Easter, and on the Purification, Annunciation, and Visitation of Mary; *green* in Epiphany-tide until Septuagesima, as well as in Trinity-tide; *red* on Pentecost, Trinity, and the feasts of St. John and the Apostles; *black* on Good Friday, on days of repentance, and at funeral services. The minimum, in our view, would be a *black* parament for Lent, days of repentance (including for ordinary Sundays after Trinity) and for funeral services, and one with a color, perhaps dark green, for other days. If there is the ability and desire to add a third one, either red or violet should be chosen, and they should be divided thus: either *dark green* for Advent and Epiphany to Septuagesima, and *red* for the three high feasts and other notable feasts; or *violet* for Advent, Epiphanytide, and Trinity-tide, and *dark green* for high feasts, etc.

Concerning *gold or silver borders* for paraments, one should be attentive, rather than negligent, or the latter will soon turn black. If gold is not feasible, let it simply be of wool. But in any case, "away with all frivolous passementerie or appliqué glass pearls, enamel, and the like, and instead let there be simple embroidery in woolen thread or cord," etc. (Meurer).[410]

---

[408] Christian Scriver, *Seelen-Schatz* (Magdeburg/Leipzig: Seidel/Scheidhauer, 1731), 514; quoted in R. Rocholl, *Die Realpräsenz* . . . (Gütersloh: Bertelsmann, 1875), 380. —MC.

[409] Schultze, 81. —MC.

[410] *Evangelische Kirchenzeitung* (1861), 755ff.; quoted in Schultze, 81. —MC.

The *altar cloth* covers the altar surface [or *mensa*], is invariably of snow-white linen, and on its overhanging edges may have plain embroidery or be trimmed with appropriate lacework.

Partly for decoration, partly as a reminder of Exodus 3:5, the altar steps, platform, and chancel steps are covered with a carpet. "All loud, garish patterns are to be most earnestly avoided here, especially so-called flower-carpets. Realistic imagery, including crosses, must likewise be excluded. 'It is indecent to tread the sacred underfoot.' Let the use of symbolic ornaments of flora and fauna in muted colors suffice." (Schultze)[411]

(b) The *crucifix* is an indispensible requisite of the altar. Since the cross is the most ancient of all signs which the Christian faith has produced of itself for its own testimony, it is only fitting for the crucifix to adorn our altars, corresponding to the prefigurative bronze serpent (for such time as it was used in Israel only as a memorial and not made into an idol). In truth, <285> no other image equals the cross as a sign for the completed redemption and reconciliation of the world, as well as for the proclamation thereof and its appropriation by faith (John 19:30; 3:14–15; 2 Corinthians 5). Let all the more caution therefore be taken when choosing the form of the crucifix. "The corpus of Christ will either be produced from silvered bronze or wood of natural hue. The color of silver, being more reflective of the color of the naked body, has preference over that of gold. Fragile or inauthentic materials such as zinc, cast iron, or even plaster and porcelain, should not be chosen. The cross itself may be of gilt brass, oak, walnut, or black pearwood. A naked cross without the Crucified is better avoided" (Schultze).[412]

Regarding its size, it should without fail be higher than the altar candles. It should also be in proportion to the size of the church.

It is either free-standing or built into the reredos, forming the proper center of the altar furnishings.

(c) The *altar candlesticks* are located to the left and right of the crucifix. Burning during the celebration of the Holy Supper, these not only serve as a reminder of the time of its establishment and so of the Lord's institution, but are at the same time a symbol of Christ as the light of the world which shines in the Gospel and which has thereby filled our hearts with a bright radiance so that the illumination of the knowledge of God's glory in the face of Jesus Christ (2 Corinthians 4:6) may go out through us. For this reason, the altar candlesticks in some places are already lit for the reading of the Gospel. "The question of whether candlesticks should be set on the altar is so self-evidently deserving of affirmation that a discussion of

[411] Schultze, 82. —MC.

[412] Ibid., 83. —MC.

it seems superfluous. The beautiful symbolism of the light cannot but be clear to each person" (Schultze).[413]

The *number* of the candlesticks, on the other hand, is an open question. On many altars there are four candles, either of the same or varying height, in the latter case forming a pyramid with the crucifix in the middle. Frequently, however, the use of two is preferred.

Naturally, altar candlesticks must have *a dignified appearance*. Concerning the form, one should keep to the classic examples. In any case, metal is suitable for the material, but in no case glass or porcelain.

(d) *Flower vases* occupy the place next to or between the candlesticks and the crucifix in some parts of Germany, and often in this country more recently. <286> Scriver regards these, after Song of Songs 4:5, as a symbol of the spiritual refreshment which the believer's soul finds in the heavenly Bridegroom, particularly in the Holy Supper.[414] When they are employed merely as a special decoration on feasts or celebratory occasions, real flowers are used, which are certainly the most fitting in any case. If they have their permanent place on the altar, artificial flowers may be used. In this case, however, only something tasteful and not too colorful should be permitted. But above all, let glass domes be avoided, since they are too reminiscent of a sitting room. Outside service times they may certainly be used to protect against dust; before a service or any occasion, they should be removed by the minister.

(e) The *sacred vessels* (*vasa sacra*) are the chief requirement and principal ornament of the altar whenever the Holy Supper, and thus the *full* Chief Divine Service, is celebrated. They consist of the *paten* and *pyx*, the *chalice* and *flagon*, and the *straining spoon*, all of the same material and in the same style. In the first centuries, the sacred vessels, having the ancient form, were made of glass, clay, or even wood. As the Church came into outward prosperity, only metal was used for the purpose, namely precious metal.

The *paten* has the form of a plate, the depression of which fits into the upper rim of the chalice. It is used for the distribution of the bread. When because of the number of communicants the paten is unable to contain all the hosts, which is frequently the case, the "host receptacle," or *ciborium* (from *cibus*, "food"), is called for. This is the means by which the Distribution is done in the Catholic Church, and its form is thus that of a shallow chalice furnished with a domed lid. In the Lutheran Church, a shallow cylindrical or oblong box is used as a *ciborium*, often with a lamb or a cross decorating the lid.

[413] Ibid., 86. —MC.

[414] Scriver, *Seelen-Schatz,* 514. —MC.

The *chalice*, consisting of a foot, stem with knop, and bowl (*cuppa*), is fashioned in as artistic a manner as possible, sometimes even set with precious stones. Admittedly, in the primitive conditions of earlier years in this country, with the lack of suitable chalices, a drinking glass of somewhat chalice-like shape often stood in place of the chalice. Even so, this was preferable to the Puritans' slender metal goblets which were available then. In the course of time they graduated to true chalices of tin or silver-plate with gilding inside. <287>

The chalice of the Lutheran Communion also differs from the chalice of the papistic Mass with respect to *shape*. While in the latter the *cuppa* is relatively small, being drunk only by the celebrant, in the former it is larger and especially wider at the brim, since, in keeping with Christ's institution, all drink of it. With regard to the *cuppa*, it is therefore necessary to make sure that the one administering is able to view the contents of the chalice so that he may incline it to a greater or lesser degree. "The *Renaissance* and Neo-classicism ultimately turned the chalice into a trophy divested of every churchly characteristic. The rim of the *cuppa* was curved outward, rendering the chalice unfit for administering, because the contents of such a cup have the tendency to pour out very swiftly and broadly at the slightest inclination, so that the wine will very easily be spilt on the mouth of the communicant" (Schultze).[415]

As a result of the withholding of the chalice, the Catholic Church knows of no proper *Communion flagon*, but uses for the priest only two flagonets or Mass-cruets, the one for the eucharistic wine being marked with a "V" (*vinum*), the one for the water, with which the chalice must be rinsed out afterward, with an "A" (*aqua*), both standing on a tray. Thus we are without any model. Incidentally, the flagons for the Supper, such as may be obtained here with the better chalices, are fairly suited to the purpose as far as the form is concerned. Frequently there is a cross adorning the lid. Also appropriate is a pelican, which feeds its young with the blood of its own heart. Since only gold has the ability to withstand the acidity of the wine and to prevent the accretion of verdigris, it is also very desirable to gild the interior of the flagon. When it is not gilt, it is all the more necessary to rinse and dry the flagon immediately after use.

As an addendum to the sacred vessels, the *corporal*, the *pall*, and the *veil* may be mentioned. The *corporal*, or "body cloth," is a linen cloth on which the sacred vessels are placed, the ultimate purpose of which in the Lutheran Church is to keep the white altar linen entirely clean. The *pall* is a square piece of cardboard wrapped in the same material as the altar

---

[415] Schultze, 88. —MC.

parament, or another of similar color. During the distribution of the Supper, especially when it is done by a single person, it covers the paten and chalice—the former lest any draft of air blow a host out, the latter lest anything fall into the chalice during the Distribution. The veil is a white cloth of linen or silk which is <288> frequently used to cover the vessels, collected on the south side of the altar, before and after the Distribution. The *straining spoon*, which is of the same material as the vessels, serves to enable the discreet removal of something which has fallen into the chalice or flagon.

(e) The *stand*, which we also reckon as pertaining to the altar, should be present in two forms—one for prayer, the other for reading.

The former is the *missal stand* proper. The practice of using a stand placed on top of the altar is supported by its seeming more fitting, during the singing or reading of the Collect, Preface, Our Father, and Words of Institution, for the agenda to rest on the altar in front of the liturgist instead of being held in his hand. For this reason, the largest possible letters have always been used for the agenda, as they are in the Roman Church for missals, etc. Moreover, if the agenda lies directly on the horizontal surface of the altar, it often forces the liturgist to slouch, a position detrimental to the performance of chant.

The other stand, the *lectern*, is designated for the reading of church Lessons, not only in the incidental Divine Services but also in the Chief Divine Service. Here, according to the precedent of the Ancient Church, the correct churchly practice is to read the *Epistle* and *Gospel* not at the altar but on a lectern standing off to the side of it.[416] Since this universal custom of an earlier age has still been retained in many churches of central Germany, it could find acceptance among us also, especially since the Altar Bible, which the liturgist must use for the reading of the pericopes in the event that no pericope book is in possession, is frequently quite heavy, and many liturgists, by leaning on the altar while reading, assume a position not in keeping with decorum. A disruptive pause *seems* to result from the liturgist's walking from the altar to the lectern and, where the intonation of the Creed is still in use, back to the altar. Nevertheless, no such pause exists for the congregation, since it is filled, in the case of the Epistle, by the singing of the Amen for the Collect, and in the case of the Gospel, by the intonation of the Creed or transitional organ music. <289>

[416] *) In a description of the church of Alt-Dresden from the jubilee year 1717, there is explicit mention of "a gilded brass stand" being at the entrance to the sanctuary for the reading of the Epistles and Gospels, etc. And on the title page of the Leipzig Agenda (1681), which depicts the interior of a church and the celebration of the Chief Divine Service with preaching and Communion simultaneously, a stand may also be seen on a single step at the entrance to the sanctuary, and in front of it the deacon functioning as liturgist and vested in alb.

"The first requirement for such a lectern is that it should stand perfectly sure and firm and not be too high or too low. Earlier lecterns were made of wood, later ones frequently of metal. Often an eagle, the symbol of the evangelist St. John, served as the bearer of the lectern desk, sometimes the four evangelists also appear as supports for the whole lectern, such as on a very old carved wooden lectern in the church of Freudenstadt in Württemberg" (Schultze).[417] In an Episcopal church, the present author also saw a gilt eagle installed so that the book rested on its back and outspread wings.

As already noted, the lectern was stationed *in front of the sanctuary* on a special platform. According to the Theses of the Eisenach Conference in 1861, the "Lectern belongs either in front of the altar on one of the steps which lead up from the nave to the chancel, yet without hindering the congregation's view of the altar, or else at one of the pillars of the chancel arch, to be moved back to the altar for the purpose of catechesis, Bible class, etc." Therefore, if the pulpit stands at the entrance of the chancel, it takes a position opposite the lectern.

By distinguishing the missal stand and lectern and by using the latter for all church readings, the Agenda and the so-called Altar Bible retain their own special place: the former lies on the missal stand, the latter on the lectern.

Beautifully crafted lecterns do not require a special parament. If a special covering is used for the altar-stand and lectern, the material and color must be that of the altar parament.

Note: The presence of a lectern "avoids the unseemly practice of the clerk [*Küster*] reading from the pulpit, or even from the altar" (Schultze)[418] at *services of reading*.

II. The Pulpit

1. As in the Old Testment, so also in Christian antiquity, the altar was originally the station for declaring the Word. The bishop or presbyter sat behind it, facing the congregation, and spoke out from thence to the congregation, in the process of which he nevertheless was seated while the hearers stood. Also used for the same purpose was the ambo, located on a platform for the lector and the singers in front and to the sides of the altar. Likewise, the sermon was given at the lattice or <290> screen which divided the chancel from the nave and on which, in larger churches, a special scaffold was installed for preaching, while in smaller churches the ambo by the lattice was found sufficient itself. These lattices or screens were called *cancelli*. From

[417] Schultze, 105. —MC.

[418] Ibid. For a discussion of the term *Küster*, see above, page 74, note 127.—MC.

this the preaching station acquired its name *Kanzel* [pulpit].[419] If the ambo had thus already begun to move from the most extreme point of the church to the middle, the move was completed when, in favor of the monastic orders, who from the thirteenth century had assumed the duty of preaching, the pulpit came to be set on a pillar in larger, multi-nave churches, or on the long wall in smaller churches.

Whether the correct placement of the pulpit is separate from or connected to the altar has been a subject of much debate in recent time. Building the pulpit into the altar, or even erecting it above the altar, is, according to Schultze "unstately,"[420] and according to the opinions of the Dresden Conference of 1856, "completely wrong and utterly absurd." Accordingly, Thesis 10 of the Eisenach Conference of 1861 states, "The pulpit must not be in front of, behind, or above the altar, nor within the chancel at all. Its proper location is where the chancel and nave meet, on a pillar of the chancel arch to the outside (facing the nave); in large, multi-nave churches, on one of the eastern pillars of the central nave. The height of the pulpit depends substantially on that of the galleries, and is generally to be set as low as possible so as to make the preacher visible both in and under the galleries." Others in turn assert the opposite, such as Hasse in his book, *Die Zeichensprache der evangelisch-lutherischen Kirche* [The Symbolic Language of the Evangelical-Lutheran Church] (1877). After pointing out certain troubles which arise for some of the hearers when, because of the size of the church, the pulpit must be moved to the center, he continues:

> In moderately large houses of God, all these troubles can be prevented if *altar* and *pulpit* are united in the relation of *Word* and *Sacrament*, and thus *joined together* by integrating the pulpit into the reredos in such a way that enough room remains beneath the pulpit for an altar image and the foot of the pulpit does not rest immediately on the altar table. In this way every parishioner's seat has equal value, and the congregation comes in collective devotion under the self-evident presupposition that every middle seat, at very least, has a consistently equal view of the altar. This placement of the pulpit also corresponds to the original location of the bishop's chair behind the altar-table and the later position at the front edge of the chancel.[421]

[419] Our English term, "pulpit," is in turn related to the second element of the German word for lectern (*Lesepult*). —MC.

[420] Schultze, 100. —MC.

[421] Hermann Gustav Hasse, *Die Zeichensprache der evangelisch-lutherischen Kirche* (Leipzig: Hinrichs, 1877), 81. —MC.

Nevertheless, <291> we have been unable to approve of a combined pulpit and altar. Not only does it result in the pulpit's standing somewhat high, looking up at which causes difficulty for those congregants sitting closest to it, and not only does the sanctuary then disappear, but the due importance of the altar is thereby diminished. Pulpit, altar, font—each on its own and in its place—is the most beautiful way and as such more reminiscent of 1 John 5:8: "There are three that bear witness on earth: The Spirit and the water and the blood, and these three agree." Thus separating the three sites for these three witnesses and not conflating two of them, but joining them by means of a chancel, the pulpits in our local churches have their most logical placement where the chancel and nave meet. Close attention will nevertheless be required, especially when the church is not built in a cruciform plan, that wherever there are galleries, including those galleries located on the pulpit side, the preacher can be seen from every place.

2. In probable allusion to Psalm 116:13, the usual *form* of the pulpit is that of a chalice, excepting that here and there the foot is absent and only the *cuppa* is suggested. *Yet in no instance may the* cuppa *have a large circumference.* In many places, the *pulpit stair* is attached to the sacristy, and one then ascends through a door up to the pulpit; yet in many places the door opens from the chancel. If the pulpit is set on a column, the stair more or less winds around the column. In the installation of a *pulpit-desk*, when the pulpit stands to the side of the altar, consideration should be given orienting the preacher on the diagonal so that he can see the majority of the congregants in one glance. Not to be forgotten is a *shelf* for depositing books, nor a *kneeler*, where it is the practice to make confessions at the pulpit.

Even in cases where the church is not large enough to demand a *sounding board* [*Schalldeckel*] there is usually an eager desire to install one. But how many of our local pulpits have a sounding board which is so small, it has the effect of a sugar-bowl lid, and at the same time hangs rather high above the pulpit. If it is in fact to be a *sounding board*, its diameter must exceed that of the upper lip of the pulpit somewhat, nor should it be suspended too high.

3. "Just as special attention should be given to the proper form of the altar, it should also be given to the worthy design and adornment of the *pulpit*, as the station where salvation is declared. <292> The pulpit should not be a secular work of art or a plain timber construction, but, as Word and Sacrament stand side by side, the same care should be taken with the pulpit as with the altar, and sacred ornamentation of an architectural or figurative nature lacking no less from the one than from the other. Yet the

practical requirements must not yield to the artistic aspects" (Schultze).[422] The following is the description of the pulpit of the church in Alt-Dresden from the year 1717:

> No less dignifying to the church is the pulpit of white and gilt timber construction borne aloft by six soaring angels, which is erected upon the second pillar to the left of the altar. On its sounding board, resembling a closed crown, a depiction of Faith [*Fides*] is seen holding a Crucifix in one hand, and in the other a book, on the leaves of which is written in letters of gold: "*Fides ex auditu, auditus autem per verbum Dei. Rom. X, 17.*" That is: "Faith comes from preaching, and preaching through the Word of God." Here it may be noted as unusual that, while it has only one door, it has two different stairs embracing the pillar between them, which gives an admirable appearance not only to the structure but also to those who walk upon it. As they ascend the stair of pure doctrine, likewise they are to descend the stair of holy conduct, and personally demonstrate through a Christian conversation that which they have taught others to do.[423]

Also appropriate as figurative imagery for the pulpit, in the suitable place, are, for example, the Lord in a seated position ("preaching chair"), holding an open book in His left hand and raising His right hand in benediction; also, the evangelists represented either figuratively or by their symbols; likewise, prophets and apostles, yet not the former without the latter. And as a reminder of the ministry of the New Testament, the "ministry of the Spirit, which gives the Spirit" [2 Corinthians 3:8], it is customary for the image of a dove to be mounted inside the sounding board in such a way that it appears to be hovering over the preacher.

III. The Baptismal Font

1. In the first century, Baptism was conducted in any given place. But from about the beginning of the fourth century, special *baptistries*, or *baptismal chapels*, were constructed adjacent to the church, perhaps only by a covered walkway. This geographical separation was intended to signify symbolically <293> that through Baptism the catechumens first receive acceptance into the Divine Service of Christians, and especially into the eucharistic fellowship. But because at the time it was customary for the bishop to perform the Baptism of the catechumens, only cathedral churches possessed such

[422] Schultze, 100. —MC.

[423] Paul Christian Hilscher, *Etwas zu der Kirchen-Historie in Alt-Dresden . . .* (Dresden/Leipzig: Mieth, 1721), 136f. —MC.

baptistries, and because in populous areas the number of baptismal candidates was often rather large, these baptismal chapels sometimes occupied a sizeable area. In the center of the baptistry stood the *baptismal fountain*, a sometimes exceedingly beautiful basin into which three steps led down, and around this was a large room for the many baptismal candidates and attendants. Thus the baptistry had the form of a rotunda, and later of an octagon. But as infant Baptism became the rule and adult Baptism the exception, the ancient baptistry came to be replaced by the *baptismal font*, which usually had its position to the left of the entrance, and indeed, in a special chamber of the narthex.

Since the Baptism of our children should as a rule be performed in God's house and in the presence of the congregation, the baptismal font is without doubt most suitably located *in* or immediately *before* the chancel, in the latter case somewhat elevated. By this placement, furthermore, one is reminded that Baptism "is the admission to all the good things of God and to the communion of all the saints" (Luther),[424] and in turn, that every time one worthily partakes of the Sacrament of the Altar, it is a literal renewal of the baptismal covenant and has the purpose of sustaining one in one's baptismal grace.

2. Fashioned from stone, metal, or wood, the baptismal font is *shaped* more or less like a short Romanesque or Gothic chalice, is sometimes round but usually octagonal, and harmonizes stylistically with the pulpit and the altar. Frequently it has a vaulted or domed lid. In a church in northern Germany, a suspended angel holds the lid in his hand and, during a Baptism, is made to fly upward with it by means of a counterweight. (In another church, the place of the baptismal font is represented by an angel facing the congregation in a kneeling posture, in whose hand a large baptismal basin rests.)

3. Since the Lutheran Church knows of no *consecrated* baptismal water, and always pours out the water after the ceremony, the depression of the font is customarily supplied with a removable *baptismal bowl*. This also calls for the *baptismal ewer*, for bringing the baptismal water to the font so that it can be poured by the clerk into the basin before the beginning of the ceremony, or as is the usage in many places, into the <294> baptizer's cupped hand three times during the ceremony itself. In order that the latter may dry his hands again, the baptismal font is suppiled with a *baptismal towel*, which the clerk has ready in his possession. Frequently in the past, the *baptismal gown* was a requisite for the font, and it still is, albeit seldom, here and there. It is a white, sleeveless wrap which is put on or simply spread over the child after his Baptism, during which the baptizer, with the laying on of hands (here and there including those of the godparents) speaks the *votum baptismale* ("the

[424] Cf. Luther, "The Order of Baptism" (1523), AE 53:103. —MC.

Almighty God and Father of our Lord Jesus Christ, who has begotten you again," etc.). But as for dressing the font, the more artfully the font has been crafted, the more superfluous it is.

Note: when private Confession was still the dominant form of Confession in the Lutheran Church, there were special confessional chairs, preferably located within the chancel, so that the penitent and the confessor, while visible to everyone, could be heard by no one. Evidence that a confessional chair for Lutheran private Confession was fashioned differently from that used for Catholic auricular Confession is found, among other places, in illustrations which are still available, two of which lie in the present author's sight: one in Cubach's Prayerbook (1688),[425] the other in Nürnberg preacher J. C. [B. W.] Marperger's Communion Book (1776).[426] Both have no legs but large sides, and rest on a step on which the penitent knelt. In the first image, the back ascends somewhat higher, and a small, simple baldachin rests on top of it. Next to it in a niche is an image depicting Peter weeping and the rooster crowing. (Evidently, the minister acting as liturgist used this chair also during the Chief Divine Service, while the one who had to give the sermon waited in the sacristy until his entrance. But the liturgist never removed his ministerial vestments when he wished to hear the sermon outside of the sacristy; so he might well have his seat in the sanctuary or the front of the nave.)

425 Michael Cubach, *Einer gläubigen und andächtigen Seelen vermehrtes tägliches Bet-, Buß-, Lob- und Danck-Opffer*... (1688), expanded afterward, with notable preface by Christian Scriver. In one edition (Leipzig: Weidmann, 1728), a pertinent engraving appears in the background of a miniature on the frontispiece, p. 6 (unnumbered), as well as on p. 491 (unnumbered), where the chair is partially obscured by a pillar. Another image more clearly representing this scene is found on the altar of the St. Nikolaikirche in Brieg. See Helmut Schatz, *Historische Bilder zum ev.-luth. Gottesdienst—Eine Dokumentation*, (Ansbach: Atelier 23, 2004), 25f. —MC.

426 Bernhard Walther Marperger, *Neues Communion-Büchlein für die Liebhaber des rechtschaffenen Wesens in Christo Jesu*... (Nürnberg: Raspe, 1776), image facing p. 21. In the foreground, a female penitent on left, with back to pillar and wearing long head-covering, stands with hands folded before confessor, vested in black gown and ruff and seated in high-backed "shriving seat" with scroll-cut sides decorated with acanthus designs. A niche in the background houses a depiction of the crucifixion. —MC.